WAIMH

HANDBOOK OF

Infant
Mental Health

VOLUME ONE

Perspectives on Infant Mental Health

WAIMH
HANDBOOK OF
Infant
Mental Health

Joy D. Osofsky and Hiram E. Fitzgerald / Editors

VOLUME ONE
Perspectives on Infant Mental Health

WORLD ASSOCIATION FOR INFANT MENTAL HEALTH

John Wiley & Sons, Inc.

New York • Chichester • Weinheim • Brisbane • Singapore • Toronto

Library of Congress Cataloging-in-Publication Data:
WAIMH Handbook of infant mental health / World Association for Infant Mental Health ; edited by
   Joy D. Osofsky and Hiram E. Fitzgerald.
      p.   cm.
   Includes bibliographical references and indexes.
   Contents: v. 1. Perspectives on infant mental health — v. 2. Early intervention, evaluation, and
assessment — v. 3. Parenting and child care — v. 4. Infant mental health groups at high risk.
   Other title: WAIMH handbook of infant mental health.
   ISBN 0-471-18988-X (set : alk. paper). — ISBN 0-471-18941-3 (v. 1 : cloth : alk. paper) —
ISBN 0-471-18944-8 (v. 2 : cloth : alk. paper). — ISBN 0-471-18946-4 (v. 3 : cloth : alk. paper). —
ISBN 0-471-18947-2 (v. 4 : cloth : alk. paper)
   1. Infants—Mental health Handbooks, manuals, etc.   2. Infant psychiatry Handbooks, manu-
als, etc.   3. Child psychopathology—Prevention Handbooks, manuals, etc.   I. Osofsky, Joy D.
II. Fitzgerald, Hiram E.   III. World Association for Infant Mental Health.   IV. Title: WAIMH
handbook of infant mental health.
   [DNLM: 1. Child Development.   2. Infant.   3. Child Psychology.   4. Parenting.   5.
Early Intervention (Education)   6. Developmental Disabilities—prevention & control.   WS 105
H2363 2000]
RJ502.5.H362   2000
618.92′89—dc21   99-11893
                                                                                                      CIP

Printed in the United States of America.

10 9 8 7 6 5 4 3 2 1

Contributors

LAUREN R. BARTON, MA
Department of Psychology, Michigan State University, East Lansing, Michigan

MARIA YELLOW HORSE BRAVE HEART, MSW, PH.D.
Graduate School of Social Work, University of Denver, Denver, Colorado

SALVADOR CELIA, M.D.
Medical School of the Lutheran University, Puerto Allegre, Brazil

MIGUEL CHERRO-AGUERRE, M.D.
Child and Adolescent Psychiatric Clinic School of Medicine of the University of the Republic, Montevideo, Uruguay

PETER DE CHATEAU, M.D.
Department of Child Psychiatry, University of Nijmegen, The Netherlands

MARGUERITE DUNITZ-SCHEER, M.D.
University Children's Hospital, Graz, Austria

HIRAM E. FITZGERALD, PH.D.
Institute for Children, Youth, and Families, Michigan State University, East Lansing, Michigan

ROWENA FONG, PH.D., MSW
School of Social Work, University of Hawaii Manoa, Honolulu, Hawaii

YOKO HAMADA, M.D.
Faculty of Environmental Information, Keio University, Tokyo, Japan

SERGE LEBOVICI, M.D.
Institute de Puericulture de Paris, Paris, France

PIA RISHOLM MOTHANDER, PH.D.
Department of Psychology, Uppsala University, Uppsala, Sweden

RIVKAT J. MUHAMEDRAHIMOV, PH.D.
Lekotek, Saint Petersburg, Russia

KEIGO, OKONOGI, M.D.
Neuro-Psychiatric Department, Keio University School of Medicine, Tokyo, Japan

PETER JARON ZWI SCHEER, M.D.
University Children's Hospital, Graz, Austria

PAUL SPICER, PH.D.
National Center for American Indian and Alaska Native Mental Health Research, University of Colorado Health Sciences Center, Denver, Colorado

BEULAH WARREN, MA
Family Futures, Sydney, Australia

v

Contents

Foreword

Yvon Gauthier

I had the privilege to participate in the first international congress of the World Association for Infant Mental Health, then the World Association of Infant Psychiatry, held in Portugal in 1980. There was a very special feeling throughout this congress, a feeling that researchers and clinicians from several countries were for the first time putting together their observations about infants, and discovering their importance. Most probably, these people knew one another's writings and had met before in other situations, but there was, in their presentations and discussions an emotional tone that I personally felt intensely. And I often heard others talk about it in similar terms over the years. Can we say that this was the beginning of an infant mental health movement? We evidently need more historical facts before answering this question. But as I look back on it, this 1980 congress stands in my mind as a historical mark in terms of an international beginning of knowledge transfer in the infant mental health domain. The publication of this WAIMH handbook 20 years later is an international attempt, sponsored by WAIMH, to mark the progress made during those two decades, and to propose important directions in many areas of this most dynamic field.

In many parts of the world, ideas and practices concerned with infants and young families are gaining in importance. We may note that Spitz's and Bowlby's early works gradually had an influence on practices of institutional life and adoption all over the world, and that foster homes have become standard practice in many countries, in spite of their frequent inadequacies. Attachment-exploration phenomena are being studied in several countries, with findings that show cultural variations in infant care (see Bretherton and Waters, 1985; Waters, Vaughn, Posada, & Kondo-Ikemura, 1995). Can we predict that this movement will continue to have a considerable influence all over the world, particularly in less developed countries? It is very interesting and important that several chapters of this handbook develop cross-cultural perspectives in infant mental health, showing that this movement has already crossed several frontiers. Prepared by specialists in their own countries, they demonstrate the variety of approaches used to understand and help families who are dealing with problematic infants and young children, while taking into account culture-relevant elements involved in understanding and intervention.

Several theoretical currents are influential in infant mental health, but psychoanalysis, clinically and theoretically, holds a special place in our field. We may remember the importance that psychoanalysis has given to infancy in its theoretical development. Of course, for Freud, infancy meant the verbal child, and more specifically the 3- to 6-year-old during the Oedipal phase. Melanie Klein placed emphasis on earlier phases, though in doing so she attributed to the very young infant very destructive imaginary strivings and projections that she reconstructed from her treatment of older mostly psychotic children.

We know how much Bowlby questioned some of these psychoanalytic hypotheses. His observations of very young children in situations of separation, among other influences, led him to develop his theory of attachment, which has come to play a crucial role in research and clinical activities. With the contributions of Mary Ainsworth, Mary Main, and many others, attachment concepts have become central to research and clinical activities in many countries and have opened the way to a deeper understanding of both normal and psychopathological development. Infant mental health

is deeply influenced by the attachment paradigm.

We also have to note that family systems and family therapy are closely tied to attachment theory (Byng-Hall, 1990; Stevenson-Hinde, 1990); and thus also are very useful in infant mental health practice. Fundamental research done on the early father-mother-baby interactions (for instance in Lausanne, Corboz-Warnery, Fivaz-Depeursinge, Bettens, & Favez, 1993) is also bringing an interesting contribution to our practice.

It has almost become a postulate in our field that early intervention frequently leads to symptomatic and internal changes within the parent-child dyad or triad. More research is needed, but already significant results are available (Cramer et al., 1990; Landy et al., 1998; Robert-Tissot et al., 1996). Stern (1995) has developed the idea that early intervention for which there are many possible "ports of entry," has a good chance of mobilizing a system that has great mobility and offers true opportunities for change at this stage of life. This mobility has been well demonstrated all through this phase of life, from early pregnancy to age 2 to 3. We can now really talk of perinatality as a phase of life where an intervention, even of small proportions, can move the system in a durable manner (Gauthier, 1998).

There is an important corollary to this appreciation of the importance of early intervention: Several disciplines are involved in the care of infants, young children, and their families and must be aware that their role is essential. First-line workers, whatever their original discipline—nurse, midwife, child care worker, obstetrician, pediatrician, etc.—have to be trained in a truly systemic orientation. Examples of different types of training in this direction are reported in this handbook, opening the way to an essential transfer of knowledge between disciplines.

It also becomes clearer as we study infants and young families that parenting, mothering, and fathering do not start at birth, but are present as soon as a child is expected. Therefore, professionals have to become involved even during pregnancy, for there is evidence that even before birth the child becomes invested with affects and images that may influence development. Bydlowski (1997), Raphael-Leff (1993), and Molénat (1993), among others, have described well how this developmental phase is often marked by a "permeability of the unconscious" that often allows significant therapeutic work.

From a similar perspective, Fraiberg's clinical studies opened the way to the concept of intergenerational transmission, which finds interesting confirmation in recent research on transmission of attachment patterns (Benoit & Parker, 1994; Fonagy, Steele, Moran, Steele, & Higgitt, 1993). Important changes are being observed in the responsibilities that parents assume in the care of their children, just as greatly differing societies and cultures are developing new ways of socializing the infant and the young child. This handbook will bring us up to date on such issues.

Research on brain development shows the importance of the early years and the essential role of the environment in its development (Schore, 1994, 1996). Early intervention is essential for all, but particularly for high risk populations, since we now know that poverty and psychopathology are intricately connected, and that early intervention is essential to avoid repetitions and reach parents' desire for a new experience, one different from their own childhood, with their child. We also know that several situations constitute a risk for the coming child: Prematurity, substance abuse, depression, adolescent pregnancy, death of a previous child, and traumatized childhood are all conditions that call for early preventive intervention from professionals who are naturally in contact with mothers and fathers.

This handbook is an unusual sharing of knowledge from experts in several disciplines and all parts of the world, whose work focuses on infants and young families. It expresses the conviction, which has gradually come to all professionals working in this area of infant mental health, that early intervention is the best way to prevent the severe difficulties in the development of children and adults that often lead to psychopathology. Although such early intervention may be costly, it is certainly less so than later psychopathology is to societies. Let us hope that this major effort will be much read all over the world, so that it influences, in all parts of our global environment, the development of social policies that encourage and support an early involvement with infants and families.

References

Benoit, D., & Parker, K. C. H. (1994). Stability and transmission of attachment across three generations. *Child Development,* 65, 1444–1456.

Bretherton, I., & Waters, E. (Eds.). (1985). Growing points of attachment: Theory and research. *Monographs of the Society for Research in Child Development, 50* (1–2, Serial No. 209).

Bydlowski, M. (1997). *La dette de vie: Itinéraire psychanalytique de la maternité* (Le fil rouge). Paris: Presses Universitaires de France.

Byng-Hall, J. (1990). Attachment theory and family therapy: A clinical view. *Infant Mental Health Journal, 11*(3), 228–236.

Corboz-Warnery, A., Fivaz-Depeursinge, E., Bettens, C. G., & Favez, N. (1993). Systemic analysis of father-mother-baby interactions: The Lausanne triadic play. *Infant Mental Health Journal, 14*(4), 298–316.

Cramer, B., Robert-Tissot, C., Stern, D. N., Serpa-Rusconi, S., De Muralt, M., Besson, G., Palacio-Espasa, F., Bachmann, J. P., Knauer, D., Berney, C., & d'Arcis, U. (1990). Outcome evaluation in brief mother-infant psychotherapy: A preliminary report. *Infant Mental Health Journal, 11*(3), 278–300.

Fonagy, P., Steele, M., Moran, G., Steele, H., & Higgitt, A. (1993). Measuring the ghost in the nursery: An empirical study of the relation between parents' mental representations of childhood experiences and their infants' security of attachment. *Journal of the American Psychoanalytic Association, 41,* 957–989.

Gauthier, Y. (1998). Du projet d'enfant aux premières semaines de la vie: Perspectives psychanalytiques. In P. Mazet & S. Lebovici (Eds.), *Psychiatrie périnatale. Parents et bébés: Du projet d'enfant aux premiers mois de vie.* (Monographies de la psychiatrie de l'enfant). Paris: Presses Universitaires de France.

Landy, S., Peters, R.DeV., Arnold, R., Allen, B., Brookes, F., & Jewell, S. (1998). Evaluation of "Staying On Track": An early identification, tracking, and referral system. *Infant Mental Health Journal, 19*(1), 34–58.

Molénat, F. (1992). *Mères vulnérables.* Paris: Stock/Pernoud.

Raphael-Leff, J. (1993). *Pregnancy: The inside story.* Northvale, NJ, and London: Jason Aronson Inc.

Robert-Tissot, C., Cramer, B., Stern, D. N., Serpa, S. R., Bachmann, J. P., Palacio-Espasa, F., Knauer, D., De Muralt, M., Berney, C., & Mendiguren, G. (1996). Outcome evaluation in brief mother-infant psychotherapies: Report on 75 cases. *Infant Mental Health Journal, 17*(2), 97–114.

Schore, A. N. (1994). *Affect regulation and the origin of the self.* Hillsdale, NJ: Erlbaum.

Schore, A. N. (1996). The experience-dependent maturation of a regulatory system in the orbital prefrontal cortex and the origin of developmental psychopathology. *Development and Psychopathology, 8,* 59–87.

Stern, D. N. (1995). *The motherhood constellation: A unified view of parent-infant psychotherapy.* New York: Basic Books.

Stevenson-Hinde, J. (1990). Attachment within family systems: An overview. *Infant Mental Health Journal, 11*(3), 218–228.

Waters, E., Vaughn, B. E., Posada, G., & Kondo-lkemura, K. (Eds.). (1995). Caregiving, cultural and cognitive perspectives on secure-base behavior and working models: New growing points of attachment theory and research. *Monographs of the Society for Research in Child Development, 60*(2–3, Serial No. 244).

Preface

Joy D. Osofsky and Hiram E. Fitzgerald

In 1996, anticipating our 6th World Congress, we recognized with the Executive Committee of the World Association for Infant Mental Health (WAIMH) that our next World Congress planned for July 2000 would not only mark the beginning of the new millennium, but also, for WAIMH a celebration of our 20-year anniversary. Thus, the WAIMH Handbook of Infant Mental Health was "conceived" as a tribute to that occasion. We agreed to undertake the editing of a series of volumes that would present a comprehensive review and integration of work in the area of infant mental health from around the world. From the initial idea, with the help of our editors at John Wiley & Sons, we decided that four volumes were needed to truly represent the area covering the breadth of programs and approaches that would best describe the field including: I. Perspectives on Infant Mental Health; II. Early Intervention, Evaluation, and Assessment; III. Parenting and Child Care; IV. Infant Mental Health in Groups at High Risk. We were committed to making the book interdisciplinary and international to reflect the vision of WAIMH.

Many people have been very helpful and encouraging in bringing this major effort to an excellent conclusion. First, we want to thank the Executive Committee of WAIMH including Yvon Gauthier, Peter de Chateau, Tuula Tamminen, Elizabeth Tuters, Miguel Hoffmann, Antoine Guedeney, and Bob Emde who encouraged us from the outset. They thought it was an exciting and very worthwhile undertaking, and have been extremely helpful in assisting us in bringing many chapters to completion and editing others when we needed their help. Second, we are very appreciative of the vision and foresight of Kelly Franklin, first our editor and now publisher, who brought us to New York to discuss how Wiley could play a role in advancing the field of infant mental health. We hope that you will agree that her encouragement of us to develop the *WAIMH Handbook of Infant Mental Health* and her saying, "You can do four volumes!" was fortuitous.

We each have individual people to recognize and thank. I (JDO) want to thank my colleagues, especially Martin Drell, Head of the Division of Infant, Child and Adolescent Psychiatry at Louisiana State University Health Sciences Center who not only were available and supportive of this work, but offered inspiration as well. Through the Harris Center for Infant Mental Health that I direct at LSUHSC, I am constantly exposed to the excitement in our faculty and trainees as they learn more about and provide better interventions and treatment for infants and their families. In such an environment that values making a difference in the earliest years of life, the development of this publication has been encouraged and valued. My support staff for this book, including some who have moved on to complete their graduate education, have included Bridget Scott, Ana Linares, and Angela Black. I am appreciative of their careful record keeping and help with organizing this project. Of course my family, as always, has been very patient with me and encouraging as I spend endless hours in front of the computer writing and/or editing. Perhaps the best part of that support is seeing how my three growing and grown children have learned to value education, writing, and helping others. My husband, Howard, has always been there for me with encouragement and pride as such a major project has come to completion. I thank him for always providing a "secure base" and for his love and steadiness for all of us.

I (HEF) too have many individuals to thank, starting with my wife Dolores. Not only has she been a steadfast companion for the past 37 years, but she actually holds her own place in WAIMH's history (as Paul Harvey might say, see Volume 1, Chapter 1, page 20 "for the rest of the story!"). When writing and editing there is no more treasured commodity than time, and my colleagues at Michigan State University, Rachel Schiffman, Ellen Whipple, and Holly Brophy-Herb helped to release some of that by sharing responsibility for administering the interdisciplinary graduate programs in infant studies. I learned a great deal about infancy by participating in the rearing of three individuals each of whom has blossomed into a caring, compassionate adult who values education, children, and family life. Being a grandparent, however, provides insights into infant development and parent-infant relationships not afforded to parents as they play out the daily routine. So, thanks to Sean, Ryan, Mara, and Mallory for refreshing and renewing my opportunities to view again the truly wonderous early beginnings of human devleopment.

Finally, we want to thank the many infants, toddlers and families who have really "taught us all we know" about infant mental health. Without them, we would not only be less knowledgeable, but also, we would never have had the opportunity to appreciate the magic of human development. Combined we have probably directly sampled a small portion of the lifecourse of thousands of infants and their caregivers. The diversity of human development, the resilience to adverse outcome, and both the compassion and inhumanity of humankind, each, in its own way, challenges infant mental health specialists to hone their scientific and clinical skills, and to participate in advocating for policies that enhance the quality of life, especially during the early years.

These volumes are a beginning, not an end. They are intended to provoke discussion about the field of infant mental health and to frame a definition of that field. They unambiguously join scientific and clinical perspectives and boldly speak to public policy issues. We invite each of you to join this effort to help shape a perspective, one that will play out across disciplines, across national boundaries, and across the full spectrum of human development.

Joy D. Osofsky
New Orleans, Louisiana

Hiram E. Fitzgerald
East Lansing, Michigan

WAIMH

HANDBOOK OF

Infant
Mental Health

VOLUME ONE

Perspectives on Infant Mental Health

1

Infant Mental Health: Origins and Emergence of an Interdisciplinary Field

Hiram E. Fitzgerald and Lauren R. Barton

1
—

Advice to Persons About to Write History—Don't
    Lord Acton (1887)

Introduction

The infant mental health field is relatively young and continues to expand, evolve, and define itself. Infant mental health focuses on the social and emotional well-being of infants and their caregivers and the various contexts within which caregiving takes place. Infant mental health, therefore, focuses on relationships; infant development is conceptualized as always embedded within emergent, active systems of relationships. By definition the infant is born into a social world (Bell, 1968; Rheingold, 1968). Moreover, it is increasingly clear that the infant's social relationships begin to be structured even before birth by such factors as parents' motivation for parenthood (Leifer, 1977) as well as their fantasies and expectancies about their baby. For example, Lebovici (1983) describes the mother's "creative anticipations" as the means by which she transforms her fantasies into attributions about her baby when it is born. Lebovici asserts that such fantasies come about as the mother thinks about her fetus, and "the baby invests the mother with affect even before knowing her cognitively. This in turn helps the mother to establish her concept of herself as a mother" (Lebovici, 1984, p. 329).

Infant mental health is rooted in the understanding that developmental outcomes emerge from infant characteristics, caregiver-infant relationships, and the environmental contexts within which infant-parent relationships take place. From an infant mental health perspective, "parents are looked at as interacting participants in the developmental process, which does not permit a dichotomization of nature and nurture" (Shapiro, 1976, p. 4). Winnicott (1964/1987) captured the essence of the caregiver-infant relationship when reflecting upon his prior comment that there was no such thing as a baby, "meaning that if you set out to describe a baby, you will find you are describing a baby and *someone*. A baby cannot exist alone, but is essentially part of a relationship" (p. 88). Infant mental health specialists also are concerned about the effects of contextual factors such as poverty, violence, addiction, and homelessness on socioemotional development and therefore actively use intervention and prevention strategies in their efforts to ameliorate disturbances to the developmental process. "Infancy, then, involves not only the baby and the holding mother, but the father and the surrounding environment as well" (Call, 1984, p. 186).

The origins of this focus on emergence, regulation, and systemic organization are to be found in evolutionary, systems, and psychoanalytic theories, each of which is conceptualized as a theory of change. Evolutionary, systems, and psychoanalytic theories each challenged the status quo of its day, each capitalized on the prevailing zeitgeist, and each had an impact that extended far beyond its original context. The broad impact of these theories of change was to fundamentally change the way that scientists, clinicians, and policy advocates describe, investigate, intervene, and advocate for infants and their families.

Obviously, we did not heed Lord Acton's sage advice! However, we use it as a springboard to disclaim any attempt on our part to provide a comprehensive history of infant mental health. We have been informed by a much larger literature than anticipated, and have discovered a much deeper history than we thought possible. Keeping to the concept of a handbook, we present a sketch, an overview of influential theories, individuals, and professional associations in the emergence of infant mental health.

Each of the theories of change we refer to—evolutionary, systems, and psychoanalytic—originated in the biological sciences, and each focused primarily on issues related to how the origins of behavior affect behavioral outcomes. Moreover, each is implicitly a developmental theory in that it attempts to account for change. Evolutionary theory contributed the concept of

adaptation and suggested that it was as valid to use descriptive and experimental scientific methods to study the ontogeny of behavior as it was to study phylogeny (Haeckel, 1879). Evolutionary theory provided an intellectual revolution that led investigators to posit connections between behavioral economy and natural selection (Baldwin, 1895), to theorize about the organization of behavioral systems (Werner, 1948), to accept that aspects of development were self-organizing and emergent (Schneirla, 1957), and to propose that developmental pathways were circumscribed by the environments in which they emerged (Waddington, 1956). Systems theory contributed a conceptual framework, constructed a language that enabled disciplines to communicate more effectively, and facilitated interdisciplinary exchanges by drawing attention to self-organizing characteristics of systems and to their interdependence. Psychoanalytic theory provided the first formal theory that proposed infancy as an important period in the life cycle and hypothesized that the events of infancy have long-term consequences. We have organized our discussion of these theories in the context of the emergence of infant mental health, rather than by the historical dates of their appearance in the general literature. As we add comments to support our selection of the change theories that give infant mental health its substance, we will promote René Spitz and Selma Fraiberg as the founders of the interdisciplinary field of infant mental health. We also describe the organization of the World Association for Infant Mental Health and discuss the definition of infant mental health, realizing that we are unlikely to achieve in one chapter what four volumes have been assembled to address.

Theories of Change

Central to the development of the infant mental health movement is the notion that infancy is a circumscribed period of life during which environmental influences can have a substantial impact on later development. This idea emerged about 150 years ago (Kagan, Kearsley, & Zelazo, 1978). Prior to the 1800s, the term *infant* referred to school-age children, not to babies (Aries, 1962). The idea that nurturance was an important aspect of development existed as early as the eighteenth century Enlightenment, the historical period that DeMause refers to as the "Intrusive Mode of parent-infant relations" (De-Mause, 1974). Despite the enlightened recognition of the importance of nurturance for child development, infancy was not viewed as an especially important time in human development, nor were the outcomes of child development in general so heavily bound to mother love (Kagan et al., 1978).

The concept that the first few years of life constitute a special period within human development emerged during the late nineteenth and early twentieth centuries, fueled perhaps by the publication of a number of baby biographies (Hall, 1896, 1897; Major, 1906; Preyer, 1888; Shinn, 1894). Although Sigismund (1856) may

have been the first person to publish a baby biography, Darwin's systematic observations of his infant son were written in 1842, though not published until 35 years later (1877). Such ethnographic renditions of the daily behavior of infants were influenced by the naturalistic observational methodology of evolutionary biology, which also focused attention on adaptation as a central theme of phylogeny and ontogeny. The concept of adaptation and its focus on species evolution in response to demands of the environment stands as one of three key concepts in the ancestry of infant mental health.

Evolutionary Theory and Infant Mental Health: Focus on Adaptive Behavior

Evolutionary theory focused on adaptive behavior and the organism-environment relationship. It set the stage for new ways of thinking about development. Nearly a century before Darwin and Wallace published their theories on evolution, a German zoologist (Wolff, 1733–1794) offered a novel explanation for development that he deduced from his studies of the embryological development of chickens. Wolff opposed the ovulists (Schwammerdam, 1646–1716) and the animal cultists (van Leeuwenhoek, 1632–1723), two preformationist schools, by suggesting that the embryo did not develop from an already completed whole, but rather was governed by a process of new formation from originally unorganized material, through the process of differentiation. Thus, changes during embryological development were

6

linked to environmental events and to interactions among the parts of the differentiating organism. In other words, Wolff proposed that embryological development was epigenetic; the zygote was not simply the additive product of the sperm and ovum, but was a unique organism whose genesis (development) was uniquely bound to its environment. The scientific community of the mid–eighteenth century was not yet ready to accept this theory as a broad principle of development. In contrast, evolutionary theory engaged debate about the origins of species, offered a naturalistic observational methodology for study of ontogenetic development, and opened a window from which one could view phylogeny retrospectively, and ontogeny prospectively. Evolutionary theory stimulated descriptive studies of early development; these eventually pushed experimental studies of development, and in combination with a pervasive emphasis on behavior, eventually led to discovery of "the competent infant" (Stone, Smith, & Murphy, 1973).

Early in the twentieth century, scientific inquiry focused on laboratory studies of the infant's sensory, perceptual, and motor abilities. For example, Brackbill's (1964) bibliography on infant research lists 1,733 citations of empirical studies, the majority of which were conducted prior to World War II and focused on sensory-perceptual responsivity, motor development, and learning. Arnold Gesell launched the infant assessment movement, initiated the use of motion picture photography as a research tool, and demonstrated the utility of the longitudinal method for investigating

developmental change (Gesell, 1928; Gesell & Halverson, 1942). Mary Shirley (1931) published detailed descriptions of the development of motor behavior, as did Myrtle McGraw (1935). McGraw also directed attention to the importance of twin studies for investigating the relationship between biological and environmental contributions to development. Major longitudinal studies of human development were established in this era, as were child welfare stations devoted to studies of child development and to dissemination of knowledge about child development. Although the longitudinal studies established in the 1920s and 1930s are significant in their own right for the data generated across successive generations, they also provided a foundation for the subsequent reconceptualization of development itself. The philosophy of science that was fundamental to the social and behavioral sciences prior to World War II was challenged by a new way of thinking about the developing organism. The behaviorist concept of the passive infant with little or no consciousness at birth (tabula rasa) was rejected and replaced by a variety of organismic, constructivist, systemic theories that emphasized the infant's active engagement of objects and events in the environment, including social objects.

By the 1960s researchers from a wide variety of disciplines were actively engaged in the study of infancy. From early in the decade into the 1970s, the literature mirrored that of the early twentieth century, with emphasis on experimental studies of the infant's sensory-perceptual (Cohen & Salapatek, 1975), learning (Fitzgerald &

Brackbill, 1976; Fitzgerald & Porges, 1971), and cognitive abilities (Kagan, 1970). Results of these investigations challenged the common view that the newborn was a passive recipient of environmental stimulation in possession of a tabula rasa consciousness. Research laboratories were established at most major research universities in the United States. Such laboratories included those established by William Kessen at Yale (visual processing), Lewis Lipsitt at Brown (sensory processing and operant learning), Yvonne Brackbill at Denver (psychophysiology of learning), Frances Graham at Wisconsin (psychophysiology of attention), Wendell Jeffries at Los Angeles (attention and habituation), Robert Fantz in Cleveland (visual processing of social stimuli), and Jerome Kagan at Harvard (attention and cognitive processing). Within a decade students from these laboratories had established their own research centers and the frontal assault on infant development was solidly under way. The results were fast coming and by 1973 the infant was officially declared to be competent (Stone, Smith, & Murphy, 1973). This intensive study of the behavioral and perceptual-cognitive abilities of the infant produced one of the more intriguing paradoxes of science: The intensely mechanistic empirical studies of the 1960s were in large measure responsible for demonstrating the inadequacy of the mechanistic model for explaining infant behavior and development. They provided convincing evidence that the human infant was an active information processor and was very much engaged in adapting to its environment while simultaneously influencing the environment to which it was adapting.

Systems Theory and Infant Mental Health: The Unity of Science

Ludwig von Bertalanffy (1900–1972) provided the second influence on infant mental health when he challenged the prevailing philosophy of science with his organismic biology (1928/1934) and proposed an alternative approach to science that eventually became known as general systems theory (von Bertalanffy, 1950, 1968). Systems theory emerged as a reaction to nomothetic, linear causal models such as those characterizing theoretical physics during the early part of the twentieth century. As physics and biology attempted to explain problems of organized complexity involving multiple sources of variation, it became evident that new theoretical formulations were necessary. Bertalanffy (1951; 1962), impressed by the order, organization, and maintenance he observed in the face of continuous change, regulation, goal-seeking, and apparent purposiveness of behavior, began to formulate an alternative to classical models in science. His general systems theory defined living systems as hierarchically organized (Werner, 1957), self-maintaining, and open, and specified key principles that describe system dynamics.

If a system is defined as a set of components that, when coupled together, form a functional whole that generates emergent properties unique to the system itself, three major themes become evident: the components, the feedback structures, and the new emergent properties (Levine & Fitzgerald, 1992). These themes have influenced the way researchers model and clinicians intervene in the processes influencing healthy infant development. Figure 1.1 illustrates three family systems, each of which engages systems external to it (exogenous).

From a systems perspective, analysis of the individual child must first take into account the presenting state characteristics of each individual in the family system. Then one must know the presenting state characteristics of each dyad (triad, etc.) in order to assess the degree to which the child is connected to family members and the quality of those relationships. Family functioning depends on the degree to which the family is connected to systems external to it (what we have labeled exogenous: school, workplace, religious center, supplemental child care site, etc.) and the barriers that may make access to exogenous systems difficult. Living systems are open systems, and one of the major tasks for systems science is to assess the open system's ability to cope with uncontrollable endogenous variables (an autistic child, an abusive parent, a single parent), to traverse boundaries between endogenous and exogenous factors, and to suggest better ways for the system to transact with outside conditions (psychotherapy, employment, a court order, school). In a sense, systems scientists use their analytic tools to find better coping mechanisms for the system under study or in treatment. The coping mechanisms can be represented as a set of one or more feedback loops whose behavior buffers the system against extreme outside

influences (Levine & Fitzgerald, 1992). Because systems are posited to be self-organizing, they are by definition equifinal, that is, the end point reached by the system is independent of its initial conditions (Anderson & Anderson, 1954).

Central to the impact of systems theory on infant mental health is its impact on the field's conceptualization of development itself. If development is "the act or process of causing to develop," and if we define *develop* as "to grow, unfold, take shape, become larger and more complex, evolve by natural process" (Wyld, 1938, p. 301), then development is little more than a synonym for maturation. Considerable evidence exists to support an alternative definition of development, one that casts development in terms of dynamic processes, organism-environment transactions, and probabilistic-contextual influences on organizing systems. Schneirla (1957) defined development as "a pattern of changes occurring in a system through time" (p. 78), with special emphasis on "progressive changes in the organization of an individual considered as a functional adaptive system throughout its life history" (p. 79). Werner (1957) formulated the orthogenetic principle by which development "proceeds from a state of relative globality and lack of differentiation to a state of increasing differentiation, articulation, and hierarchic integration" (p. 126).

In its contemporary form, development

is characterized by an increase of complexity of organization (i.e., the emergence of new structural and functional properties and competencies) at all levels of analysis . . . as a consequence of horizontal and vertical

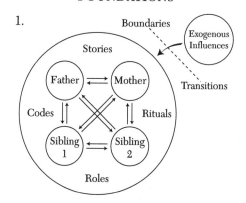

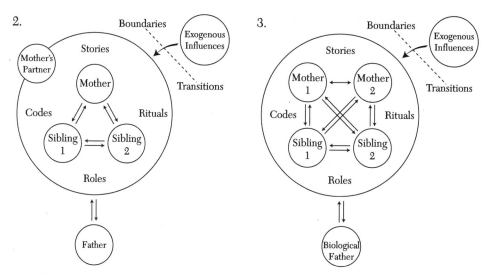

FIGURE 1.1

Possible transactional linkages in a primary family system (1) consisting of a mother, father, and their children, (2) in which the parents have divorced and the mother has recoupled, or (3) headed by two lesbian women with a known biological father who is not part of the system. Other configurations are possible depending upon the structure of the primary family system and the exogenous adjunctive systems that interact with it. From "The Family as a Unity of Interacting Personalities" (pp. 35–59), by A. Loukas, G. R. Twitchell, L. A. Piejak, H. E. Fitzgerald, and R. A. Zucker, 1998, in L. L'Abate (Ed.), *Family Psychopathology: The Relational Roots of Dysfunctional Behavior,* New York: Guilford. Reproduced with permission.

coactions among the organism's parts, including organism-environment coactions. (Gottlieb, 1991, p. 7)

The contemporary developmentalist, therefore, views adaptive behavior and adaptive functioning as emergent, epigenetic, systemic, organized, constructive, hierarchically integrated (Ford & Lerner, 1992; Gottlieb, 1991; Miller, 1978; Sameroff, 1995), and potentially chaotic (Levine & Fitzgerald, 1992; Thelen & Smith, 1992). All of these contemporary variations on the general systems theme in one way or another connect back in time to von Bertalanffy, and all have had a historical impact on the way infancy and developmental process itself is conceptualized today.

Infancy is a fertile age for examining the emergence and integration of biopsychosocial systems as well as for investigating the organization of these systems within multiple social-cultural contexts. Studies of the organization of social-emotional systems (Sander, 1987), emotional development and the differentiation of ego structures (Sroufe, 1979), social networks (Lewis, 1987), behavioral organization (Als, Lester, Tronic & Brazelton, 1982), infant-caregiver modulation (Brazelton, 1982), determinants of parenting (Belsky, 1984), and the importance of context (Lerner, 1984) to one degree or another reflect the influence of systems thinking on the organization of behavior. Attachment theory was strongly influenced by control systems (Bowlby, 1951, 1969). Inge Bretherton's (1987) control systems model of the attachment system illustrates an attempt to clarify the complexity of the attachment process. Her model depicts the information flow among the subsystems constituting the attachment system. In this model, the filial attachment system monitors two types of information: clues to danger and accessibility to the attachment figure. Bretherton conceptualizes this as a continuously active system that monitors and regulates the activation and deactivation of attachment behaviors.

Apropos of infant mental health, the influence of systems theory and evolutionary theory was not restricted to the scientific study of infants. It also had an impact on theories related to therapeutic interventions with infants. Contemporary clinical approaches developed by Greenspan (1981), Stern (1985), and Minde and Minde (1986) also reflect a systems perspective. But it was the ego psychologists of the 1930s and 1940s who seem to have been profoundly influenced by systems theory as they reshaped psychoanalytic theory of personality to focus on object relations and self-object differentiation during infancy and early childhood. In their volume highlighting articles published in the *Journal of the American Academy of Child Psychiatry*, Rexford, Sander, and Shapiro (1976) bound systems theory tightly to infant psychiatry:

The plan of the papers in this volume offers one framework by which the variety of contributors relevant to the task of the clinician can be brought together, namely, that of the systems point of view. . . . This fluid state of adaptation emerges from the continuing adaptations of the various systems involved in organizing the infant's behavior. (p. xvi)

The developmental perspective causes one to search for developmental processes, or as Emde (1981) has argued, it enables consideration of systems sensitivity, which he defines as "an intuitive, empathic registration by the therapist of the quality of functioning of complex personality subsystems and their interactions" (p. 5).

Psychoanalytic Theory and Infant Mental Health: Subject-Object Relationships

Three years before the publication of *The Origin of Species* (Darwin, 1859), Sigmund Freud was born in Freiburg (in what was then Czechoslovakia). Educated in medicine, he specialized in neurology, and when he was 44, he published his first work on psychoanalytic theory. In so doing, Freud set into motion the third key influence on infant mental health (Freud, 1900/1932). Psychoanalytic theory supported infancy as a special period in the formation of personality and emotional development (Freud, 1909) and laid a foundation for the emergence of ego psychology and its focus on subject-object relations (Roiphe, 1979). Whereas basic researchers played an undeniably important role in describing and discovering the sophisticated processes infants use to guide their adaptation to the demands of the environment, clinical investigators already were a step ahead with respect to their conceptual understanding of the active role that the infant played in the adaptation process. René Spitz, said to be one of the first individuals to complete an analysis with Freud, was to emerge as the most influential figure in the history of infant mental health. In fact, one can think of Spitz as the individual who provided the theoretical foundations for infant psychiatry, and Selma Fraiberg as the individual who both pushed its application to other clinical fields and facilitated infant psychiatry's transformation to a more inclusive field of infant mental health (Bonkowski & Yanos, 1992).

Sigmund Freud's (1856–1939) theory of personality stimulated considerable controversy over such topics as the role of instincts in human behavior, the structure of the mind, the function of conscious and unconscious processes, the stage sequencing of personality, and the various intricate relationships between parent and child that he thought defined the individual's personality. Freudian theory was the first major theory to attribute special importance to the early interactions between children and their parents. However, it did not place adequate emphasis on ego functions or take adequate account of social and cultural influences on personality development. During the 1920s a number of psychoanalytic revisionists focused more intensely on ego psychology and the significance of object relations for later development (Roiphe, 1979). Efforts to blend the psychosexual stages of development into social and cultural contexts are characteristic of neo-Freudian theorists such as Erik Erikson and Margaret Mahler.

Whereas Freud stressed the biological determinants of personality and the functions of the id and superego, Erikson stressed personality development in light of the individual's historical and cultural past. Moreover, Erikson was concerned primarily with the development of ego functions. For Erikson, personality is not fixed or final; it is subject to change over the life course. The individual is always in a state of becoming. Erikson used the Freudian term libidinal energy to refer to the regulatory force that drives epigenetic development, with each stage of psychosocial development posing a dilemma or dialectical conflict that required resolution. Each stage marked a turning point or choice point in the organization of personality. Central to infancy and early childhood is the infant's need to develop a sense of trust in its environment. This sense of trust prepares the individual to become an autonomous and self-initiated individual.

Margaret Mahler's work focused on the organization and emergence of an intrapsychic sense of self—that is, an awareness that the self exists as a separate being. The infant accomplishes this developmental task through a process of separation and individuation (Mahler, Pine, & Bergman, 1975). Initially the infant's intrapsychic awareness must be satisfied by the caregiver. Toward the end of the first month of life the infant develops a sense of unity or symbiosis with that caregiver, especially mediated by physical contact. The infant cannot maintain a symbiotic state with the caregiver if a sense of self-identity is to be achieved. As the infant separates from the caregiver, he or she simultaneously begins to organize a sense of being. From Mahler's perspective, this is not a sense of "who I am" but a sense of "that I am"—that I exist as a separate, distinct entity. Although Erikson and Mahler penned influential revisions of Freudian theory and focused attention on the period of infancy, neither had much success in bringing about adoption of his innovative theoretical ideas in the broader infant research community. Indeed, Erikson's theory seemed to have a more powerful impact on adolescence and issues of identity formation.

Conversely, after World War II a number of researchers who were more outwardly influenced by evolutionary and systems approaches to the study of development turned their attention to assessing the impact of environmental events on the infant's social and emotional behavior. Seminal publications of the time included those of Ribble (1943) on "the rights of infants," Spitz and Wolf (1946) on anaclitic depression, Spitz (1945, 1965) and Goldfarb (1943) on the effects of institutionalization, A. Freud and Burlingham (1944) on separation, and Bowlby (1951) on maternal deprivation. René Spitz emerged from this era as a leading spokesperson for infant psychiatry, the forerunner of what we now know as infant mental health.

Spitz (1965) was the first individual to formally propose a nosological classification of infant psychiatric disturbances, anticipating by nearly 30 years the diagnostic classification system developed by Zero to Three (1994; see Table 1.1). He also contributed two seminal ideas that were to have a significant impact on both the scientific and clinical communities with respect to studies of subject-object differentiation: his concept of dialogue and his description of events that served to organize subject-object relationships (Spitz, 1959).

Emde (1983) notes that Spitz's emphasis on dialogue captured the importance of

TABLE 1.1

Focus on Emotional Development: Spitz's Etiological Classification of Psychogenic Diseases of Infancy According to Maternal Attitudes and the 0 to 3 Diagnostic Classification of Mental Health and Development Disorders of Infancy and Early Childhood

	Spitz's Classification (1965)		0 to 3 Classification System
	Etiological Factor Provided by Maternal Attitudes	Infant's Disease	
Psychotixic (Quality)	Overt Primal Rejection	Coma in Newborn (Ribble)	Axis I: Primary diagnosis
	Primary Anxious Over-Permissiveness	Three-Month Colic	Traumatic Stress Disorder
	Hostility in the Guise of		Disorders of Affect
	Anxiety	Infantile Eczema	Adjustment Disorder
	Oscillation between		Regulatory Disorders
	Pampering and Hostility	Hypermotility (rocking)	Sleep Behavior Disorder
	Cyclical Mood Swings	Fecal Play	Eating Behavior Disorder
	Hostility Consciously	Aggressive Hyperthymic	Disorders of Relating & Communicating
	Compensated	(Bowlby)	Axix II: Relational Classification
			Axis III: Medical and Developmental Diagnoses
Deficiency (Quantity)	Partial Emotional Deprivation	Anaclitic Depression	Axis IV: Psychosocial Stressors
	Complete Emotional Deprivation	Marasmus	Axis V: Functional Emotional/Developmental Level

Note. From The First Year of Life (p. 209), by R. A. Spitz, 1965, New York: International Universities Press; and from Diagnostic Classification of Mental Health and Developmental Disorders of Infancy and Early Childhood: 0–3 (pp. 75–82), by Zero to Three, 1994, Washington, DC: Zero to Three, The National Center for Infants, Toddlers and Families. Copyright 1994 by Zero to Three. Adapted with permission.

14

the mother-infant relationship and by so doing broadened the concept of object relations and drew attention to the infant as an active participant in dyadic communication. The influence of systems thinking is evident in Spitz's observation about the nature of mother-infant communication. "It is a dialogue of action and response which goes on in the form of a circular process within the dyad, as a continuous mutually stimulating feedback circuit. . . ." (in Emde, 1983, p. 152). In his edited collection of Spitz's papers, Emde (1983) quotes Spitz as saying, "Every successive organizer in the further course of development introduces a new formula of relations, successively more complex and better adapted" (p. 201) and goes on to comment that "as a developmental theoretician, Spitz was intensely preoccupied with the dynamics of how such major reorganizations could take place" (p. 201).

Spitz was among the first to propose that the infant participated in the organization of three explicit organizers of the psyche that played a transformational role in development. The first organizer, the social smile, marked the transformation from passive involvement to active involvement in the socialization process. Spitz attached great importance to the infant's smile response to the human face, provided one of the earliest ethologically based descriptions of the development of social wariness as reflected by differential smiling, and observed the importance of motion as part of the stimulus characteristics that prompt infants to orient to the adult face (Spitz, 1965). The second organizer, 8-month anxiety, indicated to Spitz that the infant has

consolidated not just a cognitive representation of the libidinal object (familiar caregiver), but also an affective representation. Spitz (1965) writes, "It is evident that the object has been established not only in the optic (cognitive) sector but also—and perhaps we should say *primarily*—in the affective sector" (p. 161). Communication is the third organizer of the psyche, especially as reflected in the semantic no. Spitz believed that the toddler's active resistance expressed to the libidinal object marked a more substantive transformation in the toddler's social and personality development. The libidinal object that the infant could not bear to be separate from in late infancy now is resisted. "The 'No,' in gesture and in word, is the semantic expression of negation and judgment; at the same time this is the first abstraction formed by the child, the first abstract concept in the sense of adult mentation" (Spitz, 1965, p. 189). Spitz was well aware of the dynamic processes regulating the emergence of the organizers and that their emergence itself transformed the infant and transformed the infant's relationships with others. "It is a dialogue of action and response which goes on in the form of a circular process within the dyad, as continuous mutually stimulating feedback circuit . . . an archaic form of conversation" (Spitz, cited in Emde, 1983, p. 152).

Today, infant mental health specialists are more likely to attribute significance to the first few years of life because of the importance of emergent, dynamic, and organizing systems than from a sense that specific events during infancy necessarily have an impact over the life course (Emde,

1981; Sameroff, 1983). Contemporary knowledge of brain development provides vivid confirmation of the plasticity that extends to all aspects of systemic organization, particularly during the early years of development (Lerner, 1984).

Selma Fraiberg's work with parents of blind infants provides an excellent illustration of systemic reorganization and plasticity. Parents of blind infants were taught to use tactile and auditory stimulation to solicit, maintain, and enhance social behaviors (organizers) and to achieve their dialogue through nonvisual means. Fraiberg (1918–1981) was to become a powerful spokesperson for the infant mental health movement. In 1958, Fraiberg's *The Magic Years* focused public attention on the early years of development: In a 15-year period over one million copies of the volume were sold. Less well known to the general public were her publications on blind infants and their families (Fraiberg, 1968), including studies of sensory-motor competence (Adelson & Fraiberg, 1972, 1974, 1976; Fraiberg, Siegel, & Gibson, 1966), mother-infant communication (Fraiberg, 1974; Fraiberg, Smith, & Adelson, 1969), social behavior (Fraiberg, 1970, 1971), and ego development (Fraiberg & Freedman, 1964).

In 1972, Fraiberg established the Child Development Project at the University of Michigan. The project's goal was to develop a home visitation psychotherapeutic model of intervention for mother-infant dyads. She and her colleagues subsequently contributed to the study of adolescent pregnancy programs (Aradine, Shapiro, & Fraiberg, 1978; Fraiberg, 1971; Shapiro, Fraiberg, & Adelson, 1976), and

to the field of social work (Fraiberg, 1978). Her work reflected a commitment to the scientific study of infancy; the integration of psychoanalytic theory with the basic data of child development; and the conviction that to be maximally effective, the study of infancy must be multidisciplinary.

Fraiberg was unequivocal in her recognition that scientific study of the infant and clinical preventive intervention programs were only two aspects of the infant mental health triad; the third was advocacy. For example, in her comments on infant mental health prepared for Emde's volume paying tribute to René Spitz, Fraiberg notes that

> when social policy or law does not acknowledge the primacy of infant-parent relations for optimal development of every child, or functions through archaic practice to disrupt these bonds, the mental health professional must speak for children and their rights to bring about enlightened policies and practices that can in themselves prevent damage to countless numbers of children. (p. 442)

Fraiberg was especially good at speaking for infants. As E. James Anthony noted (1984), Selma was especially skilled at "making the obscurities and complexities of the human condition clear, concise, and comprehensible" (p. xxxiii). Moreover, she found a way for babies to speak about unresolved issues that confounded their parents' abilities to provide loving relationships, a phenomenon she referred to as "ghosts in the nursery" (Fraiberg, Adelson, & Shapiro 1975).

By the mid-1970s infant mental health

had found its theoretic in ego psychology, especially the theoretical contributions of René Spitz; had a solid link to scientific studies of the infant and of infant-caregiver relationships; and had an extraordinarily effective advocate in Selma Fraiberg. What it lacked was a more formal structure to promote discussion, encourage scientific and clinical studies, and speak to policy issues affecting infants and their caregivers. Interestingly enough, events within infant psychiatry and within social work were to have a profound effect on the emergence of professional organizations exclusively devoted to infant mental health.

Professionalization of Infant Mental Health: WAIPAD + IAIMH = WAIMH

The World Association for Infant Mental Health was officially established in 1992. Perhaps appropriately, WAIMH emerged from the union of two parent associations, one with its origins primarily in the field of psychiatry (World Association for Infant Psychiatry and Allied Disciplines, WAIPAD), and the other with its origins primarily in fields other than psychiatry (International Association for Infant Mental Health, IAIMH). However, the first professional organization devoted exclusively to infant mental health was the Michigan Association for Infant Mental Health (MiAIMH), an organization that had direct connections to the work of Selma Fraiberg and that played a key historical role in the professionalization of the field.

IAIMH

In 1973 and in 1974, Betty Tableman, director for prevention in the Michigan Department of Mental Health, persuaded Fraiberg to train individuals already working at community mental health agencies as a way of implementing infant mental health services throughout Michigan (Shapiro, Adelson, & Tableman, 1978, 1980, 1982). The 12 individuals enrolled in these two training groups, among the first formally trained community-based infant mental health specialists, were to become founders of MiAIMH.

After completing their formal training, the 12 continued to meet regularly to discuss clinical issues and to plan ways to disseminate the infant mental health perspective to other professionals throughout Michigan (Adelson, Shapiro & Bennett, 1982; Tableman, 1982a, 1982b). Few could have anticipated the events that were to transpire as a result of those first informal meetings. As a first step in dissemination, a one-day workshop was held, attended by 80 persons. Encouraged by the enthusiastic response to the workshop, in 1976 the group decided to conduct a 2-day conference in Ann Arbor, Michigan. Because the University of Michigan conference center required users to be sponsored by an organization, the planning group created and incorporated The Michigan Association for Infant Mental Health (1977) as the umbrella organization for the training conference. Conference planners had hoped for an attendance of 300 in order to make expenses, but were overwhelmed when nearly 800 registrations poured in from

Michigan, other states, and Canada (Tableman, 1982a). Each year at the annual conference, MiAIMH honors the memory of Selma Fraiberg by presenting an award in her name to a person or program in the state of Michigan for outstanding contributions to infants and their families. An award to honor Betty Tableman also is presented to an individual or organization that has made a significant impact on policy issues related to infants and their families.

During the January 1979 meeting of the MiAIMH board of directors, it was decided to sponsor a professional journal of international scope consistent with MiAIMH's educational mission. In 1980 the first issue of the *Infant Mental Health Journal* (IMHJ) was published under the editorship of Jack Stack. At that same meeting, the MiAIMH Board also approved development of an international society, one that would help promote development of infant mental health associations that would reflect the purposes of the international organization but also would be uniquely suited to local needs (Fitzgerald, 1985; Shapiro, Adelson, & Tableman, 1978; Tableman, 1982a). On April 27, 1979, the MiAIMH board of directors approved two proposals offered by Jack Stack. The first was to establish IAIMH; the second, to establish the *Infant Mental Health Journal* as MiAIMH's official publication, with IAIMH having cosponsorship as well as ownership of the logo that appeared on the journal for the first 17 years of its existence. Human Sciences Press was selected as the publisher, and Jack Stack was installed as founding editor. Michael Trout was selected by the organizing IAIMH board as

its first president. Members of the MiAIMH board who voted to create both the journal and the IAIMH were Michael Trout (president), Ruth Szabo, Jack Stack, Ann Saffer, Judith Evans, Mary Scoblic, Stan Garwood, Thomas Barrett, Mary K. Peterson, Barbara Banet, Alice Marie Carter, and Hiram Fitzgerald.

During the first few years the IMHJ subscription list grew rapidly and the number of submissions to the journal increased proportionally. Jack Stack turned the editorial duties over to Sharon Bradley Johnson, and things continued to progress well until a variety of production difficulties arose that threatened the quality of the journal. Publication of the journal fell more than a year behind schedule, galley proofs came to the editor with portions of one article appearing in another, pages missing, and typos rampant. The editor resigned in frustration, and Hiram Fitzgerald assumed editorial responsibilities and began to negotiate with the publisher to transfer copyright ownership of the journal to MiAIMH. Following a long and difficult legal process, and with the extraordinary assistance of Clinical Psychology Publishing Company (CPPC), a small publishing firm in Vermont, MiAIMH gained ownership of the journal and secured a publishing contract with CPPC that continued until 1998 when John Wiley & Sons purchased CPPC.

WAIPAD

Although the pathway from Spitz to WAIPAD is not quite as clear as that from Fraiberg to IAIMH, Spitz's early use of the term infant psychiatry (1950) clearly set the stage for the emergence of infant psychiatry as a specialized subfield within child psychiatry. But the more proximal catalysts for the formation of WAIPAD were Justin Call and Eleanor Galenson. In 1974 the American Academy of Child and Adolescent Psychiatry established the Committee on Infant Psychiatry, with Justin Call as chairperson. As Call notes in a letter to Yvon Gauthier written in 1991, the committee was established so that "psychiatrists who were interested in infancy could get together in the workings of that committee and relate our work to the field of infancy and still maintain our identity within the field of Child Psychiatry" (Call, 1991). In fact, Call had been involved therapeutically with infants and young children for some time (e.g., Call, 1957; 1975), as had such pioneers as Benedek (1938), Bowlby (1951), Brody (1956), Erikson (1950), Fish (1957), A. Freud (Freud & Burlingham, 1944), Greenacre (1945), Hartmann (1939), Lourie (1949), Mahler (1952), and Winnicott (1941, 1953, 1964/1987, 1965). Without question there was a rich base of theory, research, and clinical practice that motivated individuals such as Call and Galenson to organize a more formal structure for discussion of the issues related to psychiatric issues during the early years of life.

In 1980, Call contacted Serge Lebovici and discussed the possibility of forming the World Association of Infant Psychiatry (WAIP), a move that Lebovici (2000) recalls opposing at first because he did not want to see increasing specialization within the field of psychiatry. However, it was agreed to conduct a world congress, and in April 1980 the congress was held in Estoril, Portugal, and E. James Anthony was selected to serve as the first president of the association. The congress was dedicated to René Spitz (1887–1974) in honor of his contributions to the field of infant psychiatry, contributions that Fraiberg (1983) contended led directly to creation of the field of infant mental health. According to Lebovici, one consequence of the congress was the establishment of an interdisciplinary group in France focusing on issues related to what we might now refer to as relationship disturbances (AETPN: Association pour l'Étude des Travaux Psychiatriques sur le Nourrisson; see Lebovici, 2000). AETPN accepted responsibility for organizing WAIP's second world congress, which was held at Cannes. The Cannes meeting was notable, not only because nearly 1500 people attended, but because WAIP changed its name to WAIPAD and Robert Emde was elected to be president of the society.

WAIMH

During the time when MiAIMH was having difficulties with the original publisher of the *Infant Mental Health Journal,* Hiram Fitzgerald had invited Robert Emde to present a colloquium at Michigan State University. After the colloquium they engaged in a conversation about the growing number of infancy organizations, which included not only WAIPAD and IAIMH, but also the International Society of Infant Studies and the training center then known as the National Center for Clinical Infant

Studies. They discussed the possibility of having both IAIMH and WAIPAD cosponsor the IMHJ and the possibility of asking Joy Osofsky to become editor of the journal. A follow-up meeting was scheduled to take place at the biennial meeting of the Society for Research in Child Development in Toronto, and the courtship of IAIMH and WAIPAD began.

The planning committee that met in Toronto included Robert Emde (president of WAIPAD), Richard Barthel (president of IAIMH), Joy Osofsky (proposed editor of the IMHJ), Dolores Fitzgerald (IAIMH administrative assistant), and Hiram Fitzgerald (executive officer of IAIMH and editor of the IMHJ). The discussion went well, and not only did Osofsky agree to a 5-year term as editor, Fitzgerald agreed to serve as program chair for WAIPAD's 1988 world congress. Emde played a key role in carrying the merger message to WAIPAD. Everything was in place for members of each organization to get to know one another. Moreover, a committee was established to review possibilities for merging the two organizations into a strong interdisciplinary and international force for infant mental health. WAIMH was conceived!

Prenatal development went smoothly. During the first trimester, Joy Osofsky became editor of the IMHJ (1988, a position she will continue to hold until at least 2002). During the second trimester, WAIPAD successfully held its fourth world congress in Lugano, Switzerland, and newly elected president Serge Lebovici appointed a merger/bylaws committee to prepare a recommendation for merger to

be considered by the directors of both WAIPAD and IAIMH. At the end of the third trimester, the bylaws committee (Robert Emde, Joy Osofsky, Hiram Fitzgerald, Sonya Bemporad, Serge Lebovici, Yvon Gauthier, and Justin Call) presented its recommendations to a joint meeting of the IAIMH and WAIPAD held in Chicago in September 1992. The members of IAIMH voted to dissolve as a corporation, WAIPAD voted to change its bylaws and name, and members of each association ratified the establishment of the World Association for Infant Mental Health. Joy Osofsky was elected the first president of WAIMH; Hiram Fitzgerald agreed to a 10-year term as executive director; and a central office for the association was established at Michigan State University, first in the Department of Psychology and then within the Institute for Children, Youth, and Families. The new organization and bylaws retained the affiliate structure established by IAIMH. During its 12 years of existence IAIMH helped to establish affiliate associations in Texas (1980), Delaware Valley and Illinois (1981), Mexico, Ontario, and Iowa (1982), Virginia and North Carolina (1983), Quebec and Maryland (1985), Minnesota (1986), Maine (1987), Australia (1988), New Jersey (1990), Oklahoma (1991), and the Nordic countries (1992). Since 1992, WAIMH has added affiliates in Louisiana and Greece (1993), France (1994), Kansas and Russia (St. Petersburg, 1995), the United Kingdom, the Netherlands, and Germany-Austria-Switzerland (1996), Finland and Italy (1998), and currently has active associations emerging in South Africa, Brussels-

Luxemburg, British Columbia (Canada), and the state of Washington. WAIMH currently has affiliate organizations established or in development in 24 countries, and individual members reside in 43 countries.

WAIMH has matured as a parent organization, but its basic goals are consistent with those of all of its affiliates. Specifically, WAIMH:

- Promotes education, research, and study of the effects of emotional development during infancy on later normal and psychopathological development
- Promotes research and study of the mental health of the parents, families, and other caregivers of infants.
- Promotes the development of scientifically based programs of care, intervention, and prevention of mental impairment in infancy.
- Facilitates international cooperation among individuals concerned with promoting optimal development of infants and their families.
- Maintains with MiAIMH a video library of films about infant development, infant mental health, and family relationships, as well as a historical archive of the field.
- Sponsors the *Infant Mental Health Journal* and its newsletter, *The Signal.*
- Sponsors regional and world congresses devoted to scientific, clinical, and educational work with infants, their caregivers, and their cultural contexts.

So the pathways that had their origins in the infant psychiatry of René Spitz and the clinical social work of Selma Fraiberg merged and shaped WAIMH into an interdisciplinary, multicultural organization focusing on the mental health needs of infants and their families.

Definition of Infant Mental Health

Infant mental health is difficult to define because it is such a pervasive concept. At one level, it focuses on the social and emotional well-being of infants and their caregivers. Any event or set of events that affects infant/family well-being is an issue of appropriate concern for infant mental health: premature birth, perinatal complications, inadequate prenatal care, infant mortality and morbidity (and parental grief), physical disability, mental retardation, poverty, undernutrition, single parenting, supplemental caregiving, parental psychopathology, parental stress, abusive parenting, parental substance abuse, and marital conflict.

Is infant mental health an educational discipline? Yes. Programs involving parent effectiveness training, infant care and development, training of supplemental caregivers, and training of infant specialists all legitimately fall under the rubric of infant mental health. Is infant mental health a clinical field? Yes. Nurses, social workers, psychologists, physicians, physical therapists, audiologists and speech pathologists, and other health care professionals interact with infants and/or their caregivers in a variety of clinical settings. Is infant mental health a research discipline? Yes. Investigators from a wide variety of disciplines engage in basic and applied research as well as clinical studies in order to build on the cumulative body of knowledge about infant development, caregiver-infant relationships, and ecological or contextual influences on development. It is from such cumulative knowledge that prevention and intervention programs are best conceptualized, implemented, and evaluated.

The fact that infant mental health encompasses all of the above necessarily leads to its multidisciplinary character. No single discipline can lay claim to all the knowledge necessary to promote optimal development of infants and their caregivers. Professionals from many disciplines may at one time or another come into contact with infants and their caregivers. One could argue that a researcher investigating basic skills of auditory perception during infancy is not engaged in infant mental health work. At one level this may be true. The researcher may have little interest in issues related to application of the basic perceptual phenomenon detailed in his or her work. At another level, however, such investigation could easily fall within the purview of infant mental health. Research that uncovered information or techniques useful in helping deaf infants enhance their orientation to objects and events in their environments could thus ultimately yield changes in ego development, self-concept formation, competence motivation, autonomy striving, and caregiver-infant relationships.

One way to ascertain the scope of a discipline is by examining the contents of the articles published in its journals. We recently completed such an examination of the *Infant Mental Health Journal* covering the first 18.5 years of its existence (spring 1980 to summer 1998). First we wanted to know what kinds of articles were appearing in the journal, so we classified each as an empirical study (empirical program evaluations/assessments/tools), a clinical study (treatment and case studies, program descriptions), a theoretical or content review article, or a book review. We found that 42 percent of the articles were empirical, 28 percent were clinical, 20 percent were theoretical or content reviews, and 10 percent were book reviews. This simple analysis suggests a rather nice blend of empirical, clinical, and theoretical approaches that seems quite appropriate for a clinical science.

Next we categorized all articles into themes and topics (see Table 1.2). *Topic* refers to the specific content of an article, whereas *theme* represents a higher level categorization. For example, the topics feeding, sleep disturbance, and temperament are subsumed under the theme self-regulation. Each article could be classified with up to two representative topics, but only assigned one primary theme. If infant mental health was defined by the themes most represented in the *Infant Mental Health Journal,* then we would be a discipline concerned with infant mental health services and the field of infant mental health itself (31.6 percent of 484 total articles), caregiver-infant interactions (24.4 percent), conditions placing infants at risk (22.3 percent), infant development outcomes (9.9 percent), methodology/

TABLE 1.2

Topics Addressed in Articles Published in the *Infant Mental Health Journal*
from Spring 1980 through Summer 1998

Topics	Total	1980–86	1987–92	1993–98
Infant Development/Outcomes	**104**	**41**	**25**	**38**
Infant development (multiple areas)	11	5	4	2
Social-Emotional	30	11	10	9
Cognition	25	4	3	18
Neuromotor	15	8	3	4
Vision & Audition	1	1	0	0
Language/Communication	20	11	4	5
Infant state	1	1	0	0
Sex differences	1	0	1	0
Self-Regulation	**26**	**5**	**8**	**13**
Nursing/Feeding	7	0	1	6
Sleep disturbances	7	1	2	4
Temperament	12	4	5	3
IMH Services/Field	**233**	**104**	**72**	**53**
Community programs/Prevention	14	10	2	2
IMH specialists/Interdisciplinary	16	10	3	3
IMH—Training	8	3	3	2
IMH Field	14	2	8	4
IMH services/Early intervention	90	33	31	26
In memoriam	3	2	1	0
Home-based interventions	13	8	3	2
Health care/Maternity/NICU	11	7	2	2
Historical practices	5	1	2	2
Parent education/Training/Support	24	20	3	1
Psychotherapy	30	7	14	9
Public policy issues	4	1	3	0
Methodology/Assessment	**69**	**25**	**20**	**24**
Assessment issues	54	22	15	17
Methodological issues	15	3	5	7
Conditions That May Place Families/Infants at Risk	**233**	**83**	**73**	**77**
Maternal depression	24	1	8	15
Infants/Children with disabilities	18	8	4	6
Multirisk infants and familes	11	8	2	1
Poor home environment	5	2	3	0
Failure to thrive	6	2	3	1

(continued)

TABLE 1.2 (Continued)

Topics	Total	1980–86	1987–92	1993–98
Colic	8	0	5	3
Child maltreatment/abuse	16	8	6	2
Psychopathology	13	7	4	2
Premature/LBW	36	15	14	7
Day care	12	6	6	0
Grieving/Death/Loss	9	2	1	6
Separation (including for employment)	5	3	2	0
Perceived attractiveness	3	2	0	1
Social support/Network	9	6	2	1
Stress/Coping	14	2	4	8
Observers of violence	6	0	0	6
Adolescent parents	20	8	8	4
Cesarean birth/Birthing	3	2	1	0
Substance use/Drug exposure	14	0	0	14
Father absence	1	1	0	0
Caregiver Interactions/Influence/Role	***251***	***76***	***92***	***83***
Parenting				
Fathers and infants	15	13	2	0
Grandparental role	1	1	0	0
Parenting behaviors/Skills/Interactions	103	37	34	32
Parents' perceptions/Attitudes/Beliefs	58	13	24	21
Cognitions				
Custody/Legal issues	5	3	1	1
Attachment	59	7	29	23
Marital interactions/Satisfaction	10	2	2	6
Transition to parenthood	1	0	1	0
Cross-Cultural Studies/Non-U.S. Samples	***19***	***1***	***12***	***6***

assessment (9.5 percent), self-regulation (1.9 percent) and cross-cultural studies (0.4 percent).

Table 1.2 indicates the distribution of major themes for articles published in the journal organized in 6-year cohorts. If we defined infant mental health by the topics that appear in the journal, then the definition would be cohort dependent, because the emphasis on specific topics changes over time. Scanning across the columns in Table 1.2, note that the field seemed to be losing interest in prematurity/low birthweight (36 articles total, but only 7 in the past 6 years) and fathers (15 articles, 2 in the past 6 years—although this will change with the special issue on fathers published in 1999). Perhaps the most dramatic drop in interest is associated with parent education/training/support. Of the 24 articles published over the 18-year period, only 4 were published during the past 12 years.

Prominent among the topics gaining in interest are maternal depression (24 articles, 15 in the last 6 years), attachment (59 articles, only 7 of which appeared in the first 6 volumes), cognitive development (25 articles, 18 in the past 6 years), and substance abuse (14 articles, all of which appeared in the past 6 years). Studies of social-emotional development, infant mental health (IMH) services, assessment issues, and parent perceptions/attitudes seem to hold their interest across the three cohorts.

We can also ask questions about how representative articles in the journal are of diverse human cultures. If one examines the country of origin of senior authors and includes all articles published regardless of the nature of the article, one finds that the senior author for 356 of 488 publications resided in the United States (Table 1.3). However, senior authors represent a total of 23 countries, with the top five—the United States, Canada, the United Kingdom, France, Switzerland, and Israel—accounting for 439 of the 488 articles. Although the number of articles published by United States-based authors is disproportionate, it is fair to say that there is some degree of diversity in the articles published in the IMHJ. South America, Africa, and Asia have particularly low frequencies relative to the portion of the world's infants that these countries represent. These data are not substantively different from those obtained when one scans all major scientific databases in an effort to compile a world literature on scientific studies of infants of color (Fitzgerald et al., 1999). It is clear

that much work needs to be done to chronicle the rich cultural variation in infant development and family life so that the resultant knowledge of infant development, infant-caregiver relationships, and the cultural context of early development describes the species, rather than representing a narrow account of development in a particular cultural context.

Finally, in determining which authors were more successful in surviving the peer review process, we discovered some interesting trends (Table 1.4). For example, Tiffany Field is the most published author in the history of the journal, with nicely balanced frequencies across the three cohorts. The second most published author, Hiram Fitzgerald, had 10 of 13 articles published in the journal's first 6 years, whereas the third on the list, Daniel Stern, had all of his 10 articles published since 1987. If one counts only senior-authored papers, then there is a much longer list of authors, but Tiffany Field continues to stay at the top (Table 1.5).

Defining a field by the contents of its journal may be instructive, but it is not satisfying because it provides only one window into the breadth of a field that because of its multidisciplinary and international character may involve hundreds of journals, books, and other forms of knowledge generation and dissemination. A more formal definition is desired. In 1997, the Maine Association for Infant Mental Health's quality assurance committee defined infant mental health

as the ability of infants to develop physically, cognitively, and socially in a manner which

TABLE 1.3

Country of Senior Author for Papers Published in the Infant Mental Health Journal 1980–1998 by Type of Article

	1	2	3	4	5	6	7	8	9	10	11	12	13	14	15	16	17	18
United States	1	29	25	85	48	17	4	8	15	38	6	9	35	12	16	4	3	356
New Zealand	1																	1
England/U.K.	1	2	6			2	1		1				1	4	3			19
Switzerland	3	3	3	1	1	2		1	1					3	1			15
Japan	2		1		1									2				6
Italy	3							2										7
Canada	1		3	5	1	2	2		1	2	3			2	1			23
Uruguay	1			1						1								3
Australia	1		1										1					3
Netherlands	1		2	1	1							1						6
Sweden			2		4		1			1								8
Israel	1		1	3	1	1			1			1	1	1				11
South Africa				1														1
France	1		4		2	1	1						1	3				15
Chili					1													1

26

	1	2	3	4	5	6	7	8	9	10	11	12	13	14	15	16	17	18
Greece		1					1											2
Finland					1					1								2
Russia				1														1
Brazil					1													1
Portugal										1								1
Germany											1				1			2
Austria														1				1
Argentina									1				1					2
Unknown									1								1	1
Total	104	43	8	64	7	24	10	35	20	48	10	11	39	27	21	4	3	488
% from U.S.	100	67.4	5	78.7	78.0	46.05	67.15	79.2	60	81.8	.97	84.4	76.2	4.4	6.2	1	0	7

Note. 1 = Bibliography; 2 = Case study; 3 = Commentary or position papers; 4 = Correlational study; 5 = Descriptive study; 7 = Historical; 8 = Instrument critique, descriptive; 9 = Instrument critique, validation; 10 = Program description; 11 = Program evaluation; 12 = Review article, position paper; 13 = Review article, topical area; 14 = Theoretical; 15 = Therapeutic technique; 16 = Review article, broad work in the field; 17 = Review article, multiple programs, 18 = Totals. (Analysis excludes all published book/video reviews.)

TABLE 1.4

Individuals with Three or More Senior Authored Papers in the *Infant Mental Health Journal*,
from Spring 1980 to Spring 1998

	1980–86	1987–92	1993–98	Total
Boger, Robert P.	3	0	0	3
Bradley, Robert H.	3	0	0	3
Bradley-Johnson, Sharon	3	0	0	3
Bretherton, Inge	0	2	1	3
Cramer, Bertrand	0	2	3	5
Crittenden, Patricia M.	1	2	0	3
Dunst, Carl J.	4	0	0	4
Emde, Robert N.	0	3	3	6
Field, Tiffany M.	5	5	0	10
Fonagy, Peter	0	1	2	3
Frodi, Ann M.	5	1	0	6
Guedeney, Antoine	0	1	3	4
Halpern, Robert	2	1	0	3
Heinicke, Christoph M.	0	1	2	3
Lebovici, Serge	0	1	3	4
Lewis, Michael	2	1	0	3
McGreal, Cathleen Erin	2	1	0	3
Solyorm, Antal E.	5	0	0	5
Stern, Daniel N.	0	2	1	3
Thomas, Jean M.	0	0	3	3
Trout, Michael David	2	1	0	3
Zeanah, Charles H.	0	2	2	4

allows them to master the primary emotional tasks of early childhood without serious disruption caused by harmful life events. Because infants grow in a context of nurturing environments, infant mental health involves the psychological balance of the infant-family system. (p. 3)

Alicia Lieberman (1998) has proposed five principles that she believes define the point of view underlying infant mental health, particularly within the context of clinical interventions: (1) Infants are social organisms who exist in relationships, most of which are dyad specific; (2) individual differences are an integral component of the infant's functioning; (3) every infant exists in a particular environmental context that can substantively influence the person's functioning; (4) infant mental health practitioners make an effort to understand how behaviors feel from the inside, not just how they look from the outside; and (5) the intervener's own feelings and behaviors have a major impact on the intervention.

Osofsky (1995), in linking infant mental health with psychoanalysis, discusses important research directions for infant men-

TABLE 1.5

Individuals with Five or More Authored Papers Published in the *Infant Mental Health Journal* between 1980 and 1988

	1980–86	1987–92	1993–98	Total
Barnard, Kathryn	0	4	2	6
Boger, Robert P.	7	0	0	7
Cramer, Bertrand	0	2	5	7
Emde, Robert N.	0	4	3	7
Field, Tiffany M.	6	5	9	20
Fitzgerald, Hiram E.	10	1	2	13
Frodi, Ann M.	6	1	0	7
Harris, Lauren Julius	5	1	0	6
Lebovici, Serge	0	1	5	6
Lester, Barry M.	0	4	2	6
Osofsky, Joy D.	0	3	2	5
Pickens, Jeffrey	0	0	6	6
Richter, Richard A.	5	0	0	5
Solyom, Antal E.	5	0	0	5
Stern, Daniel N.	0	6	4	10
Zeanah, Charles H.	0	4	4	8

tal health. Areas currently receiving major emphasis include: (1) concern with nosology and diagnosis in infancy and early childhood, (2) efforts to gain more understanding of the intersubjective world of shared affective and cognitive meaning between infant and caregiver, (3) interest in intergenerational issues and risks, including continuities and discontinuities and attachment relationships, and (4) concern with the development of effective preventive intervention strategies, especially for infants at high psychosocial risk.

Miguel Hoffman (1994) suggests that ethical issues related to optimal development of infants and young children are essential ingredients of infant mental health and draws attention to six types of poverty that he believes should reside within the domain of infant mental health (Hoffman,

1995). These domains reach far beyond issues of economic poverty. The six types are: poverty of subsistence (food and shelter), poverty of protection (bad health systems, violence), poverty of affection (exploitative relationships), poverty of understanding (poor education), poverty of participation (marginalization of women, children, and minorities), and poverty of identity (due to forced migration, exile, or imposed foreign values). Hoffmann refers to eight "fronts of the mental health of early infancy" (1995, p. 13) that span research, clinical, educational, and social policy settings and issues (see Figure 1.2). Jordan (1997) notes that infant mental health specialists must take into account historical and cultural factors as they affect family life and gender role if we are to fully understand the boundaries that envelop infants and toddlers in their cultural contexts.

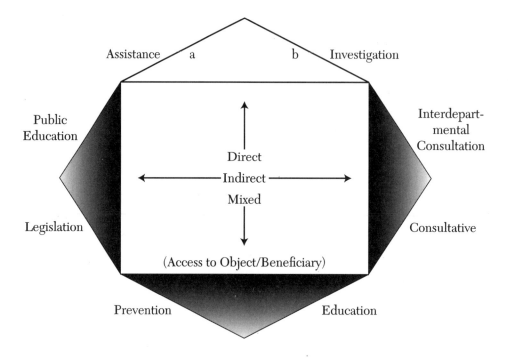

FIGURE 1.2

Eight components of infant mental health. From "Some Thoughts on Infant Mental Health,"
by J. M. Hoffman, *The Signal, 3,* pp. 12–13. Reprinted with permission of the
World Association for Infant Mental Health.

Conclusion

The challenges before us are significant, and few of the problems we face have simple solutions. When one considers the number of children living in poverty throughout the world, the level of demand for quality supplemental care, the substantial increase in single-parent families, the needs of adolescent mothers, the number of children scarred by abuse, neglect, or war, the disruption in family life caused by alcoholism and other drugs, the pervasive alienation and isolation of young parents from intergenerational sources of support, and the need for effective interventions for infants with handicapping conditions, it is clear to us that our potential for success rests on the collective efforts of theoreticians, researchers, practitioners, and child advocates. Further, there is an urgency to find ways to translate theory, research, and practice into programs that make sense to parents and politicians, because infant mental health must also be community based and politically wise if it is to be successful. Infant mental health views individuals and their families systemically. It seeks alternative developmental pathways, focuses on the contextual events of infancy, searches for answers through basic and applied research, strives to connect infants more effectively with their caregiving environments, concentrates on networking of services and interdisciplinary cooperation, and thereby strives to promote the optimal development of infants and their families.

References

Adelson, E., & Fraiberg, S. (1972). Mouth and hand in the early development of blind infants. In J. Bosma (Ed.), *Third symposium in oral sensation and perception.* Springfield, IL: Charles C. Thomas.

Adelson, E., & Fraiberg, S. (1974). Gross motor development in infants blind from birth. *Child Development, 45,* 114–126.

Adelson, E., & Fraiberg, S. (1976). Sensory deficit and motor development in infants blind from birth. In Z. S. Jastzembska (Ed.), *The effects of blindness and other impairments on early development.* Washington, DC: The American Council for the Blind.

Adelson, E., Shapiro, V., & Bennett, J. (1982). The training of community mental health clinicians as infant specialists. *Infant Mental Health Journal, 3,* 77–83.

Als, H., Lester, B. M., Tronick, E. Z., & Brazelton, T. B. (1982). Toward a research instrument for the assessment of preterm infants' behavior (APIB). In H. E. Fitzgerald, B. M. Lester, & M. W. Yogman (Eds.), *Theory and research in behavioral pediatrics* (Vol. 1, pp. 35–63). New York: Plenum.

Anderson, H. H., & Anderson, G. L. (1954). Social development. In L. Carmichael (Ed.), *Manual of child psychology* (pp. 1162–1216). New York: Wiley.

Anthony, E. J. (1984). The influence babies bring to bear on their upbringing. In J. D. Call, E. Gelenson, & R. L. Tyson (Eds.), *Frontiers of infant psychiatry* (Vol. 2, pp. 259–266). New York: Basic Books.

Aradine, C., Shapiro, V., & Fraiberg, S. (1978). Collaborative treatment fosters attachment: Nurse and therapist collaborate in the care of an adolescent high-risk mother pregnant with her second child. *American Journal of Maternal and Child Nursing, 3,* 92–98.

Aries, P. (1962). *Centuries of childhood: A social history of the family.* New York: Vintage.

Baldwin, J. M. (1895). *Mental development in the child and race.* New York: Macmillan.

Bell, R. Q. (1968). A reinterpretation of the direction of effects in studies of socialization. *Psychological Review, 75,* 81–95.

Belsky, J. (1984). The determinants of parenting: A process model. *Child Development, 55,* 83–96.

Benedek, T. (1938). Adaptation to reality in early infancy. *Psychoanalytic Quarterly, 7,* 200–214.

Bertalanffy, L. von. (1928/1934). Kritische theorie der Formbildung (Modern theories of development). New York: Harper Torchbooks edition published 1962.

Bertalanffy, L. von. (1950). The theory of open systems in physics and biology. *Science, 3,* 23–29.

Bertalanffy, L. von. (1951). Problems of general system theory. *Human Biology, 23,* 302–312.

Bertalanffy, L. von. (1962). General systems theory—a critical review. *General Systems, 7,* 1–20.

Bertalanffy, L. von. (1968). *General system theory.* New York: Braziller.

Bonkowski, S. E., & Yanos, J. H. (1992). Infant mental health: An expanding field for social work. *Social Work, 37,* 144–148.

Bowlby, J. (1951). *Maternal care and mental health* (Monograph Series No. 2). Geneva, Switzerland: World Health Organization.

Bowlby, J. (1969). *Attachment.* New York: Basic Books.

Brackbill, Y. (Ed.). (1964). *Research on infant behavior: A cross-indexed bibliography.* Baltimore, MD: Williams & Wilkins Company.

Brazelton, T. B. (1982). Early intervention: What does it mean? In H. E. Fitzgerald, B. M. Lester, & M. W. Yogman (Eds.), *Theory and research in behavioral pediatrics* (Vol. 1, pp. 1–34). New York: Plenum.

Bretherton, I. (1987). New perspectives on attachment relations: Security, communication, and internal working models. In J. D. Osofsky (Ed.), *Handbook of infant development* (pp. 1061–1100). New York: Wiley.

Brody, S. (1956). *Patterns of mothering.* New York: International Universities Press.

Call, J. D. (1957). Interlocking affective freeze between an autistic child and his "as-if" mother. In G. C. Morrison (Ed.), *Emergencies in child psychiatry: Emotional crisis of children, youth, and their families* (pp. 248–273). Springfield, IL: Charles C. Thomas.

Call, J. D. (1975). Psychoanalytically based therapy for children and their parents. In J. Dryud & D. X. Freedman (Eds.), *American handbook of psychiatry* (Vol. 5, pp. 206–234). New York: Basic Books.

Call, J. D. (1984). From early patterns of communication to the grammar of experience and syntax in infancy. In J. D. Call, E. Galenson, & R. L. Tyson (Eds.), *Frontiers of infant psychiatry* (Vol. 2, pp. 16–29). New York: Basic Books.

Call, J. D. (1991). Correspondence to Yvon Gauthier.

Cohen, L., & Salapatek, P. (Eds.). (1975). *Infant perception: From sensation to cognition: Vol. 1. Basic visual processes.* New York: Academic.

Darwin, C. (1859). *On the origin of species by means of natural selection, or the preservation of favored races in the struggle for life.* London: John Murray.

Darwin, C. (1877) A biographical sketch of an infant. *Mind, 2,* 285–294.

DeMause, L. (1974). The evolution of children. In L. DeMause (Ed.), *The history of childhood.* New York: Psychohistory Press.

Emde, R. N. (1981). Searching for perspectives: Systems sensitivity and opportunities in studying the infancy of the organizing child of the universe. In K. Bloom (Ed.), *Prospective issues in infancy research* (pp. 1–23). Hillsdale, NJ: Erlbaum.

Emde, R. N. (1983). *René A. Spitz: Dialogues from infancy. Selected papers.* New York: International Universities Press.

Erikson, E. H. (1950). *Childhood and society.* New York: Norton.

Fish, B. (1957). The detection of schizophrenia in infancy. *Journal of Nervous and Mental Disease, 125,* 1–24.

Fitzgerald, H. E. (1985). The Michigan Association for Infant Mental Health: Historical Context and Contemporary Status. *Prevention in Human Services, 3,* 35–44.

Fitzgerald, H. E., & Brackbill, Y. (1976). Infant classical conditioning: Development and constraints. *Psychological Bulletin, 83,* 353–376.

Fitzgerald, H. E., Johnson, R. B., Castellino, D. R., Van Egeren, L. A., Johnson, C. B., & Judge-Lawton, M. (Eds.). (1999). *Infancy and culture: An international re-*

view and source book. New York: Garland.

Fitzgerald, H. E., & Porges, S. W. (1971). A decade of infant conditioning and learning research. *Merrill-Palmer Quarterly, 17*, 79–117.

Ford, D. H., & Lerner, R. M. (1992). *Developmental systems theory*. Newbury Park, CA: Sage publications.

Fraiberg, S. (1958). *The magic years*. New York: Charles Scribner's Sons.

Fraiberg, S. (1968). Parallel and divergent patterns in blind and sighted infants. *Psychoanalytic Study of the Child, 23*, 264–300.

Fraiberg, S. (1970). Smiling and stranger reaction in blind infants. In J. Hellmuth (Ed.), *The exceptional infant* (Vol. 2, pp. 110–127). New York: Brunner/Mazel.

Fraiberg, S. (1971). Intervention in infancy. *Journal of the American Academy of Child Psychiatry, 10*, 381–405.

Fraiberg, S. (1974). Blind infants and their mothers: An examination of the sign system. In M. Lewis & L. A. Rosenblum (Eds.), *The effect of the infant on its caregiver* (pp. 215–232). New York: Wiley-Interscience.

Fraiberg, S. (1978). Psychoanalysis and social work: A reexamination of the issues. *Smith College Studies in Social Work, 48*, 87–106.

Fraiberg, S., Adelson, E., & Shapiro, V. (1975). Ghosts in the nursery: A psychoanalytic approach to the problems of impaired infant-mother relationships. *Journal of the American Academy of Child Psychiatry, 14*, 387–421.

Fraiberg, S., & Freedman, D. (1964). Studies in the ego development of the congenitally blind child. *Psychoanalytic Study of the Child, 19*, 113–169.

Fraiberg, S., Siegel, B., & Gibson, R. (1966).

The role of sound in the search behavior of a blind infant. *Psychoanalytic Study of the Child, 21*, 327–357.

Fraiberg, S., Smith, M., & Adelson, E. (1969). An educational program for blind infants. *Journal of Special Education, 3*, 121–139.

Freud, A., & Burlingham, D. (1944). *Infants without families*. New York: International Universities Press.

Freud, S. (1932). The interpretation of dreams. In J. Strachey (Ed.), *Standard Edition*, (vol. 4 & 5). London: Hogarth. (Original work published 1900)

Freud, S. (1955). Notes upon a case of obsessional neurosis. In J. Strachey (Ed.), *Standard Edition* (Vol. 10, pp. 153–318). London: Hogarth. (Original work published 1909)

Gesell, A. L. (1928). *Infancy and human growth*. New York: Macmillan.

Gesell, A. L., & Halverson, H. M. (1942). The daily maturation of infant behavior: A cinema study of postures, movements, and laterality. *Journal of Genetic Psychology, 61*, 3–32.

Goldfarb, W. (1943). Infant rearing and problem behavior. *American Journal of Orthopsychiatry, 13*, 249–365.

Gottlieb, G. (1991). Experiential canalization of behavioral development: Theory. *Developmental Psychology, 27*, 4–13.

Greenacre, P. (1945). The biological economy of birth. *Psychoanalytic Studies of the Child, 1*, 31–51.

Greenspan, S. I. (1981). *Psychotherapy and adaptation in infancy and early childhood*. New York: International Universities Press.

Haeckel, E. (1879). *The evolution of man: A popular exposition of the principal points of human ontogeny and phylogeny*. New York: Appleton.

Hall, W. S. (1896). The first five hundred days of a child's life. *The Child Study Monthly, 2,* 330–342, 394–407.

Hall, W. S. (1897). The first five hundred days of a child's life. *The Child Study Monthly, 2,* 458–473, 522–537.

Hartmann, H. (1939). *Ego psychology and the problem of adaptation.* New York: International Universities Press.

Hoffman, J. M. (1994). The fish is in the water and the water is in the fish. *The Signal, 2,* 5–6.

Hoffman, J. M. (1995). Some thoughts on infant mental health. *The Signal, 3,* 12–13.

Jordon, B. (1997). Gender, politics, and infant mental health. *The Signal, 5,* 1–5.

Kagan, J. (1970). Attention and psychological change in the young child. *Science, 170,* 826–832.

Kagan, J., Kearsley, R. B., & Zelazo, P. R. (1978). *Infancy: Its place in human development.* Cambridge, MA: Harvard University Press.

Lebovici, S. (1983). Le Nourisson, la mère et le psychanalyse [The newborn, the mother, and the psychoanalyst]. Paris: Le Centurion.

Lebovici, S. (1984). Comments concerning the concept of fantasmic interaction. In J. D. Call, E. Galenson, & R. L. Tyson (Eds.), *Frontiers of infant psychiatry* (Vol. 2, pp. 323–334). New York: Basic Books.

Lebovici, S. (2000). Cross-cultural perspectives on infant mental health: A French view on the history of infant and child psychiatry. In J. D. Osofsky & H. E. Fitzgerald (Eds.), *WAIMH Handbook on Infant Mental Health Vol. 1: Perspectives on Infant Mental Health* (pp. 123–152). New York: Wiley.

Leifer, M. (1977). Psychological changes accompanying pregnancy and motherhood. *Genetic Psychology Monographs, 95,* 55–96.

Lerner, R. M. (1984). *On the nature of human plasticity.* New York: Cambridge University Press.

Levine, R. & Fitzgerald, H. E. (1992). *Analysis of dynamic psychological systems* (Vol. 1). New York: Plenum.

Lewis, M. (1987). Social development in infancy and early childhood. In J. D. Osofsky (Ed.), *Handbook of infant development* (2nd ed., pp. 419–493). New York: Wiley.

Lieberman, A. (1998). A perspective on infant mental health. *The Signal, 6,* 11–12.

Loukas, A., Twitchell, G. R. Piejak, L. A., Fitzgerald, H. E., & Zucker, R. A. (1998). The family as a unit of interacting personalities. In L. L'Abate (Ed.), *Family psychopathology: The relational roots of dysfunctional behavior* (pp. 35–59). New York: Guilford.

Lourie, R. S. (1949). Studies on bed rocking, head banging, and related rhythmic patterns. *Clinical Proceedings Children's Hospital, 5,* 295–302.

Mahler, M. S. (1952). On child psychosis and schizophrenia. *The Psychoanalytic Study of the Child, 7,* 286–305.

Mahler, M. S., Pine, F., & Bergman, A. (1975). *The psychological birth of the human infant.* New York: Basic Books.

Major, D. R. (1906). *First steps in mental growth.* New York: Macmillan.

McGraw, M. B. (1935). *Growth: A study of Johnny and Jimmy.* New York: Appleton-Century-Crofts.

Miller, J. G. (1978). *Living systems.* New York: McGraw-Hill.

Minde, K., & Minde, R. (1986). *Infant psychiatry.* Beverly Hills, CA: Sage Publications.

Osofsky, J. D. (1995). Infant Mental Health: Research and Clinical Directions. *Newsletter of the International Psychoanalytic Association.*

Preyer, W. (1888). *The mind of the child, Part I: The senses and the will* (2nd. ed.; H. W. Bram, Trans.). New York: D. Appleton & Company.

Rexford, E. N., Sander, L. W., & Shapiro, T. (Eds.). (1976). *Infant psychiatry: A synthesis.* New Haven: Yale University Press.

Rheingold, H. L. (1968). The social and socializing infant. In D. A. Goslin (Ed.), *Handbook of socialization: Theory and research.* Chicago: Rand McNally.

Ribble, M. (1943). *The rights of infants.* New York: Columbia University Press.

Roiphe, H. (1979). A theoretical overview of preoedipal development. In J. D. Call (Ed.), *Basic handbook of child psychiatry.* (pp. 118–126). New York: Basic Books.

Sameroff, A. (1983). Developmental systems: Contexts and evolution. In W. Kessen (Ed.), *Handbook of child psychology* (pp. 237–294). New York: Wiley.

Sameroff, A. (1995). General systems theory and developmental psychopathology. In D. Cicchetti & D. J. Cohen (Eds.), *Developmental psychopathology: Vol. 1. Theory and methods* (pp. 659–695). New York: Wiley.

Sander, L. (1987). A 25-year follow-up: Some reflections on personality development over the long term. *Infant Mental Health Journal, 8,* 210–220.

Schneirla, T. C. (1957). The concept of development in comparative psychology. In D. B. Harris (Ed.), *The concept of development* (pp. 78–108). Minneapolis, MN: University of Minnesota Press.

Shapiro, T. (1976). A psychiatrist for infants? In E. N. Rexford, L. W. Sander, & T. Shapiro (Eds.), *Infant psychiatry* (pp. 3–6). New Haven, CT: Yale University Press.

Shapiro, V., Adelson, E., & Tableman, B. (1978). A model for the introduction of in-fant mental health services to community mental health agencies. *Journal of the American Academy of Child Psychiatry, 17,* 283–355.

Shapiro, V., Adelson, E., & Tableman, B. (1980). Beginning at the beginning: The introduction of mental health services to community mental health. In S. Fraiberg (Ed.), *Clinical studies in infant mental health: The first year of life* (pp. 271–278). New York: Basic Books.

Shapiro, V., Adelson, E., & Tableman, B. (1982). The introduction of infant mental health services in Michigan. *Infant Mental Health Journal, 3,* 69–141.

Shapiro, V., Fraiberg, S., & Adelson, E. (1976). Infant parent psychotherapy on behalf of a child in a critical nutritional state. *Psychoanalytic Study of the Child, 31*

Shinn, M. W. (1894). *Notes on the development of a child.* Berkeley, CA: University of California Press.

Shirley, M. M. (1931). *The first two years, a study of twenty-five babies: Vol. 1. Postural and locomotor development.* Minneapolis, MN: University of Minnesota Press.

Sigismund, B. (1856). *Kind und Welt: Die fünf ersten Perioden des Kindesalters.* Braunschweig, Germany: Vieweg und Sohn.

Spitz, R. A. (1945). Hospitalism. *The Psychoanalytic Study of the Child, 1,* 53–74.

Spitz, R. A. (1950). Psychiatric therapy in infancy. *The American Journal of Orthopsychiatry, 20,* 623–633.

Spitz, R. A. (1959). *A genetic field theory of ego formation.* New York: International Universities Press.

Spitz, R. A. (1965). *The first year of life.* New York: International Universities Press.

Spitz, R. A., & Wolf, K. W. (1946). The smiling response: A contribution to the onto-genesis of social relations. *Genetic Psychology Monographs, 34,* 57–125.

Sroufe, L. A. (1979). Socioemotional development. In J. D. Osofsky (Ed.), *Handbook of infant development* (pp. 465–518). New York: Wiley.

Stern, D. N. (1985). *The interpersonal world of the infant.* New York: Basic Books.

Stone, L. J., Smith, H. R., & Murphy, L. B. (Eds.). (1973). *The competent infant.* New York: Basic Books.

Tableman, B. (1982a). Infant mental health: A new frontier. *Infant Mental Health Journal, 3,* 72–76.

Tableman, B. (1982b). What happened after training: The development of infant mental health services. *Infant Mental Health Journal, 3,* 84–89.

Thelen, E., & Smith, L. B. (1992). *A dynamic systems approach to the development of cognition and action.* Cambridge, MA: MIT Press.

Waddington, C. H. (1956). *Principles of embryology.* New York: Macmillan.

Winnicott, D. W. (1941). The observation of infants in a set situation. *International Journal of Psychoanalysis, 22,* 229–249.

Werner, H. (1948). *Comparative psychology of mental development.* New York: International Universities Press.

Werner, H. (1957). The concept of development from a comparative and organismic point of view. In D. B. Harris (Ed.), *The concept of development* (pp. 125–148). Minneapolis, MN: University of Minnesota Press.

Winnicott, D. W. (1953). Transitional objects and transitional phenomena. *International Journal of Psycho-Analysis, 34,* 89–97.

Winnicott, D. W. (1987). *The child, the family, and the outside world.* Reading, MA: Addison-Wesley. (Original work published 1964)

Winnicott, D. W. (1965). *The maturation process and the facilitating environment.* New York: International Universities Press.

Wyld, H. C. (1938). *The universal dictionary of the English language.* Chicago, IL: Standard American Corporation.

Zero to Three. (1994). *Diagnostic classification of mental health and developmental disorders of infancy and early childhood: 0–3.* Washington, DC: Zero to Three: The National Center for Infants, Toddlers, and Families.

2

Cross-Cultural Perspectives on Infant Mental Health: Japan

Keigo Okonogi and Yoko Hamada

2

Introduction: Japan's Involvement in WAIMH

Japanese researchers took part in WAIMH (World Association for Infant Psychiatry & Allied Disciplines, WAIPAD) for the first time in 1986, at the Third World Congress held in Stockholm. Keigo Okonogi and Hisako Watanabe attended the congress, and were so deeply impressed that immediately after returning home, they organized a study group, the Keio Meeting of Infant Psychiatry, and began activities to spread information about infant psychiatry in Japan. Since then, Japanese researchers have participated in subsequent world congresses held once every three years, and have continued to present their findings.

In 1988, *Frontiers of Infant Psychiatry*, (Call, Galenson, & Tyson, 1984) a collection of papers presented at the First World Congress, was published with a Japanese translation by Okonogi et al. The book helped popularize the phrase *infant psychiatry* in Japan. Also in 1988, researchers in Pacific Rim countries, most notably Japan and the United States, held a WAIPAD regional meeting in Hawaii. Okonogi served as WAIMH's regional vice president, while Watanabe was elected as a member of the executive committee. In 1994, the WAIMH regional meeting was held in Tokyo with Okonogi as chairman. Many key members of WAIMH, including Serge Lebovici, Robert Emde, Joy Osofsky, Bertrand Cramer, Peter Fonagy, and others, attended this highly successful event.

Numerous WAIMH researchers continued to visit Japan after the Tokyo regional meeting to give lectures and hold seminars, while Okonogi, Watanabe, and other Japanese members conducted vigorous educational activities in various parts of Japan. As a result of their efforts, the concepts and principles of infant mental health have been promoted steadily in Japan. For example, a growing number of studies on infant mental health are being presented at meetings of existing scientific associations in the field of pediatrics, obstetrics, and infant psychiatry. Research groups and academic associations related to infant mental health, meanwhile, are being organized in Japan.

The Japanese Association for Medical and Psychological Study of Infants and Four Winds are two leading infant mental health organizations currently operating in Japan. Others include infant observation groups, developmental psychology researcher groups, and a group of psychologists who work at Neonatal Intensive Care Unit (NICU).

History of Mother-Child Health in Japan

Establishment of Mother-Child Health System

After World War II, various mother-child health measures were implemented, primarily to improve infant and maternal mortality rates. At present, all pregnant women who notify public offices of their pregnancies are issued documents called "pocket books for mothers and babies" and become eligible to receive two free health examinations for pregnant women, in the early and later stages of their pregnancies. After delivery, they can receive a variety of tests and checkups for their children, including screening tests for congenital metabolic disorders, two infant health examinations (between ages 3 and 6 months, and between ages 9 and 11 months), screening tests for neuroblastoma, and subsequent health examinations at 18 months and 3 years of age. These tests are all provided free of charge, and are taken by nearly 100 percent of the subjects. If abnormalities are detected in any of these tests, assistance is provided so that children may receive higher level medical treatment.

As a result of these measures, infant mortality, which occurred in over 60 out of 1,000 births in 1950, dropped to 4.3 out of 1,000 births in 1995, the lowest level in the world. Meanwhile, both the number of births and birthrates have continued to decrease in recent years. The number of babies born in 1995 fell to 1.19 million, and the total fertility rate (the number of children a woman bears in her lifetime) plunged to 1.42. Consequently, the focus of mother-child health measures, which traditionally was disease prevention, has recently shifted to mental health, with particular emphasis on creating a system to support child rearing (Health and Welfare Statistics Association, 1997).

Recent Trends as Seen from Mother-Child Health Statistics

Bankon-ka (postponing marriage; getting married at an older age) and *shoshi-ka* (having fewer children) are two phenomena that have recently become topics of heated discussion in Japan. They are manifested in men and women getting married at older ages, in women giving birth at older ages (in proportion to those who postpone marriage and in keeping with the trend toward later marriage), and in lowering of birthrates. In 1995, the average age at which people got married for the first time was 28.5 years for men and 26.3 years for women. Both average ages were more than one year higher than they were 20 years ago. Similarly, the average age at which women gave birth to their first child was 27.5 years, which was close to two years older than the average age 20 years ago (Health and Welfare Statistics Association, 1997; Ministry of Health and Welfare, Japan, 1998).

One of the unique aspects of Japan is the low percentage of babies born out of wedlock—about 1 percent—and the fact that this percentage has remained unchanged for the past 20 years. In other words, despite the rapid changes in society and the advancement of *bankon-ka,* the Japanese seem to have adhered doggedly to the fundamental framework of family—that is, to get married and bear children. Conversely, there is a strong tendency for people not to have children unless they are married. The rise in marriage age, therefore, leads to a rise in childbearing age, and to fewer children. Statistically, a higher percentage of children conceived out of wedlock are aborted artificially compared to those conceived by married parents, clearly showing that people try to avoid pregnancies and childbirth out of wedlock (Ministry of Health and Welfare, Japan, 1998).

Under the Mother's Body Protection Law, abortions are conducted legally in Japan, either to protect the mother's health or for financial reasons. In 1995, as many as 342,720 fetuses, or 22.4 percent of the 1.53 million babies conceived that year, were aborted. The availability of abortion prevents an increase in the number of infants born under inferior conditions, as often occurs in teenage pregnancies. There is also a possibility that this option helps reduce excessive psychological, social, and economic stress among women, promotes healthy development of infants, and prevents child abuse.

Japan has numerous advantages in terms of infant mental health, compared with developed countries in Europe and the United States. First, the number of Japanese who are dependent on drugs such as narcotics and stimulants is relatively small (although the use of such drugs has been increasing among teenagers in recent years), so that births of "drug babies" and fetal alcohol syndrome babies are extremely rare. Second, the number of HIV-infected patients is small in Japan, so the incidence of mother-child HIV infections and AIDS babies is low. And third, Japan is more or less a homogeneous country where only one language is spoken. In general, people enjoy high educational levels, and their lives are protected by social security and universal health programs. As a result, only a small number of people, such as those living in slums, are severely impoverished, and problems related to child abuse are relatively uncommon. In 1996, a total of 4,102 abuse cases were reported to child consultation centers throughout Japan. Although the number has been increasing sharply in recent years, it still represents only a small percentage of the population. Meanwhile, Japan has its own distinct problems. Numerous cases of abuse do not come out in the open because the people are still bound strongly to the traditional concept of family. And because a foster child-parent system has not yet taken hold in Japan, it is difficult to provide adequate care to children who have been isolated or separated from problem families.

The Japanese I FEEL Pictures Studies

Development of the Japanese I FEEL Pictures Test

Infant Facial Expressions of Emotions from Looking at Pictures (I FEEL Pictures) is a research tool, developed by Emde, Osofsky et al (Emde, 1993). The standard set of I FEEL Pictures consists of 30 pictures of infant facial expressions (Emde, Osofsky, and Butterfield, 1987). All pictures are of one-year-olds and typical of everyday life, most of them expressing blended or ambiguous emotions. By asking parents and other adults their judgement of infants' emotion, we can explore adult interpretation of the infant facial expressions, which may affect everyday parent-infant interaction. Although this tool can be used in various ways, standardized administration technique is as follows (Butterfield and Ridgeway, 1993); respondent is given the I FEEL Pictures booklet along with a corresponding numbered response

sheet and directed to tell the strongest and clearest feeling that each baby is expressing, in one word if possible. The word responses are then classified into emotional categories according to standardized Lexicon, which the Colorado group had developed through their infant emotion research, as well as classified according to emotional intensity and hedonic tone.

When Okonogi saw this technique at the third world congress of WAIPAD in Stockholm, Sweden, he was fascinated, and decided to get permission from Emde to use the I FEEL Pictures Test in Japan. Okonogi organized the I FEEL Pictures group in his country and started administering the technique to Japanese subjects in 1987.

To analyze the responses of Japanese subjects, we found that translating the English lexicon into Japanese was not enough. We thus decided to develop our own category system as follows. The free responses of 30 of the subjects were selected randomly and classified using the KJ method. The KJ Method was invented by J. Kawakita (Kawakita, 1967) which involved integrating various ideas during a brainstorming session, using small cards and a large room. Each responding word of 30 subjects is made into small card and distributed in a room. Five members of the research group are assembled in the room and had a session, placing the responding word cards so that similar responses come closer. Each researcher independently moved the cards according to his/her own idea, and finally separate concept groups were established after the session. These concept groups formed the basis for the new category system based on the responses of Japanese subjects using Japanese language (Mochimaru, Hamada, Fukatsu, 1988). Although this system had many points in common with the original system, it also presented a number of unique characteristics. For example, we included the word *refusal* in the *fear* category, and a new category, *withdrawn,* was added. The results of this preliminary study were presented at the Pacific Rim congress of WAIPAD, held in Honolulu, Hawaii, in 1988.

While proceeding with the study described above, we realized that it was vital for the respondent to have a sense of kinship with the photographic stimuli. Unless those images were familiar to them, their answers might be purely conjectural and hence reflect less of a personal "pull." Because the I FEEL Pictures Test presented only Caucasian and African-American infants as models, it held little familiarity for many Japanese subjects; therefore, we felt it necessary to reconstitute the I FEEL Pictures with Japanese babies as models (the Japanese I FEEL Pictures).

Twenty-five 12-month-old infants were selected and their parents were asked if their infants' pictures could be used for the Japanese I FEEL Pictures guidelines. Three professional photographers took pictures of the infants at their homes. Approximately 3,500 pictures were taken, and 20 representative shots of each of the 25 babies were printed. Five members of the study group spent 15 hr choosing approximately 100 pictures for use in the test. Among the criteria for selection were photographic quality, angle of view (frontal

shot or head turned no more than 45 degrees away), and exclusion of the mother's face, toys, or other objects. Given successive pictures of the same infant's expression, the shot having the best photographic quality was chosen. In some cases, pictures were touched up to eliminate unwanted backgrounds and surroundings. The selected pictures were grouped by the KJ method described above on the basis of the aforementioned Japanese category system.

Four days after the pictures were selected, the same group members narrowed down the number of pictures to 68. They added another six pictures in which backgrounds had been blotted out (in order to evaluate the effect of the background), bringing the total to 74.

These 74 pictures were shown to 52 adult subjects who included medical doctors, clinical psychologists, nurses, and psychology students. They were asked to describe the emotions they read in the pictures, using a free response method. After all the responses had been gathered, four members classified them according to the KJ method and prepared a new category system that consisted of 27 categories and was more detailed than the previous I FEEL Pictures system. The new system included such categories as boredom, perseverance, loneliness, serenity, and object-seeking *(amae).*

Four researchers then coded the responses of the 52 subjects according to this new system. The results were pooled, and a principal component analysis was made, using 74 photographic stimuli as items and 27 categories as samples. The results of the analysis indicated an eigen value of 18.58 for the first principal component, 13.27 for the second, 9.7 for the third, and a cumulative contribution ratio of 53.4 percent down to the third principal component.

The four members then made a final selection of the photographic stimuli. The criteria they used were as follows: (1) configuration of the principal component; (2) photographic quality; (3) diversity in the degree of ambiguity (pictures in which feeling could be easily recognized were included as well as those in which feelings were difficult to judge); (4) scattering of response categories; (5) equal representation of the infants used as models; and (6) selection of pictures in which the percentage of categorized responses was close to that of the original I FEEL Pictures. By this procedure, 30 pictures were finally selected for use in the Japanese I FEEL Pictures Test. (Inoue, Okonogi, & Takiguchi, 1989; Inoue, Hamada, & Okonogi, 1990, 1993)

Preliminary Studies

To test the validity and reliability of Japanese I FEEL Pictures, we conducted the following studies in 1988. A total of 167 female college students in Tokyo, aged 19 to 20, were chosen as subjects. Their responses to the I FEEL Pictures and the Japanese I FEEL Pictures were compared. The photographs of each test were made into slides for presentation, and the subjects used free responses to describe the kinds of emotions or feelings they thought the infants in the pictures had. One month later, 151 of the students were retested, using the Japanese pictures. All

the responses were categorized twice by two independent raters into 27 previously developed categories.

To examine the correspondence between the two picture sets, we analyzed the correlation and the mean difference between the two sets for frequency of use for each category. There was a significant correlation at $p < .1$ level between the frequency of use for each category in the two sets, which showed that the two picture sets measured the same physiological aspects. Interestingly, there were differences in the respondents' attributions for the 27 categories in the two picture sets. The Japanese subjects had significantly more responses in categories such as bubbling joy, shyness, anger, sleep, self-assertiveness, object seeking (*amae*), no emotion, seeking attention, envy, boredom, perseverance, and will. The original American pictures had more responses in thinking, loneliness, sadness, anxiety, fear, suspicion, surprise, and attention categories.

To examine the reliability of the Japanese I FEEL Pictures, we administered this technique on two occasions, one month apart, to the same subjects. The results indicated that there was a significant correlation between test and retest results for all 27 categories.

We administered the Self-rating Depression Scale (SDS, Zung, 1965) as well as the I FEEL Pictures Test to the female students, and the relations between I FEEL responses and SDS ratings were studied. Those who used the category *suspicion* more frequently showed lower SDS scores than those using it with intermediate or low frequency. Those who used *surprise* less frequently, moreover, showed higher SDS scores than those using it with intermediate or high frequency (Hamada, Inoue, & Okonogi, 1989; Inoue, Hamada, & Okonogi, 1990).

Revision of the Category System

We subsequently revised our category system, as we found that 27 categories were far too many, and that several categories were not reliable. We repeated the KJ method, and after heated discussion, established a new 18-category system. This new system included the following categories: joy, shame, tired, thinking, anger, sadness, sleepiness, anxiety, frustration, self-assertion, fear, attention/doubt/surprise, object-seeking, pain, desire, jealousy, perseverance, and not otherwise categorized (e.g. words describe behavior, such as "he is crying," words without emotion, interjection, etc.). Several of these categories were common to the American system.

Process of Standardization

We then continued our testing of the Japanese I FEEL Pictures Test to expand the number and variety of subjects. In 1990 and 1991, we visited a well-baby clinic in Tokyo where we obtained the responses of 137 mothers with infants, and attended prenatal maternity classes at public health centers and hospitals where we obtained the responses of 121 pregnant women. All the responses were coded into 18 categories of emotions, and we calculated frequencies of use per category, per subject,

and per photo. We then compared the responses of the two groups (pregnant women and mothers with infants).

In this comparison, 11 out of 30 Japanese I FEEL Pictures yielded significant differences between the two groups in terms of frequency of use of each category. Mothers with infants more frequently used the categories "attention/doubt/surprise" for Pictures 1 and 10, and "sadness" for Pictures 2, 16, and 19. On the other hand, categories that pregnant women used significantly more frequently than the other group were "joy" for Pictures 1 and 24; "frustration" for Pictures 10, 11, 19, and 28; "pain" for Picture 2; "attention/doubt/surprise" for Picture 9; and "anger" for Picture 11. The two groups' mean frequencies of use for each category were compared, and significant differences were found in 8 of the 18 categories. Pregnant women used "anger," "anxiety," "frustration," and "pain" significantly more frequently, whereas mothers with infants used "sadness," "sleepiness," "self-assertiveness," and "desire" more frequently.

We confirmed the difference in responses to the Japanese I FEEL Pictures between pregnant women and mothers, which we had already noticed (and felt intuitively) during our everyday practice. Pregnant women tended to respond more emotionally than the other group, while mothers were more reality oriented. In other words, they judged infants' emotions in the context of their caregiving behaviors. This difference seemed to stem from the mothers' actual child-rearing experiences.

We then gathered the responses of male university students and compared them with those of their female counterparts. Female students interpreted the pictures as showing "desire" more often than the male students. Compared to mothers, however, both male and female students interpreted fewer pictures as showing "desire." "Object-seeking *(amae)*" was the reaction seen most frequently among mothers and pregnant women, followed by female students, then male students.

In addition, four members of the group visited Hawaii to gather the responses of non-Japanese subjects. An interesting finding was obtained for Pictures 5 and 22, in which many Japanese subjects perceived *amae* feelings; none of the University of Hawaii students showed reactions that could be classified under the "object-seeking" category. Since they did not know the word *amae* itself, they naturally did not use that word. However, for these students the pictures did not evoke any reactions or emotions that could be classified under the "object-seeking" category, such as "a feeling of wanting to be loved" or "a desire to seek its mother."

Clinical Applications for Mothers Who Abuse Their Infants or Complain of Difficulty in Child Rearing

Psychiatrists are visited by mothers who abuse their children, refuse to bring them up, or complain of difficulty in child rearing. We administered the Japanese I FEEL Pictures Test to these mothers and compared the responses with their clinical findings.

According to their responses, the moth-

ers were classified into the following six types:

1. Depressive type: Those who used the "sleepiness" category more frequently (seven or eight responses out of the 30 pictures) than the mothers who had no child-rearing problems (about two or three such responses, on average). Emotional communication during clinical interviews with these depressive mothers was usually restrained. Their reduced activity levels may have been projected onto the pictures.

2. Rejective type: These mothers often gave rejective responses, such as "the baby is fussy" or "doesn't like something" to pictures that yielded positive responses from normal mothers, such as "happy," "satisfied," or "feels secure."

3. Split type: These mothers responded to the pictures in almost the same manner as normal mothers, but clinically, they abused or rejected their children. In other words, the mental state shown through the I FEEL Pictures responses was split off from that observed in actual daily situations.

4. Paranoid type: These mothers gave delusive responses to the infants' facial expressions, providing dark interpretations to people's feelings, such as "the baby is up to something," "is thinking of something unpleasant," or "is smiling at some sinister thought." These mothers projected their own anxieties and fears onto their children, which tended to lead to delusion. These mothers became fearful of their children and abused them.

5. Deviation type: These mothers showed regressive behavior when responding to the pictures. For instance, they would spend abnormally long periods of time on a certain picture, or were unable to make responses and rejected the test midway.

6. Others.

We also administered the Japanese I FEEL Pictures Test to 103 mothers of 4-month-old or 9-month-old infants during their children's regular health checkups held at public health centers in Hiroshima. After analyzing the mothers' responses to the pictures, we identified 29 subjects whose responses suggested the possible presence of child-rearing problems. Of these, 7 were classified as depressive type, 5 as rejective type, 1 as paranoid type, 12 as deviation type, and 4 as other types.

Six months later, we carried out a follow-up survey via public health nurses visiting each of the mothers at their homes. This follow-up included 19 of the 29 mothers whose responses showed potential problems, and 8 mothers, or 42.1 percent, were identified as having some child-rearing problems. Five depressive type mothers out of 7 were followed up, and 2 had problems. One rejective type mother out of 5 was followed up and was found to have a problem. Nine out of 12 deviation type mothers were followed up, and 5 had problems. Of the 74 mothers who were judged to be free of problems based on the I FEEL responses, 11 were followed up, and 2 mothers, or 18.1 percent, were identified as having some problems.

This pilot study gauged the potential of the Japanese I FEEL Pictures Test in predicting possible mother-child relationship problems. It showed that administering the Japanese I FEEL Pictures Test to mothers during babies' regular health checkups may help in the early detection of problems in mother-child relationships and in providing assistance to these mothers. Special attention must be paid to those mothers identified as deviation types—those who took an excessively long time thinking of a response, who complained that it was hard for them to understand, who discontinued their participation in the test midway through it, or who appeared to lack confidence (Fukatsu, Mori, & Okonogi, 1996).

Outlook of the Japanese I FEEL Pictures Study and Future Research Plans

Naoki Hirano, one of the joint researchers, used the data accumulated thus far to identify the categories that subjects had applied the most frequently to each picture ("popular responses"). He then classified the 30 pictures into seven groups or categories, including joy, fear, and attention/interest. Using these categories, he determined a subject's tendency to read infants' emotions, and studied how much he or she deviated from the popular responses indicating the mean tendencies (Hirano, Hamada, & Okonogi, 1997).

We have established a standard Japanese I FEEL Pictures implementation method in detail, and are presently gathering data. The pictures are now being used in such diverse fields as studies of newborns, mental health in school settings, and disabled children.

Studies by Japanese Psychoanalysts on Mother-Child Relationships

Cultural Characteristics of Japanese Mother-Child Relationships

The following cultural characteristics are found in Japanese mother-child relationships:

1. Parents sleep side by side with their child(ren) placed between them, like the Chinese character (*kawa*, "river"). Okonogi has long advocated the theory of *kawanoji bunka,* or a culture represented by the Chinese character *kawa.* This character, which consists of three vertical lines, metaphorically describes the way Japanese infants sleep at home: The shorter line in the center represents the child, and the two longer lines on either side represent the father and the mother. Generally speaking, Japanese infants sleep in the same room as their parents until they reach the age of 3 or 4. In the 1960s, parents and their children still slept side by side, literally like the character *kawa.* Today, infants sleep in the same room as their parents, but often on their own beds, separate from their parents. Very few babies—at least until they reach the age of 1—sleep alone in their own rooms, separate from their parents, as is common in Europe and the United States. This indicates that Japanese children grow up harboring a sense of one-ness with their parents. In other words, children are raised in a psychological situation in which the generation boundary between a child and his parents is ambiguous.

2. Japanese people place more importance on parent-child relationships than on husband-wife relationships. Parents concentrate on having their children sleep soundly. Because of this, they tend to suppress themselves during sexual intercourse, and often make sex in haste while being extremely cautious not to wake up the children. At Japanese homes, people tend to call each other by the names that the youngest member of the family uses (such as mother, father, or older brother). As shown in this example, after the first child is born, Japanese families become child-oriented: Wives call their husbands "father" and husbands call their wives "mother." Sex between a married couple becomes secondary in importance, while non-sexual intimate emotion between parents and children is encouraged and valued. Takeo Doi (1962) studied this emotion from the perspective of *amae* (Doi, 1973).

3. Many Japanese families are child-centered. Evaluated from the perspective of American family psychiatry, Japanese families have the psychological characteristics of child-centered families. They may also be diagnosed as immature families, meaning that the parents remain strongly attached to their own parents.

4. Families often have absent fathers and strong mother-child ties. Before World War II, Japanese people lived in extended families spanning three genera-

tions. As heads of families, fathers exercised supreme authority and power. During the 50 years after the war, however, the number of nuclear families increased dramatically. A majority of today's Japanese families are centered around close mother-child relationships, with fathers nowhere to be seen. This is what families experience psychologically: While fathers spend all their time and energy working and associating with other men, mothers enjoy cozy, intimate relationships with their children at home. As a result, the mother-child relationship has become stronger than ever before. Children have become even more dependent on their mothers although, at the same-time, they grow up feeling a narcissistic sense of omnipotence toward their mothers. Children normally experience inner conflicts when they try to separate themselves from their mothers. But because they have remained so close to their mothers, Japanese children suffer more strongly than others. The conflict becomes even more pronounced during adolescence; in the course of weaning themselves from their mothers, children often direct their resulting aggression toward their mothers. In fact, many children suffer because they can separate themselves from their mothers only in such a negative manner. This is a theme that appears in Ajase complex, and is studied through Ajase's rancor toward his mother, as discussed later in this paper.

5. Mothers feel guilty about wishing to abort or kill their children. In Japan, mothers have long been solely responsible for raising the children. At the same time, if a woman became pregnant and the couple did not want to have children, or if they were unable to raise the baby for whatever reason, it was her job to abort the fetus or kill the baby after birth. For 400 to 500 years, until about 100 years ago, numerous Japanese children were either aborted or killed immediately after birth due to the family's inability to feed them. This was the mother's responsibility. Research indicates, on the other hand, that fathers took on this role in Europe and America. The *Kanmuryojukyo*, a Japanese Buddhist scripture centering on the salvation of the mother, played an important role in relieving a mother of her pain, distress, and sense of guilt for having committed infanticide. The story of Ajase was told as this scripture spread in Japan. This provides one of the cultural backdrops to the study of Ajase complex.

Psychoanalytic Studies on Mother-Child Relationships in Japan: *Amae* and the Ajase Complex

Two major studies by Japanese psychoanalysts who discuss the cultural characteristics of Japanese mother-child relationships enumerated above. The work of Takeo Doi explores *amae;* Heisaku Kosawa and Keigo Okonogi have written a study of the Ajase complex. The former focuses on the emotions and adaptation mechanisms in the Japanese relationships of attachment and dependence seen during the early stages of a mother-child relationship. The latter discusses two aspects of Japanese mother-child relationships: a woman's sometimes agonizing conflict over whether to bear a child, and the rancor, conflict, and aggression that children feel toward their mothers when they must wean themselves from their mothers after growing up closely attached to them.

Takeo Doi, one of Japan's foremost psychoanalysts, presented a unique theory on *amae*. (Doi, 1973) This theory originated as a study on *amae*, a word found only in the Japanese language. Later, the study was expanded by Robert Emde and other researchers who recognized that, although the word *amae* may not exist in other languages, the emotion of *amae* and a form of interpersonal relationship characterized by *amae* is universally evident.

Doi has recently (1992) defined the word *amae* as follows:

> The concept deriving from the Japanese word *amae* is introduced as that which bridges dependence and attachment, two conceptually different states. The word primarily refers to what an infant feels when seeking his or her mother, but it can also apply to an adult to indicate the presence of a similar feeling of being emotionally close to another. Significantly, the feeling of *amae* is not mediated by words, though it can be acknowledged as such on reflection. Also, when frustrated, it can easily lead to a desire for such a feeling. (Doi, 1992)

Doi further states:

> That being the case, I hope you will not be surprised to hear that there is a concept in Japanese that bridges dependence and attachment, two concepts which are conceptually separate in English. That concept is *amae* and I shall explain how it combines the two meanings. (Doi, 1992, p. 8)

He then explains the prototype of *amae.*

> *Amae* is a noun form of *amaeru*, an intransitive verb meaning "to depend and presume upon another's love or bask in another's indulgence." It has the same root as the word *amai,* an adjective meaning "sweet." Thus *amae* can suggest something sweet and desirable. Perhaps what is most significant about the word *amae* is that it definitely links with the psychology of infancy, for we say about a baby that is *amaeru*-ing when it begins to recognize the mother and seek her, that is to say, long before it begins to speak. Please note that *amae* here refers to the feeling of attachment that is observable. Later, when a child begins to speak, he or she will eventually learn that such a feeling is called *amae.* But that does not change the situation that the feeling of *amae* is something to be conveyed nonverbally. (Doi, 1992, p. 8)

Meanwhile, Robert Emde discusses the significance of Doi's concept of *amae* introduced above from the standpoint of his infant research.

> Takeo Doi's (1992) construct of *amae* refers to a form of intimacy that is central in Japanese culture but also has features that apply to human relationships across cultures. Doi reviews that the prototypic function of *amae* refers to a principle of organization that is motivational throughout the life span of the individual in the context of other caring relationships. *Amae*, except under unusual circumstances, operates silently, beyond con-

sciousness. It involves monitoring the feelings and sensitivities of one's partners according to what feels right There is a sense of dependency, reciprocity, and obligation, and it operates "sweetly." *Amae* does not depend on verbal description and it is deeply embedded in everyday nonverbal, as well as verbal, interchanges. It seems difficult to articulate in Japanese, and it is no wonder that the construct is not easily susceptible to translation. (Emde, 1992, p. 35)

Emde explains that he was attracted to Doi's construct of *amae*

because it seemed to be referring to similar processes under study by our Colorado group; *amae* seemed to offer the promise of expanding our knowledge about mutuality, with respect to both its cultural and biologically based (i.e., universal) origins. (Emde, 1992, p. 35)

Emde states:

Our theory portrays a number of aspects of the early relationship experience and implicitly shares points of emphasis with Doi's theory. These include: (a) the biological preparedness for processes of relatedness; (b) the positive contributions to relatedness that are based in the internalized procedures of everyday caregiving experiences; and (c) the moral processes in early development that contribute to both *amae* and an emotionally guided sense of self. (Emde, 1992, p. 36)

According to Emde,

amae is a dyadic construct involving reciprocity in an intimate relationship. Without

reciprocity there is no *amae*. In the earliest caregiving relationship, the mother is reliably caring, communicating love, and is dependable; the infant, in turn, offers devotion, learning, and obedience. Moreover, the infant, who internalizes the procedures related to *amae*, is internalizing and consolidating many subtle procedures and rules about everyday social reciprocity and about what to do in given circumstances. Similar considerations have led us to our theory of a "basic morality." We have come to the view that the early self is a moral self, developing under expectable circumstances from the operation of the basic motives in the context of the caregiving relationship experience. (Emde, 1992, p. 38)

Emde sets forth the following research task in positioning the concept of *amae* within the context of his group's overall infant research:

our theory holds that there are basic processes of morality in the child that become established and go forward in development, providing there is adequate support in terms of the caregiving relationship experience. And how does this relate to *amae?* Can the universal features of *amae* be considered as special instances of the more general propensity for a basic morality we have described as a result of our research with Western infants? In addition to the rich culturally specific aspects of *amae*, I agree with Doi that there may be important aspects of *amae* that are universal and that may not be encompassed by our current theories. It is also the case, however, that there are some significant areas of overlap of *amae* theory with our emerging theory of an early moral self. Such areas, in terms of our theory, include internalized procedures for regulating reciprocity, everyday rules (e.g., about what to do, when to do it, and what belongs where), empathy, and the internalization of standards. *Amae* involves all of these areas. (Emde, 1992, pp. 38–39)

And seeking answers to the following questions, he says, is a task all future researches on *amae* should address:

We now turn our attention to similar research questions about *amae*. What are the influences of child gender on the course of *amae?* Is a mother's *amae* with her boy characterized by more mutuality and with her girl by more of other kinds of interactions? What about other child effects on the caregiver, such as effects of temperament or birth order? To what extent are these *amae* conflicts that cross gender and cross generations? Are there conflicts, for example, between son-mother *amae* and son-wife *amae?* These are only a few of the intriguing research questions that could be asked about *amae* once operationalization takes place. (Emde, 1992, p. 41)

In his definition of *amae,* Doi explained the fact that *amae* was not only an emotion that occurred in an infant within a mother-child relationship, but rather, it was an emotion that was experienced also by adults in their interpersonal relationships in general (Doi, 1992).

Interestingly, the word *amae* can be predicated not only of a child, but also an adult when he or she displays a certain behavior vis-à-vis another that indicates the presence of a feeling of being emotionally close, something similar to what prevails between a baby and its mother. In other words, the assumption is that there is a continuity between children and adults so far as *amae* is concerned. Thus we may use the word *amae* to describe the relationship between lovers, friends, husband and wife, teacher and student, even employer and employee. (Doi, 1993, p. 8)

And Doi (1992) states that *amae* involves psychological dependence that a certain person feels on another person, and because of this, it includes a sense of vulnerability and instability.

I think it must be clear from what has been said above that *amae* involves a certain psychological dependence, because one who wants to *amaeru* requires another person who senses one's need and can meet it. Thus *amae* is vulnerable and, being susceptible to frustration, it undergoes various transformations. (Doi, 1992, p. 9)

Okonogi, for his part, states that *amae* is a concept that should be understood from both interpersonal and intra-individual perspectives. (Okonogi, 1992) Patterns of *amae*, like patterns of attachment, can be seen in insecure, as well as secure, forms. Moreover, interactive routines involving *amae* can involve negative emotions as well as positive emotions, and these may function as motivators of behavior. The word *amae* is generally used in the Japanese language with a variety of emotions depending on different interpersonal interactions:

- When an adult identifies with an infant or a child and directs appropriate emotional availability, the affect of dependence and attachment that the adult recognizes in the child is called *amae* (the prototype of the word).

- When an adult has little empathy with the dependency or attachment shown by the child, the adult negatively perceives that the child is "*amaeru*-ing." Experiencing such discommunications, the child begins to test adults to see if they have empathy with him or her. In other words, the child begins to formulate certain psychological functions linked with *amae* such as reading other people's expressions—*hitom ishiri* (stranger anxiety) or *enryo* (hesitation or reserve).

- When the child is good at actively manipulating the emotions of adults and creates such a state of affect as to satisfy his or her dependence or attachment, he or she is said to be an *amaeru*-ing child.

- When the child, although he or she is actually dependent on or loved by adults, denies the fact and behaves innocently or defiantly, the child is said to be in a state of *amae*.

The usage of the word *amae* described above can be observed in exactly the same manner in interactions between adults. In theorizing *amae* as described above, Okonogi feels that the most important task is gaining understanding of the following two aspects: first, the negative image or emotion that the mother reflects on the child in mother-child interactions, and second, the negative ideas and emotions that the child experiences toward parents or adults who forgive his or her *amae*. Not all parents are the same. As already stated, some parents sincerely find pleasure in ac-

cepting a child's *amae*, whereas others perceive *amae* as something bad from the beginning. Still others are convinced that discipline consists of refusing *amae* and not allowing a child to *amaeru*. In clinical work with infants and children, Okonogi feels that a major theme is treating the mother's negative emotional projections on the child's *amae*.

Moreover, a child, when his or her *amae* is accepted by an adult, often feels anxious, rather than simply happy or satisfied. This anxiety, which we call "engulfment anxiety," is the fear that, as a result of having your *amae* accepted by an adult, you lose yourself, being exploited and engulfed by them. The prototype of this negative aspect of interpersonal relationships involving *amae* was first discussed by Kosawa and further developed by Okonogi, in the theory of the Ajase complex, whose main theme is ambivalent mutual interactions between a mother and child (Kosawa, 1953, 1954; Okonogi, 1988, 1991). Further discussion of *amae* from this perspective is needed.

The Ajase complex is an original theory developed by Heisaku Kosawa (1953, 1954) and subsequently expanded by Keigo Okonogi (1988, 1991). Whereas Freud based his Oedipus complex on a Greek tragedy, Kosawa developed his theory of the Ajase complex from stories found in Buddhist scripture. The story of Ajase centers on the Buddhist concept of reincarnation.

THE STORY OF AJASE AND HIS MOTHER: HEISAKU KOSAWA'S VERSION

Well known to the Buddhist world, Ajase's story appears with many variations in the scriptures of ancient India. These scriptures entered Japan by way of China and Korea from approximately A.D. 700 to 1000. Kosawa modeled his theory on the version of Ajase's story appearing in the *Kanmuryojukyo*, a Buddhist scripture centering on the salvation of the mother. In this instance, the woman saved by the Buddha is Ajase's mother, Idaike.

The wife of King Binbashara, the ruler of an ancient Indian kingdom, Idaike feared that as her beauty faded she was losing her husband's love. She consulted a soothsayer, who told her that a sage living in the forest would die in 3 years' time, to be reborn as her son. However, Idaike was too anxious to wait 3 years; desperate to have a child, she killed the sage. As he was dying, the sage cursed Idaike, telling her that, reincarnated as her son, he would one day kill the king. Idaike became pregnant at this moment. The unborn Ajase had thus already been murdered by his mother's egotism. Moreover, fearing the wrath of the sage reincarnated in her womb, Idaike attempted to kill her son by giving birth to him from the summit of a high tower. Ajase survived; however, having broken his little finger as a result of his fall, he was nicknamed "the prince with the broken finger."

Ajase passed a happy childhood. However, on reaching adolescence, he learned from Daibadatta, the enemy of Buddha, that his mother had attempted to kill him at his birth; he had only to look at his broken little finger for proof. The Sanskrit word *Ajatasatru* means both "broken finger" and "prenatal rancor" (a term to be discussed below). Disillusioned with the mother he had idealized, Ajase attempted to kill her.

He was subsequently overcome by guilt, however, and developed a severe skin disease, characterized by festering sores so offensive in odor that no one dared approach him—except for his mother, Idaike. Despite his mother's devoted care, Ajase did not readily recover; he even attempted several times to kill her. Seeking relief, Idaike went to the Buddha and told him of her sufferings. The Buddha's teachings healed her inner conflict, and she returned to continue to care for Ajase. Eventually, the prince was cured to become a widely respected ruler. This is the version of the Ajase story that Kosawa wrote in the 1950s, based on the *Kanmuryojukyo* (Kosawa, 1954).

THEMES OF THE AJASE COMPLEX
According to Okonogi, the Ajase complex consists of the following three themes (Okonogi, 1988).

1. The mother's conflict between the wish for a child and infanticidal wishes. Queen Idaike wished to have a child in order to protect her status as queen and maintain her husband's love—she took the extreme action of killing the sage to achieve her desires. However, believing that the birth of the reincarnated sage would bring disastrous results, Idaike began to fear the child in her womb. She then attempted to kill her child by giving birth to him from the top of a high tower.

   The story of Ajase illustrates two conflicting emotions on the part of the mother. On the one hand, she wishes to have a child in order to protect herself, and to achieve her own desires. On the other hand, projecting persecutory imagery and hatred onto her baby, she becomes fearful of the child's birth and attempts to kill him.

According to Serge Lebovici (1988), such conflict depicts the mother's ambivalence concerning her *bébé imaginaire.* The egocentric conflict of the mother—her wishes both to have a child and to eliminate her baby—arouse persecutory anxiety through projection onto the child she carries. This unconscious maternal conflict appears clearly in the Ajase story.

2. The child's prenatal rancor and matricidal wishes. Ajase experienced rage toward his origins from the moment of conception. As a reincarnation of the murdered sage, that is, he desired to kill his mother even before his birth. In Buddhism, this anger experienced toward birth itself is termed *misho-on,* or prenatal rancor.

   Kosawa compared the Oedipus complex and the Ajase complex as follows: "Freud's Oedipus complex originates in a conflict involving the libido, with the son's love for his mother and hatred for his father. The Ajase complex, on the other hand, concerns the more fundamental question of birth or origins." Kosawa further contended that whereas incestuous desire and patricide formed the core of the Oedipus complex, the Ajase complex centered on the themes of matricide and prenatal resentment.

3. Two types of guilt, and the mother's forgiveness. The paper Kosawa originally submitted to Freud concerning the Ajase complex bore the title "Two Types of Guilt" (see Kosawa, 1954). ("The Ajase Complex" was rather its subtitle.) In this paper, Kosawa asserted the following: When a child makes a mistake or does something wrong, he or she first experiences guilt as a fear of punishment. However, human beings have another sense of guilt, one of a higher dimension than mere fear of punishment. This second type of guilt is experienced when the child who fears punishment is forgiven his or her wrongdoing.

In terms of the Buddhist legend, Ajase suffered feelings of guilt when confronted by a minister with his desire to kill his mother. Shocked at his own contemplated matricide, he began to shake and became deathly ill. Idaike, however, forgave her son and nursed him devotedly. Under his mother's care, Ajase experienced a more profound sense of guilt, one of heartfelt remorse.

Kosawa termed this guilt resulting from forgiveness *zangeshin* or "repentance." He emphasized the need to differentiate between repentance and the guilt related to punishment. This repentance-type guilt compares with Klein's depressive/reparative guilt. The Ajase story may thus be viewed as depicting the transition from a punitive to a reparative type of guilt. (Kosawa may in fact have read Klein's *The Psycho-Analysis of Children* before writing his thesis.)

Ramon Ganzarain, an American psychoanalyst who studied the Ajase complex, has delineated several defense mechanisms in its treatment of guilt, including denial and confusion.

Other researchers have discussed the Ajase complex from the field of infant mental health. We once received the following remarks from Professor Theodore Lidz concerning the Ajase story (Lidz, 1985). In his view, children should be raised by both parents; the conflict of the Ajase story originates when a father declines an active role and leaves a child's fate in the hands of the mother. Ajase's difficulties, in other words, began with the tragedy of a mother losing her husband's—or, in a broader sense, a man's—support.

Lidz's interpretation is also relevant in light of the sociohistorical background of the Ajase legend in Japan. Behind the legend lay the problem of guilt over infanticide, particularly abortion, since Japanese women have traditionally been assigned responsibility for disposing of unwanted children. The depiction of Idaike's salvation in the *Kanmuryojukyo* played an important role in assuaging mothers' guilt over infanticide.

Luis Feder, a Mexican psychoanalyst, has long studied preconceptive ambivalence, a concept representing maternal conflicts on being pregnant. As an actual example told in a myth of a mother suffering from preconceptive ambivalence, he cited Jocasta, the mother of Oedipus.

Jocasta's husband Laius, when staying as a guest at a certain palace on the Peloponnisos peninsula, tempted the king's beautiful son into a homosexual relationship. The young boy, deeply ashamed of this fact, killed himself. Enraged with Laius's sin, Zeus cursed Laius, saying, "If you ever have a son, he will kill you when he grows up." Learning about this god's curse, Laius gave up the hope of ever having a child, and abandoned having sexual intercourse with his wife Jocasta. But Jocasta, not being told of this curse, desperately wanted to have a child. So she served alcoholic drinks to make him drunk, seduced him, and had sexual intercourse. She became pregnant as a result. However, when Laius told her about Zeus's curse, Jocasta was overcome with fear for the child she had conceived, and disposed of the newborn in a river. This abandoned child was Oedipus, and Feder contends that the conflict Jocasta felt toward Oedipus is one of the examples of preconceptive ambivalence. Feder also explained that his studies on preconceptive ambivalence and Okonogi's study on the Ajase complex both dealt with similar themes.

Meanwhile, Joan Raphael-Leff, a British psychoanalyst engaged in infant mental health, took note of the similarity between the conflict Jocasta felt about the desire to have her child Oedipus and infanticidal wishes, and the conflict Idaike had toward her son Ajase. She wrote a paper entitled "Mother of Ajase and Jocasta," and presented it at an international conference (1992).

Okonogi and Fukatsu (Fukatsu, Mori, & Okonogi, 1996) studied Idaike's conflicts toward Ajase using Lebovici's (1988) concept of the *bébé imaginaire* and a mother's projections of the *bébé imaginaire* onto her actual baby (Okonogi & Fukutsu, 1993).

Changes in modern society have brought about the collapse of the maternal love myth. Like other countries, Japan is seeing an increase in mothers who suffer from this preconceptive ambivalence. Studies on the Ajase complex mentioned thus far are therefore expected to become increasingly significant in the field of infant mental health.

Major Clinical Studies and Research on Infant Mental Health in Japan

The following list includes some of Japan's leading clinicians and researchers on infant mental health.

Keigo Okonogi, Yoko Hamada, Chikako Fukatsu, and Sachiko Mori of Keio University, Kako Inoue of Yokohama National University, and Naoki Hirano of Hokkaido University of Education have been studying the development and application of the aforementioned Japanese I FEEL Pictures. Okonogi, Hamada, and Fukatsu, moreover, practice mother-child psychotherapy for mothers having difficulty in child rearing, and study intergenerational transmission and other themes in clinical situations.

Hisako Watanabe, a lecturer at the Department of Pediatrics, School of Medicine, Keio University, is one of the pioneers who introduced infant mental health into Japan. She also serves as WAIMH's regional vice president. Watanabe has organized infant observation groups, given numerous lectures throughout Japan, and made substantial contributions to promoting infant mental health in Japan (Watanabe, 1987, 1992).

Ryuji Kobayashi, professor of Tokai University's School of Health Science, is an infant psychiatrist specializing in the treatment of infants with autistic spectrum disorders and their mothers. Kobayashi uses mother-child units equipped with play rooms and observation booths for active treatment of relationship disturbances of infants with autistic spectrum disorders and their mothers. In particular, he took note of approach-avoidance motivational conflicts, a vicious cycle that autistic infants often fall into, and includes holding sessions as part of the treatment program (Kobayashi, Shiraishi, & Ishigaki, 1997).

Chihoko Tanaka (Department of Educational Psychology, Graduate School of Education, Tokyo University), together with Yoshiko Niwa, has long been conducting clinical studies and research on the mother-child relationship of children with Down syndrome. Their findings were published in the *Infant Mental Health Journal* (Tanaka & Niwa, 1991, 1994). Tanaka has also published several books on mother-infant psychotherapy, and played an important role in spreading knowledge about infant mental health in Japan.

Keiko Yoshida, Department of Psychiatry, Kyushu University, received training at a London hospital with a mother-child unit. She currently conducts research on postpartum depression.

Yoko Hashimoto, a clinical psychologist at the Neonatal Center, Western Yokohama Hospital, School of Medicine, St. Marianna University, is widely regarded as a pioneer of the infant mental health approach taken at NICU in Japan.

Tomoko Takamura, a staff member at the National Institute of Special Education, has been conducting longitudinal developmental research on infants with extremely low birth weight (Takamura, 1997).

Nobuo Masataka of Kyoto University's Primate Institute uses the simultaneous mother-infant voice analysis method to study affect attunement and other mother-child relationships from an ethological approach. He studies the motherese with which infants acquire a language, and conducts comparative studies between humans and other primates.

Afterword

As we have stated in this paper, Japan has distinct cultural characteristics, yet is undergoing social changes similar to those taking place in Europe and America. We believe that the study and practice of infant mental health in our country will be influenced by these two conflicting directions. We sincerely hope that infant mental health will continue to develop in Japan in close cooperation with WAIMH.

References

Butterfield, P. M., & Ridgeway, D. (1993). The I FEEL Pictures: Description, Administration, and Lexicon. In R. N. Emde, J. D. Osofsky, & P. M. Butterfield (Eds.), The I FEEL Pictures: A new instrument for interpreting emotions (pp. 73–95). Madison: International Universities Press.

Call, J. D., Galenson, E., & Tyson, R. L. (Eds.). (Japanese translation ed. Okonogi, K.). (1988). Frontiers of Infant Psychiatry. Iwasaki-gakujutu-shuppansha, Tokyo. (In Japanese)

Doi, T. (1973a). *The anatomy of dependence* (J. Bester, Trans.). Tokyo: Kodansha.

Doi, T. (1992). On the concept of *amae*. *Infant Mental Health Journal, 13*(1), 7–11.

Emde, R. N. (1993). The collaborative History of the I FEEL Pictures. In R. N. Emde, J. D. Osofsky, & P. M. Butterfield (Eds.), The I FEEL Pictures: a new instrument for interpreting emotions (pp. 53–72). Madison: International Universities Press.

Emde, R. (1992). *Amae*, intimacy, and the early moral self. *Infant Mental Health Journal, 13*(1), 34–42.

Emde, R. N., Osofsky, J. D., & Butterfield, P. M. (1987). The I FEEL Picture booklet. Denver: University of Colorado.

Fukatsu, C., Mori, S., & Okonogi, K. (1996). *Clinical applications of the Japanese I FEEL Pictures Test (JIFPT) to mothers who abuse their children or complain of difficulty in childrearing*. Paper presented at the Sixth World Congress of WAIMH, Tampere, Finland.

Ganzarain, R. (1989). Various guilt feelings in psychoanalysis. *Japanese Journal of Psychoanalysis, 32*, 93–102. (In Japanese)

Hamada, Y., Inoue, K. K., Okonogi, K., et al. (1989). Japanese 'I FEEL Picture Test' II: Cross Cultural Aspects. Paper presented at 4th world congress of World Association for Infant Psychiatry and Allied Disciplines, Lugano, Switzerland.

Health and Welfare Statistics Association. (1997). Trends of people's Health, 1997. *Welfare Index, 44*(9), 44–116. (In Japanese)

Hirano, N., Hamada, Y., Okonogi, K., et al. (1997). A study of the Japanese I FEEL Pictures: A consideration of its characteristics from the responses given by mother subjects. *Journal of Japanese Clinical Psychology, 15,* 144–151. (In Japanese)

Inoue, K. K., Hamada, Y., Okonogi, K., et al. (1990): Development of the Japanese I FEEL Pictures Test. *Japanese Journal of Family Therapy, 7,* 114–124. (In Japanese)

Inoue, K. K., Hamada, Y., Okonogi, K., et al. (1993). The Japanese I FEEL Pictures. In R. N. Emde, J. D. Osofsky, & P. Butterfield (Eds.), *The I FEEL Pictures: A new instrument for interpreting emotions.* New York: International University Press.

Inoue, K. K., Okonogi, K., Takiguchi, T., et al. (1989). Japanese 'I FEEL Picture Test' I: Comparison with American Version. Paper presented at 4th world congress of World Association for Infant Psychiatry and Allied Disciplines, Lugano, Switzerland.

Kawakita, J. (1967). Conceptualization. Chuokoronsha, Tokyo. (In Japanese)

Klein, M. (1932). The psychoanalysis of children. The writings of Melanie Klein. London: Hogarth.

Kobayashi, R., Shiraishi, M., Ishigaki, C., et al. (1997). Affective communication of infants with autistic spectrum disorders and internal representation of their mothers. *Japanese Journal of Medical Psychological Study of Infants, 6,* 9–20. (In Japanese)

Kosawa, H. (1953). Final Kosawa version of Ajase story. In translator's afterword, Zoku-seishinbunseki Nyumon, Nihonkyobunsha, Tokyo. (In Japanese)

Kosawa, H. (1953). Final Kosawa version of the Ajase story, 1953, in the translator's afterword, *Japanese version of Neue Folge der Verlesungen zur Einfuhrung in die Psychoanalyse, 1932.*

Kosawa, H. (1954). Two kinds of guilt, 1934. *Japanese Journal of Psychoanalysis, 1.*

Lebovici, S. (1988). Fantasmatic interaction and intergenerational transmission. *Infant Mental Health Journal, 9*(1), 10–19.

Ministry of Health and Welfare, Japan. (1998). *Annual Report on Health and Welfare, 1998 Ministry of Health and Welfare White Paper.* Tokyo: Author.

Mochimaru, F., Hamada, Y., Fukatsu, C., et al. (1988). Findings and analysis of "I-Feel Pictures" in Japanese pregnant women. paper presented at World Association for Infant Psychiatry and Allied Disciplines, Pacific Rim Congress, Honolulu.

Okonogi, K. (1978) The Ajase complex of the Japanese (1). *Japan Echo, 5,* 88–105.

Okonogi, K. (1979). The Ajase complex of the Japanese (2). *Japan Echo, 6,* 104–118.

Okonogi, K. (1989). Ajase Complex: Clinical and Historical Review. *Japanese Journal of Psychoanalysis, 32,* 103–116. (In Japanese)

Okonogi, K. (1991). Le complex d'Ajase. *Devnir, no. 4,* 71–102.

Okonogi, K. (1992). *Amae* as seen in diverse interpersonal relations. *Infant Mental Health Journal, 13*(1), 18–25.

Okonogi, K., & Fukatsu, C. (1993) Imaginary baby, Ajase complex and intergenerational transmission. *Japanese Journal of Psychoanalysis, 36,* 539–554. (In Japanese)

Raphael-Leff, J. (1992). *Mother of Ajase and Jocasta, 1992.* Invited Paper presented at the Tokyo Meeting of Infant Psychiatry, Tokyo.

Takamura, T. (1997). Psychological viewpoints in the follow-up study of very low birth weight infants. *Neonatal Care, 10,* 55–59. (In Japanese)

Tanaka, C., & Niwa, Y. (1991). The adaptation process of mothers to the birth of children with Down's syndrome and its psycho-therapeutic assistance. *Infant Mental Health Journal, 12,* 41–54.

Tanaka, C., & Niwa, Y. (1994). A psychotherapeutic technique for mother-child intervention: A case study of a Japanese Down's syndrome child. *Infant Mental Health Journal, 15,* 244–261.

Watanabe, H. (1987). Establishing emotional mutuality not formed in infancy with Japanese families. *Infant Mental Health Journal, 3,* 398–408.

Watanabe, H. (1992). Difficulties in *amae:* A clinical perspective. *Infant Mental Health Journal, 13*(1), 26–33.

Zung, W. W. K. (1965). A self-rating depression scale. *Archives of General Psychiatry, 12,* 63–70.

3

Longitudinal Aspects of
Early Parent-Infant Interactions
and Contacts with
Mental Health Agencies

Peter de Château

3

Introduction

In the early 1970s studies were conducted on neonatal care routines in hospitals (De Château, 1976). The main reason for these studies was the feeling that, for instance, separation of mother and infant immediately after delivery was unnecessary from a medical point of view and could be harmful to the developing relationship. Although no cause-effect could be proven, correlations were found between these early routines and later outcomes.

Over the last few decades, hospital personnel have been trained to provide high quality physical care both to the mother and her infant. However, relatively little attention has been paid to the importance of the neonatal period for the development of the parent-infant relationship. Many routines in our neonatal and maternity wards, such as separation, were introduced to prevent infection and to improve the treatment of the newborn (De Château, 1976). Although it was soon recognized that this approach had an adverse effect on the mother-infant relationship, many parents still encounter difficulties gaining full physical and mental access to their newborns, especially if these newborns are premature or sick. In an experimental study De Château and Wiberg (1977a, 1977b) worked to keep the mother and infant together immediately after delivery. Correlations were found between the early interactional behavioral circumstances and later outcome measures, such as parental attitudes toward child-rearing practices, family planning, the solving of conflicts between mother and child, aspects

of child development, and measures of psychological arousal in children.

Day care has also been an important topic of discussion for many years. Here Sweden will be presented as an example. Public child care in Sweden includes care for children of preschool age and after-school activities for older children. The aim is to provide children with a stimulating and secure environment while giving men and women equal opportunities to combine family life with paid work or study.

Additionally, a case study on infantile autism demonstrates that communications between parents and the medical system are not always optimal.

Finally, the results of a prospective longitudinal epidemiological study on mental health in infants and children are presented. These results will show that early risks may be long-term risks. This 30-year follow-up study, with the aid of official registers on young infants and on children (De Château, 1991) who were treated at the Child Guidance Clinic in Stockholm, Sweden, suggested that in the long run, the decisions made in this clinic did not correlate with more favorable later development and socially acceptable positions in society. Many of the alternative explanations for these results are extensively discussed at the end of this chapter.

Early Mother-Infant Interaction and Later Outcome

Infant and Maternal Capacity

Newborns can stretch out their arms and by doing so send a message to the environment. During the first few hours postpartum they become capable of doing many other things. After being put on the maternal abdomen, they are, for instance, capable of moving upward to the nipple in order to suckle. About 30 percent of healthy fullterm newborns actually reach this goal within one to 1½ hr postpartum, while the majority are capable of partly fulfilling this task (Rigardt & Alade, 1990; Widström, Wahlberg, & Matthiesen, 1990). This sequence of behaviors that results in rooting is well-known in mammals and is most probably of survival value for the offspring. In response to this infant behavior, the mother will most likely pick up the baby. Anticipatory behavior and preprogramming of the mother guarantee that this process will be complete. During pregnancy, maternal preparation for this process is sensitized and practiced. In addition, early experiences from the mother's own childhood and her relationship with her parents contribute to this process (Nilsson & Almgren, 1970; Uddenberg, 1974).

Studies on healthy women's perinatal emotional adjustment have shown that psychiatric symptoms and conflicts are correlated with the woman's prenatal social circumstances, personal relationships, and psychological background and conditions during her childhood and adolescence. These factors also influence the way parents prepare for parenthood, behave with their baby, and respond to the baby's signals. An example of this part of the developing anticipatory process can be observed in a new mother's interactive behavior with her infant and the high correlations with earlier beliefs and fantasies about the baby.

To further illustrate this point, maternal holding behavior will be used as an example. About 80 percent of mothers at hospitals with rooming-in care hold their babies on their left arm while sitting, irrespective of left- or right-handedness and a number of other factors (De Château, 1976). One month prior to delivery, primigravidae with normal pregnancies were interviewed during a routine prenatal visit to the hospital (De Château, Mäki, & Nyberg, 1982). All the infants were delivered healthy and full-term. During the first postnatal week, the way a mother held her newborn was studied. The mothers who held their babies on their left arm had been better prepared for delivery and having a baby, perceived bodily changes differently, expressed the desire to return to work sooner after parturition, and were married to or living with more highly educated men than the right-holding mothers. These results suggest that one month before delivery, the mothers who held their infant on the left side differed in certain respects from the mothers who held their baby on the right side during the first postnatal week. From other studies it is known that the proportion of mothers who hold their baby on the right is higher after the mother and infant have been separated, which suggests that perinatal maternal anxiety and uncertainty influence this maternal behavior (De Château, Holmberg, & Winberg, 1978; Salk, 1960, 1970). In addition, more right-holding mothers reported that during their stay on the maternity ward, it had taken them longer to relate to and accept their feelings toward the growing fetus or newborn than left-holding mothers. A follow-up study 3 years after delivery showed that both primiparous and multiparous right-holding mothers had more frequent contact with a child health center and received significantly more home visits from the health care nurses during the follow-up period.

Two explanations have been offered for the preference for holding an infant on a particular side. Salk (1960, 1970) discussed the influence of the maternal heartbeat as an imprinting stimulant that has a soothing effect on the infant, while Weiland and Sperber (1970) postulated that preference for holding a baby on the left arm serves primarily to relieve anxiety in the adult carrier. Results of our own studies support both hypotheses. However, the infant may also play a key role in molding maternal behavior patterns. An infant's response to stimulation with sound, light, and touch has proven to be asymmetrical under certain conditions. Correlations exist between the initial head-turning response of infants 2 days postpartum and maternal holding preference 2 to 3 weeks later (Ginsberg, Fling, Hope, Musgrove, & Andrews, 1979). This could imply that right-holding also is appropriate in normal newborns that show left-side preference in their behavior responses. In sick, premature, and/or separated newborns, deviation could be a sign of disturbed neonatal behavior, because the percentage that show right-turning responses to stimuli is higher.

Meshing of the mother-infant dyad reflects the inborn or imprinted capacities of both individuals. A number of studies have addressed the reactive capacity of the newborn and its influence on the environment.

Bowlby stated that the infant's smiling, crying, clinging, sucking, and following are activities that may produce and facilitate maternal behavior; the behavior is intended to achieve attachment and maternal care. Although some authors (De Château, 1976) are critical of Bowlby's explanation for all five types of infant behavior—questioning, for example, whether it functions to bring about proximity of the mother and result in mutual attachment—they all agree that smiling plays a role in the growing mother-infant relationship. Infant crying may have different causes and can be seen as a method of communication with the adult. Using spectrographic analysis, Wasz-Hiickert, Lind, Vuorenkoski, Partanen, and Valanne (1968) were able to identify four types of infant cry in the neonatal period: the birth cry, the hunger cry, the pain cry, and the pleasure cry. These different types of cry may be signals that function to produce specific responses in the mother. In lactating primiparous mothers, the hunger cry caused an increase in the temperature of the breasts. Experience seems to influence the level of this reaction: The longer the mothers listened to their own infant's crying, the higher their skin temperature became. Some mothers showed a weak reaction, while others showed a strong one.

Blauvelt and McKenna (1968) studied infants' special capacity to respond to the environment provided by their mothers. Tactile stimulation of an infant's face from the ears to the lips resulted in turning of the infant's face toward the mother. This head turning and orienting toward the mother's face might stimulate maternal care. Turkewitz, Moreau, and Birch (1968) noted that normal infants were more responsive to stimulation in the right perioral region than in the left. As described above, an infant's preference for turning to the right and looking to the right may be a species-specific adaptation to maternal holding on the left. By looking and turning to the right, the baby can see its mother. On the other hand, an infant's preference for looking and turning to the right could also be a signal in favor of being held in the left arm.

Infant adaptive behavior is highly suitable for the creation of a representational world of this sort, as described by Lebovici (1995). In a similar way to the feeding situation, the holding situation may encompass repetitive elements that are necessary for the development of mental representations and a sense of self. After birth, the infant gradually learns to appreciate its mother, and this becomes more specific the more the infant is exposed to her. Symptoms of distress during feeding by care providers other than the mother may be partly explained by this observation. In many clinical cases of feeding problems in adolescents (anorexia, bulimia), a thorough anamnestic interview often reveals a history of very early feeding difficulties. Either the infant was difficult in the neonatal period, or interaction during early feeding sessions did not proceed smoothly. The clinical importance of this observation is clear (De Château, 1996).

Postnatal Contact

Primiparous mothers and their infants who had an extra 15 to 20 minutes skin-to-skin and suckling contact during the first hour after delivery displayed different behavior, breast-fed their infants several months longer, and expressed different opinions about child rearing practices during follow-up at 36 hr, 3 months, and 12 months compared to a control group of primiparous mothers and infants who received routine care immediately after birth (De Château, 1976). In this experimental study routine care immediately following delivery consisted of the following procedures: The baby was put on the delivery table, mouth and upper airways were rinsed, and the stomach was emptied. Face, trunk, and legs were wiped dry with a towel, and the infant was shown to the mother for a brief glance, but usually she did not touch him. After cord clamping the baby was taken to another part of the delivery room for weighing, bathing, physical examination, and dressing. After that the mother was helped to deliver the placenta and washed and cleaned, and the baby with clothes on was put into a crib and covered with a blanket. The crib was placed beside the mother's bed so that she could watch her baby and touch its face. In contrast, in the extra-contact group, after clamping the cord, the midwife put the naked infant on the mother's abdomen, and the infant's back was covered with a blanket. The skin-to-skin contact began approximately 8 to 10 min postpartum. Some 5 min later the midwife moved the baby upward onto the mother's chest and helped him to suckle from his mother's breast. This extra contact lasted for about 10 to 15 min, and after this the procedure described for the routine care group was continued.

The material for this study consisted of 42 mother-infant pairs, of which 22 were given extra contact and 20 routine care. The basic criteria for participation in this study were that mothers and infants should be healthy and live in the hospital catching area and that pregnancy and delivery should have been normal. A comparison between the two groups on maternal age, social background, medical condition during pregnancy and delivery, and the condition and sex of the newborns were comparable in the two groups. Other criteria that all mother-infant pairs had to meet were described as optimal obstetrical condition elsewhere (De Château, 1976). The selection procedure for the study was carried out by the midwives when mothers arrived at the hospital for delivery. Mothers were randomly assigned to either group, so that preliminary selection was based solely on existing data concerning previous obstetric history, present pregnancy, and residence within the hospital area.

The methodology used at 36 hr postpartum included direct observation of mother and infant behavior and was standardized in a previously tested way with sufficient interobserver reliability. Later, at 3 months during a home visit, mother-infant interactional behavior was studied in a standardized, controlled way during a free play activity, and the mothers were given a personal interview. At 1 year during a follow-up at the hospital, mother-infant behavior during a task-oriented activity was observed, using a previously developed and controlled standardized method (De Château & Wiberg, 1984). Moreover, this time a personal interview with the

mothers was made, the Gesell Developmental Schedule was used for the children, and the duration of breast-feeding was ascertained in order to evaluate both groups.

At this point mothers with extra contact were more frequently holding their children with positive empathy, were exhibiting more touching, and were talking positively more frequently than mothers with routine care. On the developmental scale, children with extra contact were ahead of those in the routine care group. Finally, mothers with extra contact breast-fed the infants an average of 2½ months longer than mothers with routine care.

Several other studies of paranatal caregiving procedures have indicated that the period around birth is of special importance for the development of the parent-child relationship. Some of these results seem to find support from other studies, while others fail to confirm them. Interestingly enough, the influence of extra contact was, at all four follow-ups, more pronounced in mother-boy than in mother-girl pairs.

In view of the results of these follow-up studies and the controversy about the importance of early postnatal interaction, it was considered of interest to make a fourth follow-up study 3 years after delivery. The main consideration in this study was to examine how extra skin-to-skin and suckling contact immediately following delivery, in contrast to routine care, might influence development of the mother-child relationship, while taking the sex of the child into account (De Château & Wiberg, 1977a, 1977b, 1984).

At the 3-year follow-up, the mothers

and children were invited to spend a day at the hospital. The evaluation procedure included questionnaires, interviews, developmental screening, measurement of hormone levels, and analysis of videotapes of the mothers and children during free play (Wiberg, Humble, & De Château, 1980).

The questionnaires and interviews revealed only a few differences between the mothers in the two groups. When asked in retrospect about the period immediately after delivery, a large portion of the mothers in the routine care group described the time with their infant as insufficient. Very few mothers in the extra contact group expressed this opinion. This was the only significant difference between the mothers in the two groups. Trends were found on the following issues: Although actual care facilities for the children and time spent outside the home were almost identical in the two groups, a larger portion of the mothers in the routine care group expressed the wish to spend more time with their 3-year-old child. During the three year followup period, mothers in the extra contact group had twice as many children as mothers in the routine care group. However, babies that were born to mothers in the routine care group were more closely spaced than those in the extra contact group. The number of ongoing pregnancies at the time of follow-up was the same in each group.

Two significant differences were found between the two groups of children. The extra contact children had become stubborn at a younger age than the children in the routine care group. A larger proportion of the extra contact children were content during the day at 18 months. Language de-

velopment, measured in terms of success in mastering two-word sentences at the age of 18 months, seemed to have been a little faster in the extra contact children.

According to parental judgment, the children's language development in the extra contact group should have been somewhat faster, a finding in agreement with other studies (Ringler, Trause, & Klaus, 1976; Ringler, Trause, Klaus, & Kennell, 1978). Söderbergh (1982), using the videotapes of our free play follow-up, reported on the possible connection between early extra contact during the first hour postpartum and linguistic development 3 years later. The linguistic effects of early contact, if present, are supposed to be reciprocal, although the evaluation of the dyad's interaction has been treated as an entity with the mother as the most responsible partner, being the linguistically more mature of the two. Of the dyads showing the best dialogues, all were early contact pairs. The poorest linguistic interactions were found in the control pairs. Of the remaining pairs in the middle of the scale, there was an even distribution between early contact and routine care. However, these results do not allow us to draw any definite conclusions.

Demographic characteristics were similar in the two groups for such traits as parental occupation, satisfaction with employment, and time off because of illness. Day care and other child care arrangements were almost identical. The general health and the number of visits to hospitals and baby clinics were also similar in the two groups.

The results of the Denver Developmental Screening Test (DDST) are classified into the following three categories: normal, questionable, and abnormal. The data showed a normal age distribution, and there were no differences between the two groups as a whole or between boys and girls. None of the children had a developmental delay. Efforts were made to test the children alone, but in about half of the cases one of the parents was present. Twice as many boys as girls were accompanied by a parent. The proportions were similar in the two groups.

Adrenaline and noradrenaline excretion values in the two groups of boys and girls and mothers and fathers during mother-child play, separation, lunch, and rest in the hospital were measured. Because the traveling time to the hospital and the means of transportation differed between families, only measurements obtained at noon, 1:00 P.M., and 3:30 P.M. were used. Catecholamine excretion rates per kilogram body weight and per minute were about twice as high in the children as in the parents. Analyses of variance for repeated measurements were performed and revealed that the difference in noradrenaline excretion between the routine care and extra contact mothers was significant. However, because the data for several subjects was not available, the number of subjects in the ANOVA was small; thus paired t tests were also performed. One trend found was that the extra contact mothers and the extra contact boys excreted more adrenaline and noradrenaline. There was no significant difference in cortisol excretion between the two groups.

In order to understand how the video-tapes were analyzed and what the results may mean, a detailed description of the methodology, technique of analyzing, and different variables observed is now given. For the videotape recording of mother and child interaction, they were invited to play with dolls in a dollhouse for about 30 min. A videotape recording of the session was made, and in order to facilitate the recording, the dollhouse was constructed without a roof. It contained four furnished rooms: kitchen, bathroom, bedroom, and living room. The dolls were intended to represent the members of the child's own family and chosen individually to suit each mother-child dyad: normally father, mother, child, and any other family members. The mother and her child were instructed to sit on a mattress 3 m from the camera in a corner of the laboratory with the dollhouse between them. A microphone was suspended 1 m over the play corner.

The mother and child received the following instructions before the play started: "We want you to play together and show what happens on an ordinary day at home in your family. A videorecording of the play session is going to be made. If possible, we want you to play for half an hour, that is, as long as the videotape lasts." These instructions, that the play should mirror the usual routines in the family, may be said to have determined the character of the interaction between mother and child. Of the total of 30 min of recording, the mother and child were alone for approximately 20 min. The examiner was present for 5 min at the beginning of the session and at the end of the session.

The interactional pattern of communication between mother and child is crucial in the development of the play situation. In a pilot study it was observed that 30 min is too long for the 3-year-old to play with the same dolls and dollhouse. All the mothers and the children experienced stress through this arrangement. With this in mind, the instruction about half an hour's play with the same toys was used in order to induce conflicts. In this way the everyday conflicts were included, such as when mother and/or child wanted to do something else, and it was possible to study conflicts and eventual conflict resolution.

All families were asked to watch a playback of their own videotape together with the examiners in order to give the family an opportunity to see what actually was recorded and also to get an opinion about the recording. None of the parents expressed doubts about the representativeness of the recorded interactions between mother and child. Permission was obtained from all the parents to use the videotapes for further analyses.

Both quantitative and qualitative analyses were made. In the quantitative analyses, maternal behavior included eight items: active touching, caressing, hugging, kissing, direct eye-to-eye contact, looking at, smiling/laughing, and talking. Child behavior items were: active touching, caressing, hugging, sitting close to, sitting far from, looking at, smiling/laughing, and talking. Two observers analyzed each tape simultaneously but independently without knowing to which group each mother-child couple belonged. The videotapes were analyzed in random order. Of a total of 30 min

recording, two 5-min intervals were analyzed: the first from 10 to 15 min elapsed time, and the second from 20 to 25 min elapsed time, when mother and child were alone in the laboratory. The choice of two intervals allowed for analysis over time. Each 5-min interval was divided into 20 sequences of 15 s in order to observe the behavior of the mother and child in detail. Behavior that occurred during each of the 20 observation periods was noted and scored as a unit. In the final analysis the scores of all items of behavior were added up and the sum was used as a measure of the frequency of the particular behavior. The maximum score for any item during one of the two scoring periods was therefore 20. The correlation coefficient (r) between the observers was above .95 for all behavioral items used.

In the qualitative analysis of the interaction the following criteria were used to describe and compare the qualitative aspects of the interaction between mother and child in a free play situation: The contents of the variable should be (1) observable, (2) relevant according to the level of development of 3-year-old children, and (3) present on the majority of the videotapes. The interactional variables analyzed were the mother's manner of conduct, the child's manner of conduct, emotional climate, playing, and conflicts. Details and definitions of these different interactional variables are given elsewhere (Wiberg, Humble, & De Château, 1989).

Three naive observers made independent qualitative analyses of the tapes in random order. The mother's manner of conduct and the child's manner of conduct were analyzed in six 5-min intervals. The advantage of not breaking up the analyses into too short sequences was that it afforded the possibility of experiencing and understanding the interaction between mother and child. Evaluations were made of behavior that was regarded as most dominant. Dominant here means behavior that was typical and central for the course of events. Once these evaluations had been carried out, the separate judgments of the three observers were incorporated into joint observational records and the frequencies added up and used for analysis. The interobserveral reliability in terms of levels of agreement among the three observers ranged from 90 to 97 percent and was lowest in the mother's and child's manner of conduct.

In the quantitative analysis of mother and child behavior during videotaped free play, no significant difference was found between the two groups (routine care versus extra contact) as a whole, but the following trends were noticed: Mothers in the extra contact group smiled/laughed and touched their children more actively than the mothers in the routine care group. Children in the extra contact group smiled/laughed more toward their mother and were also sitting further away from her than the children in the routine care group. A within-group comparison based on the sex of the child revealed the following effects: Extra contact girls touched their mothers more than the extra contact boys did. Routine care girls looked significantly more often at their mothers ($p < .05$); they also smiled and laughed more often than the boys did. Mothers in the routine care group looked more frequently at daughters than at sons. Extra contact mothers with boys smiled/laughed more often than routine care mothers with boys.

In the qualitative analysis of the videotapes of mother-child interaction, two significant differences were found between the routine care and extra contact groups (Fig. 3.1). The extra contact mothers gave more encouragement and instructions to their children than the routine care mothers did. Small trends noticed included the extra contact mothers' being somewhat more authoritarian and demanding than the routine care mothers, while the opposite was found for support and laissez-faire behavior. The children's conduct was comparable in the two groups.

The emotional climate during interaction was assessed on a five-point scale. The mean value in the extra contact group was 3.4, while in the routine care group it was 3.3. The extra contact girls and their mothers had the highest mean value (3.6). Verbal communication type was measured in four categories. Monologue by the child, parallel monologue, and maternal one-way communication were observed with the same frequency in the two groups; the last was more common in the mothers with boys. Dialogues between mother and child were somewhat more common in the extra contact group. Level of play was similar in the two groups. Four out of the 11 boys in the extra contact group displayed the highest level of play, that is, role-playing. Only 1 out of the 11 routine care boys was judged to have achieved the same level of play.

Conflicts arose in all the mother-child dyads, with the exception of one mother-

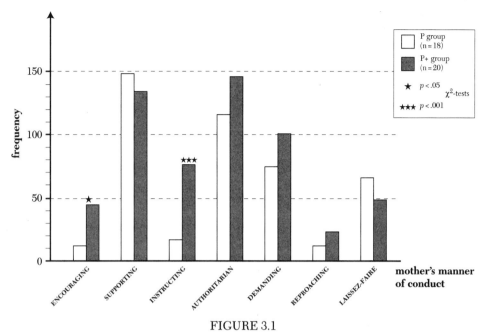

FIGURE 3.1

Results of the qualitative analysis of the mother's interactive behavior during free play.
Γ(Γ+) = primiparous mothers and routine care infants (extra contact) after delivery. From
"Long-term Effect on Mother-Infant Behaviour of Extra Contact During the First Hour Post
Partum. V. Follow-up at Three Years," by B. Wiberg, K. Humble, and P. De Château, 1989,
Scandinavian Journal of Social Medicine, 17, pp. 181–191. Reproduced with permission.

daughter pair in the extra contact group. Conflicts appeared at approximately the same time in all the dyads in the two groups. In the routine care group, conflicts arose after a mean of 14.7 min on the videotape, while in the extra contact group this occurred after a mean of 12.8 min. Articulated conflicts were more common in the extra contact group. Regardless of the type of conflict, significantly more conflicts were resolved in the extra contact group. Six out of the 11 extra contact mother-son dyads resolved their conflicts, in contrast with 2 out of the 11 routine care mother-son pairs. Perhaps the most interesting results were connected with hormone analysis. Differences between extra contact

mother-infant dyads and routine care mother-infant dyads confirmed previous findings that adrenaline and noradrenaline excretions are sensitive measures of psychological arousal in children as well as in adults (Lundberg, De Château, Winberg, & Frankenhaueser, 1981).

It is of special interest to note that although the absolute levels of catecholamine excretion per kilogram body weight differed between the children and adults, the magnitude of the response was almost identical. Urinary levels of catecholamines seem to provide a useful index of psychological arousal in young children, but direct levels of subjective intensity may be difficult to measure. This study also compared the urinary excretion levels of adrenaline and noradrenaline in the children and their parents under different conditions at the hospital follow-up. The only consistent pattern seemed to be a somewhat higher catecholamine level in the extra contact mothers than in the routine care mothers. A similar but weaker relationship was found for boys. The difference in catecholamine excretion between the two groups increased throughout the day. This varied with increasing stress and was most obvious after the videotaping of the mother and child at play. The level of stress expressed by the increase in catecholamine excretion was highly correlated with the nature of the conflicts that were observed during the free play session. In the extra contact group, more articulated verbal conflicts arose (see Fig. 3.2) than in the routine care group. The excretion of catecholamine in the former group was significantly higher during that sampling period and the next one. The general trend in the extra contact group during the day at the hospital was an increase in catecholamine excretion in the mothers and boys, but a smaller increase in the girls. This was not the case in the routine care group.

During the free play session, mother-child interaction in the extra contact group was characterized by maternal encourag-

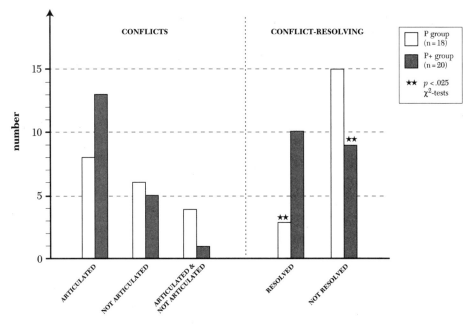

FIGURE 3.2

Results of the analysis of conflicts during mother and child free play. P(P+) = primiparous mothers and routine care infants (extra contact) after delivery. From "Long-term Effect on Mother-Infant Behaviour of Extra Contact During the First Hour Post Partum. V. Follow-up at Three Years," by B. Wiberg, K. Humble, and P. De Château, 1989, *Scandinavian Journal of Social Medicine, 17,* pp. 181–191. Reproduced with permission.

ing and instructing behavior. In the routine care group, the mothers tended to be less demanding and displayed more laissez-faire behavior. These findings are in agreement with the results of previous studies in which stress was induced by achievement tasks. The extra contact mothers excreted more catecholamine and were more demanding, gave more instructions and encouragement, and thus created an atmosphere in which their children, especially the boys, would perform better. The sex differences observed in these children are consistent with those found in other studies on adults and children.

The results of this study support the earlier contention that mother-infant postnatal contact can influence the development of the mother-child relationship in several respects, even on a long-term basis.

Child Care—Day Care

Changing from family care to out-of-home care is an important transition for young children and their families. Social circumstances and benefits can influence its course, at least in the short term (Clark et al., 1993). Although the results of research on possible long-term effects of early mother-infant interaction have been controversial, several studies have shown correlations between early postnatal events and routines and later outcome. Other studies have failed to show such connections (Wiberg, Humble, & De Château, 1989). A major change in child care prac-

tices comes, however, with the introduction of out-of-home care for many infants and young children. Although reasons for change may seem obvious studies of the development of major theoretical concepts over the last decade do not give unambiguous support (Stern, 1995). Adaptation to out-of-home care may be difficult and will proceed according to a number of unknown factors. However, some information on this transition is available.

For instance, Clark and coworkers (1997) recently published a very interesting paper on the length of maternity leave and the quality of mother-infant interactions. In Clark's study, shorter maternity leave correlated with depressive symptoms in the mother and a more difficult temperament in the infant as perceived by the mother. These mothers also demonstrated less positive affect, sensitivity, and responsiveness in the interactions with their infants at 4 months.

In Sweden the Paid Parental Leave Act provides for many forms of paid parental leave. For instance, it allows fathers the right to 2 weeks' leave at 90 percent of the regular salary at the time of the child's birth. It also gives fathers the opportunity to take care of other children in the family while mothers are in the maternity ward, and gives all family members the opportunity to spend a week together adjusting to the newest member. Of Swedish fathers, 85 percent use this right (De Château, 1952).

Secondly, the act entitles either parent to be off work for up to 12 months full-time after childbirth, or 24 months part-time, with financial compensation equivalent to 100 percent of the normal salary. The parents can divide this time between them as they see fit. The act also entitles one parent to be off work an additional 3 months full-time, 6 months half-time, or 12 months at 25 percent off, at a lower level of compensation.

Recent statistics on how fathers use their right to parental leave show that approximately 35 percent took at least some paid parental leave during their child's first year, and that the average leave taken was 1½ months. One result of the Paid Parental Leave Act is that practically all Swedish children up to the age of 1 year are at home with at least one parent, and that during their first year, relatively few children are placed in child care outside the home. Recent data on the work patterns of Swedish mothers with young children also show that extrafamilial child care is not used until the children are 9 to 12 months old, and that the number of children receiving care outside the home becomes significant only after 12 months of age.

A general preschool program with objectives and content for all preschools and leisure-time centers was completed some 10 years ago. This program includes municipal and staff planning, and the organization of activities. The preschool staff contributes to a secure, stimulating environment for raising children and acts as a complement to what the home offers. In cooperation with parents, the preschool must pursue activities designed to:

1. Support and stimulate children's learning ability and social, emotional, motor, linguistic, and intellectual development.

2. Strengthen children's social, linguistic, and cultural identity, pass on their cultural heritage, and broaden their knowledge.

3. Provide good and safe care while parents work or study.

4. Raise children in a democratic spirit of responsibility and lay the foundation for the will to participate in development of the society.

Activities should be shaped by the children's views with the aim of broadening their horizons. The methods of the preschool imply that daily situations, children's games and adult work, and immediate surroundings are used as natural situations for learning. The activities of preschools should be planned based on the children's interests, experiences, and needs. The aims of child care are thus well defined and a consensus is reached. Many children, however, do not have places in municipal day care because of a shortage of places, staff, and money. Families whose children do not attend public day care either change their working hours so that one parent is always at home with the children, take turns with neighbors, involve grandparents, or hire private child-minders.

In the Netherlands paid parental leave has also been introduced, but in a less generous and centralized way. Here the total length of parental leave is 4 to 6 months, and discussion is going on about the prolongation of this period of time. The main argument in favor of this prolongation is one put forth in many other countries, that more and better interaction between parents and small children is needed in order to stimulate normal and healthy development. In many European countries consultation bureaus or child health centers have been in operation for many years, and almost 100 percent of all preschool children visit these clinics on a regular basis. Before the establishment of child health centers, physical checkups during the preschool years were made on a regular basis. The current general tendency is that fewer physical handicaps and diseases are found in this group than was the case 10 to 20 years ago. Therefore, the work of these centers has changed to identifying children in poor social, economic, and psychological circumstances and at risk for developmental delay. Children in need of special support include the physically disabled and intellectually handicapped, those with a hearing impairment, visual disability, or speech impediment, the medically handicapped, and those with social and psychological problems. Governments have not always been too eager to meet these new demands, while the number of schoolchildren with behavioral problems is growing.

Clinical Infantile Autism Case Study

Autistic Disorder (AD) is currently considered a developmental disability with multiple, but usually unknown, biologically based etiologies (Gillberg, 1995; Gillberg & Coleman, 1996). It is characterized by cognitive, communicative, and social deficits. Language retardation is an almost invariable feature of AD and is generally the primary reason for a psychiatric examination. So far there have been few systematic studies on preverbal vocalizations in autistic children. However, clinical observations and parental reports suggest that in such children, the development of babbling is usually delayed; in some children, it may be reduced in amount and deviant in quality (Ricks, 1972; Rutter, Bartak, & Newman, 1971).

In the youngest age groups, language impairment is especially notable; apart from IQ, it has proven to be the best predictor of the later psychosocial outcome in autistic children. Capute et al. (1986) showed that the early attainment of language milestones is predictive of cognition in infancy. Massie and Rosenthal (1984) and Adrien et al. (1990) demonstrated the value of home videos for studying the early behavior of children who are later diagnosed as autistic. We briefly present one of our patients as a case study.

Our patient (R) was videotaped by her parents several times from birth to 14 months of age (Eriksson & De Château, 1992). When she was referred to our clinic at the age of 2 years, 7 months, videotaping was continued in order to further document this case. R is the second child in the family. She was born after a normal pregnancy and delivered at 42 weeks' gestation with normal Apgar scores. Her birthweight was 5,390 g, length 57 cm, and head circumference 36 cm. Her mother's blood glucose levels were checked during pregnancy and found to be within the normal range. According to the parents, R developed normally during the first year. Her communicative behavior was also normal. She smiled, laughed, babbled, and played peek-a-boo. She played with toys in an age-appropriate manner. At 12 to 13 months, the parents first noticed that R was losing interest in her surroundings. As yet there was no indication of R having any disorder. We could confirm the child's history reported by the parents by looking at the videotapes. At 8 months R waved good-bye and played peek-a-boo. At 11 to 12 months of age she walked without support. She babbled in an age-appropriate way with repeated syllables, played with a car, ate well, and pointed at objects when asked. At 13 months of age she was very quiet and hardly used any language at all. She was less active in play, sitting on the floor and playing with a book in a stereotyped repetitive way. She seemed more withdrawn and showed little interest when the parents called her name. When R was 2 years old, her mother told the doctor of the child health clinic that her speech was delayed. She was referred to our hospital at 2.7 years of age. She then showed all the symptoms of AD according to the *DSM-IV* criteria (American Psychiatric Association, 1994). She was withdrawn and preoccupied with rocking or spinning her mother's hair. She showed no interest in other people or playthings. She did not utter any words but only monotonous sounds, except for some phrases from a children's song. Our examination revealed that R's gross motor development corresponded to 2.2 years of age, her fine motor skills to 1 year, and her mental development, measured using the Griffith scale, to 1.6 years of age. The somatic examination, CT scan, MRI, and EEG were all normal. Metabolic screening was normal. Screening for infections known to

affect the brain was negative, and her brain stem audiometry was normal. The videotapes from 11 to 12 months and from 31 months were analyzed by two independent observers using the Childhood Autism Rating Scale (CARS; Schopler, Reichler, DeVellis, & Daly, 1980). At 12 months, R's score was 15 to 15.5 points, which represents nonautistic behavior. In contrast with this observation, her score on the CARS at 31 months was 48.5 to 49 points, which reflects the typical behavior of an autistic child (>30 points = AD). The videotapes recorded by the parents were sometimes of poor quality, but clear enough to observe the quality of R's development. The quantity of different types of communicative behavior could not be estimated, because the videotapes showed only short sequences of R's behavior. Although R seemed to have developed normally during her first year without any delays, she became withdrawn in a period of only a few months, without any obvious medical or biological reason. At 12 months of age, her score on the CARS was within the normal range, and although her autistic symptoms could be detected on the videotape, her mother had not spotted this until her child was 2.3 years old. In R's record from the child health clinic only a tendency toward strabismus was noted. The videotapes provided us with a unique opportunity to study her preverbal communicative behavior. Her stages of speech development during the first year were normal. At 13 months, her preverbal vocalization was deviant in both quality and quantity, as described earlier. This case report is interesting because the videotapes enabled us to confirm the parents' report that R developed normally during her first year. It also showed us that if communicative screening tests had been used routinely at the child health clinic, R's divergent and peculiar behavior would have been noted at a much earlier age and she and her family would most probably have received adequate help at the time. This case report also showed that as early as 12 months of age, the parents noted aberrant behavior in their infant. Earlier normal interaction and attachment behavior had changed, leaving the parents confused and worried. Obviously the parents had drawn the correct conclusion from their observations. These suspicions were later confirmed by the development of full-blown Autistic Disorder.

Thirty-Year Follow-Up Study in Child Guidance Clinics

During the period 1953 to 1955, a total of 2,364 children aged 0 to 18 years were discharged from the Child Guidance Clinic (CGC) in Stockholm. A subgroup of 125 infants (68 boys, 57 girls), who represented 5.2 percent of the primary group, were under the age of 3 years at the time of discharge. Thirty years later, a follow-up study was conducted on these individuals by examining official registers. The parents had all consulted the CGC because they had been experiencing problems with their children. However, many of the parents showed psychiatric symptoms themselves (Curman & Nylander, 1975, 1976; De Château, 1993). The infants' and parents'

psychiatric diagnoses and treatment during initial contact with the CGC are summarized in Table 3.1.

Seventy-seven percent of the infants were judged to have normal mental health or to display mild environmental reactions. Behavioral disorders, mental retardation, and psychosomatic diseases accounted for 23 percent of the diagnoses. The distribution of the diagnoses among sexes was almost identical, with the exception of mental retardation, for which the sex ratio was nine boys to one girl. The parents showed a greater preponderance of mental disturbances than the infants did. In 41 percent of the families, mental disturbances were present in a slightly higher proportion of the families with boys.

The parents who consulted the CGC reported an average of 2.4 symptoms per infant. The most common symptoms were insomnia, aggressive behavior, eating disorders, extreme anxiety, and hyperactivity. Half of the infants were treated for less than 6 months, while the other half received treatment that lasted for more than 6 months (Table 4.2). In 21 cases (17 percent) the infant was placed in foster care or in an institution. The parents agreed with this decision in less than half of these cases. Fourteen of these infants were boys. During follow-up 30 years after discharge, the following sources of information were used: registers kept by child and adolescent psychiatric care clinics or centers and mental hospitals for inpatients; the Social Welfare Board Register; the Register of Criminal Offenses (criminal register); the National Board of Excise Register; the Temperance Board Register (temperance

TABLE 3.1

Infant and Parental Psychiatric Diagnoses and Treatment at the Child Guidance Clinics
from 1953 to 1955

	Boys (n = 68)	Girls (n = 57)	Total (N = 125)
Infant diagnosis			
Healthy	18 (26%)	11 (18%)	29 (23%)
Mild environmental reactions	32 (45%)	36 (63%)	68 (54%)
Behavior disorder	6 (9%)	9 (15%)	15 (12%)
Mental retardation	9 (13%)	1 (2%)	10 (8%)
Psychosomatic disease	3 (4%)	1 (2%)	4 (3%)
Parental diagnosis			
Neurosis	28 (41%)	18 (26%)	46 (37%)
Psychiatric illness	2 (3%)	0 (0%)	2 (2%)
Mental retardation	3 (4%)	0 (0%)	3 (2%)
Maternal diagnosis	21 (31%)	13 (19%)	34 (27%)
Paternal diagnosis	12 (18%)	6 (9%)	18 (14%)
Contact/treatment			
Shorter than 6 months	34 (50%)	30 (53%)	64 (51%)
Longer than 6 months	34 (50%)	27 (47%)	61 (49%)
Compulsory placement	7 (10%)	5 (7%)	12 (10%)
Voluntary placement	7 (10%)	2 (3%)	9 (7%)

board); and the National Social Insurance Board Register (insurance board).

Seventy-five of the 125 infants (60 percent) who were discharged from the CGC between 1953 and 1955 appeared in one of the five registers used for follow-up 30 years later. This proportion was similar to that in the whole group of 2,364 children aged 0 to 18 years (62.9 percent). Records were found most commonly in two of the registers, those kept by the psychiatric clinics and the Social Welfare Board, but many of these patients appeared in more than one of the registers during the follow-up period (Tables 3.2 and 3.3).

Twenty-nine infants (23 percent) were suffering from behavioral disturbances or mental or psychosomatic diseases. At fol-low-up, the 10 patients (8 percent) with mental retardation all had the same diagnosis and were therefore excluded from this part of the analysis of psychiatric symptoms. More of the females who had a psychiatric diagnosis during infancy sought psychiatric help as adults than the males with a similar diagnosis. In the mentally normal infants, the proportions were similar. A total of 55 percent of the individuals who appeared in the register(s) had a parent with a mental deficiency. This was found in only 21 percent of the nonregistered infants ($X2$ = 6.1; p < .01). More boys (48 percent) than girls (26 percent) had a parent with a mental deficiency ($X2$ = 7.8; p < .005). Table 4.1 shows that 51 out of the 125 infants had either one or two parents

TABLE 3.2
Number of Patients in Different Registers during the Follow-Up Period

	Boys (n = 68)	Girls (n = 57)	Total (n = 125)
Psychiatric institution	29 (43%)	24 (42%)	53 (42%)
Social Welfare Board	36 (53%)	20 (35%)	56 (45%)
Criminal register	13 (19%)	2 (4%)	15 (12%)
Temperance board	13 (19%)	2 (4%)	15 (12%)
Insurance board	4 (6%)	2 (4%)	6 (4%)

with a psychiatric diagnosis. At follow-up, 43 of these individuals were identified in one or several of the registers, as opposed to 32 out of the 74 in whom this factor was lacking ($X2 = 21.2; p < .01$). Both of the parents of eight individuals had a diagnosis of mental insufficiency. All but one of these parents were judged to be neurotic at the CGC (the exception, who had a diagnosis of reactive psychosis, was the father of a boy). In six cases, the infant was found to be healthy. Although there were only a few cases, the proportion of individuals noted in one or more registers appeared to be about the same as in the total group.

There were no differences in the number of consultations and treatments given at the CGC or in the duration of consultation and treatment between the sexes.

However, after consultation, placement outside the home was more common in boys than in girls (21 percent versus 12 percent). Voluntary placement was also more common for the boys. Regardless of the mode of placement, the outcome of the 21 infants placed outside the biological home did not differ from that of the total infant group. Of these 21 infants, 62 percent appeared in one or more of the registers at some point during the follow-up period.

Sixty percent of the youngest patients who were examined at the Stockholm CGC during the 1950s appeared in one or several of the government registers 30 years later. A similar proportion of records was found in a follow-up study on children of 0 to 18 years of age covering the same period of time, using the same technique (De

TABLE 3.3
Number of Patients on Various Registers during the Follow-Up Period

	Boys (n = 68)	Girls (n = 57)	Total (n = 125)
In one register	21 (31%)	17 (30%)	38 (30%)
In two registers	9 (13%)	7 (12%)	16 (13%)
In three registers	16 (24%)	4 (7%)	20 (16%)
In four registers	1 (1%)	0 (0%)	1 (1%)
Total	47 (69%)	28 (49%)	75 (60%)

Château & Nylander, in press). The notion that early treatment influences the prognosis in a positive way could therefore not be substantiated by the results of this study. This does not imply that we should not increase our efforts to identify very young individuals who need psychiatric care and treatment. Instead, it forces us to critically reflect on our methods and to adjust them in such a way that they become more effective. In this study, the number of subjects who were suffering from a psychiatric illness and needed help from the Social Welfare Bureau was much larger than the number in the general population of a comparable age in Stockholm (De Château & Nylander, in press). This cohort is unique in many respects (Curman & Nylander, 1976), and therefore no valid control group is available. Inclusion of patients occurred only during a limited period of time. They were discharged either after psychiatric care and treatment had resulted in adequate social adjustment, or because the parents were unwilling to continue attending the CGC. The children in the sample did not display any severe social maladjustments or psychiatric or psychological problems (Curman & Nylander, 1976; De Château, 1990). Seventy-six percent of the sample of infants were considered to be healthy or to have shown mild reactions to their environment at that time by the CGC staff.

Nevertheless, our follow-up clearly demonstrated that the outcome was far from encouraging. At the CGC, many of the disorders were judged to be relatively mild and not to pose much threat to the children's mental health and development.

The question arises as to whether these judgments were well founded and whether it may have been possible to detect or foresee all the difficulties and hardships. In the 1950s, it was generally accepted that it was very important to refer patients to the CGC during an early stage of their maladjustment. However, children under the age of 3 constituted only 5 percent of the total cohort. In our experience, professional help is sought for children not because they are in urgent need of it, but because they are causing serious problems in their environment. If this is true, then it is not surprising that as adults they show such poor social adjustment and have so many other problems and difficulties (De Château, 1991).

Alternative explanations for the correlations found in this study must be discussed. Altogether a great number of items concerning the families was registered and used in the follow-up. However, only few strong correlations were found between these registered items and later outcome (e.g., male sex and parental diagnosis at CGC).

Conclusion

In this chapter, a number of selected examples are given to illustrate the possible connections between early interactional experiences and later normal or psychopathological development. In a recent review of the relationships between mental disorders in childhood and in adulthood, Rutter (1995) concluded that there is strong and specific continuity of depressive disorders.

Information can also be gathered from studies on risks at birth. In an investigation on neonatal separation, Barnett et al. (1970) allowed a group of mothers to enter the premature baby nursery from the 2nd day after birth and to touch and handle the infant in the incubator. Compared to the mothers without this extra contact, the mothers in the experimental group showed greater commitment to their infants, more confidence in their mothering skills, and greater care-providing skills; they also provided the infant with more stimulation. Leifer et al. (1972) found differences in maternal attachment behavior, smiling, and close bodily contact between mothers of full-term versus preterm infants. Lower maternal self-confidence (Seashore, 1973) was found in the primiparous mothers who had been separated from their premature infant for 3 to 12 weeks than in the primiparous mothers who had been permitted to have physical interaction and contact during this period. This difference was not found in multiparous mothers. In a retrospective study, Stern (1973) found that prematurity and separation were strongly correlated with child abuse. In a classical carefully controlled prospective study on 670 infants, Werner et al. (1967) provided evidence that if an infant had suffered some disadvantage at birth (e.g., perinatal asphyxia), then poor environmental circumstances reinforced the existing disadvantage. Conversely, favorable postnatal social influences compensated for the existing disadvantage. In our own studies, right-holding behavior was high in mothers who had been separated from their infant and was also related to more pre- and post-

natal anxiety in the relationship with the infant (De Château, Mäki, & Nyberg, 1982). Many men and women begin parenthood with feelings of insecurity and low self-confidence about their competence as prospective parents. The reasons for this are complicated. Frequently feelings of inadequacy go back to the individual's own early experiences and relationship with his or her own parents. Psychological, medical, and social information, as well as support, may neutralize part of this anxiety. However, adjustment to the parental role, sensitivity to the infant's needs, and the ability to meet the infant's demands are probably more emotional/empathic than cognitive (Winberg & De Château, 1982). If men are not as well prepared in this respect as women, as is indirectly indicated by their behavior, more effort should be made to activate and promote their feelings.

Studies on correlates of early mother-infant interaction generate a number of interesting issues. The relatively short period of extra contact during the first hour after delivery can in itself hardly explain the differences in mother-infant interaction and child behavior later on. During this early contact, however, mother and infant may have had the opportunity to exchange signals that stimulate mother-infant synchrony. Consequently, development of the mother-infant relationship may proceed more smoothly. Other variables, such as the personality of the mother, family and social background, and parental age and health, are possibly of equal importance, as may also be the mother's relationship with her husband, her own parents, planning and course of pregnancy, mode of delivery and so on. From a biological point of view, taking care of a newborn child is a delicate matter. The optimal physical condition for the newborn child is characterized by fairly narrow boundaries, which is also the case with regard to many physiological processes. Parents and scientists are not always aware of these boundaries, and their importance has not always been carefully observed. There should be no great departures from a newborn infant's needs. During the sensitive phase of very early development, these needs are probably best served by patterns of maternal and paternal behavior that for the most part are genetically determined. Perhaps our task should be to provide parents with conditions in our delivery, maternity, and neonatal wards that most closely meet their needs and those of their newborn infant.

The conclusion that can be drawn from these studies and its impact on perinatal care is impressive. However, this in itself constitutes a danger. If a new routine is introduced to replace an old one, then its practical application must take place with great sensitivity. Such a change should not be too rigorous, even when there is evidence of a positive implication for perinatal care. Right from the start, infants differ markedly from each other; their families have different capabilities and backgrounds. Any system must be flexible enough to meet the individual requirements of each and every family. The danger of too much generalization on the basis of contemporary research into mother-infant relationships is not just an illusion.

Our case report on a girl with Autistic

Disorder gives rise to another important question regarding nonoptimal communication between parents and the existing medical system. The parents were convinced that their little girl had a serious delay in development and emotional interaction at a much earlier stage than the medical establishment. Consequently, it took quite some time to find the right channels through which treatment, support, and help could be provided. Delay in correct management is still frequently observed, especially in cases of severely affected young children, and this has great bearing on the possibilities for treatment and future development.

The outcome of the longitudinal, prospective follow-up study on a group of former CGC patients does not seem very encouraging. A major finding was that the majority of this very young CGC population, who had mild adjustment problems, suffered from a number of difficulties later on. Significant predictive factors were the sex of the child and the CGC diagnosis of the parents. These findings were supported by comparable studies on older children (Dahl, 1965; Sundby, Sommarchild, & Kreyberg, 1968). The implication of these findings for practical purposes is that even mild or moderate adjustment problems in early infancy may lead to severe maladjustment in adulthood. Evaluation methods during the 1950s may have been less than adequate, and the severity of the problems may therefore not have been correctly diagnosed. On the other hand, we believe that diagnostic skills during the initial phase of contact with the CGC were of good quality. Discrepancies between these two observations are still poorly under-stood and clearly need more detailed study (De Château, 1991).

Our own experience shows quite clearly that early interactional patterns have a bearing on later development. Correlations between early interactional patterns and the later mother-infant relationship illustrate such a connection. However, little is known about the processes by which such continuity is mediated.

References

Adrien J. L., Faure, M., Perrot, A., Hameury, L., Garreau, B., Barthélémy, C., & Sauvage, D. (1990). Autism and family home movies: Preliminary findings. *Journal of Autism and Developmental Disorders, 21,* 43–49.

American Psychiatric Association. (1994). *Diagnostic and statistical manual of mental disorders* (4th ed.). Washington DC: Author.

Barnett, C. R., Leiderman, P. H., Grobstern, R., & Klaus, M. H. (1970). Neonatal separation, the maternal side of interactional deprivation. *Pediatrics, 45,* 197–205.

Blauvelt, H. N., & MacKenna, J. (1968). Mother-neonate interaction: capacity of the human newborn for orientation. In B. Voss (Ed). *Determinants of infant behaviour* (pp. 3–27). New York: Wiley.

Capute, A., Palmer, F., Shapiro, B., Wachtel, R., Schmidt, S., & Ross, A. (1986). Clinical Linguistic and Auditory Milestone Scale: Prediction of cognition in infancy. *Developmental Medicine and Child Neurology, 28,* 762–771.

Clark, R., Paulson, A., & Conlin, S. (1993). Assessment of Developmental Status and Parent-Infant Relationships. In C. H. Zeanah (Ed.), *Handbook of Infant Mental Health* (pp. 191–219). New York: Guilford.

Cohn, D. J., Paul, R., & Volkmar, F. R. (1987). Issues in the classification of pervasive developmental disorders. In D. J. Cohen & A. Donellan (Eds.), *Handbook of autism and pervasive developmental disorders* (pp. 20–40). New York: Wiley.

Curman, H., & Nylander, I. (1975). Clientele at the Stockholm Child and Youth Guidance Clinics, *Discharged as Having Completed Treatment During the Years 1953–1955.* Privately published, Stockholm.

Curman, H., & Nylander, I. (1976). A 10-year prospective follow-up study of 2268 cases at the Child Guidance Clinics in Stockholm. *Acta Paediatrica Scandinavica:* Suppl. 260.

Dahl, V. (1965). *The Course of Mental Disorders in Childhood.* Copenhagen: Munksgaard.

De Château, P. (1976). *Neonatal care routines. Influences on maternal behaviour and on breastfeeding.* Umeå University Medical Dissertation, New Series, No. 20.

De Château, P., & Wiberg, B. (1977a). Long-term effect on mother-infant behaviour of extra contact during the first hour post partum. I. First observations at 36 hours. *Acta Paediatrica Scandinavica, 66,* 137–144.

De Château, P., & Wiberg, B. (1977b). Long-term effect on mother-infant behaviour of extra contact during the first hour post partum. II. A follow-up at three months. *Acta Paediatrica Scandinavica, 66,* 145–151.

De Château, P., Holmberg, H., & Winberg, J. (1978). Left-side preference in holding and carrying newborn infants. I. Mothers holding and carrying during the first week of life. *Acta Paediatrica Scandinavica, 67,* 169–175.

De Château, P., Mäki, N., & Nyberg, B. (1982). Left-side preference in holding and carrying newborn infants. III. Perception of pregnancy and subsequent holding and carrying behaviour. *Journal of Psychosomatic Obstetrics and Gynaecology, 1–2,* 72–76.

De Château, P., & Wiberg, B. (1984). Long-term effect on mother-infant behaviour of extra contact during the first hour post partum. III. Follow-up at one year. *Scandinavian Journal of Social Medicine, 12,* 91–103.

De Château, P. (1990). Mortality and aggressiveness in a 30-year follow-up in Child Guidance Clinics in Stockholm. *Acta Psychiatrica Scandinavica, 81,* 472–476.

De Château, P. (1991). A 30-year prospective follow-up study of 125 infants in Child Guidance Clinics in Stockholm. *Infant Mental Health Journal, 12,* 116–125.

De Château, P. (1992). A Challenge for Day Care in Sweden: Prevention and Infant Mental Health. *Annals RCPSC, 25*(1), 29–32.

De Château, P. (1993). Long-term follow-up of infants at Child Guidance Clinics in Stockholm. *Journal of Reproductive and Infant Psychology, 11,* 243–248.

De Château, P. (1997). The importance of early mother-infant interactional studies for child psychiatry. In W. Koops, J. B. Hoeksma, & D. C. van den Boom (Eds.), *Development of interaction and attachment: traditional and non-traditional approaches* (pp. 59–78). Amsterdam: North-Holland.

De Château, P., & Nylander, I. (in press). A 30-year follow-up study of 2193 cases at the Child Guidance Clinics in Stockholm. *Acta Paediatrica Scandinavica.*

Eriksson, A. S., & De Château, P. (1992). Brief Report: A girl aged two years and seven months with Autistic Disorder videotaped from birth. *Journal of Autism and Developmental Disorders, 22,* 127–129.

Gillberg, C. (1995). The prevalence of autism and autism spectrum disorders. In F. C. Verhulst & H. M. Koot (Eds.), *The Epidemiology of Child and Adolescent Psychopathology* (pp. 227–257). Oxford: Oxford University Press.

Gillberg, C., & Coleman, M. (1996). Autism and medical disorders: A review of the literature. *Developmental Medicine and Child Neurology, 38,* 191–202.

Ginsberg, H. J., Fling, S., Hope, M. L., Musgrove, D., & Andrews, C. (1979). Maternal Holding Preferences: Consequence of Newborn Headturning Response. *Child Development, 30,* 280–281.

Lebovici, S. (1995). The infant's creativity and competences. *Infant Mental Health Journal, 16,* 5–11.

Leifer, A., Leiderman, P. H., Barnett, C., & Williams, J. (1972). Effects of mother-infant separation on maternal attachment behaviour. *Child Development, 43,* 1203–1218.

Lundberg, U., De Château, P., Winberg, J., & Frankenhaueser, M. (1981). Catecholamine and cortisol excretion patterns in three-year-old children and their parents. *Journal of Human Stress, 7:3.*

Massie, H. N., & Rosenthal, J. (1984). *Childhood psychosis in the first four years of life.* New York: McGraw-Hill.

Nilsson, A., & Almgren, P. E. (1970). Paranatal emotional adjustment. *Acta Psychiatrica Scandinavica*, Suppl. 220.

Ricks, D. M. (1972). *The beginning of verbal communication in normal and autistic children.* Unpublished, MD thesis, University of London.

Rigardt, L., & Alade, M. O. (1990). Effectual delivery room routines on success of first breadfeed. *The Lancet, 336,* 1105–1107.

Ringler, N. M., Trause, M. A., & Klaus, M. H. (1976). Mother's speech to her two-year-old, its effect on speech and language comprehension at 5 years. *Pediatr Res, 10,* 307–311.

Ringler, N. M., Trause, M. A., Klaus, M. H., & Kennell, J. H. (1978). The effects of extra post partum contacts and maternal speech patterns on children's I.Q., speech and language comprehension at five. *Child Development, 49,* 862–865.

Rutter, M., Bartak, L., & Newman, S. (1971). Autism—A central disorder of cognition and language? In M. Rutter (Ed.), *Infantile Autism: Concept, characteristics and treatment* (pp. 148–171). Edinburgh: Churchill-Livingstone.

Rutter, M. (1995). Relationships between mental disorders in childhood and adulthood. *Acta Psychiatrica Scandinavica, 91,* 73–85.

Salk, L. (1960). The effects of the normal heartbeat sound on the behaviour of the new born infant: implications for mental health. *World Mental Health, 12,* 168–175.

Salk, L. (1970). The critical nature of the post partum period in the human for the establishment of the mother-infant bond: A controlled study. *Diseases of the Nervous System,* Suppl. 11, 110–115.

Schopler, E., Reichler, R. J., De Vellis, R. F., & Daly, K. (1980). Toward objective classification of childhood autism. Childhood Autism Rating Scale (CARS). *Journal of Autism and Developmental Disorders, 11,* 92–103.

Seashore, M. J., Leifer, A. D., Barnett, C. R., & Leiderman, P. H. (1973). The effects of denial of early mother-infant interaction on maternal self-confidence. *Journal of Personality and Social Psychology, 26*(3), 369–378.

Söderbergh, R. (1982). Linguistic effects by three years of age of extra contact during the first hour post partum. In C. E. Johnson & C. Larson Thew (Eds.), *Proceedings of the second international congress for the study of child language* (pp. 429–441). Washington, DC: University Press of America.

Stern, D. N. (1995). *The motherhood constellation.* New York: Basic Books.

Stern, L. (1973). Prematurity as a factor of child abuse. *Hospital Practice,* 177–123.

Sundby, H. S., Sommarchild, H., & Kreyberg, P. Ch. (1968). *Prognosis in Child Psychiatry.* Oslo: Universitets-forlaget.

Turkewitz, G., Moreau, T., & Birch, H. G. (1968). Relation between birth condition and neuro-behavioural organization in the neonate. *Paediatric Research, 2,* 243–249.

Uddenberg, N. (1974). Reproductive adaptation in mother and daughter. *Acta Psychiatrica Scandinavica,* Suppl. 254.

Wasz-Höckert, O., Lind, J., Vuorenkoski, V., Partanen, T., & Valanné, E. (1968). The infant cry: a spectographic and auditory analysis. *Clinics in Development Medicine, 29.* London: Heineman.

Weiland, I. H., & Sperber, Z. (1970). Patterns of mother-infant contact: the significance of lateral preference. *Journal of Genetic Psychology, 117,* 157–165.

Werner, E., Simonian, K., Bierman, J. H., & French, F. E. (1967). Cumulative effect of perinatal complications and deprived environment on physical, intellectual and social development of pre-school children. *Pediatrics, 39,* 490–502.

Wiberg, B., Humble, K., & De Château, P. (1989). Long-term effect on mother-infant behaviour of extra contact during the first hour post partum. V. Follow-up at three years. *Scandinavian Journal of Social Medicine, 17,* 181–191.

Widström, A. M., Wahlberg, V., & Matthiessen, A. S. (1990). Short-term effects of early suckling and touch of the nipple on maternal behaviour. *Early Human Development, 21,* 153–163.

Winberg, J., & De Château, P. (1982). Early social development: Studies of infant-mother interaction and relationships. In W. Hartupp (Ed.), *Review of Child Development Research,* pp. 1–44. Chicago: University of Chicago Press.

4

Cross-Cultural Perspectives on Infant Mental Health: Development of Infant Mental Health in Australia

Beulah Warren

4

I've often thought, as old as I am, that it would have been lovely to have known a father and a mother, to know parents even for a little while, just to have had the opportunity of having a mother tuck you into bed and give you a goodnight kiss—but it was never to be.

Confidential evidence age 65, Tasmania: child fostered at 2 months in 1936.

Evidence given to the *National Inquiry into the Separation of Aboriginal and Torres Strait Islander Children from their Families*, 1997.

Past Carin'
Our first child took, in days like these,
A cruel week in dyin',
All day upon her father's knees,

Or on my poor breast lyin';
The tears we shed—the prayers we said,
Were awful, wild—despairin'
I've pulled three through and buried two,
Since then—and I'm past carin'.

Henry Lawson cited in Gandevia (1978)

For general objectionableness there are none to compare with the Australian baby . . . the middle and lower classes are not content with baby's supremacy in the household. . . . Wherever his mother goes, baby is also taken. . . . He squalls at concerts; you have to hold him while his mother gets out of the omnibus, and to kiss him if you are visiting the house.

Twopenny, 1883 cited in Burns & Goodnow (1979, p. 54)

A Brief History of the Family in Australia

The Arrival of the Europeans

Australia, home to indigenous Aborigines for thousands of years, was first populated by Europeans in 1788. Captain Cook had claimed and named the southern land mass New South Wales in 1770. It was Governor Philip who brought the first fleet from England to Australia with about 600 male and 190 female convicts, a handful of children of convicts, and some 200 military and civil personnel to oversee the convicts (Burns & Goodnow, 1979). It was a very difficult beginning—a reluctant workforce, disease, and in the second year, threatened starvation for the occupants of the fledgling colony due to failure of the crops. Further transportations of convicts occurred into the nineteenth century (Clark, 1962).

Within a few years, free settlers began arriving from Great Britain, in particular Ireland and Scotland. A trickle of immigrants arrived from Europe, America, and China; greater numbers followed the discovery of gold in the 1840s. During the nineteenth century, Australia was a pioneer country. Once the barrier to expansion to the west of the initial colony at Sydney Cove had been removed by crossing the coastal mountain range in 1813, settlers began occupying land farther and farther inland. In addition to the spread west inland from Sydney, other remote coastal colonies were established to the south, north, and west.

The population increased dramatically with government-assisted passage from England in 1832. Women began accompanying the men inland and set up homes in remote areas, often working alongside the men, clearing the land, nurturing fledgling crops and a few animals. Women also had the task of producing, raising and educating the children. The child population rose from 20 to 40 percent of the total population and remained so for the remainder of the century, although child mortality, in particular infant mortality, remained high (Burns & Goodnow, 1979). Something akin to a family lifestyle began to evolve.

The "Typical Australian Family"— Cornerstone of Society

Toward the end of the nineteenth century, the typical Australian family emerged. Contemporary observers commented on the general happiness of Australian marriages. "Husband and wife have grown rich together. . . . Domestic occupations so occupy the thoughts of wives, and business those of husbands, as to leave few moments of vacuity for Satan to introduce mischief into" (Twopenny, 1883, Cited in Burns & Goodnow, 1979, p. 28). Burns and Good-

The following individuals were interviewed for this chapter: Bryanne Barnett, associate professor, School of Psychiatry, University of New South Wales, Australia; Kerryl Egan, psychologist and psychotherapist, Sydney, Australia; Isla Lonie, psychiatrist and psychotherapist, Sydney, Australia; David Lonie, child psychiatrist and psychotherapist, Sydney, Australia; and Marianne Nicholson, early childhood nurse, South Eastern Area Health Service, Sydney, Australia.

now state that this pattern was well established by the 1880s and has remained up to the latter half of the twentieth century. Major elements of the Australian family include "small family size, a belief in the centrality of children in the marriage, a marked sexual division of labour, an intense engagement in domesticity by women and their consequent low profile in public life" (Burns & Goodnow, 1979, p. 28). West (1997) has suggested that the lives of Australian women were dominated for approximately 100 years, 1850–1950, by the practice of separate spheres, man's sphere being business and public life, while woman's sphere was the home. That women were chiefly responsible for both home and family was due to the influence of earlier evangelical Christian belief on middle-class women.

Caroline Chisholm, one of the most influential philanthropists in Australia, had, in the mid–nineteenth century, seen the family as the salvation of the Australian colonies. This view was endorsed by Henry Parkes, a visionary political figure of pre-Federation Australia, 20 years later (Clark, 1981; West, 1997). Official recognition of this Australian family was given with the introduction of the minimum wage in 1907. "This was in fact a family wage, set at a figure calculated as sufficient to allow an unskilled labourer, his wife and three children to live in 'frugal comfort'" (Burns & Goodnow, 1979, p. 28).

The ideal of the Australian family has remained throughout the years, evolving to become the "white picket fence" idealization of the current conservative government of 1999.

The Pivotal Role of Women in Family Life

Within the concept of the typical Australian family sits the competence of the Australian mother and her centrality within the family, irrespective of social class (Burns & Goodnow, 1979). In both urban and rural settings, parenting was always predominantly the responsibility and prerogative of the mother, with women devoting much of their time to children and households (Burns & Goodnow, 1979). Man's lack of involvement in the family has not been without criticism. In 1975 the Royal Commission on Human Relationships received a submission from the Anglican Church arguing that many important family concerns are left to the woman, "not because of the male's greater respect for his partner, but because of his own laziness and unwillingness to accept responsibility" (West, 1997, p. 22). As recently as the 1960s, a comparison of Australian children with children in several other countries found that the Australian children saw their mother as much more involved in making decisions and implementing them about household issues and child rearing (Adler, 1966).

Throughout the 210 years of European presence in Australia, single mothers, whether widowed, deserted, or otherwise, have been a sizable proportion of all mothers. In the early years of the nineteenth century, ⅔ of new births were reported to be illegitimate (Kennedy, 1982). Many of these single mothers experienced a difficult time fending for themselves and their children. Although Australia had universal elementary education relatively early (all colonies legislated to that effect between 1872 and 1895), the education received was sex-determined, with girls being educated for domesticity (Burns & Goodnow, 1979). If a woman lost her partner, there were very few possibilities of employment, the socially acceptable means being domestic service, to which she usually could not take her children. Small children were reportedly left unattended at home. In response to this, the voluntary Kindergarten Union and the Sydney Day Nursery Association were formed in 1895 and 1905 respectively to provide a safe and caring environment for young children while mothers worked (J. Fitzgerald, Kindergarten Union, personal communication, December, 1998; Kelly, 1988).

Infant survival was a primary issue until well into the twentieth century. The authorities began to acknowledge that if those women solely responsible for the care of their children were compelled to work, then often the children suffered. They did not have the welfare of the infants exclusively in mind, however, when they enacted legislation to improve the lot of children. Political leaders were concerned with the decreasing birthrate and the need for a productive adult population. An examination of parliamentary debates early in the twentieth century reveals the mixed motives of politicians:

The widow, the orphan and the babe in arms are the first call upon us. . . . Little children are our human sunshine . . . where a mother is engaged in rearing a family of children, she is doing her duty to the State if she rears that family satisfactorily. If at the same time she has to go out into the world to try to earn a livelihood, that work cannot be satisfactorily carried out. The children will suffer and the State will suffer when those children grow up by reason of the fact the work was not properly done. (New South Wales Parliamentary Debates, 1923, cited in Burnes & Goodnow, 1979, p. 50)

Two pieces of legislation were of great significance for women and children. In 1941 national child endowment was introduced. From the beginning it was available to all families, paid to the mother to guarantee that it was spent for what it was intended: "the maintenance, training and advancement of the endowed child." The Hansard record of the time states that the universality of the endowment was justified as it was "an investment in humanity . . . writing into the statute book our realisation of the national significance of family life . . . to ease the disability which must be suffered by the larger family regardless of the wage standard" (Hansard, Australian Parliamentary, 1941, pp. 419, 430). The second significant piece of legislation was in 1942, the national means-tested widow's pension. From the beginning this pension was available to all deserted women, deserted wives, divorcees, wives of mental patients and prisoners, and deserted de facto wives (Burns & Goodnow, 1979).

Watershed of World War II

Although World War I affected most Australian families, in particular because of the loss of many males of marriageable age, World War II had a more dramatic impact on the Australian way of life. A significant proportion of healthy adult males participated in the war; women took work outside the home; large numbers of American servicemen were stationed or took leave in Australia. Following the war, immigration increased. Because of the suffering in England many children were sent to Australia, often under misinformed circumstances, to be fostered or sent to institutions, under the auspices of organizations such as The Fairbridge Foundation or Barnardo's. Seventy thousand British children were sent to Australia under the child migration scheme that ended in 1967 (Gill, 1998).

The immigration policy was expanded. A relatively small number of immigrants from Europe had arrived prior to the war, but from postwar Europe, large numbers of refugees emigrated to Australia; the population rose dramatically, and there was also a dramatic change in the composition of the population. Prior to the war, the nonaboriginal population was predominantly white Anglo-Saxons and Celts from the United Kingdom. Today there are Australians from over 200 countries, and 23 percent of Australians were born overseas (Australian Bureau of Statistics, 1996).

The Period Since World War II

Following the war, married women who had been in the workforce returned to their domestic duties. The 1950s in Australia was a period of full employment, with only 15 percent of women aged 15 to 64 in the workforce (Arndt, 1998b). The "typical Australian family," the nuclear family, again came into vogue and marriage was on the increase. The birthrate peaked in 1952 (Mackay, 1998). With the introduction of the oral contraceptive pill in the 1960s, women for the first time could control their reproduction. Family size began to decrease, with a steady decline in the birthrate since 1974 (Mackay, 1998). Women began to become better educated and to stay in the workforce or return to the workforce after a short absence for childbearing.

In 1972, a Labor government was voted into power after 23 years of conservative government. The new government set about implementing extensive social reform, including the single mother's pension in 1974, abolition of university fees, and funding for child care centers. In the last two decades, there has been a decline in marriages and an increase in the number of babies born to single mothers, with a 70 percent increase in the past decade. In 1998, 27 percent of children were born to unmarried mothers. In 1975, of families with dependent children, 9 percent were single-parent families, compared with about 19 percent in 1996 (Arndt, 1998a).

After years of full employment, the number of people unemployed began to increase in the late 1970s and 1980s; in the late 1990s, the figure remains over 8 percent. There are other indicators of social change; for example, an increase in the divorce rate. Now, $\frac{1}{3}$ to $\frac{1}{2}$ of new marriages end in divorce (ABS, 1996). There is also a dramatic increase in the number of children referred to the Child Protection

Agency and an increase in the number of children and young people registered as homeless. University fees have been reintroduced and there has been a consequent reduction in applications for places. Children remain the victims of political decisions and their social consequences.

An Overview of the Social Welfare of Children in Australia

Early Rapid Increase in the Number of Children

Initially, the children of the colony were of little consequence. However, within a few years the number of children rose from 36 (1788) to 200 in 1792, and within 7 years young children constituted 17 percent of the population (Gandevia, 1978). More importantly, ⅔ of new births were reported to be illegitimate, and many of those neglected. An increasing number of children were the responsibility of women dependent on welfare. Those responsible for the spiritual welfare of the colony were concerned that the children not grow up to emulate their depraved parents, but that they be trained to become "honest and industrious" members of society (Kennedy, 1982).

Establishment of Schools for the Colony's Children

The Reverend Richard Johnson is credited with the establishment of schools and orphanages where the new generation could be separated from their parents. With the support of the military authorities, approximately half the children of the colony, including some as young as 2 years of age, were in school by the time the first colony was a decade old (Burns & Goodnow, 1979). Although it must have been apparent that the children could not be cared for by deserted women who had no support nor the opportunity to earn an income, their destitute condition was attributed to the parent's lack of moral influence, rather than prevailing social conditions (Kennedy, 1982). The high percentage of children involved in schools and orphanages continued into the next century. The "typical" Australian family was not the experience of a large number of children, nor is it today.

During the 1980s, then Prime Minister Bob Hawke pronounced that there would be no child living in poverty by 1990. However, according to Judy Cashmore, chairperson of the New South Wales Child Protection Council (1998), a recent publication has indicated that 16.3 percent of children are living in poverty (King, 1998).

The Profile of the Disadvantaged Child

At the end of the last century the profile of the disadvantaged child was one living in an institution or with a destitute single parent, or perhaps oscillating between the two; children in large families where the father could not earn enough to support the family; or a child in an isolated rural family, isolated not only from other families but often also from the father, who was away for long periods trying to earn some money. For many life was hard. Visits to the cemeteries of country towns tell of the appallingly high infant mortality rate (see Henry Lawson's poem, "Past Carin'," at the beginning of the chapter). Raising children to the age where they could be useful on the family property or farm, or able to support themselves, was an often unachievable goal in the first 140 years of the colonies. Isolated rural families had no access to basic health services. Accidents, childbirth, and illness were managed by the woman of the household, or with the help of neighbors. It was not until 1933, when the innovative Far West Children's Health Scheme began, that the extent of health problems among outback children became apparent. Initially the children were taken for a holiday by the sea, but it was soon apparent that most of the children were in need of medical attention, and so the program was extended to address health problems (Burns & Goodnow, 1979).

The Golden Age of Child Welfare Legislation

The years between 1890 and 1930 have been referred to as the golden age of child welfare legislation, as a spate of legislation was enacted that greatly improved the situation for not only poor children but all children (Burns & Goodnow, 1979). More importantly for infants, infant mortality came under scrutiny. Because of the declining birthrate during the depression of the 1890s, in 1903 the New South Wales government appointed a Royal Commission on the Decline of the Birthrate. Infant mortality, although good by overseas standards, was high (11 to 12 percent), in particular in the cities (14 to 20 percent) and among infants born illegitimately, for whom the rate was three times higher (Burns & Goodnow, 1979). The major causes of death were recognized as social: a combination of weaning early from breast milk or supplementing infant diet with other food or milk, unhygienic living conditions, and the ignorance of young mothers (Burns & Goodnow, 1979). The infant welfare movement arose in response to these findings. It stressed breast-feeding, education of mothers, home visiting, and specialized clinics. In the 10 years from 1904, when the Infant Protection Bill was passed (Macartney-Bourne, 1993), there was a sharp increase in the proportion of breast-fed babies—from 72 to 94 percent—and infant mortality was virtually halved—from 116 to 68 per thousand births (Burns & Goodnow, 1979).

The efforts to improve the infant mortality rate were extraordinarily successful, with employed health visitors reaching 20 percent of all infants in Sydney by 1911. By 1930, every township and suburb had its Baby Health Centre where all mothers could take their infants for free advice on health and related issues (Burns & Goodnow, 1979). The strength of the Baby Health Centre Service has been its universality. It has been used by mothers of all social classes and, although it came under criticism during the 1960s and 1970s for being too allied with the medical model (Gandevia, 1978), it remains a service utilized by more than 90 percent of new mothers at least once (Macartney-Bourne, 1998). Currently 460 Early Childhood Health Centres (ECHCs) operate throughout New South Wales (Macartney-Bourne, 1993). From 1900, the School Medical Services addressed the needs of children of school age, monitoring the improvement in the health of children over the next 20 years and effectively screening for problems associated with the depression of the 1930s (Burns & Goodnow, 1979).

Separation of Children from Parents

Children have been separated from their parent "for their own good" since the earliest days of the colony. As stated previously, in the early nineteenth century, two out of three children in the colony were illegitimate, many born to deserted convict mothers (Kennedy, 1982). Others were orphaned. Where a mother died, often the father could not care for his children and also hold down a job. The social structure of the time created many children who could be perceived as in need of care. The philanthropists who founded charity schools believed that the only way to save these children was to remove them from their parents. In addition to teaching morality, these schools aimed to prepare their pupils to be literate workers, competent in a trade or skill (Kennedy, 1982).

In the recent National Inquiry into the Separation of Aboriginal and Torres Strait Islander Children from their Families (Wilson, 1997), it was stated,

> The developmental needs of children were imperfectly understood until the 1950s and even later. However, there was an early appreciation of the damage incurred in institutions (highlighted by the NSW Public Charities Commission Inquiry in 1874). Non-indigenous children soon benefited from this new awareness. Indigenous children did not. Their needs were met only to a limited

extent in some institutions during this period. (p. 169)

The Latter Half of the Twentieth Century

The 1950s and 1960s saw a dramatic increase in the standards of health, nutrition, education, welfare, and material comfort in Australia. There was also an increasing community awareness of the effects of separation on children. It was as if, with infants physically surviving, society could turn to the quality of their existence, and the mental health of infants. There was a sharp reduction in the number of babies given up for adoption, and the practice of separating Aboriginal babies from their families and communities, which had gone on since before the middle of the previous century, began to decrease. It was in the early 1970s, following the election of a Labor government with a policy platform of Aboriginal self-determination and the funding of indigenous groups to challenge the very high rates of removal of the indigenous children, that a sharp decline in their removal occurred (Wilson, 1997).

It was also in the 1960s that the effects of institutionalization on both adults and children began to infiltrate the community. The seminal work by Erving Goffman, *Asylums,* was published by Doubleday in 1961, and by Penguin in 1968. The effect was to bring the treatment of the mentally ill under public scrutiny. Large psychiatric institutions became more open to the community as a consequence of the Royal Commission into Mental Health, appointed in 1963. By the end of the 1960s new medications made it possible for many psychiatric patients to be treated in the community. Although there was some awareness of the effects of institutions on children as highlighted in the New South Wales Public Charities Commission Inquiry in 1874, (Wilson, 1997) it was in the 1970s that large children's homes, established and managed by charities, were closed or restructured to provide accommodation in family-size group homes, or services provided to whole families at centers where parents received counseling and participated in self help educational and therapeutic groups and children attended day care.

The Association for the Welfare of Children in Hospital was formed in 1973 to address the separation of infants and children in the hospital from their parents.

> The provision of paediatric health care which also meets the psycho-social needs of children and their families is indeed an ideal which had stirred hearts and minds in earlier times and in far away places before it inspired Australians and, ultimately, called into being the Association for the Welfare of Children in Hospital. (Langley, 1986)

From the earliest days, vast distances separated colonial (and later state) capitals such as Sydney, Melbourne, Brisbane, and Perth, with consequent regional differences in emphasis and rate of change. That so much of this change has occurred unevenly throughout Australia, in particular between urban and rural Australia, is a concern in the late 1990s. For example, Australia's infant mortality rate in 1996 was 5.8 per 1,000 live births. However, the death rate for Aboriginal and Torres Strait Islander infants was almost four times that of the rest of Australia (ABS, 1997).

Social/Political Influences on Infant Mental Health in Australia

Social and political influences on infant mental health can be identified embedded in the historical events recounted, together with geographic factors. These influences include:

- Geographic isolation and distance of Australia from other countries, in particular Europe, where the majority of Australians have their roots.
- Geographic isolation and distance from resources for many people within Australia.
- Political leaders and philanthropists who knew what was "best" for children. Social control by the ruling class was often effected through the philanthropy of the elite; in particular, through charitable upper-class women addressing the poorer and the indigenous families (Kennedy, 1982). Emotional ties of children to parents were ignored until the 1950s.
- The life circumstances of those in poverty, with few opportunities for appropriate employment that allowed for care of children; neglect of children was seen to be because of moral degradation and not acknowledged to be part of the pervading social conditions, such as no extended family to help in times of crisis.

- Pioneering life, which was a very difficult experience for colonial women (West, 1997). There was a stoicism about illness and personal sorrow that meant that children experienced little warmth and affection.
- Children's needs being subsumed to the needs of the adults of society; for example, the female and male orphan schools served the function of "preparing children so they were acceptable to employers at an early age" (Kennedy, 1982, p. 19). Religion was also used to instill the work discipline.
- Religion, especially Protestant nonconformism, which served the needs of the leaders of the colony by instilling the work discipline and the glorification of self-denial and menial tasks. The function of the charity schools was "to impart instruction, establish in the children a religious and moral character, as well as to make them more serviceable in the sphere of life in which they are likely to move" (Kennedy, 1982, p. 23).
- Moral character, the cultivation of which was elevated to an art form in the children's institutions, with death elevated in status, in the latter part of the nineteenth century. "Nothing was regarded as more edifying than the death of a model child" (Kennedy, 1982, p. 23).
- Universal primary education established between 1872 and 1895 implied that there was a high level of public literacy; however, there was criticism of what was being taught. Rote learning was encouraged, while personal development was extracurricular. Education of the total child with the capacity to question

was not the concern of the schools even as recently as the mid-1950s (Burns & Goodnow, 1979). Butts, an American educationist, refers to a conversation with a history teacher who felt that schools had a responsibility to teach facts alone. "Children should not try to analyse life until it comes naturally, and anyway most people get along all right without analysing things too carefully" (Butts, 1955, p. 40).

Two Hundred Years of Denial of Emotional Pain

The emotional threads that are woven through the history of Australia have relevance to our understanding of infant mental health in Australia at the end of the 20th century. There has been a pervasive denial of the pain of loss.

- Succeeding generations of Australians have struggled with issues of separation and loss from their birthplace. Sometimes it was a relief to be in a new country—for example for some of the early convicts and later refugees—but for most there has been considerable pain at separation from the familiar. For many there was the shock of an entirely different, harsh landscape and a pioneering culture lacking refinement—true culture shock.
- Children have been separated from their parents "for their own good" since the earliest days of the colony. It was assumed that convicts were not appropriate parents and children needed to be taught to be responsible skilled citizens.

The initial nonexistence of extended family meant that many of the illegitimate and orphaned children of the colony were institutionalized.

- Within rural families many children were sent to board in country towns or to boarding school, in particular for secondary education, although some went as young as 5 or 6. In the cities, children of more affluent families have been separated from their parents and sent to board at one of the elite private single-sex schools, some for both primary and secondary education.

- It has not been acceptable to own or talk about feelings. The accepted behavior following separation or loss was to get on with the task at hand, not dwell on the pain, except to dull the pain with alcohol or other substances.

Increasing Societal and Professional Awareness of Infant Mental Health through the 1960s, 1970s and 1980s

- The importance of the family to the mental health of its members began to be understood with the publication of works, for example, by Bateson and Jackson (Bateson, Jackson, Haley, & Weakland, 1956; Jackson, 1960). The treatment of mentally ill patients underwent a radical change with the introduction of therapeutic communities in psychiatric hospitals, and the insistence that families be involved by participating in group therapy; for example Fraser House at North Ryde Psychiatric Hospital and Bayview House at Callan Park Hospital, Sydney.

- Parents whose children were born in the late 1960s and 1970s were born into postwar affluence, had experienced an adolescence, and entered the workforce at a time of full employment. These parents had time and were conscious of the responsibility of parenting over and above issues of survival and education, but were also experiencing uncertainty about their capacity to parent. Evidence given to the Royal Commission on Human Relationships in 1977 stated that "these young people [embarking on the first pregnancy] do not have firmly established experience in child-rearing and go into parenthood with tremendous fear, doubt, guilt, and other problems."

- During the 1960s with the introduction of the pill and increased education, women began to look at the quality of life for the fewer babies they were producing. Infant mortality had been stabilized for the majority of the population but (note that infant mortality among the Aboriginal population was still high and remains so in the 1990s). Society, and health professionals in particular, was in a position to focus attention on the quality of experience of the future generations.

- Concern was being raised at the consequences of childbirth taking on the status of illness and increasing intervention in the birth process. The medical profession was looking at the effects of birthing practices on newborns. Research into the effects of medication was conducted in the 1970s; for example, the effects of epidural anesthesia on newborns and their mothers (Murray, Dolby, Nation, & Thomas, 1981). It was not simply the biological or physical consequences of these practices that were studied, but also the behavioral outcomes for mother and infant.

- Young couples were asking for fathers to be present at birth (B. Barnett, personal communication, October 9, 1997). Some fathers were keen, but others were dubious, wondering how they would cope but not wanting to lose face. These fathers did not have role models of fathers present at the birth of babies.

- Childbirth had been removed from the province of the home with the gradual decline of domiciliary midwifery and the subsequent advent of childbirth moving to hospitals, first small cottage hospitals and then to maternity wards of general hospitals, in the 1940s and 1950s. In addition, with the growing knowledge of infection, newborns and mothers were increasingly separated after the birth and while they were in hospital. There was growing concern at this turn of events, so that the study conducted by Klaus and Kennell (Klaus et al., 1972), which examined the consequences on the relationship of not separating mother and baby postpartum, affected Australian obstetric practices.

- The negative effects of separation on infants and young children began to filter into the community consciousness. The Robertsons had made their film on the consequences of short-term separation of infants from their parents, and hospital practices began to change with the lobbying of the Association for the Welfare of Children in Hospital from 1973.

- Child development courses at universi-

ties began to include the work of Bowlby, the Robertsons, and in the 1970s, Ainsworth and her students.

- By the end of the 1970s research was being conducted into the consequences of medical practices on infant development, in particular, the consequences of a premature birth on later development (for example, Kitchen et al., 1980; Yu & Wood, 1978). Publication of "The Battered Child Syndrome" (Kempe, Silverman, Steele, Droegemueller, & Silver, 1962) had awakened the world to child abuse, and one of the identified at-risk groups was premature infants. Methods of intervention to reduce the risks associated with prematurity were investigated. For example, Dolby and her associates found that parents of those premature infants identified as "difficult infants" appeared to benefit dramatically from early support. At follow-up at 6 months, parents of these infants who had received support were more affectionate and verbally responsive toward their infants, and more aware and active in meeting their infants' developmental needs (Dolby, English, & Murray, 1982).

- Parenting in its various forms was examined. Professor Gordon Parker, of the University of New South Wales, examined the consequences of overprotective parenting for children and their development (Parker, 1983).

- Funding bodies, in particular the government, began to question practices that did not take into account the emotional life of the child. For example, a mother-infant residential unit for mothers and infants who were having difficulties postbirth, was told that a condition of funding would be the appointment of a child psychiatrist to their board (D. Lonie, personal communication, December 16th, 1997). Medical personnel on the board wondered what purpose a child psychiatrist would serve. A consultant child psychiatrist was appointed to the unit's honorary medical staff in 1979, and a psychiatrist has been on the board since 1980.

- As large institutions that had been responsible for housing children at risk began closing, other ways of working with families to protect children from child abuse and neglect began to emerge. In addition to working more directly with families to protect children, in 1977 New South Wales doctors were mandated to report suspected incidents of child abuse and neglect.

- Infant behavior per se became a focus of investigation, for example, Murray on crying (1979). This new area of research and clinical observation of the individual characteristics of the infant was consolidated by the visit to Australia of Dr. T. Berry Brazelton in 1978, and the training of local professionals in using the Neonatal Behavioral Assessment Scale (Brazelton, 1973).

- From the late 1950s through the 1960s and 1970s the Royal Alexander Hospital for Children (RAHC) was at the forefront of efforts to understand the emotional needs of infants. Professor Julian Katz, a child psychiatrist, had worked with Bowlby and was strongly versed in attachment theory and Winnicott's work. He taught generations of psychi-

atric registrars and professionals of other disciplines from his firsthand experience. During 1973 the Association for the Welfare of Children in Hospital was established, and Dr. John Bowlby met with the officeholders on a visit to Sydney and the RAHC. At the same time, exciting clinical work was being carried out in the wards, with efforts being made to work with parents on the oncology wards, to support staff through therapeutic groups, and to better understand the needs of the infants through careful observations of their behavior. In the 1970s a team was set up by Dr. John Yu to study the emotional health of children in hospital and to make recommendations. As a consequence, unrestricted visiting became policy, accommodation for parents was planned, and the establishment of social workers on staff increased (Norma Tracy, personal communication, December 5, 1998).

- The practice of infant observation as part of psychoanalytic training began in 1968. Infant observation became more widely available a few years later when two professionals who had undergone training at the Tavistock Clinic in London, Dr. Avril Earnshaw and Peter Blake, returned to Australia and offered to train others in Sydney.

- Increased anxiety during pregnancy in first-time mothers was recognized as a necessary preparation for childbearing and parenting but also as having the potential to interfere with the management of labor and bonding with the baby (Barnett & Parker, 1985). Dr. Bryanne Barnett was able to demonstrate the effectiveness of an intervention by both professionals and lay persons in reducing anxiety in highly anxious groups. The professional intervention of support, antianxiety measures, promotion of self-esteem and confidence, and attention to the quality of the mother-infant, mother-father, and father-child interactions significantly lowered anxiety levels (Barnett & Parker, 1985). Performed in 1980–1981, this was also the first research using the strange situation paradigm (Barnett, Blignault, Holmes, Payne, & Parker, 1987).

The Discipline of Infant Mental Health in Australia

Two Publications That Influenced Clinical Practice and Teaching

Two seminal books of the 1980s had a profound effect on the establishment of the discipline of infant mental health in Australia. The first of these was *Clinical Studies in Infant Mental Health—The First Year of Life* by Selma Fraiberg (1980), which outlined the work of the Child Development Project, a program attached to the Department of Psychiatry, University of Michigan Medical School, Ann Arbor. The treatment program outlined was based on the work of Selma Fraiberg and Jeree Pawl, and its combination of home visiting, developmental guidance, practical support, and infant-parent psychotherapy struck a powerful chord with some clinicians who were working with infants and their families. Fraiberg outlined a way of

working with those families who did not respond to more traditional developmental guidance or follow-up recommendations.

The second significant publication was Daniel Stern's book, *The Interpersonal World of the Infant* (1985), which alerted many adult as well as child psychotherapists to the "dialogue between the infant as revealed by the experimental approach and as clinically reconstructed" (p. ix; I. Lonie, personal communication, December 6, 1977, D. Lonie, personal communication, B. Barnett, personal communication, Oct. 9, 1997 and K. Egan, personal communication, December 2, 1997). Dr. Bryanne Barnett referred to using the material of Stern and others in conferences and student lectures, and remembers the buzz of excitement as the implications for practice became apparent.

The Early Intervention Programme (EIP)

Several authors of this period (for example, Brazelton, 1983; Helfer, 1987) were writing of a window of opportunity around the time of the birth of a baby; that parents were available to be co-opted into protecting and nurturing their baby, and there was opportunity to focus and build on the strengths of the infant, the parents, and the parent-infant relationship before problems had exacerbated. Gaile Shea-Everidge (1986) used such concepts to develop a protocol for the establishment of an infant-parent support program, the Early Intervention Programme (EIP), for the Benevolent Society of New South Wales, in Sydney. This innovative home visiting program of a multidisciplinary team of professionals was funded by the New South Wales Government Department of Health. Dr. Shea-Everidge not only drew on overseas studies and clinical interventions outlined in the literature, but interviewed local researchers and clinicians. The study conducted by Dr. Bryanne Barnett (Barnett & Parker, 1985) with first-time mothers with high anxiety was one such resource. Another resource was a team of psychologists and physiotherapists: Dr. Robyn Dolby, Mrs. Beulah Warren, Ms. Vickie Mead, and Mrs. Jan Heath, at the Royal Hospital for Women, who were conducting a follow-up study with premature infants and their families (Dolby, Warren, Meade, & Heath, 1987). This study included meeting parents in the neonatal intensive care unit (NICU) before they took their baby home, offering psychological support to parents, obtaining the parents' perceptions of their baby's behavior as well as a developmental assessment of the infant as the basis for intervention—elements that Shea-Everidge indicated were compatible with the protocol of the new program, EIP, that she was writing. Fraiberg's (1980) model, invitation to the family, was to be the framework for the EIP, which was established in 1987. The multidisciplinary team of seven participated in intensive training to enable each member to work as a primary therapist with the mother-infant dyad to strengthen their relationship. The program, funded for regular group and individual supervision, became a model of preventive work with families with new infants. The majority of referrals

to EIP came from the large maternity hospital to which it was attached and where, in the first 2 years, at least ⅓ of the infants were born premature. The EIP recently celebrated 10 years of working with families of infants with a conference and the publication of a book, both titled *Inner Worlds—Outer Realities: The Prevention of Child Abuse and Neglect through Early Intervention* (Donnolley & Edwards, 1998).

Isolation Broken Down, Distance Overcome

Isolation and distance have always played a significant role in shaping life in Australia, and the understanding of infant mental health is no exception. The lower prices and increasing popularity of international airline services in the late 1960s made attendance at international conferences possible. The first congress of the World Association for Infant Psychiatry (WAIP) held in Cascais, Portugal, in 1980, alerted Australians to international interest in infants. The International Association for Child and Adolescent Psychiatry and Allied Professions (IACAPAP) held a congress in Australia in 1978. One of the attendees was Bianca Gordon of the Anna Freud Centre, London, who had published an article the year before on her work as a consultant, using psychodynamic principles, to nurses in a neonatal nursery. Dr. Gordon was persuaded to give an extempore presentation about her work, to the fascination of Australian clinicians. Another paper, by an American analyst, described the analysis of a healthy woman during her pregnancy

(D. Lonie, personal communication, December 16, 1997).

At the next IACAPAP conference in 1982 in Dublin, WAIP had a half-day symposium. Australians also met Professor Jim Herzog, an adult and child psychoanalyst from Harvard University, and heard a presentation of his work. In 1986, at the third WAIPAD congress in Stockholm, Sweden, the number of Australians and New Zealanders attending had grown, and an invitation on behalf of the Psychotherapy Association of Australia was issued to Professor Herzog to visit Australia. In 1987, Professor Herzog visited Sydney, Melbourne, and Adelaide, making a considerable contribution on infancy to the work of adult psychotherapists, focusing on new developments in infant research and their application to theory and practice.

Divergent Beginnings, Common Outcome

Following the WAIPAD third world congress in 1986, those who had attended began to discuss the possibility of forming an Australian branch of WAIPAD. An Australasian vice presidency had been created at the WAIPAD congress. Those who had already attended the international congresses and were at the forefront of the push were primarily child psychiatrists from Sydney and Melbourne. The topic was discussed at a meeting of the Psychotherapy Association of Australia in Melbourne in late 1987. The WAIPAD Pacific Rim conference in Honolulu in April 1988 provided further impetus for a number of child psychiatrists to begin meeting

as an Australian WAIPAD. Meanwhile, adult psychotherapists and others were struck by the work of Stern and the new research on infants and how that research challenged current perceptions of the infant. "It was a huge opening, also the sense that something new, genuinely new, was happening and it had great explanatory power" (K. Egan, personal communication, December 2, 1997). Academics conducting research in early development at Macquarie University, Sydney, were approached, and the psychotherapists interested were directed to attend the International Society for Infant Studies biennial conference being held in April of 1988. This was an instant introduction to the field for Ms. Kerryl Egan, clinical psychologist and psychotherapist, who was to return to Australia and establish the Australian Association of Infant Mental Health Inc. before the year ended. The conference provided exposure to many key people involved in infant studies, and opportunity to discuss with directors of the International Association of Infant Mental Health (IAIMH) the possible relationship between an Australian association and IAIMH. Back in Australia, Kerryl sought out those who were working in the field with mothers and their infants to ascertain their interest and enlist their cooperation in forming an association. Earlier in the year, team members of the Early Intervention Program (EIP) and others working in the field formed an interest group to meet and discuss issues relevant to working with parents and infants. It was this group that Kerryl approached to enlist cooperation to establish an Australian Association of

Infant Mental Health, as well as the child psychiatrists who were meeting as WAIPAD Australia.

The Australian Association of Infant Mental Health Inc.—AAIMHI

In the minutes of the inaugural meeting of the AAIMHI held at the Institute of Psychiatry, on September 14, 1988, Kerryl Egan, the foundation president, reported as follows:

> The concept grew from her experiences in a study group and was consolidated by the prospect of becoming affiliated with the IAIMH. In discussing with colleagues the possibility of establishing an association, she also became aware of a number of existing networks, isolated from one another but sharing common ground. It is envisaged that the Association will provide a forum for communication between such groups, and for multi-faceted discussion in the area of infant development.

There were 16 foundation members: three staff members of the EIP, adult and child psychiatrists, adult and child psychotherapists, an occupational therapist, a speech pathologist, a social worker, and an academic child psychologist. The original committee of management was drawn from the above membership. It was proposed at that meeting that the committee be enhanced by the inclusion of persons from the following disciplines:

- Nursing, a representative from early childhood health centers
- A representative from the child protection services
- A social worker, representing those who work with drug-addicted mothers
- A paediatrician
- A physiotherapist

Thus, from its inauguration AAIMHI has been an inclusive, broad-based association of persons with the stated objectives to:

1. Improve professional and public recognition that infancy is an important period in psychosocial development;
2. Improve awareness that psychological and biological development processes are interrelated;
3. Provide a forum for multidisciplinary interaction and cooperation;
4. Establish and maintain discussion and exchange of information on both national and international levels;
5. Provide members with access to the latest research findings and observations on development in infants;
6. Facilitate the integration of such findings into clinical practice and community life;
7. Work for the improvement of the mental health and development of all infants and families;
8. Provide where possible reports and submissions to governments, other authorities, organizations, and individuals on matters relating to infants and family health and welfare; and
9. Adopt such other objectives as the association shall approve by special resolu-

tion at a general meeting (AAIMHI 1988a, 1988b; AAIMHI statement of objectives, 1992).

Struggling Beginnings

Initially the association struggled financially but immediately planned to hold a series of Saturday morning workshops and bimonthly seminars; publish a newsletter; and begin dialogue with the fledgling local WAIPAD group. The first Saturday workshop in February 1989, "Do Babies Have Feelings: The Emerging Self: Implications for Practice," attracted 65 participants. The speakers were Dr. Curtis Samuels, Dr. Russell Meares, and Dr. Bruce Tonge.

Balancing the budget, holding regular seminars, and getting a newsletter catab lished were the preoccupations of the foundation committee through 1989 and 1990. The workshop "Do Babies Have Feelings?" was followed by such seminars as "Infant Observation," "Attachment Theory and Practical Implications," "Infants in Hospital," "Giving Birth to Feelings," "The Transition from Coupling to Parenting," and "Crying Babies" and the workshops "Maternal Grief" and "The Neonatal Behavioral Assessment Scale" (Brazelton 1984), to name a few. Renate Barth, a psychologist on the EIP team, undertook to be the first editor of the newsletter. Number 1 was published May 8, 1989, with a letter from the president, a calendar of events of the association and other relevant seminars and conferences, and an article giving an explanation and suggested management of colic within the framework of self-regulation theory.

The dialogue with those who proposed a WAIPAD branch continued, and plans were made for AAIMHI to join with WAIPAD to hold a conference. The inaugural infant mental health conference in Australia was the Pacific Rim meeting of WAIPAD, "Mothers, Fathers and Infants: Transition to Parenthood," held in Melbourne, Victoria, April 26–28, 1991. The planning and delivery of the meeting was the achievement of the newly formed AAIMHI and those associated with WAIPAD in New South Wales, working with the WAIPAD Association of Victoria. The plenary speakers included Dr. Tiffany Field, Dr. Graeme Russell, and Dr. Kyle Pruett, and the following topics were addressed in workshops and seminars:

- Attachment (parent-infant and infant-parent)
- The infant in hospital (preterm infants, perinatal death, handicapped infants)
- Reproductive technology (transition to parenthood following a period of infertility)
- Internal working models (the parent and infant within)
- Disturbances of early relationships (child abuse and neglect)
- Infant observation (psychoanalytic perspectives)
- Early intervention (role of the maternal and early childhood nurse, early intervention programs)

This international meeting was successful in many ways. It brought together professionals interested in infant mental health from all over Australia (there were over 300 registrants); it was financially successful, providing a core fund for future meetings; and it was hoped that with so many professionals enthusiastically returning to all states, public awareness of the needs of infants would be increased. In planning for the conference it became clear to members of the committees that the two groups in New South Wales should amalgamate (D. Lonie, personal communication, December 16, 1997). As AAIMHI had a formal structure and was affiliated with the International Association of Infant Mental Health, the New South Wales WAIPAD committee decided to disband and give their support to AAIMHI.

When the two international organizations, WAIPAD and IAIMH, joined together in September 1992, AAIMHI, through its affiliation with IAIMH, became affiliated with WAIMH. At this point there were thus two Australian infant mental health associations, AAIMHI and WAIMH (Vic); the latter formally established itself at a meeting on July 22, 1992 (Paul, 1993). The regional vice president, Dr. David Lonie, began discussions with the presidents of the two associations as to how they should operate together, whether as two separate organizations relating through the regional vice president, or as a national organization with state committees (Lonie, 1993). As the discussion continued, with regular updates published in the newsletter, the solution evolved. With each successful conference, the membership of AAIMHI throughout Australia increased. Members in different centers began to meet together to address local needs and formed local committees representing state branches. The hard-

working committee in South Australia was the first to formally launch a state branch. The Inaugural Conference and Launch of the South Australian Branch of AAIMHI was held in October 1994. Dr. David Lonie opened the conference and Dr. Sula Wolff, honorary fellow of the University of Edinburgh Department of Psychiatry, gave the keynote address: "The Scope of Infant Mental Health: Pointers to Helpful Interventions." By September 1996, the states of Western Australia and Queensland also had active branches. A federal organization with active state chapters appeared to be the way forward. To this end, the members of WAIMH (Vic) consulted with legal practitioners to determine whether the existing AAIMHI constitution could be altered to accommodate the growing, truly national organization. At the AGM during the third national conference in Melbourne, December 1996, the membership was given the opportunity to discuss the proposed changes. State committees agreed to examine the document and refer back to the ad hoc constitutional committee.

At the fourth national conference, October 1997, hosted by the recently formed South Australian Branch of AAIMHI, a special meeting was held with representatives of WAIMH (Vic), AAIMHI members from the executive committees of the South Australia, Western Australia, and Queensland branches. Points of concern raised from different members were collated and taken back to the solicitors. Draft documents were again circulated to representatives from each state branch and comments invited to enable the new constitution to be finalized, presented, and approved by the membership at a special meeting in June 1998. AAIMHI now has a small national executive committee with representatives from each of the state branches. The quarterly newsletter and the annual national conference will be the responsibility of the national committee and delegated to a state branch.

National Conferences and Visiting International Educators

AAIMHI members who had been involved in the successful Pacific Rim meeting of the World Association for Infant Psychiatry and Allied Disciplines, "Mothers, Fathers and Infants: Transition to Parenthood," held in Melbourne, April 1991, were greatly encouraged and determined to try and make a national conference an annual event. In October 1991, AAIMHI joined with the Australian Early Intervention Association to present a conference, "Under 5 and at Risk." Dr. Arnold Sameroff, Dr. Susan McDonough of Brown University, and Dr. Ruth Schmidt-Neven of the Royal Children's Hospital in Melbourne, were the plenary speakers. Several AAIMHI and WAIMH (Vic) members presented papers and workshops at the 1992 Chicago meeting of WAIPAD and IAIMH, and participated in the vote for the merged WAIMH.

The School of Behavioural Sciences at Macquarie University, Sydney, in conjunction with the School of Psychiatry at the University of New South Wales, began a longitudinal study of a cohort of Sydney infants, known as the Sydney Family Emotional Development Study. As infant attachment was going to be a critical factor

to be measured, it was decided to bring an experienced academic and qualified trainer on the Strange Situation procedure and attachment theory to train a core group of researchers and clinicians. Dr. Robert Marvin of the University of Virginia, Charlottesville, conducted a 2-week attachment workshop on the use of the Strange Situation procedure with infants in 1993 and returned to conduct a further training workshop in the use of this technique with toddlers in July 1994. The result has been an increased use of the Strange Situation procedure as a measurement tool in research. Since attachment experts from both the United Kingdom and the United States gathered in Australia that July, and in recognition of the International Year of the Family, AAIMHI hosted in Sydney a 2-day conference, "Principles of Attachment Theory: Relevance to Intervention with Infants and Caregivers." Dr. Marvin presented his work on attachment of children with a disability; Dr. Lynne Murray and Dr. Peter Cooper of Cambridge University brought those in attendance up to date with research on the effects of postnatal depression on infants and the Cambridge Study; and Dr. Mary Sue Moore of Boulder, Colorado, brought together threads from the other presentations to outline implications for the management of infants, the consequences of trauma, and the relationship between infants and their parents. This conference provided an opportunity for a broad range of people working with infants, their parents, and caregivers, to gain a greater knowledge of attachment theory and current research in the area.

Our next national conference was the Third Pacific Rim meeting of the World Association for Infant Mental Health, "The Baby, Family and Culture—The Challenges of Infancy, Research and Clinical Work." The scientific program was in the hands of the WAIMH (Vic) committee, and the conference was hosted by the AAIMHI committee in Sydney in April 1995. An impressive array of international speakers joined local presenters, including Dr. Hiram Fitzgerald, executive director of WAIMH from Lansing, Michigan; Dr. Hisako Watanabe from Yokohama, Japan; Dr. Antoine Guédeney from Paris, France; Dr. Charles Zeanah from New Orleans, Louisiana; Mrs. Dilys Daws from London; Dr. Mary Sue Moore from Colorado; Dr. Eric Rayner from London; Dr. Ann Morgan from Melbourne, Australia; and Mrs. Elvie Kelly from Melbourne, Australia. The conference was held back-to-back with the Pacific Rim Marcé meeting in order to encourage cross-fertilization. Many international and local speakers, not to mention conference delegates, took advantage of the arrangement and attended and enjoyed both meetings. Over 200 professionals from all over Australia attended the AAIMHI conference and, as reported in the Newsletter, were exposed to a "rich feast." "The quality of the papers and their scope were a convincing indication of the interest there is in Australia in Infant Mental Health" ("Editorial," 1995). The conference had also given membership a boost so that at the end of June 1995 there were 191 members, from all states except Tasmania and the Northern Territory. Immediately following the conference, the Victorian branch collaborated with the Melbourne Institute of Psychoanalysis to present a 1-day colloquium on infancy and psychoanalysis. A summary of the event, as well as of the plenary sessions of the conference, was published in the newsletter so that all members could share the information and experience.

Many members of AAIMHI attended and presented at the WAIMH's sixth world congress in Tampere, Finland, July 1996, but many more were able to attend the association's annual national clinical meeting held in Melbourne, Victoria, in December 1996, "The Interplay of Infants, Parents and Therapists." The international speakers were Ms. Juliet Hopkins of the Tavistock Clinic, London, and Dr. Mary Sue Moore, Community Infant Program, of Boulder, Colorado. Particular highlights were the quality of the clinical material presented by local clinicians, and the inaugural D. W. Winnicott Memorial Lecture given by Ms. Juliet Hopkins, "The Dangers and Deprivations of Too Good Mothering." The 1997 annual national conference, with two additional days of workshops, was hosted by the South Australian branch and held in Adelaide, October 1997. Dr. Anne Sved-Williams and Ros Powrie, the scientific coconvenors, brought together three outstanding figures from the international arena as well as presenters from Australia and New Zealand to produce a conference of "excellent academic and practical merit" (Sved-Williams, 1997). International luminaries were Professor Marinus van IJzendoorn, professor of psychology at Leiden University in the Netherlands, Dr. Martha Erikson of the STEEP Project, Rochester,

Minnesota, and Dr. Hisako Watanabe, child psychiatrist, Keio University Hospital, Tokyo, Japan.

AAIMHI joined with the Perinatal Society of Australia and New Zealand, the Australian Neonatal Nurses' Association, and the New Children's Hospital, Westmead, to bring Professor Heidelise Als of the Boston Children's Hospital, and associate professor of psychology (psychiatry) at the Harvard Medical School to Australia. In addition to being a plenary speaker at the second annual Perinatal Society of Australia and New Zealand Congress, Dr. Als presented a seminar in Sydney, "Newborn Developmental Care in NICU," in March 1998. The fifth annual meeting, held in Sydney in September 1998, drew participants from all states and New Zealand. "'With No Language But a Cry'—Trauma in Infancy," the meeting focused on understanding the enduring consequences of various forms of trauma in infancy and was directed by keynote speakers Dr. Mary Sue Moore and Ms. Janet Dean, Boulder, Colorado, Dr. John Byng-Hall, cofounder of the Family Therapy Training Program at the Tavistock, and Professor Barry Nurcombe, chair, Department of Child Psychiatry, University of Queensland, Brisbane, Australia.

Academic Courses in Infant Mental Health

Although the annual conferences, individual seminars, and short courses conducted by the association were successful in meeting some of the educational needs of the growing number of professionals, it be-

came apparent that there was a need for a more formal course of study in infant mental health. The Victorian branch of the association, in particular Dr. Campbell Paul, Ms. Brigid Jordon, and Frances Thompson-Salo, was instrumental in setting up the first post graduate diploma and master's in infant mental health at the University of Melbourne in 1996. The New South Wales Branch, in collaboration with the New South Wales Institute of Psychiatry, has followed with a postgraduate course in infant mental health. The first intake of 15 were enrolled in the 2-year course in July, 1998.

AAIMHI Finds Its Political Voice

In 1996 a major event occurred in Australian political and social history in the form of the National Inquiry into the Separation of Aboriginal and Torres Strait Island Children from their Families. A number of members of AAIMHI made personal submissions, but more significantly, the executive committee decided a submission from AAIMHI would declare publicly that we have a major interest in the well-being of infants and their families. The committee decided to address the transgenerational issues in terms of attachment theory. The final document was prepared by a postgraduate student of the Institute of Early Childhood Studies, Macquarie University, and edited by committee member Julie Campbell with the help of other committee members. The submission addressed the question, "What are the effects on the child of separation from a primary carer at birth, in infancy, in later childhood?" Explanation was given of how an infant develops in interaction with his or her primary caregivers; how, within the earliest relationship, usually with the mother, an infant builds up a mental picture of him- or herself, of the carer, and also of how the carer has responded to cries for help over the early months of life; and how this mental picture of oneself in relation to one's carer is the basis for interactions in later life. An outline was given of the consequences for those infants who had experienced little, no, or interrupted mothering and included the following statement:

> It has been argued (Bowlby, 1988) that early loss of a mother or prolonged separation from her before age 11 is conducive to subsequent depression, choice of an inappropriate partner, and difficulties in parenting the next generation. Anti-social activity, violence, depression and suicide have also been suggested as likely results of the severe disruption of affectional bonds (Bowlby, 1979). (Wilson, 1997).

This statement was used in the report of the inquiry to give focus to the many submissions made to the inquiry by Aboriginal people detailing the tragic loss and self-destructive behavior in their lives (note the opening quotation of this chapter). AAIMHI felt it had made a significant contribution.

The association has since made submissions to two New South Wales government inquiries. The first was the inquiry into Parenting Education and Support Programs in New South Wales in February 1998. Three members of the AAIMHI

committee made a presentation in person. Their presentation was appreciated by the chairman of the government Standing Committee on Social Issues, and the chairperson suggested that AAIMHI should make a submission to another government inquiry into the establishment of a New South Wales children's commission. This was completed in haste as the closure for submissions was imminent. AAIMHI was also asked to write the chapter on the developmental needs of children for the New South Wales government report on parenting education and support programs. Dr. Marija Radojevic accepted the responsibility.

Current Issues in Infant Mental Health in Australia

In researching the information for this chapter a sample of professionals involved in infant mental health were interviewed. One of the questions asked of them was, what did they think were the current infant mental health issues in Australia?

The Welfare of Children

Issues related to the welfare of children include the nonaccidental deaths of infants even though they and their parents may be known to the child protection agency; the increasing number of homeless children and young adolescents, which many feel relates back to early parent-infant relationships; and the failure of child protection, juvenile justice, and other relevant agencies to recognize the need for attachment-informed interventions in early life to prevent subsequent health and forensic problems. The increasing number of divorces where very young children are involved and the subsequent risk of the young children not having equal access to both parents is also a matter of concern. Associated with this factor is the continuing need to encourage and keep fathers involved with their babies and infants. Recent Australian research shows that many of these issues are linked to families experiencing economic stress and living in crime-prone neighborhoods. Child neglect was found to be the strongest causal factor of juvenile participation in crime (Weatherburn & Lind, 1998). The infant mental health professionals felt that the resolution of the economic issues would be the greatest factor influencing the welfare of children. Increasing unemployment and greater numbers of part-time workers meant there is less money available, often in families previously more affluent, which puts additional stress on family relationships both between parents and children and parents and each other. A recent study of marital issues in Australian society found that "socio-economic status predicts marital quality" (Amato & Booth, cited by Bone, 1998).

In spite of such concerns, some felt that perhaps there was an increasing community awareness of the importance of attachment and of early infant-parent relationships. This encouragement resulted from some politicians' responses to the report of the National Inquiry into the Separation of Aboriginal and Torres Strait Islander Children from Their Families referred to earlier. The minister for Aboriginal affairs acknowledged that money was needed for counseling services and support networks for those who had experienced early separation from family and culture. This was tacit acknowledgement that severe disruption to the child-parent relationship would have serious consequences in the life of the adult. Perhaps the allocation of resources to meet these needs of Aboriginal people will lead to recognition that allocating resources to ensure that infants are nurtured and protected is money well spent.

Political Obsession with a Platform of "Law and Order"

As each state and federal election of the past few years has come around, both major political parties have canvassed voters on adopting policies of "getting tough on crime." This has occurred even though it is known that a high proportion of those apprehended are themselves victims of abuse and neglect and that indigenous persons are overrepresented in the prison population, with a ratio of 15.7:1 of indigenous to nonindigenous rates of imprisonment for 1997 (Australian Bureau of Statistics. National Correctional Services Statistics Unit, 1997). Although it is acknowledged that Aborigines who experienced dislocation from family and culture in infancy and early childhood would find it difficult to parent (Wilson, 1997), there is not the follow-through to understanding that children thus neglected are more likely to be those participating in misdemeanors and criminal activity, and that early intervention with education and support would thus be more appropriate than prison sentences. It is known that indigenous mothers tend to be younger than nonindigenous mothers, with indigenous teenagers being 5 times more likely to be mothers than nonindigenous teenagers. The babies of indigenous mothers are 2 to 3 times more likely to be of low birthweight and about 2 to 4 times more likely to die at birth than are babies of nonindigenous mothers (Australian Bureau of Statistics, 1997). Recent research indicates that low birthweight, often a consequence of poor nutrition or infectious illness during pregnancy, is implicated in the fatal diseases of adulthood—diabetes, high blood pressure, and kidney and heart disease—that kill Aborigines, on average, 20 years younger than other Australians (Mathews, 1998). In at least two states where the Aboriginal population often live in isolated communities, Aboriginal people are implementing programs developed by Aboriginal people and medical workers to facilitate young Aboriginal pregnant women accessing medical facilities. One such scheme, "Strong Women, Strong Babies, Strong Culture," focuses on five areas—nutrition, dangers, protection and prevention, sharing, and caring—and has been so successful that the state government has agreed to fund and expand the program (Strong Women Program, 1998).

The Distribution of Scarce Resources

There is concern at the increasing pressure on front line workers of both health and education to meet the mental health needs of the community. These workers, trained to work with persons of healthy communities, are underresourced and undertrained in responding to mental health needs. There is also the difficult issue of distributing limited funding. Children and adolescents in crisis, i.e., those experiencing abuse, neglect, and homelessness, and an increasing number committing suicide are more pressing on the public purse than the perceived needs of infants. Likewise, while the demands of women with postnatal depression find a response from funding bodies, the infants of the same mothers are often overlooked. In funding services to mothers, the needs of infants should be acknowledged and accommodated (D. Lonie and B. Barnett, personal communication, October 9, 1997). There is a tendency for this not to occur. There is also the struggle for resources between the aged and new parents, given that increasing numbers of baby boomers are reaching the age of retirement and requiring more health services.

Unfulfilled Expectations

Many young women, born to women educated in the 1960s and 1970s, have grown up and been educated to expect that they can pursue a career and have a family in a relationship where parenting will be equally shared. In this time of change, however, men are not educated with the same expectation. Corporations large and small are not known for their support of family life or recognition of the need for the father to work shorter days and be available to his partner and child. It can be taken as a given that new mothers usually find the demands of a newborn baby extremely taxing. If there is an involved and caring partner, the load is lessened, but it is still more than the average couple can manage. We have created a society of nuclear, single-parent or blended families, or families with same-sex parents, isolated from family support for one reason or another and living in suburbs and towns not known for providing mutual caring and understanding. In contemporary Australia there seems to be a prevailing attitude that the newborn baby should accommodate the needs of the parents; that is, the newborn baby should behave differently from how newborn babies have behaved since time immemorial.

Too often, we are encouraging and attempting to find answers to the wrong questions. Instead of asking, "How can I get my baby to stop crying, to get in a routine, to sleep more—that is, to fit in with my lifestyle," we should be helping new parents ask, "Where can we get the help, support, and resources to enable us to meet the needs of our baby, in particular in these first months of life?" given that we know the future life of this new person depends on the availability of caring parents.

Conclusion

The history of modern Australia is of a population in constant transition. Initially this land of ancient Aboriginal culture was largely subsumed by an Anglo/Celtic presence. The primarily British culture then gave way to an identifiable Australian, reasonably homogeneous culture. This earlier Australian way of life has now been subsumed by multiculturalism, characteristi-

cally rich and varied. A new inclusive Australian identity may be in the making, based on the maturity of reconciliation. Time will tell. With economic changes that have occurred in the 1980s and 1990s and the threat of increase rather than decrease in unemployment, there is fear of a change from a largely egalitarian society to one with distinctive class differences: an educated wealthy class and a less educated, poor working class. Should this change occur, and many commentators say there is a trend in that direction, the consequences will be a continuing increase in the neglect of infants and young children. Infant mental health workers in Australia must be not only clinically skilled but also politically active and vigilant, prepared to advocate on behalf of infants.

References

AAIMHI statement of objectives. (1992, Autumn). *Australian Association for Infant Mental Health Newsletter*, p. 8.

Adler, D. (1966). The contemporary Australian family. *Human Relations, 19*(3).

Arndt, B. (1998a, February 14). 70% jump in births to single mothers. *The Sydney Morning Herald*, p. 3, Spectrum p. 1, 6.

Arndt, B. (1998b, April 21). The stalled revolution. *The Sydney Morning Herald*, p. 8.

Australia, House of Representatives. (1941, April 3). Child Endowment Bill. *Debates* (Vol. HR, pp. 419, 430).

Australian Association for Infant Mental Health Incorporated. (1988a). *Minutes of the inaugural meeting of AAIMHI, held at the Institute of Psychiatry, Rozelle, Sep-*

tember 14. (Available from AAIMHI Secretary)

Australian Association for Infant Mental Health Incorporated. (1988b). *Rules.* Sydney. (Available from AAIMHI Secretary)

Australian Bureau of Statistics. (1996). Births, Australia. ABS Catalogue number 3301.0.

Australian Bureau of Statistics. (1997). *The health and welfare of Australian Aboriginal and Torres Strait Islander Peoples.* ABS Catalogue number 4704.0.

Australian Bureau of Statistics. National Correctional Services Statistical Unit. (1997) *Indigenous imprisonment, March, 1997: Prisons March quarter, 1997.* A report prepared for the Corrective Services Ministers Council by NCSSU, ABS.

Barnett, B., Blignault, I., Holmes, S., Payne, A., & Parker, G. (1987). Quality of attachment in a sample of 1-year-old Australian children. *American Academy of Child and Adolescent Psychiatry, 26,* 303–307.

Barnett, B., & Parker, G. (1985). Professional and non-professional intervention for highly anxious primiparous mothers. *British Journal of Psychiatry, 146,* 287–293.

Bateson, G., Jackson, D. D., Haley, J., & Weakland, J. H. (1956). Toward a theory of schizophrenia. *Behavioral Science, 1,* 251–264.

Bone, P. (1998, March 3). Love and security is what matters most. *The Sydney Morning Herald.*

Brazelton, T. B. (1973). Neonatal Behavioral Assessment Scale. *Clinics in Developmental Medicine,* No. 50.

Brazelton, T. B. (1983). Testimony to the House of Representatives Select Committee on Children, Youth and Families, 28th April [Abstract]. *Zero to Three, 3*(4).

Brazelton, T. B. (1984). Neonatal Behavioral Assessment Scale (2nd ed.). *Clinics in Developmental Medicine,* No. 88. London: Spastics International Medical Publications.

Burns, A., & Goodnow, J. (1979). *Children and families in Australia: Contemporary issues and problems.* Sydney, Australia: George Allen and Unwin.

Butts, R. F. (1955). *Assumptions underlying Australian education.* Melbourne, Australia: ACER.

Cashmore, J. (1998, January 3). Time for our children to be seen and heard. *The Sydney Morning Herald,* p. 47.

Clark, C. M. H. (1962). *A history of Australia: Part 1. From the earliest times to the age of Macquarie.* Carlton, Australia: Melbourne University Press.

Clark, C. M. H. (1981). *A history of Australia: Part 5. The people make laws.* Carlton, Australia: Melbourne University Press.

Dolby, R., English, B., & Murray, A. (1982). Hospital practices that strengthen parent-infant attachment. In K. Oates (Ed.), *Child abuse: A community concern* (pp. 57–73). Sydney, Australia: Butterworths.

Dolby, R., Warren, B., Meade, V., & Heath, J. (1987, May). *Preventive Care for Low Birthweight Infants.* Paper presented at the International Physiotherapy Conference, Sydney.

Donnolley, S., & Edwards, J. (Eds.). (1998). *Inner worlds—Outer realities: The prevention of child abuse and neglect through early intervention.* Sydney, Australia: Benevolent Society of NSW.

Editorial. (1995, June). *AAIMHI Newsletter, 7,* 1.

Fraiberg, S. (Ed.). (1980). *Clinical studies in infant mental health—The first year of life.* New York: Basic Books.

Gandevia, B. (1978). *Tears often shed: Child*

health and welfare in Australia from 1788. Sydney, Australia: Pergamon.

Gill, A. (1998, June 5). Lost tribe. *The Sydney Morning Herald,* p. 12.

Goffman, E. (1961). Asylums. London: Doubleday.

Helfer, R. E. (1987). The perinatal period, a window of opportunity for enhancing parent-infant communication: An approach to prevention. *Child Abuse and Neglect, 11,* 565–579.

Jackson, D. D. (Ed.). (1960). *The etiology of schizophrenia.* New York: Basic Books.

Kempe, C. H., Silverman, F. N., Steele, B. F., Droegemueller, W., & Silver, H. K. (1962). The battered child syndrome. *Journal of the American Medical Association, 181,* 17–24.

Kennedy, R. (1982). *Australian welfare history.* Melbourne, Australia: The Macmillan Company of Australia Pty Ltd.

King, A. (1998). Income poverty since the early 1970s. In R. Fincher & J. Nieuwenhuysen (Eds.), *Australian poverty: Then and now* (pp. 71–102). Melbourne, Australia: Melbourne University Press.

Kitchen, W. H., Ryan, M. M., Rickards, A., McDougall, A. B., Billson, F. A., Keir, E. H., & Naylor, F. D. (1980). A longitudinal study of very low-birthweight infants: IV. An overview of performance at eight years of age. *Developmental Medicine and Child Neurology, 22,* 172–188.

Klaus, M. K., Jerauld, R., Kreger, N. C., McAlpine, W., Steffa, B. S., & Kennell, J. H. (1972). Maternal attachment: Importance of the first post-partum days. *The New England Journal of Medicine, 9,* 460–463.

Kelly, J. (1988). *Not merely minded: Care and education of young children of working women in Sydney. The Sydney Day Nurseries & Nursery Schools Association*

1905–1945. Unpublished doctoral dissertation, University of Sydney, Sydney, Australia.

Langley, E. M. (1986). *The Australian Association for the Welfare of Children in Hospital: The first ten years.* Parramatta, Australia: AAWCH.

Lonie, D. (1993, April). World Association for Infant Mental Health. *AAIMHI Newsletter,* p. 11.

Macartney-Bourne, F. (1993). *A genuine love of children: A quality assurance project customer satisfaction survey.* Sydney: Central Eastern Sydney Area Health Services.

Macartney-Bourne, F. (1998). *Results of a three month pilot study in South Eastern Sydney Area Health Service, Eastern Sector.* Unpublished manuscript. (Available from author)

Mackay, H. (1998, May 23). Birthrate blues rather than optimism. *The Sydney Morning Herald,* p. 32.

Mathews, J. (1998, April). *Indigenous health.* Paper presented at the Perinatal Society of Australia and New Zealand Second Annual Congress, Alice Springs, Northern Territory, Australia.

Murray, A. D. (1979). Infant crying as an elicitor of parental behavior: An examination of two models. *Psychological Bulletin, 86,* 191–215.

Murray, A. D., Dolby, R. M., Nation, R. L., & Thomas, D. B. (1981). Effects of epidural anesthesia on newborns and their mothers. *Child Development, 52,* 71–82.

Parker, G. (1983). *Parental overprotection: A risk factor in psychosocial development.* New York: Grune and Stratton.

Paul, C. (1993, April). Infant Psychiatry in Victoria. *AAIMHI Newsletter, 5,* 10.

Robertson, J. (1969). *John.* (film) Series: Young children in brief separation. Concord Films Council, Naeton, Ipswich Suffolk, U.K.

Royal Commission on Human Relationships. (1977). *Final Report: Volume 2. Education for human relationships.* Canberra, Australia: Australian Government Publishing Service.

Shea-Everidge, G. (1986). *The Early Intervention Programme: A programme designed to reduce the incidence of child abuse within families.* Sydney, Australia: The Benevolent Society of NSW.

Stern, D. N. (1985). *The interpersonal world of the infant.* New York: Basic Books.

Sved-Williams, A. (1997, December). Conference report—AAIMHI national conference, Adelaide, October, 1997. *AAIMHI Newsletter, 9,* 1.

Strong Woman Program. (1998). *The Strong Women, Babies, Culture Program.* Darwin, Northern Territory, Australia: Territory Health Services.

Weatherburn, D., & Lind, B. (1998). Poverty, parenting, peers and crime-prone neighborhoods. *Australian Institute of Criminology Trends & Issues,* No. 85.

West, J. (1997). *Daughters of freedom.* Sutherland, Australia: Albatross Books Pty Ltd.

Wilson, R. (1997). *Bringing them home. Report of the National Inquiry into the separation of Aboriginal and Torres Strait Islander children from their families.* Canberra, Australia: Australian Government.

Yu, V. Y. H., & Wood, C. (1978). Perinatal asphyxia and outcome of very low birthweight infants. *Medical Journal of Australia, 2,* 578–581.

5

Cross-Cultural Perspectives
on Infant Mental Health: A
French View on the History of
Infant and Child Psychiatry

Serge Lebovici

5

A Personal Experience

A personal experience has enabled me to gain perspective and to become familiar with the events that took place before and during World War II. This once-in-a-lifetime experience helped me provide an account of the development of child psychopathology in France since the beginning of this century. Child psychiatry developed recently in France. The first chair of child psychiatry, held by Georges Heuyer, was established as recently as 1955. However, a department of child psychiatry did exist before that, at the Necker-Enfants Malades hospital, in Paris.

I have a "screen memory" going back to this period, before World War II: Being on call at the Bicêtre hospital, I was sometimes called to the Vallée Foundation. There I saw children who were hitting themselves on their heads. After this visit, I was filled with a great uneasiness. One understands, under these circumstances, that René Spitz's (1965) revelations on hospitalism, as well as the moving documents that I still have the opportunity to show to students, could only, with hindsight, open my eyes. With this same perspective, I completed my training in pediatrics during the war at the Necker-Enfants Malades hospital. A few memories from this period have

become very important, because of their obvious relationships with the screen memory that I just described.

As a resident at the day nursery for children who were admitted to the hospital, I had been struck by the importance given to maintaining hygiene. If somebody entered the department, he or she had to wear the same mask as the nurses; contagion was to be avoided. One can understand why, in this situation, the babies' contact with adults was rather scant. The babies, often suffering from severe enteritis, had little contact with their parents, because transportation was difficult, and because the visiting hours were limited to about 1½ hr each day. The babies were hardly ever held in anybody's arms, because the day nursery was so understaffed. Two young women who were breast-feeding their own babies took better care of the abandoned babies by giving a portion of their milk to the children who were the most sick. Otherwise, the children's meal consisted of a bottle that the babies had to become accustomed to drinking from while lying or sitting in their beds. The bottles were tied with a string to a bar on the bed, and were placed in the babies' mouths. If the baby dropped it, the bottle didn't fall on the floor, but the meal remained unfinished unless a soft-hearted adult came by and put the nipple back into the baby's mouth. In short, we were working in conditions reminiscent of those existing today in Romanian orphanages.

Diarrhea due to enteritis was severe and often fatal. It was assumed that this diarrhea was related to an infection of the upper respiratory system. It was also thought that many ear infections had a very important etiological role, because they were often followed by mastoiditis. Babies with mastoiditis, usually from 6 months to 1 year of age, were operated on without any anesthesia. It was considered that putting a bottle in their mouth while their mastoid was opened with a hammer should suffice. The imposition of this twofold trial, of enteritis and of surgery without anesthesia, resulted in babies who, if they survived, could not develop normally, despite their possible "resilience."

Last, I was also in charge of a department where children with chicken pox were admitted. We noticed that some children would constantly shake their heads on their pillows. The chief of the department thought that these children were suffering from encephalitis. I was therefore entrusted with writing a paper on "pendulum encephalitis." However, the research I was conducting in this department showed me that the children in fact were suffering from separation from their parents. Because the infants had no appetite, the chief of the department decided he wanted to cure this problem. He was naive and quite brave, and he thought "good air from the ocean" would do the trick. So he placed a basin filled with salty water and a fan at the head of the children's beds. This simple device was aimed at reproducing an ocean climate, and was probably a kind of acknowledgment that the atmosphere surrounding these children was quite deleterious to them.

One can therefore understand, after this picturesque and often tragic account, that, having started a psychoanalysis at the end of the war with Sacha Nacht, who, like me, was a volunteer in the Free French Forces, I was more than ready to receive, with great emotion, Spitz's (1965) discoveries on hospitalism. It is impossible to recall in detail the memories of this period, which pertain mainly to the development of psychoanalytic psychopathology applied to children. Here it should be sufficient to mention a few colleagues who shared my interest in young children. This was particularly the case for Evelyne Kestemberg and René Diatkine, as well as Donald Buckle, an Australian psychiatrist with psychoanalytic training. He was employed by the World Health Organization (WHO) and gave me an opportunity to work with this organization, through which I built my first relationship with John Bowlby, whom I met in Geneva when he was writing his work on lack of maternal care.

The Implementation of Community Psychiatry: Sectorization

In 1960, in France, the principle of community psychiatry (sectorization) was adopted. This implementation of so-called sectors was meant to benefit a population of 60,000 inhabitants, whereas the inter-

sectors of child and adolescent psychiatry filled the needs of 180,000 inhabitants.

In the psychiatric hospitals, as the asylums from the time before World War II were called, and which have now become the *centres hospitaliers spécialisés* (CHS: specialized hospital centers), patients were to be treated with the aim that their stay be the shortest possible and that their care mainly take place in an outpatient setting. Philippe Paumelle and I, soon to be joined by René Diatkine, had good reasons to suggest that the 13th District of Paris should be the center of this effort, which was soon designated a pilot experience. Therefore, and according to what the official texts that justified such an association were expecting, the care of adult mental patients involved approaching their families, and, if necessary, helping their children. Conversely, the treatment of children in outpatient clinics could lead to the discovery of mental disturbances in their parents. Most of these disturbances were characterologic personality organizations that no standard treatment could cure. But the families who consulted could be offered psychosocial casework, which led to the discussion of their social rehabilitation.

Sector psychiatry was also a sort of community psychiatry, in the English sense of this term. Network assistance was to be implemented, leading necessarily to getting in touch with the pediatricians who treated the children. It was under these circumstances that I had the opportunity to meet the pediatricians who were in charge of the care of babies and their mothers in the state-run outpatient maternal and infantile protection centers (*protection maternelle*

et infantile: PMI), and in the neighborhood day nurseries, where mothers frequently brought babies to me asking what I thought of their condition. I had met Myriam David in a seminar organized by the WHO before she started working with me. She had alluded to her work on the attachment ties between the baby and its mother, a work that was published with Geneviève Appel (David & Appel, 1983). This was the first publication in French on interactive psychopathology and the only French publication quoted by Bowlby in his book on separation.

The investigations that were carried out in the 13th District of Paris led to studying the possibility of making an early diagnosis of psychosis in the small child. As mentioned earlier, I had become interested in this issue during the prewar period, from which I had a screen memory concerning children suffering from hospitalism. A few cases will be mentioned.

I knew that autism had been described by Kanner, but it was impossible to get his publications because in those times, English or American texts were out of reach. Nevertheless, a few words had made a great impression on people's minds. For example, I considered autism to be close to the so-called schizophrenic psychoses of small children. In 1947, I had published a case of child schizophrenia in which I had mentioned the word autism (Lebovici, 1949). Hubert was a 2-year-old child who was called the "little lion." Once in a while, although he could never express himself through words, he would start crawling on all fours on his bed and start screaming. He had been found in his nurse's bed when she had been dead for the past 24 hours. Hubert never talked. During his adolescence, he was admitted to the hospital under Henri Ey's supervision; Ey attended my conference and was somewhat irritated when he heard me defend the hypothesis of a traumatic etiology for this case. This young patient died in the hospital, swallowing through the wrong pipe and choking after he had stuffed himself with bread. It is easy to imagine Henri Ey's triumph when he wrote to me several years later to tell me that I had made a mistake because Hubert's twin sister was schizophrenic and had just been admitted in his own department following the death of their parents. The origin of this schizophrenia was necessarily genetic, according to Ey, because the children were twins, even though they were heterozygous.

In the meanwhile, I had had the opportunity to travel abroad and to meet Anna Freud, although I did not have a chance to spend time with her. René Spitz was now a professor in Geneva, and I had organized the publication of his books by the Presses Universitaires de France in Paris. We became friends, and he often talked about his conversations with Anna Freud and reflected on Bowlby's controversial work in relation to psychoanalysis.

The great majority of French analysts still do not consider Bowlby's work to be psychoanalytic. On the other hand, René Zazzo, who was an opponent of psychoanalysis because of his persistent involvement in the French Communist Party, was won over by Bowlby's theory. He organized a roundtable on that topic. The book that resulted from this event contained contributions that ranged from moderately positive, to resolutely enthusiastic (Widlöcher, 1986). Today, in France, the situation has not changed much. Nevertheless, Mary Ainsworth's and Mary Main's work is widely used in experimental and clinical research (Ainsworth, Blehar, Waters, & Wall, 1978; Main et al., 1985). This is particularly the case in Lausanne, where Blaise Pierrehumbert (1996) has developed a test, the CAMIR, which is the study of the intergenerational transmission of attachment in the adult. In England, Fonagy and his colleagues Howard and Miriam Steele (Steele, Steele, & Fonagy, 1996) have carried out longitudinal studies on the transmission of attachment between parents and infants. American psychoanalysts who have studied development are enthusiastic about Bowlby's theory.

I was fortunate to meet Winnicott when I first left France after the war. I was very impressed by his attitude during therapeutic consultations, and I am proud to say that I had become one of his friends. During these same years, I was introduced to Kleinian theory by Henri Ezriel. I met Melanie Klein when she came to visit us in Paris, but I am more familiar with her followers, Paula Heimann and Hannah Segal. We had discussions during the 1953 session of the Institute of Psychoanalysis of Paris, when they came to collaborate with investigations led by the International Psychoanalytical Association and during symposia organized by the WHO. Of these two disciples I was most friendly with Hannah Segal; I also knew Ilse Helman, who like Segal was a follower of Anna Freud. My knowledge of Meltzer and Bion comes mainly from books, although they have gained many disciples in France.

My relationship with Anna Freud developed when I was president of the IPA (International Psychoanalytic Association). The congress of this association was held in London in 1975, and Anna Freud presided with pleasure over the precongress, which was devoted to the training of child psychoanalysts. Nevertheless, she always remained hostile to the atypical psychotherapeutic approach. After her research on infants in nurseries during the war, she remained loyal to the metapsychological study of lines of development. Although her investigations on this topic became decisive, she is seldom read and hardly appreciated in France. Another memory concerning Anna Freud goes back to 1980, the year when Evelyne Kestemberg presided over a European symposium on child psychoanalysis that took place in Geneva. There Anna Freud met little Hans, who had become the director of the Geneva Opera. She also claimed that psychoanalysts over 60 weren't able to treat children any longer, since they couldn't sit on their knees and play with them. At that time, although I was on very good terms with her, when I presented her with a therapeutic case, her comment was brief: "I have already heard Winnicott tell stories like that!"

How French Psychoanalysts Became Interested in the Baby

It is well established that a few neurologists have been true forerunners in France, and that they played a remarkable role on the international scene in the description of the newborn's early skills. A few names should be mentioned here: André Thomas, his student Saint Anne Dargassies, and Julian de Ajuriaguerra. These physicians were the founders of the French school of neurophysiology. The clinicians from this school are remarkable and were called upon often when parents had serious concerns about possible lags in their infant's development. Their present perspectives are close to those of cognitive scientists, who consider that the newborn's skills are genetically programmed (Mehler, 1993).

The following presentation mentions the research work of various French investigators, many of whom lacked direct experience with babies. Nevertheless, they are most often psychiatrists with a pediatric background, or psychologists, who have become pioneers in the field of infant psychoanalysis in France and elsewhere.

Michel Soulé has always established excellent collaborations with pediatricians, particularly when he was the assistant of Professor Lelong, with whom I had the opportunity to be invited to Stockholm, by the WHO. There I heard about the work of Gesell and his followers, among whom was Ernst Kris. Kris had shown the importance of epigenetic factors in the child's development. The dangers of admitting a child to a hospital had been well described at the Karolinska Institute, where this symposium was taking place (see the film by Robertson, *A Child Goes to the Hospital*).

After Lelong's retirement, Soulé, together with Léon Kreisler (a pediatrician trained in psychoanalysis), played an important role at the Saint Vincent de Paul hospital, a teaching children's hospital in Paris. Soulé, with the collaboration of Janine Noël, has clearly shown the dangers of a dysfunctional economic and social situation for children's development. They have brought to light the importance of social indicators such as broken marriages and badly tolerated pregnancies in this context. While labeling individuals has been criticized, it remains essential to be aware of the negative effects of physical abuse and severe neglect on development. Kreisler has also worked with Pierre Marty, the founder of the Paris school of psychosomatics. He has confirmed in children what Marty had suggested concerning the origin of certain disorders in the adult; for instance, the geographic proximity with the mother in the case of allergic disorders (no separation anxiety and therefore no fear of strangers).

Kreisler presented observations of this kind to Soulé and to Michel Fain, and the three discussed them in *L'enfant et son corps* (*The Child and Its Body;* Kreisler, Fain, & Soulé, 1974). Since then, Kreisler has shown the importance of what he called the essential depression (*dépression essentielle*) in the baby, thus taking up Marty's description. Kreisler had the opportunity to work with Bertrand Cramer and suggested, at the same time as I did, using the notion of fantasmic interaction (Lebovici, 1988). Fain, with the help of his collaborator, Denise Braunschweig, was able to contribute to the understanding of the primary fantasies described by Freud: "the woman lover's censure" takes place at night, when the mother must prohibit close contact with her baby, and make it clear to the baby that she prefers its father. This forces this baby to become certain of the firmness of its narcissistic cathexes, in order to feel that it continues to be alive.

During all those years, relationships with my French-speaking and Latinate language–speaking colleagues grew. In Barcelona, René Diatkine contributed to the initial training of the group which is now the Spanish Society of Psychoanalysis, later taken over by the Kleinian school. I had the opportunity to travel with him to Spain several times. There I initiated the training of child psychoanalysts, who continued their training by mail. In Paris, I also benefited from the collaboration of Giovanni Bollea, who spent several years here, until he was appointed professor in Rome, and also of Matic, who became a psychoanalyst in Belgrade.

My Portuguese colleague, Joao dos Santos, who had spent several years in Paris for his training, came back to Paris for 1 year after his wife's death. He presented an interesting report on the warning signs in the young child that may foretell severe disorders later in life and may therefore call for preventive action. This work generated great interest in Portugal, where it is still considered important. During a trip where I had been commissioned by the WHO to assess the importance of preventive work in the realm of mental health, I had the opportunity to consult with Maria José Cordeiro about her research on the negative effects of the decrease of breast-feeding in urbanized populations, which had lost more traditional ways of living. Collaboration with young Portuguese university colleagues has continued on issues related to prevention in mental health.

In 1946, I went to Switzerland for a few weeks. There I met a few child psychoanalysts who were working with either Bovet in Lausanne or Repond in Sion. In Sion my colleagues and I provided important weekly consultations by using a truck to transport psychotherapists to remote village sites. That was an important decision if one wanted to apply psychoanalysis in the sectors, particularly through the means of home visits. In Lausanne, Bovet had organized meetings, where Diatkine and Ajuriaguerra, in particular, were invited. Also in Lausanne, this group of analysts all met Madeleine Rambert, who was using puppets in her psychotherapeutic work. These trips generated a strong current of integration that brought young Belgian and Swiss analysts to Paris. I will not easily forget the names of Thérèse Jacobs Van Merlen (Antwerp) and Edith Schreitzer (Neûchatel; the late Mrs. Henry Sion).

My Activity in Bobigny

In 1978, I left the Alfred Binet Center to establish a university hospital department of psychiatry at the Medical School of Bobigny, at the Université de Paris-Nord. Once more, I started working alone most of the time in a small room, and I decided to devote myself mainly to clinical approaches and research in the field of infant psychotherapy. I was assisted in this work by collaborators who joined me, among whom I count the following.

Serge Stoléru was a close colleague who became a researcher at the Institut National de la Santé et de la Recherche Médicale (INSERM: National Institute for Health and Medical Research). During our collaboration, we coauthored a book in 1983 that met with remarkable success in France (Lebovici & Stoléru, 1983). Stoléru then brought psychotherapy sessions to low income pregnant women using home-based methods inspired by the work of Fraiberg. This work, with which Martine Moralès-Huet collaborated, became the subject of her doctoral thesis in psychopathology. Currently, Stoléru is working in Professor Spira's laboratory, where he is involved with couples who have fertility problems. The aim of this work is to understand psychogenic sterility. Stoléru introduced the use of the Brazelton Neonatal Assessment Scale in France, and he created a nonstandardized projective test on parenting. The latter is a nonstandardized test representing pregnant women or parents holding a baby in their arms, in contrast to the Thematic Apperception Test (TAT), where the person is asked to invent stories from photographs. Finally, he has just developed a semistructured interview technique as a clinical approach to the young child's psychopathological problems (Stoléru, 1989).

I have also trained Martine Caron in the techniques of child observation. For some time, she worked with babies who had just undergone a liver graft. The research she did on this topic has not been published, but it is full of important information on the effects of the extreme guilt feelings of the parents and the deadly anxiety that results from such guilt feelings. Now she is the head of a specialized consultation unit at the Alfred Binet Center.

Antoine Guédeney, who had acquired solid training in research with Daniel Widlöcher, has become a very close collaborator. He has helped me become better acquainted with the problems of African migrating populations. He is interested in postpartum depression, and he plays an important role in the Marcé Society. He helps me with this work and was named secretary general of the World Association of Infant Mental Health (WAIMH) when I was the president of that association, between 1988 and 1992. He is now the head physician of the day hospital for small children at the Institut de Puériculture de Paris, and he is the editor of the journal *Devenir.*

After I became a professor at the Medical School of Bobigny, I founded the university research laboratory on psychopathology in the young child and its family. Then I suggested that a certain number of research units form a network inside the INSERM. As a result, university laboratories and the INSERM laboratory of Albert Spira and that of Claude Griscelli came together. Françoise Weil-Halpern (Lebovici & Weil-Halpern, 1989) was working at Griscelli's laboratory, and I had the opportunity to collaborate with her when we wanted to understand the development of children put into plastic bubbles at birth because of severe immune deficiency. The work of this collaborative network has been renewed three times. Jean-Pierre Visier succeeded me as coordinator, and now it is coordinated by Michèle Maury and Martine Lamour. New laboratories have joined this network, including the "young team" in Toulouse, which is

working with Elisabeth Abadie, and Dominique Cupa's team at the Paris X University. Marie-Rose Moro also joined the network, where she brings the investigations she is leading on families in exile (Moro, 1994). Inspired by present investigations on the importance of the triad from birth, the network is now working on triangulation problems. The investigations of the laboratory in Lausanne on the initial triad have been studied, and this initial triad, according to the work of Elisabeth Fivaz, leads either to the triad or to the Oedipal triangle.

At the same time, this network has acknowledged the importance of microanalytic investigations involving videotaped interactions. It is important to note that this research focuses not only on the behavior of families, but also on the behavior of the professionals, who are also involved with self-analysis and with clarification of their countertransference.

After this first network, other clinicians created research networks sponsored by the INSERM. I had the opportunity to bring my collaboration to the network on child autism. My colleagues and I are trying to contribute to this network with studies of films taken by families. For example, we are trying to study the early detection of autism within disorders of interactive attunement that are sometimes observed. It is well known that Selma Fraiberg emphasized the freezing of the glance as a first line of defense mechanism in infancy. We think that we have found confirmation of this hypothesis in the documents studied by scientists who did not know the diagnosis for the tape they were studying, and who found very vigorous confrontations in the interactive exchanges. What we should do now is see these families once more, and examine the present state of those who were children, and who are now adolescents, or even adults. This research is in agreement with other investigations led by this network, and mainly with those by Geneviève Haag, which illustrate the parallels between neurochemical changes and behavior.

The network on autism, coordinated by Pierre Ferrari, seems to have shown a possible agreement between cognitive scientists, inspired by neuropsychology, and psychoanalysis. This is an essential point if one wants to clarify the foundations of developmental psychopathology. The theory of mind indicates that intersubjectivity and the fact of using symbolic thinking both lead to the assumption that the baby confers intentions on its parents. Psychoanalysts, after Spitz, reached the same conclusion: The child must make a distinction between the maternal and the paternal functions as early as the second half of the first year of life, which results in the anxiety shown in the 8th month, which is matched with stranger fear. It is as if the stranger was submitted to the projections of the baby, who would be blaming the stranger for having made its mother disappear. The importance of this first neurotic projection is well known; it is the first model of infantile neurosis, the absence of which is disquieting. This absence can be observed in early psychosomatic manifestations. In the same way, when the baby does not organize symbolic relations with its mother, it uses her as an instrument.

English authors, mainly those who belong to the Cambridge school, thought that this absence of intersubjective relation was the cognitive foundation of autism, which could be recognized only after 2 years (Frith, 1997). As I have said, I think that autism can be predicted earlier than that, and, even if genetic factors play a major etiological role in its appearance, this leaves some hope to radically change the interactive coldness characteristic of the lack of emotional relations in these children's families. In many cases, after a therapeutic consultation, I have witnessed the disappearance of the self-sensorial manifestations (which are often severe blows to the head) through which the autistic child feels it is alive.

A third network, directed by Professor Philippe Jeammet, enabled the study of the early symptoms of bulimia in young children, whose metapsychological profiles also foretold narcissistic disturbances that are observed in borderline pathologies. Currently, the network that he coordinates is studying the psychopathology of dependence. A multicentered research program coordinates the investigations of Professor Halfon's laboratory in Lausanne with those of Professor Philippe Mazet at the Avicenne hospital. These researchers are trying to compare two samples of adolescents, in order to confirm the hypothesis that drug addiction is partly related to early attachment disorders.

Present investigations on the father's role in the contemporary family have led Martine Lamour to study this role in the French family. This research seems to support the hypothesis that intergenerational transmission and the mandate that it confers to both parents will, in the most fortunate cases, justify the father's role. He is no longer only the provider of family resources and the transmitter of his name; he is also the person who places the mother-infant relationship in context. It can also be said that the triad (Lamour, 1992) is characterized in three situations: mother-child (+ father), father-child (+ mother), and father-mother + child. It is possible that the interactive modes that are characteristic of this triad's functioning could be foretold from pregnancy, and could possibly call for preventive treatment.

A former student, Nadine Spira, a scientist at INSERM, was working for the Département d'Aide Sociale et Sanitaire (DASS: Department of Welfare and Public Health) of the Seine Saint-Denis Department. She was discouraged because it was impossible to organize preventive care programs for child abuse in poor families followed by the Protection Maternelle et Infantile (PMI: Mother and Child Protection Services). We organized an investigation that had a definite influence in this very poor department. This was an action-training research program, during which four teams of PMI volunteers were trained to apply a prevention program to families considered to be in danger. This research required a great deal of preparation. The pediatric teams involved had to open themselves to the dimension of relationships, through the discussion of clinical cases they presented, while psychiatrists had to prepare themselves to know about the babies' development. Also, during this long mutual apprenticeship, as the pediatric teams became more knowledgeable with psychoanalytic theory, we had to determine the selection criteria for families in danger of physical abuse, on one hand, and the necessary methods to assess the evolution of the cases, on the other. In these circumstances, it was suggested that pediatricians use the Bobigny Scale, a behavioral interaction scale that is widely known in France (Lamour, 1992).

This long preparatory work was accomplished by Lamour, in collaboration with several pediatricians, psychiatrists, and psychologists who took part in the publication entailed by this research (Lamour, 1992). It was facilitated by the friendship extended to me by those who were in charge of the PMI, mainly Mrs. de Chambrun and Nadine Spira. At the same time, we benefited from the preparation Lamour had been able to acquire during several training courses she attended in the United States.

This research could be criticized, since it involved only some families, and because it is difficult to think that a baby nurse in charge of administering preventive measures would have refrained from using them to benefit families that had not been included in the sample. This is a problem that concerns all research actions in the realm of health care; therefore, the therapeutic trial is not neutral. Two positive points must be emphasized. One involves the role of fathers, whose presence (which was required for participation in the project) seems to have had a very positive effect, mainly when their own parents were divorced; this result was confirmed statistically. The other point pertains to the training of pediatricians in new practices; at the same time, the psychiatrists learned from pediatricians that their usual attitude, which consisted of responding only to clearly formulated calls for help by families, was remarkably insufficient.

At this time, I had the privilege to be called to sit at the Psychological Commission of the Centre National de la Reserche Scientifique (CNRS: National Center for Scientific Research), where I met some high level researchers, who by and large were supportive of my contributions to the assessment of their colleagues' work, and of my own contributions to the understanding of the very young child's development.

The French Approach in the Field of Infant and Family Mental Health

In the 1980s, I had the opportunity to meet Justin Call. I had read his work, translated into French, on the baby's skills in handling its mother's breast during feeding, and it had impressed me very much. He wanted to found, with Eleanor Galenson, the World Association of Infant Psychiatry, specializing in approaches to work with the very young child. In principle, I was against any divisions of child psychiatry, and I had unwillingly yielded to Sherman Feinstein, with whom I established the International Association of Adolescent Psychiatry. Our colleagues were pressing more and more, asking me to contribute to the organization of an international congress on infant psy-

chiatry. It was very difficult for me to convince them that, although it didn't appear that way, there was a risk that this congress would become merely an opportunity for Americans in Europe.

The first congress of what would become the World Association of Infant Mental Health (then the World Association of Infant Psychiatry) took place in Estoril, Portugal. While there were relatively few participants, those French who were lucky enough to be there were greatly rewarded by the quality of the presentations, which led me to create a French interdisciplinary group focusing on the infant's interactive pathology. The French people who were present had the opportunity to be introduced to the work of Selma Fraiberg, who had just died. It was also in Estoril that Margaret Mahler appeared for the last time in front of French people, who did not appreciate her work very much, and who considered her as not very analytically minded.

This first French study group of psychoanalysts on infancy used to meet one Sunday a month at Bobigny to discuss observations collected in clinical work. The most fervent among the psychoanalysts were Evelyne Kestemberg, Daniel Widlöcher, and among the psychiatrists probably Ajuriaguerra.

This group, which called itself the Association pour l'Étude des Travaux Psychiatriques sur le Nourrisson (AETPN: Association for the Study of Psychiatric Work on the Infant), was entrusted in 1983 with the responsibility of organizing the World Association of Infant Psychiatry's second international congress. Its scientific committee was chaired by James Anthony, who had followed me as president of the International Association of Child and Adolescent Psychiatry and Allied Professions (IACAPAP). This congress met in Cannes and assembled more than 1,500 participants, almost half of whom were French. Members of AETPN were able to become acquainted with the remarkable studies on the importance of the baby's early skills. We benefited from the presence of Léo Rangell, Robert Emde, Daniel Stern, and Hanus Papoušek. We had the opportunity to submit to this international audience our first investigations and to introduce the notion of fantasmic interactions. Since then, the importance of French contributions was established, and in the next section describe and discuss the various activities that resulted from this development.

Interest in Psychopathology in the Young Child

From the end of World War II, and particularly since the establishment of the World Association for Infant Mental Health interest in the psychopathology of the child within French-speaking countries has not waned. In the present context, it is difficult to specify how these interests have grown. Indeed, with current technological advances, I see immediate and efficient spreading of research studies. Still, documents written in French have a rather limited distribution. Therefore, it seems to me appropriate for French scientists and clinicians to try to specify their critical contributions in the field related to clinical work

and treatment of the disorders that are detected, their diagnosis, and their classification. Clinicians should obtain all information on contributions in this field. Their taking part in actions in favor of childhood may be essential for children who are at risk because of their parents' situation and because of the critical state of our society: misery, unemployment, violence, and so forth.

Consultations for infant disorders have become much more frequent. On the whole, pediatricians are usually consulted more often than psychiatrists, whom they call upon either to become informed and to be trained, or to refer the case. It is much easier for pediatricians to build an alliance with the parents than it is for psychiatrists. The psychiatrists' clinical approach is often not well understood, in that they are often less concerned with the symptoms observed than with the transgenerational family conditions that may have contributed to these symptoms.

Indeed, there are "ghosts in the nursery!" (Fraiberg, Adelson, & Shapiro, 1985). The tree of life of each baby is built through a double process, filiation and parentalization. Consistent with American investigations, only partial knowledge can be obtained with developmental testing; in addition, observations and clinical study of parent-child interaction is needed. Koupernik and Dailly (1980) made the first attempt to describe the development of psychiatric disorders for clinicians. After this time in French literature, it was possible to consider the importance of the parents' and the children's fantasmic life, in addition to the child's cognitive development and to the programmed relations between parents and children. It is through the study of affect during parent-infant interactions that the fantasmic interaction can be described.

While caring for her baby, the mother not only holds the real child in her arms, a child that may be disappointing compared to the child she had imagined, but also the imagined or fantasized child. The imagined child is the child that she wished for during her pregnancy, who can be described by her from internalized thoughts. It is the child dedicated to the father, the child who is the result of intergenerational transmission, the child whose sex is known because of the ultrasound, the child for whom a first name is chosen, a name that implies possible family secrets. The narcissistic triumph of pregnancy proclaimed to the future maternal grandmother teaches her that she will no longer be a woman. Therefore, the mother develops a deeper relationship with her own mother as she herself becomes a mother (Bydlowski, 1997). The maternal grandmother, however, may also "take revenge," on her daughter by indicating how incompetent she is in caring for her baby.

Also, the imagined child is the child of the desire for maternity and the desire for a child; therefore, it expresses the nature and the evolution of maternal Oedipal conflicts. The grandfather is also a father for the baby. Therefore, one can understand how Jean Laplanche could write that maternal seduction is generalized, and that the mother introduces in her care the unconscious aspects of her infantile sexuality, which he calls the enigmatic signifiers (Laplanche, 1987). From this, one can under-

stand that the newborn is an object of paternal transference, and that because of this, it can be abused or have other negative feelings placed on it. In this way, adoration for the newborn depends on the fate of the maternal grandfather, whose possible death during pregnancy leads to maternal hatred against the child.

Some authors, mainly Cramer and Palacio-Espasa (1993), contend that it is not possible to act directly on the baby. Actually, the mother performs her identification projections on the baby at the level of her own fantasies, as can be understood from the preceding presentation on what the baby means for the mother. It is these projections that can be changed during the period of maternity. This discussion has shown that the psychotherapist can act directly on the baby, thus contributing to the maternalization of its mother (see Cramer & Palacio-Espasa, 1974, pp. 257–363). The baby, on the other hand, uses the sensorial and preperceptive representations of the so-called maternal care in order to build protorepresentations of this care. The relation between maternal representations of the child, colored by the mother's guilt and by the child's protorepresentations, is what we have suggested make up the fantasmic interaction. What is to be understood here is that, during the interaction, a fortuitous circumstance takes on special meaning in the interactive relationship and becomes an understandable event or scenario that can be understood only in the maternal recall.

It is important to add that the parents' behavior first depends on the evolution of their Oedipal conflict and on the nature of their relation with their own parents.

Therefore, it can be said that the transgenerational mandate entrusted to the baby is written down as part of his destiny, the family genogram that shows its manifold roots. To this filiation process corresponds the parentalization process, which is inscribed in the baby's behavior. This is how I have described the tree of life, the roots of which should be deeply fixed in the ground, but the branches of which should be sufficiently free, that is, not completely linked to transgenerational conflicts. Cultural affiliation may thus be the fortunate product of a sturdy tree of life.

Our investigations can be understood in the light of Freudian metapsychology. They are consistent with Stern's studies on the child's representational world; however, Stern does not use the notion of fantasy. Stern (1985) seems to play on the ambiguity of the term *representation*. He adopts the term's usual meaning, which assumes a thought visually represented, whereas Freud used the philosophical term *Vorstellung,* which can be translated as *thought,* setting the representation of unconscious things against the representation of words, which is then within the preconscious.

This opposition of points of view is important. The notion of scenario is implied in the notion of fantasy, where there is the production of a narrative. We are sensitive to the genetic aspect that is included; it is known that the attachment relationship is linked to cognitive factors. The importance of the programmed aspects of the interactional relationship is also known; Emde (1985) has demonstrated the "us" relation that exists from the start, with its moral prohibitions. But we also know that the birth of a child in a couple results in the activation of parental fantasies, which enable us to foretell the conditions of the Oedipal triangulation as soon as the woman is pregnant (Lebovici, 1993; Lamour, 1992).

It seems that Stern (1985) has come closer to my thinking when he describes the protonarrative envelope; these are experiences of "having been" where the child is, because of the episodic and the semantic memory that rebuilds the memories of experiences.

Ethnopsychoanalysis: A Clinical Consultation

I now describe a therapeutic consultation that illustrates my understanding of the Oedipal components of interactive behavior in an African family, and that gave me insight into the cultural habits of other countries. A 15-month-old girl from Cameroon had been brought to me by her mother, because she had stopped sleeping after her arrival in Paris, where she had met her father once again. Contrary to what I usually do, I hadn't explored her genogram, because I was wary of my cultural ignorance. The little girl and I played a game. I was hiding a piece of paper in the lower part of my jacket. She and I were celebrating her capacity to find this piece of paper. Suddenly, I ask the mother to hide the piece of paper herself, which she did by putting it close to her breasts. The little girl refused to look at her; but when I put the piece of paper behind the lower part of my jacket, she went and looked for it near my chest. Then the mother called her daughter "Mommy" and told her in a loud voice,

"Mommy, you will sleep now." Thus, she was demonstrating that she was placing the maternal transference of her daughter on me, which reduced her guilt feelings and allowed her once more to make love with her husband. As a side effect of this consultation, I had the privilege to learn that in Cameroon, one calls a girl by the grandmother's first name, or "Mommy."

During a discussion of this case with Marie-Rose Moro, I was criticized for not studying the causes of the mother's attitude, but I claimed that my empathy enabled me to act for the child's and the mother's benefit. Nevertheless, I acknowledge the validity of Nathan's theory (Nathan, 1988), in the case of large families who are distant from our culture. Maybe what keeps us apart is his desire to remain politically correct. Indeed, in the United States, there is now a will to respect immigrants' culture. But I believe that cultural autonomy is not a good rule. It seems to me that one should aim at the cultural integration of immigrants, who will thus feel as French as those who are born in France. This is probably not what happens in the case of genocides, in other words, in the case where young children witness their parents' murder or their mother's rape, and lose their individual identity. The main thing that one can do for them is then to reaffiliate them to their culture; the child of the Holocaust is the best example.

Characteristics of the Psychopathological Approach in France

Psychopathological approaches, almost all of which have a psychodynamic inspiration, are numerous. They take into account British and American investigations, mainly American, without losing a certain originality. They situate themselves more in the study and treatment of individual cases than in the application of anonymous scales that attempt to assemble normative classifications.

Psychiatric teams, who are involved with the small child, while acknowledging the importance of classifications, do not pay much attention to this issue. The present American classification, the American Psychiatric Association's *Diagnostic and Statistical Manual of Mental Disorders* (1994; *DSM-IV*) does not provide a description of attachment disorders. In the same way, the French classification of children's and adolescents' mental disorders contains a quite simple description of mental disorders at that age of life. The French classification is compatible with the International Classification of Disorders (ICD) 10. The same work group that has suggested this French classification has put together the handicaps that are linked to early mental disorders.

Léon Kreisler (1981, 1987) studied mental disorders in the infant, according to the manifest or hidden depression, that is, the essential depression. This is an important and useful description in the practical realm. A few colleagues have participated in discussions concerning the classification of early mental disorders, including Antoine Guédeney from France and Maria-José Cordeiro from Portugal. From this perspective, it is important to remember that there are rich relations between French-style psychopathology, and the psychopathology that is the focus of investigations led by some colleagues who are close to it. Cordeiro has become internationally known because of her work concerning Portuguese families who are in the process of urbanization. These families are prey to cultural conflicts that tend to alter traditions and to render the child's development uncertain.

In such circumstances, infant and family psychotherapies are extremely important. Brief psychotherapies are the subject of numerous investigations; Cramer and Palacio-Espasa (1993) represent the most systematized development in this area in Europe. These authors, studying the baby's development, provide systematized insight and find that they can use these psychotherapies when the disorders are mainly functional. The psychotherapeutic technique that they recommend aims at listening to the mother, and possibly to the father, when they talk about the origin of the disorders in the framework of intergenerational conflicts. Often, the mother talks about her child and about her own childhood while her baby plays in front of her. The two authors, based on many observations, have shown at which points the mother becomes aware of her baby's significant behaviors.

In one example, an anorexic female child's mother discussed her problems with bulimia when she was a child. When this little girl seized a piece of chocolate in order to put it to her mouth, the mother took it away from her, saying she would be dirty, and she ate the chocolate desired by the little girl. Cramer saw her a few years later (1997). He felt that the daughter, who

had become focused on cleanliness, has responded to the mother's ideal, and had repudiated her father. In this case, the collusion between the mother and daughter was not mobilized by Cramer's psychotherapeutic approach, who was not able to bring together the daughter and her father, even through transference (Lebovici, 1997). Others cases, however, have been shown to work very well with these techniques. The two authors described a special phase after a child's birth during which the child experienced the projective identifications on the part of the mother, identifications that needed to be changed through psychotherapy, so the child would not experience the negative consequences. In contrast, we have shown that the therapeutic consultation can be followed with effects that bear directly on the baby.

Mathieu was brought to us when he was 5 months old, for severe sleep disorders. He was born 11 months after his sister's sudden death. This death took place the night after the celebration of the parents' wedding anniversary. After an excellent dinner, the mother had gone to bed without checking her daughter's state. The following morning she found her dead. This event stimulated an earlier feared accusation. This little girl was cursed, because when her mother proclaimed triumphantly to her mother that she was pregnant, the (now) grandmother (referring to herself) said to her not only that she would never be a mother again, but that she was no longer a woman either, because she was married to an alcoholic husband.

The mother perceived her daughter's sudden death as a crime, and she blamed herself by distancing herself from her son, for whom she thought she was dangerous. At the same time, she was describing the close watch she was keeping on the little boy, whose insomnia reassured her that he wasn't dead. During that time the father, who was holding the child while presenting him in his arms, explained that he was not a man because he chose to be a policeman whereas his father and grandfather had been miners.

During all these accounts, the mother was observed moving away from the baby when he came close to her; she perceived herself as dangerous. At a certain moment, the baby became very fidgety. The mother handed him a cake, which he refused. Then she tried to put him straight into the father's arms, to make him stand, and the baby, who had become stiff, threw his head backward. Then I moved closer and, while continuing to talk, I stroked the baby's head and I said, "You are a beautiful baby." Three times, I saw him turn toward me and I heard him vocalize, showing he was happy. The fourth time, he buried himself in his mother's arms.

For a long time, I thought that this recorded consultation gave evidence that I was soothing the child. Bertrand Cramer, after seeing the tape, admitted that it did bear witness to the therapist's possible action on the baby. In fact, when I saw that tape again recently, I came upon a fact that nobody had noticed. The moment when the baby took refuge in the mother's arms, one could see, during a split second, that the mother turned toward me and showed me her baby, which is probably a way of telling me, "Since you want to play the man

in this dialogue, I entrust you with my baby and I give myself to you."

Thus, one can understand better what took place at the end of this consultation; the father, who has remained seated during the whole dialogue, was watching us. I probably felt that something had to be done, and I moved away. The mother was standing with Mathieu, whom she rocked. I told her, "Now, you're dancing," which she denied, feebly. Then I asked her if she often danced with her husband. The latter then spoke up and closed the situation by proclaiming, "Fortunately, she loves dancing with him; I myself don't like to dance." Thus, this man didn't want to respond to my incentive to take once again his place as a husband, which he had symbolically left to his son. Therefore, one would not be surprised to learn that the baby slept well, but that the mother left her husband and her son a few years later.

In Cramer's laboratory, there has been an effort to study the immediate and the long-term results of these brief psychotherapies. They found in several studies that interactional guidance, a treatment that aims at correcting maternal behavior by viewing it on videotape, apparently had as good results as did brief therapy, which, on the other hand, required in-depth training on the part of the psychoanalysts and psychotherapists who practiced it. These investigations require in-depth research on the nature of the relations between the mother and her baby, as well as on the transference and the countertransference of the mother and the therapist. These investigations are no doubt fascinating, but I must say that the therapeutic consultations that I practice lack the rigor of the brief psychotherapies described by Cramer. Being retired, I have at my disposal a small laboratory for teaching purposes. It is equipped with a one-way mirror and a VCR with a camera. To those who ask for an appointment with me, I give only one appointment, which will necessarily be followed by a second one, and then I let the consulting family decide if they want to come back or not. Therefore, I know only the immediate results of these consultations, which are generally very good. By mere chance, I may later learn what has happened afterward.

I have studied at length the empathic foundation of my interpretations, which are metaphorizing, and which result from *enaction*. I use this term, which means acting out, using my body marked by the interactions between the mother and the baby, with the help of my intuition gained from a narcissism that is still alive and helpful. I also think that one should retain the meaning that cognitive scientists give to the word enaction. They mean that the components that order an action unite in order to implement it and to make a decision about it, just as a queen who signs a decree "enacts" it. I justify this proposition by what Gustav Mahler has told us concerning the composition of his second symphony, *Resurrection*. He was able to write the chorus only after he had attended the funeral of his predecessor, who had been the director of the Köln orchestra. Also, this incident had a repercussion on the history of psychoanalysis. Freud had asked Federn to write the obituary of Karl Abraham, who had been his analyst, but Federn was able

to write it only after he had remembered Mahler's incident, during a long solitary walk. A. de la Grange explains that Mahler could compose only when the accumulation of his projects reached its goal, because of the emotional intensity of the work.

As can be seen, I believe that the possible therapeutic action of my consultation corresponds to the "sacred" moment when my empathy enables the family and myself to create a new situation, the situation that Daniel Widlöcher considers as resulting from a "co-thinking" (Widlöcher, 1986).

As for me, in an answer to Emde, I mention the cocreation related to empathy, in other words, to a shared feeling (Lebovici, in press). For a few weeks, after having attended the projection of a marvelous film, *The Garden of Celibidache*, directed by his son, another metaphorizing hypothesis has come to my mind. The conductor is seen conducting the rehearsal of his orchestra in Mozart's *Requiem*. He congratulates the first violins for their perfect harmony, but at the same time, he tells them, "Don't be too triumphant, and let the second violins express themselves." This metaphor is an icon of empathy. It means that empathy will be useful only if the loss of identification of the therapist enables him to identify with all the persons who are present at the consultation or who play a role in the child's life. He must accept this role as the conductor, but as a rigorous, even-handed one, a conductor who lets each kind of instrument express itself.

A French-speaking study group has tried to specify the manifold characteristics of the psychotherapeutic action in favor of very young children. It was presided over by Cramer and lead by A. Guédeney. First, I want to mention the work of Alice Doumic-Girard, who, under the direction of Pierre Mâle, used to conduct psychotherapies of very young children in the presence of their mothers and with their possible collaboration. The practice of these family psychotherapies, which involve the mother and her child, and possibly the father, reveal various influences. For example, Martine Moralès-Huet, who, in the department headed by Nicole Guédeney, has taken up the techniques she has applied with Stoléru (Stoléru & Morales, 1987) in the home-based treatment of very poor young women. A. Watillon, in Brussels, attempts to perform psychotherapies inspired by the young mother's wish to receive care. M.-R. Moro applies, to some degree, the ethnopsychoanalytic treatments recommended by T. Nathan. These recommendations do not seem entirely valid when applied to immigrants, although we understand perfectly well why interpreters should be present in this type of consultation. Finally, Rosine Debray (1987) adopts a very controversial viewpoint. She emphasizes that, according to her, brief psychotherapies are only preliminary to the mother's psychoanalysis, which is indispensable.

This brief review of the French approaches to psychology shows how difficult it is to suggest hypotheses that would be accepted by everyone, but it enables us to remember that a mother holding a baby in her arms is able to talk about herself and about the baby in a very remarkable way. She can share her thoughts, and she talks

with a preconscious sense. Bydlowski (1997) shows this in an illuminating way. At the same time, investigations on intergenerational transmission, inspired by family therapists, bear witness to the importance of each child's tree of life. This tree of life also defines the child's mandate, as does the transmission of attachment.

We can see that French clinical research has been influenced by the work of Americans specializing in development, and that it has added to this work the representation of affects as Stern has defined it by describing the attuning of affects in the modular and transmodular way Brazelton's work has been widely adopted in France. The development scale that he has described enables him "to give a new-born a good mother in ten minutes." It is understandable that his charismatic personality cannot be imitated, but we believe that, at the same time, as he has recently said, he knows how to exploit the touchpoints in development. He mentions the idea that a therapist can express feelings that the baby's development does not enable it to express. To talk for a child who is delayed is making the parents believe that this baby understands their language. It is known that Françoise Dolto and her colleagues believe that a baby who is only a few months old can understand a mother who tells it she is getting divorced. We believe from our perspective that the mother expresses herself like Brazelton, and that what she makes her baby understand are the affects that the baby feels and to which she gives meaning (i.e., touchpoints).

Tronick has promoted a research and clinical paradigm called the still face situation. This situation does not necessarily specify the mother's depression, but it allows, in the mismatch between the baby and the depressed mother, the evolution of the developing relationship. Also, several French authors have taken up Bion's theories on the mother's dreaming capacity that the therapist must be capable of, if he is to "detoxify" the baby's primary anxieties. The mother, containing her baby's projective identification, allows the emergence of the baby's psychic life. Esther Bick, from this theoretical perspective, suggests that the training of psychoanalysts should include neutral observations of the newborn in the family environment until the end of the baby's 2nd year of life. This technique is combined with weekly seminars and has widely influenced the work of Spanish psychoanalysts from Barcelona, inspired by the applications of Esther Bick's observations. In France, Didier Houzel (1987) has promoted Bion's ideas on unconscious attention, far removed from the efforts of memory, in order to use Bick's technique in preparation for psychotherapy of very disturbed children. Many study groups are organized in the same way. For example, Genevieve Haag uses these methods in her training and therapeutic work.

The Approach of Perinatal Psychiatry

The importance of postpartum neurotic disorders and of the depression that often accompanies these conditions is well known; 10 percent of women suffer from a notable depression from the end of the first month following childbirth until the end of the first year. Nothing seems to link it to the postpartum blues after release from the hospital, which is the rule in many women, especially those who are primiparous. Winnicott has shown its usefulness, calling it "the mother's madness." The mother's anxious, primary solicitude may change her into a "perfect mother."

In contrast, chromic depression seems to have far-reaching and severe effects on children. While I will not elaborate on those studies which are not specific to France, the data is impressive. In Great Britain, perinatal psychiatry is influenced mainly by adult psychiatrists who treat mothers and who have established specialized institutions for them. These seem indispensable to me when there is a pregnancy in a psychotic mother, or when the depression takes on a psychotic aspect.

In France, conversely, those who became interested in these cases are more likely to be clinicians who focus on baby psychopathology. These clinicians have been influential in creating opportunities for mother-child hospitalization in institutions. This topic has been studied intensively and has led to the organization, in 1996, of an international symposium in Monaco (Mazet & Lebovici, 1998). These problems have also been studied by other groups. The Marcé society has a French-affiliated association where N. Guédeney has presented the French translation of the Edinburgh scale, a self-administered questionnaire, which can be used to predict postnatal depression (Guédeney, Fermanian, Guelfi, & Delour, 1995). With the exception of cases where depression is obvious, it can be hidden behind a dulling of emotions or behind hypomanic attitudes and behaviors. It is important to study the disorders in the timing and fine-tuning of interactions in these cases. In addition, Bydlowski is now studying the prophylactic values of these mothers. M. Dugnat organizes in Avignon, each year, a symposium on the manifestations and consequences of postnatal depression. These meetings have been very successful because they bring together very well known specialists and people who do field work in this area.

Conclusion

We have seen that at the beginning of this century, there was not much interest in infant psychopathology in France. After World War II, psychiatrists with psychoanalytic training were well-informed about English and American investigations of the effects of separation of the child from its mother, and of the breaking of attachment relationships. Those who have followed Bowlby have understood the importance of the ties that link psychopathology to ethology, on one hand, and to their neurocognitive mechanisms, on the other. They have worked in an original fashion: They have undertaken brief psychotherapies, and they have studied the results and the mechanisms of their work. They also have carefully followed and been inspired by the work of many post-Freudian psychoanalysts. This was the case for Anna Freud, Melanie Klein, and such post-Kleinians as Bion. They were also inspired by American specialists in development,

who studied the genetic factor of the types of attachment, the role of the representations of care, and the emotional modalities of transmission. They also thought it was necessary to study the intrapsychic process that goes with the process of parentalization. They have recognized the importance of the original triad in order to study the triangulation process. Today, assembled inside the association WAIMH-France, the French-speaking association of scientists and clinicians specializing in the psychopathological study of children under 30 months old, they consider that this pathology is organized from conception to birth, from interactions between the fetus and its mother, then between the baby and its parents. Therefore, it can be understood that they have described fantasmic interactions, in addition to behavioral and emotional interactions (Lamour & Lebovici, 1991; Lebovici, 1988).

All these scientists now try to defend the specificity of a French-style psychopathology, and they will soon present to their colleagues multimedia documents—companion books and CD-ROMS—in French, English, Spanish, and Russian in order to develop a new type of interactive training. This multimedia approach may correspond better to the needs of our time, and will enable others to criticize their approach. This criticism will be even easier since it will rely on documents supplied in the CD-ROM. Thus, the critique will reflect the reactions of colleagues from other schools of thought among European analysts (Lebovici, Soule, & Diatkine, 1995).

I do not want to give the impression that I am promoting a contest between the

French or the French-speaking school and the American school. Recall that it was in Paris that WAIMH-France had the pleasure to meet and to work with individuals such as Yvon Gauthier (Montreal) and Daniel Stern (Geneva). Also, it would not be suitable to give the impression that our psychopathological approach is always greeted favorably in France. We have adversaries inside psychoanalysis—foremost among them those who claim kinship with Jacques Lacan—who put forward the theories of Françoise Dolto. Among Dolto's achievements is the establishment of *maisons vertes,* where mothers and babies are welcomed without any diagnostic approach being considered, as is shown by the experience led in Venice by Donatella Caprioglio. Unfortunately, Dolto has convinced many disciples that it is enough to speak to a baby in order to be understood by it. This belief leads to absurd psychotherapies, because they rely on the therapist's speech to cure the baby. I have explained my position on this subject, and I are much more convinced by Brazelton, who has shown that the therapist can be the baby's advocate, if he wants to give the child good parents.

Among French psychoanalysts, André Green is the strongest advocate of leaving the children's room, to find ourselves in the parents' room. They also feel that any reference to the theory of attachment is in contradiction to Freud's metapsychology.

Despite my concern not to be trapped in psychoanalytic theory, I can be criticized for not taking into account those investigations that have a more scientific aspect and imply neuropsychological research. These are the numerous investigations that take into account modern means of visualization of the functioning of the nervous system, cognitive resources, and early skills. Also, I may be criticized for not taking into account the tremendous developments of genetics, which allow the description of specific symptoms linked to the deletion of a paternal or a maternal chromosome.

Thus, modern investigations insist on the important effects of multiple biologically based syndromes. But the description of these congenital handicaps limits the psychiatrist to knowing the catalogue of these syndromes. Assuming such a limitation indicates that mental functioning can be understood through the organization of the chromosomes, when everything points to the necessity of assessing the disorders that are finally observed through their relational aspects. The study of human mental functioning, will never boil down to the study of the functioning of the human brain.

It is important for neuropsychologists and psychoanalysts to specify the definitions of terms that they use. To take only one example, note the ambiguity of the term *representation.* Freud used it in the philosophical meaning of the word *Vorstellung,* which could be translated by the word *thought.* Indeed, Freud sets the representation of things, which belongs to the unconscious, against thought expressed in words, which belongs to the preconscious. Cognitivists use the term *representations* to refer to the infinite variety of schemas expressed in our actions and in our language. Development specialists use this term to refer to thoughts represented as a show that unfolds under our eyes. This is the meaning of the word used in philosophy, and of the word *Darstellung* used by Freud.

This is to say how carefully the attempts at "translating" between neuropsychological considerations and psychoanalytic theory should be made. It seems that careful translation is possible when neurologists talk about a self linked to the synaptic reduction of neurons, and when analysts, taking up the theory of primary narcissism, consider, with Winnicott, that using the term *self* implies the knowledge of its existence and of its continuity.

Opposed to the arguments suggested by neuropsychologists are those of anthropologists: Devereux has inspired his student Nathan, who claims, as we have seen, that there is such a thing as a cultural unconscious, and that, affiliation therefore enables the curing of the observed disorders. We have widely criticized this viewpoint, which seems acceptable only in genocidal disasters.

Family specialists criticize us for not using studies of the family system sufficiently. Nevertheless, it seems to us that our investigations on interactions express our interest in the studies of the family systems. But we remain psychoanalysts. During the process of tierceization, then of triadification, the baby distinguishes its two partners (who are called its parents) and gives them a specific role only when it has reached triangulation. The Oedipal father will then play his separating role between the mother and his child. This triangulation is from now on the paradigm of psychic life.

In the interactive "taking place," the Oedipified child has the chance of being able to dream at night of its parents' union, and to organize its fantasies of the primary scene and of castration. Anyway, this very summary analysis of the foundations of normal neurotic symptoms shows that Oedipal triangulation and its mishaps constitute the basis of what has been called neurotic characters. This tends to worsen when the child is victim of severe aggression, which gives rise to a posttraumatic neurotic syndrome. Such cases are also known to result in severe mental inhibition, which may be treated with analytical psychotherapy.

On the whole, our investigations rest mainly on the study of single cases. Clinical investigations are difficult in France because the effort that is necessary to undertake them would require important means of control for the comparison of the data collected from clearly matched couples.

Nevertheless, the demonstrative conditions of single cases have been well clarified during recent research. The description of these cases could not be reduced to a demonstrative vignette. The cases my colleagues and I have presented in our multimedia product are not meant to be a reproduction of what has taken place, but rather a reconstruction of what we have thought and felt during the consultation, the excerpts of which would only present the vignettes of what occurred.

On the whole, our originality may be submitted to many criticisms, such as have already taken place in the research group WAIMH-France. It seems to have been appreciated by those whom we call the consultants. But the rapid sharing of discoveries with the whole world, and the use of the information highway, account for the contacts that enrich our knowledge. However, it should be stressed that talking or writing in another language than one's mother tongue is more difficult than is thought, especially if one wants to express a subtle thought. Therefore there will always be a relative uncertainty in any scientific exchanges among individuals who speak different languages.

I should now express here my gratitude towards my English speaking colleagues, particularly toward the small group who collaborated with my colleagues and I, and who had the extreme kindness to prepare the special issue of the *Infant Mental Health Journal* (edited by Joy D. Osofsky) on the occasion of my 80th birthday. This moving initiative has certainly contributed to making my professional experience and my research better known around the world.

French journals of child psychiatry publish the translation of many English-language works. A recent issue of *Psychiatrie de l'enfant* (Vol. 40, No. 2), includes a paper I have written on the defense and illustration of the concept of primary narcissism, that precedes the publication in French of a work by Hossein Etezady, "Primary-Secondary Narcissism: Fundamental or Obsolete Concept?" That same issue also includes a paper that involved many French collaborators who are preoccupied with the child's psychotic disorders, comparing them with multiple developmental disorders. It is noteworthy that Donald Cohen has coauthored this work.

Last, almost 10 years ago, A. Guédeney

and I contributed to the foundation of the journal *Devenir*. This journal, of a high scientific standard, is meant for the publication of French or foreign work concerning the young child's mental health. A recent issue (Vol. 10, No. 1, coordinated by Maria José Cordeiro), devoted to the study of Zero to Three's *Diagnostic Classification: 0–3*, contains articles by Robert Emde and Joy Osofsky, as well as by Jean M. Thomas and their collaborators.

We hope that these examples bear enough witness to the wealth of our exchanges, which must continue and allow the fertilization of our investigations. These exchanges were very rich during international congresses of the WAIPAD and then of the WAIMH. In particular, this was the case in the 1996 WAIMH congress in Tampere, Finland, where, thanks to spontaneous contributions, a French interpretation enabled the French delegation to follow the discussions and make their presentations. Also, the numerous regional meetings allowed for a world expansion of the exchanges: This is what Salvador Celia and Miguel Hoffmann have wished for in Latin America; Margaret Dünitz and her husband, Peter Scheer, in Austria; and Peter de Château, in the Netherlands. Also, cooperation with Japan, through Professor Okonogi and Dr. Watanabe, allowed excellent exchanges. Last, some of us were able to have discussions with teams from Eastern Europe, either in Latvia or in Moscow and Saint Petersburg, Russia. My collaboration was further strengthened through my common intensive work in the WAIMH executive committee, and thanks to its director, Hiram Fitzgerald. Thus, I have fulfilled the requirements of the title of this chapter: "Cross-Cultural Perspectives on Infant Mental Health."

References

Adelson, J. (1997). What we know about day care. *Commentary, 8,* 52–54.

Ainsworth, M. D., Blehar, M. C., Waters, E., & Walls, S. (1978). *Patterns of attachment.* Hillsdale, NJ: Erlbaum.

American Psychiatric Association. (1994). *Diagnostic and statistical manual of mental disorders* (4th ed.). Washington, DC: Author.

Bydlowski, M. (1997). *La dette de vie.* Paris: PUF.

Cohen-Solal, G. (1990). Le pédiatre, l'enfant et la mort. Paris: Odile Jacob.

Cohen-Solal, J. (1990). *Le pe'deahe, l'enfant et la neve.* Paris: Odile Jacob.

Cramer, B. (1997). *Entre filles et mères.* Paris: Calmann-Lévy.

Cramer, B., & Palacio-Espasa, F. (1974). Interventions psychotherapeutiques brèves avec parents et enfant. *Psychiatrie de l'enfant, 17*(1), 107–126.

Cramer, B., & Palacio-Espasa, F. (1993). *La technique des psychotherapies mère-bébé* (Études cliniques et theoriques). Paris: PUF.

Cyrulnik, B. (1993). *Les nourritures affectives.* Paris: Odile Jacob.

David, M., & Appel, G. (1983). Interactions mère-enfant. *Psychiatrie de l'enfant, 26*(1), 89–140.

Debray, R. (1987). *Bébés-mères en revolte.* Paris: Centurion.

Emde, R. N. (1985). The affective self: Continuities and transformations from in-fancy. In J. Call, E. Galenson, & R. L. Tyson (Eds.), *Frontiers in infant psychiatry* (Vol. 2, pp. 38–54). New York: Basic Books.

Fraiberg, S., Adelson, E., & Shapiro, V. (1975). Ghosts in the nursery: A psychoanalytic approach to the problems of impaired infant-mother relationships. *Journal of the American Academy of Child Psychiatry, 14,* 387–421.

Frith, U. (1997). *Énigme de l'autisme.* Paris: Odile Jacob.

Guédeney, N., Fermanian, J., Guelfi, J. D., & Delour, M. (1995). À propos de la traduction française de l'EPDS. *Devenir, 7,* 69–92.

Hochmann, J., & Jeannerod, R. (1993). *Esprit, où es-tu?* Paris: Odile Jacob.

Houzel, D. (1987) Le concept d'enveloppe psychique. In D. Anzieu (Ed.), *Les enveloppes psychiques* (pp. 23–54). Paris: Dunod.

Kreisler, L. (1981). *L'enfant du désordre psychosomatique.* Toulouse, France: Privat.

Kreisler, L. (1987). *Le nouvel enfant du désordre psychosomatique.* Toulouse, France: Privat.

Kreisler, L., Fain, M., & Soulé, M. (1974). *L'enfant et son corps.* Paris: PUF.

Koupernik, C., & Dailly, R. (1980). *Développement psycho-moteur du premier age* (4th ed.). Paris: PUF.

Lamour, M. (1992). On intergenerational transmission: From filiation to affiliation. *Infant Mental Health Journal, 14,* 26–72.

Lamour, M., & Lebovici, S. (1991). Les interactions du nourisson avec ses partenaires: évaluation et modes d'abord préventifs et thérapeutiques. *Psychiatrie de l'enfant, 34*(1), 171–276.

Laplanche, J. (1987). *Nouveaux fondements pour la psychoanalyse.* Paris: PUF.

Lebovici, S. (1949). Contributions a l'étude

nosologique de la schizophrenie infantile. *Évolution psychiatrique, 111,* 329–352.

Lebovici, S. (1960). L'observation de la relation objectale. *Psychiatrie de l'enfant, 3*(1).

Lebovici, S. (1988). Fantasmatic interaction and intergenerational transmission. *Infant Mental Health Journal, 9*(1), 10–19.

Lebovici, S. (1993). On intergenerational transmission: From filiation to affiliation. *Infant Mental Health Journal, 14,* 260–272.

Lebovici, S. (1995). À propos du livre de Cramer. *Psychiatrie de l'enfant.*

Lebovici, S. (1997). Défense et illustration du concept de narcissisme primaire: Les avatars du narcissisme primaire et le processus de subjectivation. *Psychiatrie de l'enfant, 40,* 429–463.

Levovici, S. (1998). *Lettre ouverte à Robert Emde.* In A. Braconnier & J. Sipos (Eds.), *Le bébé et les interactions précoces.* Paris: PUF.

Lebovici, S. (in press). Réponse à Robert Emde. *Revue internationale de psychotherapie.*

Lebovici, S., Soule, M., & Daitkine, R. (1995). *Nouveau traité de psychiatrie de l'enfant et de l'adolescent* (2nd ed., Vols. 1–4). Paris: PUF.

Lebovici, S., & Stoléru, S. (1983). *Le nourrisson, la mère et le psychoanalyste.* Paris: Centurion.

Lebovici, S., & Weil-Halpern, F. (1989). *Psychopathologie du bébé.* Paris: PUF.

Main, M., Kaplan, N., & Cassidy, J. (1985). Security in infancy, childhood, and adulthood: A move to the level of representation. In I. Bretherton & E. Waters (Vol. eds.), *Monographs of the Society for Research in Child Development: Vol. 50, (No. 1–2, Serial No. 209). Growing points of attachment theory and research* (pp. 66–104). Chicago: University of Chicago Press for the Society for Research in Child Development.

Mazet, P., & Lebovici, S. (1998). *La psychiatrie périnatale.* Paris: PUF.

Mehler, J. (1993). *Naître humain.* Paris: Odile Jacob.

Montagner, H. (1993). *L'enfant acteur de son développement.* Paris: Stock.

Moralès-Huet, M. *Thèse de troisième cycle en psychopathologie.* Doctoral thesis, Université de Paris, Paris, France.

Moro, M.-R. (1994). *Familles en exil.* Paris: PUF.

Nacht, S. (1965). Le narcissisme gardien de la vie. *Revue française de psychanalyse, 5–6,* 529–531.

Nathan, T. (1988). *Le sperme du diable* (Éléments d'ethnopsychotherapie). Paris: PUF.

N'Guyen, T. H. (1994). *De Wallon à Freud.* Paris: PUF.

N'Guyen, T. H. (1998). *La formation des attitudes: Freud and Wallon.* Paris: PUF.

Pierrehumbert, B., & Karmaniola, F. (1996). Les modeles de relations: Développement d'un autoquestionnaire d'attachement pour adultes. *Psychiatrie de l'enfant, 1,* 161–202.

Spitz, R. A. (1965). *The first year of life.* New York: International Universities Press.

Steele, H., Steele, M., & Fonagy, P. (1996). Associations among attachment classifications of mothers, fathers, and their infants: Evidence for relationship-specific perspective. *Child Development, 67,* 541–555.

Stern, D. N. (1985). *The interpersonal world of the infant.* New York: Basic Books.

Stern, D. N. (1998). The process of therapeutic change involving implicit knowledge: Some implications of developmental observations for adult psychotherapy. *Infant Mental Health Journal, 19*(3), 300–308.

Stoléru, S. (1989). Les parentification et ses

troubles. In S. Lebovici & F. Weil-Harpen (Eds.), *Psychopathologie du bébé* (pp. 113–130). Paris: PUF.

Stoléru, S., & Morales, M. (1987). *Psychotherapies neves-nourissons dans les familles à problèmes multiples.* Paris: PUF.

Wildlöcher, D. (1986). *Métapsychologie du sens.* Paris: PUF.

Wollf, P. E. (1996). The irrelevance of infants' observations and psychoanalysis. *Journal of the American Psychoanalytic Association, 44,* 369–392.

Zazzo, R., et al. (1969). *L'attachement.* Genève: Delachaux et Niestlé.

6

The Sociocultural Context
of American Indian
Infant Mental Health

Maria Yellow Horse Brave Heart and Paul Spicer

6

Introduction

Our goal in this chapter is to describe the diversity of American Indian people,[1] some of the biggest challenges that we confront in parenting our children, and the cultural resources that are available to see us through our difficulties.[2] Particular attention will be paid to the Lakota, with whom Maria Yellow Horse Brave Heart is affiliated and has worked intensively, but the implications of the Lakota experience for other native peoples will also be explored. In reviewing the available literature on American Indian parenting and infant mental health, our goal is to provide clinicians with insight into the importance of culturally based ways of addressing the problems that American Indian parents and children may experience.

The Diversity of Native North American Cultures

Readers who are unfamiliar with the native people of North America may be surprised to learn of the diversity that characterized and, to a large extent, continues to charac-

terize the population. Within the United States alone, over 500 tribes are recognized by the federal government and several more continue to fight for recognition (Bureau of Indian Affairs, 1998). Members of these tribes speak some 250 languages that belong to several different major language families (Bureau of Indian Affairs, 1998). If we add the native peoples of Canada and Mexico for consideration—and there are good reasons to include them in the cultural area of North America (Kehoe, 1992)—the diversity of the area is almost overwhelming.

The aboriginal people of North America have occupied every major ecological region of the continent, ranging from the arctic tundra of northern Canada and Alaska to the equatorial jungles of Mexico, and our distinct ways of life often reflect centuries of development and adaptation to our homelands. Given the tremendous diversity of the contemporary native population of North America, generalizations about "Indian culture" are obviously quite problematic, if not impossible. Nevertheless, certain regularities do emerge, and anthropologists have developed some important ways of thinking about the similarities and differences among native peoples.

Perhaps the easiest way of thinking

about the cultures of native North American people is the concept of culture area, which has been articulated and revised throughout the history of American anthropology (Kehoe, 1992). Fundamentally, the idea behind a culture area is that people living in close proximity within a common ecological region will tend to have similar ways of life. Thus, we expect (and to some extent find) that the people who historically lived in the southeastern United States—many of whom were forcibly relocated to Oklahoma in the 1800s—will share certain aspects of culture as a result of their common agricultural adaptation, just as the peoples of the subarctic share certain cultural traits due to the hunting and gathering that is required in their ecological niches. However, it is also important to remember that within the broad similarities that characterize a culture area there are often significant differences in terms of social organization and cultural belief systems (e.g., Champagne, 1994). Accordingly, clinicians must take care to approach each tribe individually and be prepared for aspects of their culture that may not be predicted by the generalizations about their culture area.

Culture and Parenting in Native North America

We take it as axiomatic that parenting practices have evolved and developed within local cultural worlds and that evaluations of them must be made relative to those contexts. Following the work of LeVine and his colleagues (e.g., LeVine et al., 1996), we argue that child rearing in any population must be understood as a complex product of species-specific universal constraints, population-specific socioeconomic conditions, and population-specific cultural models of parenthood (LeVine et al., 1996). Unfortunately, analyses like these have been rare among American Indian and Alaska Native peoples. There are, however, some hints in the literature about the important ways in which culture and ecology give shape to parenting in Indian and Native communities.

In a comparison of Anglo, Hopi, and Navajo mothers and their infants, for example, Callaghan (1981) found significant differences in both maternal and infant behaviors during a mutual gaze task, where mothers were directed "to get and maintain your baby's attention" (Callaghan, 1981, p. 116). He found that although all three groups spent almost exactly the same amount of time in mutual gaze, very different patterns emerged. The Anglo mothers had significantly more, but shorter, mutual gaze runs than the Navajo mothers and more mutual gaze events than did the Hopi mothers. Similarly, Anglo mothers and infants displayed significantly more total coded behaviors than did Navajo or Hopi mothers and infants, with Navajo mothers having the lowest levels of total behaviors in the comparison. These patterns suggested to Callaghan that Anglo mothers responded to the demand characteristics of the task quite differently than did Navajo and Hopi mothers: Anglo mothers were more often likely to try to make their infants look at them, even when they were not interested, while Navajo and Hopi mothers were more likely to wait until their infants were contented before attempting to engage them in mutual gaze. This was most pronounced in the case of the Hopi mothers, whose behaviors were more closely related to their infants' attention than those of either the Anglo or Navajo groups (i.e., they tended to act toward their babies only when there was mutual gaze). As one Hopi mother put it on seeing a set of videotapes, the Hopi mothers "seem to be having more of a conversation with their infants than the [Anglo] and Navajo mothers" (Callaghan, 1981, p. 129).

The hints of cultural differences that emerge in Callaghan's study are explored in greater depth in Chisholm's (1981, 1983) naturalistic studies of Navajo infancy, which are distinguished by close attention to the ecological context of parent-child interaction in Navajo and Anglo communities in northern Arizona. While the typical Navajo residence group has long been represented as a matrilocal extended family camp, Chisholm discovered that over half of the Navajo households in his study (14 of 27) were living in nuclear family camps, that is, in a camp of their own, away from either the husband's or wife's family camp. He attributed this to the deterioration of grazing land and the increasing population of both humans and sheep that made it adaptive to disperse in smaller groups. Also, the introduction of pickup trucks meant that people could live further away from their relatives to take advantage of employment opportunities yet still return on weekends to help with the livestock.

These different residential arrangements—nuclear versus extended family camps—were associated with important differences in the social context of mother-child interaction within the Navajo sample. In 1-hr spot observation periods conducted every 2 months, Chisholm found that children in nuclear family camps were significantly more likely to be at home with their mothers than were the children in extended family camps. Not surprisingly, nuclear family camps also had fewer people around during Chisholm's spot observations. Finally, the children in nuclear family camps were also significantly less likely to be actually held by their mothers, which Chisholm attributed to the lack of others to help the mother with her household work in the nuclear family camps.

There were also important differences in the social context of Anglo mother-child interaction. Anglo mothers had significantly fewer other children (only 2 of the 11 Anglo mothers had any other children) and, since they lived in the relatively urban area of Flagstaff, Arizona, the Anglo children were surrounded by nonrelatives and exposed to a constant stream of such people. This meant that, in contrast to the Navajo children, the Anglo children saw more people but were actually familiar with far fewer of the people they encountered (Chisholm, 1981). Finally, there were also significant differences between Navajo and Anglo residences. Navajo residences had significantly fewer rooms (most of the Navajo families lived in one-room dwellings called *hogans*) and the Navajo families had significantly fewer stairs, articles of furniture, dishwashers, toasters, telephones, television sets, and so on. Consequently, Anglo mothers were more likely to be away from their infants, (e.g., attending to the phone in another room), and they were also more likely to use the television set as a baby-sitter.

Given the different social contexts in which they lived, it is not surprising that there were important differences among the three groups (Navajo nuclear family, Navajo extended family, and Anglo) in terms of mother-child interaction, but what was unexpected was the direction of these differences. While one might have predicted that the Navajo nuclear family mothers and children would act more like the Anglo mothers and children, who were also in nuclear families, this was not the case. For all measures of parent-child interaction, the Navajo extended families were more similar to the Anglo families than were the Navajo nuclear families. Among the theoretically significant interaction variables in this contrast were mutual gaze, mother talking to the child, mother touching or patting the child, mother approaching and leaving the child, the child vocalizing, the child vocalizing and looking at the mother, the child approaching and leaving the mother, and the mean length of interaction. On all of these variables, the Anglo mothers and children scored the highest and the Navajo nuclear family mothers and children scored the lowest. The Navajo extended family mothers and children were always intermediate in these comparisons.

In the case of both the Anglo and the Navajo extended family mothers and children, there was more opportunity for exclusive attention between mothers and children, but for different reasons. Technological advantages and a lack of other children gave Anglo mothers more time with their infants, while for the Navajo extended family mothers had more time because of the presence of others who could help with household tasks. Navajo nuclear family mothers and children had the highest rate of others directing behavior toward their infants, but these were generally the infants' siblings, who were of less help with other household duties. Thus, the Navajo nuclear family mothers had the least opportunity for exclusive interaction with their children.

Chisholm's work is also notable for its attention to the effects of the cradleboard on mother-child interaction. Perhaps no aspect of Indian child rearing has aroused as much commentary and concern as the practice of swaddling infants on the cradleboard. This practice was hypothesized to be related to aspects of adult personality (Erikson, 1950; Gorer, 1949; Gorer & Rickman, 1949), and congenital hip disease (Rabin, Barnett, Arnold, Freiberger, & Brooks, 1965). Contrary to the available research evidence (e.g., Dennis, 1940; Kluckhohn & Leighton, 1974), Anglos in Arizona also believed that it retarded motor development (Chisholm, 1983). Although Chisholm dismissed these hypotheses for principled reasons (Chisholm, 1983), he did find reason to suspect that the soothing and calming effect of swaddling (e.g., Lipton, Steinschneider, & Richmond, 1965) might act to discourage mother-child interaction and, in turn, affect the mother-child relationship.

Chisholm found evidence that the transition to the cradleboard calmed the infant (e.g., there was decreased fretting, crying, and puckering; less nonfret vocalization; and fewer extension-flexion movements after the infant was placed on the cradleboard; Chisholm, 1983). However, these effects did not appear to have any long-term impact on the mother-child relationship. Indeed, after an exhaustive series of analyses to determine the possible effects of the cradleboard on global characteristics of mother-child interaction, Chisholm concluded that, aside from some obvious correlates of the restraint provided by the cradleboard (e.g., the child does not position him- or herself or crawl or walk when on the cradleboard), there was little consistent evidence that time on the cradleboard affected mother-child interaction in any significant way. In part, the lack of long-term effects may be attributable to some of the interactive possibilities that the cradleboard creates. Thus, although the cradleboard decreased mutual responsiveness (at least while the child was on the cradleboard), it actually increased proximity by permitting the mother and child to be close while she did her other work. Furthermore, a decline in mutual responsiveness when the child was on the cradleboard was at least somewhat offset by the particularly intense emotional exchange between mother and child during transitions off the cradleboard (Chisholm, 1983).

Chisholm's analysis reminds us that detailed studies of mother-infant interaction are not only possible but extremely valuable in different cultural contexts. The power of this approach is perhaps nowhere more evident than in the recent work of Rogoff and Mosier (1993) among Maya families from San Pedro, Guatemala, and Anglo families from Salt Lake City, Utah. The central component of this study was a controlled comparison of mother and toddler interaction in three contexts: joint exploration of novel objects, dressing the child, and the child's exploration of novel objects during adult activity.

In joint exploration of a novel object, both Salt Lake City and San Pedro mothers created bridges and structured their children's participation in activities, but there were important differences in how they did this. The Salt Lake City mothers used more talk with their toddlers, while the San Pedro caregivers more frequently used nonverbal means to orient their toddlers, and they simplified their toddlers' involvement through gestures, communicative gaze, touch, posture, and timing clues. Similarly, San Pedro toddlers also used more nonverbal communication with their mothers.

Salt Lake City mothers were also significantly more likely to talk to their children as peers and to act as their playmates, which is reflected in significantly less baby talk among the San Pedro mothers. Furthermore, San Pedro mothers were less likely to organize instruction: They provided fewer vocabulary lessons to their children and engaged in less mock excitement and praise in contrast to what seemed, for the Salt Lake City mothers, to be an effort to motivate learning. Instead, the San Pedro mothers were significantly more likely than the Salt Lake City mothers to be poised in readiness to help their children, which Rogoff and Mosier (1993) suggest is part of their greater respect for the child's autonomy in learning. It may also be related to the Maya mothers' belief that child development is something that just happens (Gaskins, 1996), a process that they follow rather than lead.[3]

Rogoff and Mosier (1993) found important differences in the management of attention, which were consistent with the idea that children in communities such as the Maya are particularly adept at learning through observation as they participate in adult activities (Rogoff, Mistry, Göncü, & Mosier, 1993). The San Pedro toddlers and their mothers were significantly more likely to attend to several events simultaneously. In contrast, the Salt Lake toddlers and their mothers were more likely to be unaware of other events when they were focused on the novel objects a contrast that was especially notable during the explorations of novel objects during adult activity (Rogoff & Mosier, 1993). As Rogoff and Mosier observe, these differences in attention are part of the larger pattern of life in the two communities that is evident throughout their data.

> Although [San Pedro] toddlers received attention, it was not to the exclusion of other on-going conversations or activities; rather, they usually appeared to be smoothly integrated into the social fabric—not the recipients of toddler-directed play, special registers of speech, or exclusive attention, but already members of the group. (Rogoff & Mosier, 1993, p. 90)

Clearly much work remains to be done to better understand the subtlety of how Indian mothers and children interact, but it is already clear that clinicians must exercise great caution and humility when working with Indian families. Certain caregiving practices that appear deficient or harmful from an Anglo perspective (e.g., the cradleboard or a lack of parental play with or instruction of the child) may well be rooted in alternative developmental pathways that are valuable in the context of life in Indian communities. In no sense do such practices imply a lack of concern for children or ignorance about their development. Indeed, from what we know about Lakota beliefs, we would suggest that children are of the utmost priority in many, if not all, Indian and Native communities.

The Traditional Lakota View of Children

Indigenous Lakota mores place the child at the center of the Lakota Nation. The Lakota word for children is *wakanheja,* a derivative of the phrase *lena wakan heca*—"these children are sacred." In the traditional context, children are viewed as spirits who are returning to earth; the Lakota child, considered a gift from the Creator, is surrounded with love, nurturing parental and extended family involvement, an active spiritual life with communal rituals, and an emphasis on abstinence from drugs and alcohol (Brave Heart, 1999b). Lakota parenting traditionally was a shared experience, not limited to the *tiwahe* (immediate family). Rather, it was conceptualized as *oyate ptayela* (taking care of the nation), a communal responsibility of the *tiospaye* (extended kinship network) and the *ospaye* (band or a collective of *tiospayes*).

Responsibility to the group and for oneself as well as commitment to natural health are reinforced within the *tiospaye*, through traditional ceremonies, and through the *Woope Sakowin,* the Seven Sacred Laws. These laws emphasize compassion, generosity, respect for all of creation, humility, the development of a great mind (including self-discipline and silent observation), wisdom, and courage to be honest and to protect the *oyate* (the Lakota Nation and all of creation). Self-sacrifice for the good of the *oyate* was an esteemed value and is evident in Lakota spirituality, particularly the *Winwanyang Wacipi* (Sun Dance), in which one fasts and prays for others.

Lakota children learned through observing and imitating the behavior of adults. They were permitted room to practice new behaviors through play. Early child rearing was permissive and nurturing as the spirit of the child and the child's inherent wisdom as a spirit returning to earth were respected. Children learned how to be good parents from their own experience of being parented as well as observing parenting in the natural world. Education occurred through experience, storytelling, and ceremonies that emphasized the *Woope Sakowin,* especially the value of self-discipline, responsibility, and commitment.

Indigenous forms of contraception were used so that births were ideally spaced 6 years apart to enable a generous amount of nurturing and attention for each child during the critical years of early development. Many traditional families had only one or two children. Both men and women prepared themselves spiritually as well as physically, mentally, and emotionally for parenthood. During prenatal development, the mother would talk to the unborn child and the child's spirit. Sage would be burned before going into labor. The baby's umbilical cord would be placed in a quilled or beaded turtle pouch and worn. This pouch was thought to help infants to heal from illnesses and gave children a sense of their place in the world. After the birth, a ceremony would be held to welcome the child's spirit back. Mothers would hold their babies up in the center of the tipi so that they could see the constellation and the stars from which their spirits had come.

It was also believed that until the soft spot on the infant's head closed, its spirit could still wander, so the mother would take care to call the child's name four times in order to call back the spirit. Birthmarks were evidence of the spirit's earlier life experience and were interpreted by an appropriate spiritual advisor. Infants were held, stimulated, and nurtured. The cradleboard was used and, as among the Navajo (Chisholm, 1983), it was seen predominantly as a nurturing, calming experience for the infant. Nursing an infant was viewed as a sacred act, and anyone present when it occurred was to remain positive and respectful. Weaning was not forced at any particular time, but was determined by the infant's readiness to move to the next developmental level.

Adolescents went through rites of passage to become men and women. Girls had ceremonies celebrating the onset of menstruation, which was viewed as a sacred and powerful time of natural purification. Since males had no physiological way of cleansing, they had to purify themselves through ceremonies (B. Kills Straight, personal communication, September 26, 1992). Both women and children were viewed as sacred beings, and domestic violence and child abuse were not tolerated in traditional Lakota society.

Modern Lakota child rearing in a drug- and alcohol-free environment retains these traditional values, and many Lakota families are striving to rekindle these practices. However, they encounter multiple obstacles to following Lakota parenting traditions, many of which can be attributed to the effects of the historical disruptions that the Lakota have endured.

The Historical Trauma Response

The native people of North America have all endured the consequences of colonialism. To a greater or lesser extent, each tribe has experienced missionary activity; the expropriation of their land; devastating loss of population due to warfare and disease; systematic attempts to destroy their traditional social, political, spiritual, and economic life; and forced acculturation in boarding schools. Rather than discuss these problems in the abstract, however, we will illustrate the implications of this history through an analysis of the Lakota historical trauma response, particularly as this has been described in the work of the first author (Brave Heart).

Lakota historical trauma is the cumula- tive emotional and psychological injury, over life spans and across generations, resulting from the history of genocide among the Lakota (Brave Heart, 1998). The Lakota historical trauma response is the constellation of features that have appeared as a result of this traumatic history, a reaction analogous to that of other groups that have experienced massive group traumas (van der Kolk, 1987; van der Kolk, McFarlane, & Weisaeth, 1996). The paired concept of historical unresolved grief is intended to describe the impaired or delayed mourning in people and communities that results from the accumulation of these traumas across the generations (Brave Heart, 1998).

Traditionally, Lakota ceremonies sustained grief management. However, the 1881 prohibition of indigenous spiritual practices impaired culturally syntonic modes of working through both normative and traumatic grief from cataclysmic events such as: (1) the 1890 assassination of Tatanka Iyotake (Sitting Bull), the personification of traditional Lakota leadership (Vestal, 1957; Utley, 1993), (2) the Wounded Knee Massacre of hundreds of Lakota ("Wounded Knee," 1990), (3) the forced removal of children to federal and mission boarding schools, and (4) the overcrowding and deficient health standards at boarding schools, which contributed to a tuberculosis death rate seven times the national average and led to the death of more than ⅓ of the Lakota population over one year of age between 1936 and 1941 (Brave Heart, 1998; Hoxie, 1989; Tanner, 1982).

The Lakota historical trauma response, as described by Brave Heart, is similar to

Jewish Holocaust survivor syndrome (Niederland, 1988) and survivor's child complex (Kestenberg, 1990). It includes: (1) depression, (2) anxiety and intrusive trauma imagery, (3) survivor guilt, (4) elevated mortality rates from cardiovascular diseases as well as suicide and other forms of violent death, (5) identification with ancestral pain and deceased ancestors, (6) psychic numbing and poor affect tolerance, and (7) unresolved grief (Brave Heart, 1998; Eitinger & Strom, 1973; Keehn, 1980; Nefzger, 1970; Sigal & Weinfeld, 1989).

We know from the literature on the intergenerational transfer of trauma that Jewish Holocaust and Japanese internment descendants have developed internal psychic representations of generational trauma that have become organizing constructs in their lives and that serve to continue the transmission of this trauma across generations (Brave Heart, 1998; Danieli, 1989; Felsen & Erlich, 1990; Nagata, 1991; Sigal & Weinfeld, 1989). For the Lakota, this process of transposition—an introjection of and commitment to ancestors while living concurrently in the past and present (Kestenberg, 1982/1990, 1989)—may be culturally amplified through the encouragement of spiritual contact with the deceased and the expansiveness of kinship lineage (Brave Heart, 1998). The perpetuation of suffering and victim identification results from allegiance to the traumatized deceased ancestors as well as identification with parental suffering (Brave Heart, 1998; Fogelman, 1991).

Other aspects of the Lakota historical trauma response need to be understood in the context of Lakota loyalty to the *tiospaye* (extended family) and the maintenance of a collective victim ego identity (Brave Heart, 1998). While many Lakota become *wakiksuyapi* (memorial people), in a manner somewhat analogous to "memorial candles" (the children of Jewish Holocaust survivors who possess a core identity with deceased ancestors; Wardi, 1990/1992), *wakiksuyapi* are not necessarily individual roles in the nuclear family. Indeed, they may be entire bands that shoulder this role for the Lakota Nation (Brave Heart, 1998, in press).

Brave Heart's formulation of the Lakota historical trauma response addresses concerns that the context of multigenerational and community trauma needs examination (Robin, Chester, & Goldman, 1996) and more accurately represents the range of American Indian trauma experience than does the standard Post-traumatic Stress Disorder (PTSD) nomenclature (Brave Heart, 1999a). Perhaps more than any other historical trauma, however, it is the legacy of Indian boarding schools that has most directly affected Indian parenting. We turn our attention next to some of the more outstanding characteristics of this particular trauma among the Lakota.

The Lakota Experience of Boarding Schools

Beginning in 1879, federal policy mandated removal of Lakota children from tribal communities and their placement in boarding schools (Brave Heart, 1998, in press; Brave Heart-Jordan, 1995). Many of these children were subjected to incarceration, physical abuse such as being shackled and chained to bedposts for weeks at a time, starvation, sexual abuse, prolonged separation from families—even death (Brave Heart, 1998; Brave Heart-Jordan, 1995; Tanner, 1982). Negative boarding school experiences were recounted by a majority of respondents in a 1992 study by Brave Heart (Brave Heart-Jordan, 1995). Physical abuse was cited by 58.1 percent with 37.9 percent having been punished for speaking Lakota and 22.6 percent reporting sexual abuse by boarding school staff. Although the mean age for beginning boarding school attendance was 8.9 years, 38.7 percent attended boarding school by age 6 and 48.4 percent by age 7, with some participants reporting boarding school placement as early as age 5. The mean distance of boarding schools from home was 123.1 miles, but the modal distance was 300 miles. Early boarding schools were sometimes over 1,000 miles away from traditional tribal communities, and children were separated from parents for several years at a time (Brave Heart-Jordan, 1995).

Lakota oral histories attest to prolonged separation from parents, the lack of nurturing substitute care in boarding schools, and abusive institutional environments (Brave Heart, 1998, in press; Brave Heart-Jordan, 1995). Role models of effective and culturally congruent parenting were also absent in the accounts of Indian boarding school survivors. Thus, for the Lakota, the legacy of boarding school abuses places parents at risk for raising offspring with punitive discipline similar to their own experiences in boarding schools (see Morrissette, 1994, for a related observation).

Clinical and research experiences among the Lakota reveal that Indian people raised in boarding school settings feel inadequate as parents (Brave Heart, 1999b). Further, descendants of boarding school attendees report a history of neglect and abuse in their own childhoods along with feelings of inadequacy and confusion as parents, particularly because of a lack of familiarity with culturally normative parenting styles (Brave Heart, 1999b). The caretaking reported by children raised in boarding schools has often been marked by an authoritarian style, inconsistent responsiveness, rejecting and critical behavior toward the child, insensitivity to the child's needs, and lack of involvement or closeness (Brave Heart, 1999b).

The Intergenerational Continuities of Parenting

There is, we think, good reason to suspect that childhood experiences like those described by former Indian boarding school students will affect their own parenting. The suggestions of such intergenerational dynamics that emerge in the work of Brave Heart gain confirmation in the research of Quinton, Rutter, and Liddle (Quinton & Rutter, 1985; Quinton, Rutter, & Liddle, 1984; Rutter & Quinton, 1984; Rutter, Quinton, & Liddle, 1983). This team of British researchers compared a group of women who, in 1964, had been in one of two children's homes (the ex-care group) with a group of women of the same age and from the same part of London who had never been in institutional care (Quinton & Rutter, 1985; Quinton, Rutter, & Liddle, 1984; Rutter & Quinton, 1984).

The results of this research suggested that those children raised in children's homes were at a significant disadvantage compared to the control group. The ex-care women were more likely to have become pregnant before their 19th birthday and they were less likely to be in a stable cohabiting relationship. Nearly ⅕ of the children of ex-care women had been placed out of the home, and fully ⅓ of the ex-care mothers had suffered a parenting breakdown during which their children had to be taken care of by someone else for at least 6 months. No evidence for either out-of-home placement or parenting breakdown was found in the control group. Similar differences were also evident in direct interview and observational measures of parenting. The ex-care mothers were also significantly more likely to suffer from psychiatric disorders, to have criminal records, and to have substantial difficulties in their interpersonal relationships. Indeed, it was difficult to distinguish the mothers' parenting difficulties from their more general psychosocial problems; in fact, there was little evidence of continuities in parenting across the two generations in the absence of other problems. Unfortunately, there are all too many parallels between the situation of these mothers in London and what we see in many contemporary Indian communities, as is so evident in what we know about the patterns of suffering in our communities.

The Levels of Distress in Current Indian Communities

Mortality statistics from the Indian Health Service (1997) begin to tell the story of the continued devastation of many Indian and Native communities. The age-adjusted mortality rate of 690.4 per 100,000 for people served by IHS is 35 percent higher than the rate of 513.3 per 100,000 for all races in the United States; the death rates for Indian people in the Bemidji, Minnesota, and Aberdeen, South Dakota, service areas of IHS[4] are each over 1,000 per 100,000. Moreover, age-adjusted IHS mortality statistics suggest that Indian and Native people are significantly more likely than the general United States population to die from alcoholism (579 percent greater rate), tuberculosis (475 percent greater rate), diabetes mellitus (23 percent greater rate), accidents (212 percent greater rate), suicide (70 percent greater rate), and homicide (41 percent greater rate). Interestingly, however, Indian and Native people are currently less likely to die from malignant neoplasms (15 percent lower rate).

Of course, given the above-noted heterogeneity of the American Indian and Alaska Native population in the United States, there is a considerable amount of variability in these data. Thus, while the rate of suicide in the California area is only half the United States rate, the rate in the Alaska area is nearly four times the U.S. rate; four other IHS area rates (Aberdeen, South Dakota; Albuquerque, New Mexico; Phoenix, Arizona; and Portland, Oregon) are at least twice the U.S. rate. Similarly, the general Indian and Native rate of death from heart disease is approximately the same as the U.S. rate (8 percent higher). However, the Albuquerque, Navajo, and California area rates are all substantially lower, while the Aberdeen and Bemidji area rates are substantially higher than the national average (Indian Health Service, 1997).

There is good reason to suspect that at least some of this distress is related to the historical traumas that Indian people have endured. For example, we know that childhood sexual abuse, reported by many boarding school survivors and descendants (Brave Heart, in press; Brave Heart-Jordan, 1995), is a significant risk factor for the development of substance abuse, depression, and/or anxiety disorders in Indian communities (Robin, Chester, & Goldman, 1996). Furthermore, within contemporary Indian communities, there are often excessive rates of trauma and PTSD among American Indian adults and youth (Brave Heart, 1999a; Manson et al., 1996), which is often comorbid with depression and substance abuse (Robin, Chester, & Goldman, 1996; Ursano, Grieger, & McCarroll, 1996).

The elevated suicide rate among the Lakota, which appears to be a manifestation of unresolved grief and pathological identification with the dead (Brave Heart, 1998), is probably best conceived of as a part of the Lakota historical trauma response. This is particularly reflected in the high correlations of suicide attempts and self-mutilation with sexual abuse, especially early in life (Bachman, 1992; Herman & van der Kolk, 1987; Brave Heart, in press; Brave Heart-Jordan, 1995). There is reason to suspect that heart disease among the Lakota may also be related to our traumatic history (Brave Heart, 1999a).

Overall, the picture that emerges from this review of mortality statistics is quite disturbing. Not only is there good reason to believe that a substantial amount of this distress is a result of past suffering, but such high mortality also means that American Indians are at higher risk for traumatic grief from early losses, further taxing families already coping with historical and other life span traumas. In what follows, we would like to focus more specifically on the problems with alcohol that plague so many Indian and Native communities, for they are implicated in many of the patterns of mortality that we have just discussed.

Alcohol Problems in American Indian Communities

Many of the problems that American Indian people have experienced as a result of alcohol abuse have by now been documented, and an emerging body of sophisticated epidemiological work suggests, at least in broad outline, some crucial dimensions of their experiences with alcohol. It has long been known, for example, that rates of alcohol-involved mortality in Indian communities are often higher than U.S. averages and, as we have just seen, deaths due to motor vehicle crashes, accidents, suicide, and homicide are often substantially higher than U.S. averages, with the exception of suicide among the elderly (May, 1996).

While there is reasonable scientific concern about attributing motor vehicle crashes, other accidents, homicides, and suicides solely to alcohol (e.g., Kunitz and Levy, 1994), there can be little doubt that alcohol is a contributing factor in many of the deaths due to these causes. Using the available literature, May (1989, 1992, 1996) argues that, for Indian people, alcohol was involved in 65 percent of all deaths in motor vehicle crashes, 25 percent of all accidental deaths, 75 percent of all suicides, and 80 percent of all homicides. Clearly, then, for a substantial number of Indian people, alcohol is a serious concern, but its impact is by no means limited to the drinkers themselves.

Indian people themselves often see alcohol as a tremendously disruptive and alien influence in their lives, especially because of the way it affects their roles and responsibilities as parents (Spicer, 1997). In a survey of federal survey providers in the Southwest, Piasecki et al. (1989) found that those children who were abused or neglected were significantly more likely to come from homes where there was parental alcohol abuse, divorce, a single parent, and a chaotic family. Research by Lujan, Debruyn, May, and Bird (1989), at around the same time and also in the Southwest, provides even more insight into these dynamics, with evidence of alcohol abuse found in 85 percent of neglect cases and 63 percent of abuse cases. Subsequent research by the same team with a control sample, however, suggests that alcohol is not necessarily the cause for child abuse and neglect, since 52 percent of the control families' homes were reported as alcohol abusing with no evidence of child abuse or neglect (DeBruyn, Lujan, & May, 1992).

This last finding indicates that, while alcohol is certainly an important part of the problem of abuse and neglect, it is by no means the only factor. The evidence of multiple problems that emerges from the work of Piasecki et al. (1989), for example, points to a constellation of difficulties in abusive and neglectful families that are more extensive than alcohol abuse and dependence. Furthermore, DeBruyn, Lujan, and May (1992) found that parents and grandparents in the target (abusing or neglectful) group of their study were significantly more likely to have evidence of a history of abuse or neglect as children, and they were also more likely to have been raised in an alcoholic family than were caregivers in the control group. These findings provide compelling support for the idea that there are strong intergenerational continuities in child abuse and neglect. Furthermore, as DeBruyn, Lujan, and May (1992) observe, there are many possible connections between the prevalence of abuse and neglect in Indian communities and the experiences of these same parents in boarding schools, a conclusion confirmed by the results of the Brave Heart studies we have already discussed (e.g., Brave Heart-Jordan, 1995).

Unfortunately, interventions in the lives of Indian children of alcoholics have often exacerbated the problems that they experience as a result of their parents' drinking. This is especially evident in the experiences of American Indian adult children of alcoholics interviewed by Spicer (Spicer, 1998b; Spicer & Fleming, in press). Intervention by the state in the lives of these children often meant that they were placed outside their natal communities and raised in non-Indian foster homes (e.g., Westermeyer 1973, 1979a, 1979b).

Those adults who grew up in foster care often describe a pervasive uncertainty about who they are and how they should behave as Indian people (Spicer 1995, 1998a, 1998b; Spicer & Fleming, in press; Westermeyer 1979a, 1979b). In turn, this lack of connection to culture has had an impact on their own parenting as they entered adulthood ill-prepared and inadequately supported by cultural knowledge and resources that might have helped them better meet the challenges of parenting (Spicer, 1998b). While passage of the Indian Child Welfare Act in 1978 offers hope that this situation may be changed for current and future generations (e g , Goodluck, 1993), ignorance of the law and enforcement remain problematic (Matheson, 1996). Moreover, the children of the former foster children interviewed by Spicer and Westermeyer are now entering parenthood themselves and little appears to have been done to help them to work through the cultural estrangement of their parents (Spicer, 1998b). The historical trauma and parenting interventions developed by Brave Heart, however, offer real hope in this regard.

A Lakota Historical Trauma Intervention

Maria Yellow Horse Brave Heart's original historical trauma intervention research incorporated an evaluation of a brief inten- sive psychoeducational group experience delivered to a group of 45 Lakota service providers and community leaders (Brave Heart, 1998; Brave Heart-Jordan, 1995). The goals of the historical trauma intervention included imparting a sense of mastery and control (van der Kolk, McFarlane, & van der Hart, 1996) to cumulative trauma survivors in a traditional Lakota context and a safe holding environment, the sacred Paha Sapa (Black Hills). Historical traumatic memories were stimulated. Opportunities were provided for both cognitive integration, necessary for effective treatment (Resick & Schnicke, 1992), and participant verbalization of traumatic experiences, which has been found to decrease psychosomatic symptoms, reduce psychic numbing, and increase affect tolerance (Brave Heart, 1999a; Harber & Pennebaker, 1992). Traditional Lakota culture and ceremonies, integrated throughout the intervention, afforded abreaction and catharsis (e.g., Silver & Wilson, 1988).

With a 75 percent valid response rate at the end of the intervention (T2), the self-report evaluation revealed that 100 percent of respondents acknowledged increased awareness of historical trauma and improved understanding of the trauma response, experienced the intervention as helpful with grief resolution, and indicated more positive feelings about themselves and about being Lakota. We used a semantic differential instrument (Osgood, Suci, & Tannenbaum, 1957/1978) for several concepts to conduct t tests for paired samples for the analysis of the change over time. At T2, ratings of "My True Self" were more positive (P = .004, $p < .01$), more potent (P = .035, p < .05), and more active (P = .006, p < .01). The American Indian holocaust (P = .000, p < .0001), which underwent the most significant change in all of the data, was more potent and more active (P = .012, p < .05) than before intervention, suggesting that it increased participants' awareness of Lakota traumatic history as a component of their current grief and psychic pain (Brave Heart, 1998; Brave Heart, 1999a). Further, sharing trauma and grief with other Lakota in a culturally traditional context provided cathartic relief. Study results revealed a decrease in negative evaluation of trauma concepts despite their increase in potency and activity coupled with an overall decrease in negative affects and an increase in positive affects over the course of the intervention (Brave Heart, 1998; Brave Heart, 1999a). The Lakota ceremonies incorporated throughout the intervention provided a safe, culturally syntonic milieu that facilitated abreaction and catharsis, fostering enhanced self-esteem, efficacy, and trauma mastery.

On the basis of this study, it appears that this model intervention for Lakota grief and trauma resolution, utilizing a culturally syntonic modality over a time-limited period, (1) provides a container and holding environment for powerful affects and testimonies, enabling the retrieval of dissociated traumatic memory (Danieli, 1989; Koller, Marmar, & Kansas, 1992), (2) optimizes the probability of successful completion, thereby fostering a sense of mastery, and (3) integrates affects and cognitions about the trauma while imparting a sense of self-control (Koller, Marmar, & Kansas, 1992; van der Kolk, 1987). The success of

this early intervention led to its incorporation and extension in a Lakota parenting curriculum also developed by Brave Heart (Brave Heart, 1999b).

Oyate Ptayela

A Lakota parenting curriculum focusing on parental healing from historical trauma and fostering a cathexis to traditional values in order to improve parenting and arrest the generational transfer of historical trauma has been qualitatively evaluated (Brave Heart, 1999b). Based upon the overwhelmingly positive response to the historical trauma intervention model, this curriculum was designed to address trauma with parents in a pilot site on a Lakota reservation. The indigenous Lakota view of parenting is the underpinning for the curriculum, with the sacred child at the center.

The sacredness of children, coupled with the *Woope Sakowin* (Seven Sacred Laws), forms the foundation for the curriculum, which is now being expanded. Embedded in traditional Lakota concepts, the first version of the curriculum is divided into four modules, four being a sacred number. There are seven sessions in keeping with the seven Lakota bands (Hunkpapa, Oglala, Sicangu, etc.), the seventh generation (the youth of today), and the need to heal so that the next seven generations of Lakota can live. Module 1 objectives are to increase awareness of historical trauma and its impact upon parenting and to introduce the *Woope Sakowin*—the embodiment of Lakota values and prescriptions for proper traditional behavior and decision-making, including parenting.

A modified version of the historical trauma healing intervention (Brave Heart-Jordan, 1995), Module I takes place in the Black Hills, the sacred center of the Lakota universe. This module incorporates (1) stimulation of generational traumatic memories with opportunities for abreaction as well as catharsis, (2) an emphasis on recathexis to the *Woope Sakowin,* and (3) facilitation of communal connection based on the indigenous construct of the *tiospaye* (Brave Heart, 1999b) in a psychoeducational group experience. Modules II through IV then occur at a reservation parent-child center, one night each week for 2 hr, conducted by two parent facilitators selected by the community and trained by the curriculum designers. Module II learning objectives include the internalization of the *Woope Sakowin* and strengthening the *tiospaye.* Module III focuses on Lakota child development, reinforcing the sacredness of children, and Module IV imparts Lakota-centric parenting skills, informed by traditional Lakota thinking about development and the *Woope Sakowin.*

The first version of the curriculum was delivered and qualitatively evaluated (Brave Heart, 1999b). Ten reservation Lakota parents from various socioeconomic and educational levels, ranging in age from late 20s to mid 60s, were recommended by the local school parent committee. Data were culled from: (1) a focus group with structured interview questions about parental experience of the curriculum, which was audiotaped; (2) field notes; and (3) an oral and written evaluation conducted by two parent facilitators at a separate interval from the focus group. The data were inductively analyzed for salient categories emerging from the data (Patton, 1990) using a constant comparative method (Strauss & Corbin, 1990).

Parents unequivocally reported a perceived positive impact of the curriculum upon their parenting and expressed an appreciation of Module I for its approach to historical trauma and its emphasis on the *Woope Sakowin.* Major emergent themes included the impact of historical trauma on parenting as well as transformation in parenting and recathexis to traditional Lakota values embodied in the *Woope Sakowin* (Brave Heart, 1999b). Parents reported increased cognizance of the generational effects of boarding school attendance and increased their communication about boarding school trauma with relatives and community members. Awareness of parenting behavior as well as attitudes toward the parental role improved after participating in the curriculum. As one parent noted: "My role and responsibility to keep the children sacred are to remain patient, to trust, to listen, to assist, and to be a better parent" (Brave Heart, 1999a). The need to focus on self-healing in order to become better parents, encapsulated in Module I—the historical trauma intervention— was reiterated by parents in the evaluation. Parents also described being more cognizant of their children from a traditional Lakota perspective: "I started telling this to my kid. I've brought the curriculum home to her . . . just taking the time and listening. . . . We tend to forget how sacred our children really are" (Brave Heart, 1999b). Moreover, parents observed improved relationships with their children.

Despite their residence in a traditionally oriented reservation district, participants were amazed by their lack of knowledge about traditional Lakota culture yet, somewhat paradoxically, also by its familiarity when it was presented to them. They also noted that they had started to use the Lakota language more with their children since their participation in the intervention. Parents were awed by the beauty of Lakota values and found that the curriculum affected their interactions with their children and grandchildren, making them more conscious of enacting the *Woope Sakowin* daily. One participant summed this up by saying: "I was raised in Indian country all my life and there's so much in the curriculum that I've learned myself and it showed me how beautiful our culture was and what we had to offer" (Brave Heart, 1999b). Other parents echoed this sentiment:

> My favorite stuff is the Seven Laws of the Lakota because when we discussed this, we didn't know these laws and we're all Lakota. . . . What stuck in my mind is that if we live by these laws then everything would be different, we'd all be living in harmony. To me, that's the traditional way to live . . . so Lakota families can be born and raised with our own Lakota values. . . . And be the strong Lakota nation that we're supposed to be. (Brave Heart, 1999b).

A by-product of the curriculum was a perceived sense of empowerment among participants and stronger communal relationships with each other, with their *tiospayes,* and within the community. That viewpoint is reflected in these words, which connect the positive impact that Lakota traditional values can make upon parenting and the general community:

> I think all of us took our children for granted, but when you look at children in this way, . . . that they are all sacred, it's good. I think the curriculum needs to be shared throughout the community, it needs to be ongoing . . . we started with a greeting. . . . We all told each other things and built community. (Brave Heart, 1999b)

Another parent continued: "We became a family here. I think that was part of the magic that developed in the training, we became empowered . . . [the Seven Laws] helped us be supportive of each other . . . grow closer. We really are a family" (Brave Heart, 1999b).

Enriched connections outside the parent group and increased involvement within the community at large were also expressed. "I found myself getting to know my relatives and going out to celebrations. . . . I found that being in this program gave me an awareness of how important these relatives are and how important being a part of the community is" (Brave Heart, 1999b). The increased social support and communal sanction for traditional Lakota values, which include placing the child at the center of a spiritually grounded, non–substance-using environment, appear to improve parenting skills and to generate support for children from the *tiospaye* and the *ospaye.* Future research is being designed to modify and expand the curriculum and involve these Lakota parents as community consultants.

The Takini Network: Continued Healing from Historical Trauma

The Takini (Survivor) Network, a collective of Lakota traditional spiritual leaders and service providers, formed in *Paha Sapa* in 1992 to address healing from historical trauma (Brave Heart, 1998; Brave Heart-Jordan, 1995). With encouragement from the Jewish Holocaust survivor community, the Takini Network is conducting prevention and intervention research, community education, and community healing aimed at validating Lakota and other Native historical trauma and providing forums for native peoples to begin to confront the traumatic past. The Takini Network is currently revising and expanding the Lakota parenting curriculum and is targeting several Lakota reservations for a more in-depth study of the curriculum's effectiveness. Takini Network faculty, trained in the historical trauma intervention model, are conducting community education on reservations in the Dakotas as well as Montana, New Mexico, Oklahoma, the Northwest, New Jersey, and Canada. The Takini Network is committed to developing further collaborative Lakota-centric research with the parents who have already gone through the first curriculum as parent leaders in breaking the generational cycle of the trauma response.

The tasks of the Takini Network are sacred; they are based on the traditional values in the face of the traumatic history of native peoples. The work is painful yet empowering. The Takini Network dedicates its efforts to the *Oyate* (the People or Nation), including the next seven generations, *hecel lena oyate kin nipi kte* (so that our people may live). The hope of the Takini Network is perhaps best expressed in the following observation, which summarizes the centrality of parenting in addressing the injuries of historical trauma among the Lakota:

> There is really no word for parenting in Lakota. The closest way to say it is *Oyate Ptayela,* which really means taking care of the Nation. And I think that's what it's going to take—we're going to have to rebuild the nation. That is our task. That is our challenge—*Oyate ptayela!* (Brave Heart, 1999b, p. 124)

Conclusion

This overview of the sociocultural context of American Indian infant mental health has emphasized the importance of appreciating American Indian and Alaska Native cultures and the strengths that they continue to provide for dealing with the problems and difficulties that confront parents and children in Indian and Native communities. While it has also been our goal to document the many struggles that our people confront, we hope that readers of this chapter will not lose sight of the fact that Indian and Native people have survived despite these problems and that we are committed to taking care of our children in ways that are consistent with our values and traditions. *Oyate ptayela!*

Notes

1. The majority of the material we discuss is concerned with the native peoples living in the lower 48 states of the United States, who are commonly referred to and refer to themselves as American Indian or Indian. Where appropriate, though, we also include material from Alaska, where the indigenous inhabitants are commonly referred to and refer to themselves as Alaska Natives. And, in one case, we include a study of the Maya, who are native to Mexico and Central America. We use "native people" as a cover term for all of these groups. While *Native American* has currency in some circles, it is important to remember that this is a political designation that refers to all indigenous peoples living within in the United States—a country whose territorial boundaries also include Pacific Island populations. We avoid *Native American* here because discussion of issues affecting the people of the Pacific takes us outside the cultural area of North America and beyond the scope of this chapter and our expertise.

2. The use of first person plural here reflects the native voice of Maria Yellow Horse Brave Heart and is intended to emphasize her connections with and commitment to native people. It also reflects our hope that Indian and Native people will find that this chapter speaks to them in their efforts to address the challenges confronting parents and children in their communities. It is not, however, meant to imply an Indian identity for Paul Spicer, who is not affiliated with any American Indian or Alaska Native group.

3. The Maya's reluctance to interfere in a child's development may also reflect respect for the child's spirit and sacredness. Among the Lakota, this is manifest in a certain degree of permissiveness with children.

4. The Indian Health Service provides care to American Indian and Alaska Native people throughout the United States. These national services are organized into 12 regional administrative units called Area Offices. These are located in Aberdeen, South Dakota; Alaska; Albuquerque, New Mexico; Bemidji, Minnesota; Billings, Michigan; California; Nashville, Tennessee; the Navajo Nation; Oklahoma City, Oklahoma; Phoenix, Arizona; Portland, Oregon; and Tucson, Arizona.

References

Bachman, R. (1992). *Death and violence on the reservation.* Westport, CT: Auburn House.

Brave Heart, M. Y. H. (1998). The return to the sacred path: Healing the historical trauma and historical unresolved grief response among the Lakota. *Smith College Studies in Social Work, 68*(3), 287–305.

Brave Heart, M. Y. H. (1999a). Gender differences in the historical trauma response among the Lakota. *Journal of Health and Social Policy, 10,* 1–21.

Brave Heart, M. Y. H. (in press). *Wakiksuyapi:* Carrying the historical trauma of the Lakota. *Tulane Studies in Social Welfare.*

Brave Heart, M. Y. H. (1999b). *Oyate Ptayela:* Rebuilding the Lakota Nation through addressing historical trauma among Lakota parents. *Journal of Human Behavior in the Social Environment.* Reprinted in H. Weaver (Ed.), *Voices of First Nations people: Considerations for human services* (pp. 109–126). New York: Haworth.

Brave Heart-Jordan, M. Y. H. (1995). *The return to the Sacred Path: Healing from historical trauma and historical unresolved grief among the Lakota.* Doctoral dissertation, Northampton, MA: Smith College School for Social Work, 1995; (copies available through the Takini Network, c/o the author, University of Denver Graduate School of Social Work, 2148 S. High St., Denver, CO 80208)

Bureau of Indian Affairs. (1998). Answers to frequently asked questions. Retrieved October 6, 1998, from the World Wide Web: http://www.doi.gov/bia/aitoday/q_and_a.html

Callaghan, J. W. (1981). A comparison of Anglo, Hopi, and Navajo mothers and infants. In T. M. Field, A. M. Sostek, P. Vietze, & P. H. Leiderman (Eds.), *Culture and early interactions* (pp. 115–147). Hillsdale, NJ: Erlbaum.

Champagne, D. (1994). Change, continuity, and variation in Native American societies as a response to conquest. In W. B. Taylor & F. Pease G. Y. (Eds.), *Violence, resistance, and survival in the Americas: Native Americans and the legacy of conquest* (pp. 208–225). Washington, DC: Smithsonian Institution Press.

Chisholm, J. S. (1981). Residence patterns and the environment of mother-infant interaction among the Navajo. In T. M. Field, A. M. Sostek, P. Vietze, & P. H. Leiderman (Eds.), *Culture and early interactions* (pp. 3–19). Hillsdale, NJ: Erlbaum.

Chisholm, J. S. (1983). *Navajo infancy: An ethological study of child development.* Hawthorne, NY: de Gruyter.

Danieli, Y. (1989). Mourning in survivors and children of survivors of the Nazi Holocaust: The role of group and community modalities. In D. R. Dietrich & P. C. Shabad (Eds.), *The problem of loss and mourning: Psychoanalytic perspectives* (pp. 427–457). Madison, CT: International Universities Press.

DeBruyn, L. M., Lujan, C. C., & May, P. A. (1992). A comparative study of abused and neglected American Indian children in the Southwest. *Social Science and Medicine, 35*(3), 305–315.

Dennis, W. (1940). *The Hopi Child.* New York: Wiley.

Eitinger, L., & Strom, A. (1973). *Mortality and morbidity after excessive stress: A follow-up investigation of Norwegian concentration camp survivors.* New York: Humanities Press.

Erikson, E. H. (1950). *Childhood and society.* New York: Norton.

Felsen, I., & Erlich, S. (1990). Identification patterns of offspring of Holocaust survivors with their parents. *American Journal of Orthopsychiatry, 60,* 506–520.

Fogelman, E. (1991). Mourning without graves. In A. Medvene (Ed.), *Storms and rainbows: The many faces of death* (pp. 25–43). Washington, DC: Lewis Press.

Gaskins, S. (1996). How Mayan parental theories come into play. In S. Harkness & C. M. Super (Eds.), *Parents' cultural belief systems: Their origins, expressions, and consequences* (pp. 345–363). New York: Guilford.

Goodluck, C. T. (1993). Social services with Native Americans: Current status of the Indian Child Welfare Act. In H. M. Pipes (Ed.), *Family ethnicity: Strength in diversity* (pp. 217–226). Newbury Park, CA: Sage.

Gorer, G. (1949). Some aspects of the psychology of the people of Great Russia. *American Slavic and East European Review, 8,* 155–160.

Gorer, G., & Rickman, J. (1949). *The people of Great Russia.* London: Cresset.

Harber, K. D., & Pennebaker, J. W. (1992). Overcoming traumatic memories. In S. A. Christianson (Ed.), *The handbook of emotion and memory: Research and theory* (pp. 359–386). Hillsdale, NJ: Erlbaum.

Herman, J. L., & van der Kolk, B. A. (1987). Traumatic origins of borderline personality disorder. In B. A. van der Kolk (Ed.), *Psy-*

chological trauma (pp. 111–126). Washington, DC: American Psychiatric Press.

Hoxie, F. E. (1989). *A final promise: The campaign to assimilate the Indians, 1880–1920*. Cambridge, MA: Harvard University Press.

Indian Health Service (1997). *Regional differences in Indian health*. Washington, DC: U.S. Department of Health and Human Services.

Keehn, R. J. (1980). Follow-up studies of World War II and Korean Conflict prisoners: Mortality to January 1, 1976. *American Journal of Epidemiology, 3*, 194–202.

Kehoe, A. B. (1992). *North American Indians: A comprehensive account* (2nd ed.). Englewood Cliffs, NJ: Prentice Hall.

Kestenberg, J. S. (1990). Survivor parents and their children. In M. S. Bergmann & M. E. Jucovy (Eds.), *Generations of the Holocaust* (pp. 83–102). New York: Columbia University Press. (Original work published 1982)

Kestenberg, J. S. (1989). Transposition revisited: Clinical, therapeutic, and developmental considerations. In P. Marcus & A. Rosenberg (Eds.), *Healing their wounds: Psychotherapy with Holocaust survivors and their families* (pp. 67–82). New York: Praeger.

Kluckhohn, C., & Leighton, D. (1974). *The Navaho*. Cambridge, MA: Harvard University Press.

Koller, P., Marmar, C. R., & Kansas, N. (1992). Psychodynamic group treatment of post-traumatic stress disorder in Vietnam veterans. *International Journal of Group Psychotherapy, 42*(2), 225–246.

Kunitz, S. J., & Levy, J. E. (1994). *Drinking careers: A twenty-five year study of three Navajo populations*. New Haven, CT: Yale University Press.

Le Vine, R. A., Dixon, S., LeVine, S., Richman, A., Leiderman, P. H., Keefer, C. H., & Brazelton, T. B. (1996). *Child Care and Culture: Lessons from Africa*. Cambridge, MA: Cambridge University Press.

Lipton, E., Steinschneider, A., & Richmond, J. (1965). Swaddling: A child care practice: Historical, cultural, and experimental observations. *Pediatrics, 35*, 519–567.

Lujan, C., DeBruyn, L. M., May, P. A., & Bird, M. E. (1989). Profile of abused and neglected children in the Southwest. *Child Abuse and Neglect, 13*, 449–461.

MacGregor, G. (1975). *Warriors without weapons*. Chicago: University of Chicago Press.

Manson, S., Beals, J., O'Nell, T., Piasecki, J., Bechtold, D., Keane, E., & Jones, M. (1996). Wounded spirits, ailing hearts: PTSD and related disorders among American Indians. In A. J. Marsella, M. J. Friedman, E. T. Gerrity, & R. M. Scurfield (Eds.), *Ethnocultural Aspects of Posttraumatic Stress Disorder* (pp. 255–283). Washington, DC: American Psychological Association Press.

Matheson, L. (1996). The Politics of the Indian Child Welfare Act. *Social Work, 41*(2), 232–235.

May, P. A. (1989). Alcohol abuse and alcoholism among American Indians: An overview. In T. D. Watts & R. Wright (Eds.), *Alcoholism in minority populations* (pp. 95–119). Springfield, IL: Charles C. Thomas.

May, P. A. (1992). Alcohol policy considerations for Indian reservations and border-town communities. *American Indian and Alaska Native Mental Health Research, 4*(3), 5–59.

May, P. A. (1996). Overview of alcohol abuse epidemiology for American Indian populations. In G. D. Sandfur, R. R. Rundfuss, & B. Cohen (Eds.), *Changing numbers, changing needs: American Indian demography and public health* (pp. 235–261). Washington, DC: National Academy Press.

Morrissette, P. J. (1994). Holocaust of First Nations people: Residual effects on parenting and treatment implications. *Contemporary Family Therapy: An International Journal, 16*(5), 381–392.

Nagata, D. (1991). Transgenerational impact of the Japanese-American internment: Clinical issues in working with children of former internees. *Psychotherapy, 28*(1), 121–128.

Nefzger, M. D. (1970). Follow-up studies of World War II and Korean War prisoners: Study plan and mortality findings. *American Journal of Epidemiology, 91*(2), 123–138.

Niederland, W. G. (1988). The clinical after effects of the Holocaust in survivors and their offspring. In R. L. Braham (Ed.), *The psychological perspectives of the Holocaust and of its aftermath* (pp. 45–52). New York: Columbia University Press.

Osgood, C. E., Suci, G. J., & Tannenbaum, P. H. (1978). *The measurement of meaning.* Urbana, IL, & Chicago: University of Illinois Press. (Original work published 1957)

Patton, M. Q. (1990). *Qualitative evaluation and research methods* (2nd ed.). Newbury Park, CA: Sage.

Piasecki, J. M., Manson, S. M., Biernoff, M. P., Hiatt, A. B., Taylor, S. S., & Bechtold, D. W. (1989). Abuse and neglect of American Indian children: Findings from a survey of federal providers. *American Indian and Alaska Native Mental Health Research, 3,* 43–62.

Quinton, D., & Rutter, M. (1985). Parenting behavior of mothers raised "in care." In A. R. Nicol (Ed.), *Longitudinal studies in child psychology and psychiatry* (pp. 157–201). New York: Wiley.

Quinton, D., & Rutter, M., & Liddle, C. (1984). Institutional rearing, parenting difficulties, and marital support. *Psychological Medicine, 14,* 107–124.

Rabin, D. L., Barnett, C. R., Arnold, W. D., Freiberger, R. H., & Brooks, G. (1965). Untreated congenital hip disease: A study of the epidemiology, natural history, and social aspects of the disease in a Navajo population [Supplement]. *American Journal of Public Health, 55*(1).

Resick, P. A., & Schnicke, M. K. (1992). Cognitive processing therapy for sexual assault victims. *Journal of Consulting and Clinical Psychology, 60*(5), 748–756.

Robin, R. W., Chester, B., & Goldman, D. (1996). Cumulative trauma and PTSD in American Indian communities. In A. J. Marsella, M. J. Friedman, E. T. Gerrity, & R. M. Scurfield (Eds.), *Ethnocultural aspects of Posttraumatic Stress Disorder* (pp. 239–253). Washington, DC: American Psychological Association Press.

Rogoff, B., Mistry, J., Goncu, A., & Mosier, C. (1993). Introduction: The concepts of guided participation and cultural universals and variation. In B. Rogoff, J. Mistry, A. Goncu, & C. Mosier (Vol. Eds.), Guided participation in cultural activity by toddlers and caregivers. *Monographs of the Society for Research on Child Development, 58*(8), 1–18.

Rogoff, B., & Mosier, C. (1993). Guided participation in San Pedro and Salt Lake. In B. Rogoff, J. Mistry, A. Goncu, & C. Mosier (Vol. Eds.), Guided participation in cultural activity by toddlers and caregivers. *Monographs of the Society for Research on Child Development, 58*(8), 59–101.

Rutter, M., & Quinton, D. (1984). Long-term follow-up of women institutionalized in childhood: Factors promoting good functioning in adult Life. *British Journal of Developmental Psychology, 2,* 191–204.

Rutter, M., Quinton, D., & Liddle, C. (1983). Parenting in two generations: Looking backwards and looking forwards. In N. Madge (Ed.), *Families at risk* (pp. 60–98). London: Heinemann Educational.

Sigal, J., & Weinfeld, M. (1989). *Trauma and rebirth: Intergenerational effects of the Holocaust.* New York: Praeger.

Silver, S. M., & Wilson, J. P. (1988). Native American healing and purification rituals for war stress. In J. P. Wilson, Z. Harel, & B. Kahana (Eds.), *Human adaptation to extreme stress: From the Holocaust to Vietnam* (pp. 337–355). New York: Plenum.

Spicer, P. (1997). Toward a (dys)functional anthropology of drinking: Ambivalence and the American Indian experience with alcohol. *Medical Anthropology Quarterly, 11,* 306–323.

Spicer, P. (1998a). Narrativity and the representation of experience in American Indian discourses about drinking. *Culture, Medicine, and Psychiatry, 22,* 139–169.

Spicer, P. (1998b). Drinking, foster care, and the intergenerational continuity of parenting in an urban Indian community. *American Indian Culture and Research Journal, 22,* 335–360.

Spicer, P., & Fleming, C. (in press). American Indian children of alcoholics. In H. E. Fitzgerald, B. M. Lester, & B. Zuckerman (Eds.), *Children of Addiction.* New York: Guilford.

Strauss, A., & Corbin, J. (1990). *Basics of qualitative research: Grounded theory procedures and techniques.* Newbury Park, CA: Sage.

Tanner, H. (1982). *A history of all the dealings of the United States government with the Sioux.* Unpublished manuscript, D'Arcy McNickle Center for the History of the American Indian, Newberry Library, Chicago.

Ursano, R. J., Grieger, T. A., & McCarroll, J. E. (1996). Prevention of posttraumatic stress: Consultation, training, and early treatment. In B. A. van der Kolk, A. C. McFarlane, & L. Weisaeth (Eds.), Traumatic stress: The effects of overwhelming experience on mind, body, and society (pp. 441–462). New York: Guilford.

Utley, R. M. (1993). *The lance and the shield: The life and times of Sitting Bull.* New York: Henry Holt & Co.

van der Kolk, B. A., McFarlane, A. C., & Weisaeth, L. (Eds.). (1996). *Traumatic stress: The effects of overwhelming experience on mind, body, and society.* New York: Guilford.

van der Kolk, B. A., McFarlane, A. C., & van der Hart, O. (1996). A general approach to treatment of Posttraumatic Stress Disorder. In B. A. van der Kolk, A. C. McFarlane, & L. Weisaeth (Eds.), Traumatic stress: The effects of overwhelming experience on mind, body, and society (pp. 417–440). New York: Guilford.

van der Kolk, B. A. (1987). *Psychological trauma.* Washington, DC: American Psychiatric Press.

Vestal, S. (1957). *Sitting Bull: Champion of the Sioux.* Boston: Houghton/Mifflin. (Original work published 1932)

Wardi, D. (1992). *Memorial candles: Children of the Holocaust.* New York: Routledge. (Original work published 1990)

Westermeyer, J. (1973). Indian powerlessness in Minnesota. *Society, 10,* 45–52.

Westermeyer, J. (1979a). Ethnic identity problems among ten Indian patients. *International Journal of Social Psychology, 25,* 188–197.

Westermeyer, J. (1979b). The apple syndrome in Minnesota: A complication of racial-ethnic discontinuity. *Journal of Operational Psychology, 10,* 134–140.

Wounded Knee remembered. (1990, December). *The Lakota Times* (Special Edition).

7

The Sociocultural Context of Infant Mental Health in the People's Republic of China

Rowena Fong

7

Introduction

Infant mental health in the People's Republic of China is a major concern to professionals, political activists, and parents and continues to receive worldwide public attention. Human rights watchers have documented maltreatment practices, largely with female infants, particularly since 1979, when a national family limitation program began. Chinese officials and China scholars, on the other hand, have refuted reports of large numbers of infants in orphanages dying from neglect and malnutrition (Spaeth, 1996).

Reports of mortality rates in orphanages cite ranges from 59.2 percent to 72.5 percent in certain provinces of China (Human Rights Watch, 1996). Even China's best-known orphanage, the Shanghai Children's Welfare Institute, estimated mortality rates as high as 90 percent in the late 1980s and early 1990s (Human Rights Watch, 1996). These claims are largely due to the repercussions of the single-child policy implemented in 1979, which limited Chinese families to having only one child due as a population control measure. However, since the 1992 passage of the Adoption Law, major efforts have been made to facilitate foreign adoptions as a means of saving maltreated infants.

Investigations of child maltreatment, mostly neglect and starvation as factors in developmental delays, continue to be problematic for American adoptive parents, who have virtually no access to Chinese biological parents or agency adoption records. The infants they have adopted face possible biological, mental health, and parenting risk factors, such as developmental delays, inappropriate attachment and bonding, and lack of parental stimulation (Johnson, 1993; Riley, 1997).

The mental health of female infants in the People's Republic of China is threatened by continued sexist attitudes and practices, despite efforts to promote unbiased population control measures in the past 20 years (Croll, Davin, & Kane, 1985; Fong, 1990; Riley, 1997). Recent reports from the Human Rights Watch in China alert the world that China, particularly since the implementation of the 1979 single-child policy, continues to treat female children and infants in a manner that jeopardizes their mental health and very existence. This population control policy has caused unexpected repercussions in

China's field of infant and child mental health and child development. Female infanticide and the spoiling of indulged only children, who had problems with obesity and overachievement, alarmed child development experts in the 1980s. Concerns for spoiling and indulgence of only children brought about significant revisions of curricula and practices in the fields of early childhood education and child development in the 1980s and early 1990s (Fong, 1990). Since the mid-1990s infant mental health and the growing concerns for neglect and abandonment have led human rights activists, adoption workers, and social service providers, especially mental health and physical disability specialists, to be aware of the special needs infants being adopted from China. Future interventions in postadoption and special needs will be important for Chinese children and their American adoptive families to survive whatever mental health problems arise (Johnson, 1993).

It is critical that mental health professionals have a contextual understanding of how China developed these severe infant mental health problems within the last two decades. This understanding can be achieved using a theoretical framework that examines the social environment and its impact on the functioning of the individual and his or her family. Urie Bronfenbrenner's (1979) theoretical model of ecology and the impact of the social environment is useful in analyzing and explaining Chinese society and its effect upon infant mental health. Bronfenbrenner's four-level model has been modified in social work to create an ecological model, also

known as the "person-in-environment" (Zastrow & Kirst-Ashman, 1987), which examines the issues from three levels of systems: macro, mezzo, and micro.

The macro level explains attitudes of Chinese society toward mental health issues and particularly toward the female sex. The mezzo level analyzes the changes in and the functioning of the single-child family—a drastic change in composition of the traditional family and functions of family members. The traditionally large extended Chinese family system still operates in other Chinese societies such as Hong Kong and Taiwan, but is quite in contrast to the single-child family, where the limitation on the number of children per family severely restricts family dynamics. The micro level examines the issues of the infant and the mental health problems that originate from a policy designed to limit population growth that has had dire consequences for females. The result has been a regression to attitudes reminiscent of feudal China, where female children were considered undesirable because they could not carry on the family name or appease the ancestors.

This chapter reviews the issues of infant mental health in China and the problems resulting from the 1979 single-child policy. The sociocultural context of the 1979 single-child policy is presented in order to explain the social and political environment of China as it affects infant mental health. A theoretical framework of the ecological model explains macro, mezzo, and micro levels of understanding societal attitudes and practices, family functioning, and infant mental health problems. Discussions about clinical implications are given, exploring risk and protective factors related to maltreatment issues, such as female infanticide, neglect, abandonment, and special needs of infants.

Theoretical Framework

It is important to have a theoretical framework to understand the sociocultural context of infants and their caregivers, as noted in the literature (Bronfenbrenner, 1986; Coll & Meyer, 1993; Fong, 1994; Le Vine, 1977; Sameroff, 1993; Whiting, 1977). Sameroff (1993) stresses the importance of viewing individual transactions as they are embedded in broader social influences. These social influences can be extended from the macro level of society to the micro level of the individual. In the case of the Chinese, the fate of infants in orphanages needs to be viewed in light of the single-child policy and the history of preferring males to females. The likelihood that a female infant will survive and enjoy good mental health is determined by adoption laws, the individual child's health, and the orphanage staff's judgment of the infant's chance of adoption. In the long run, however, a key factor is the Chinese societal attitude toward human rights for female infants and children.

Bronfenbrenner (1979) presented an ecological model or a systems theory, examining social environments as they affect individual development in three different types of systems: mesosystem, chronosystem, and exosystem. To understand the situation of China's abandoned children, Bronfenbrenner's expanded ecological model in social work, person-in-environment, will be presented in order to explain the context of the past and present impact of the social environments upon the mental health functioning of infants in the era of the single-child policy. The person-in-environment emphasis (Zastrow & Kirst-Ashman, 1987) focuses on the macro, mezzo, and micro systems in social environments. The macro system includes cultures, communities, organizations, and institutions. The mezzo system consists of families and groups. The micro system focuses on the individual. Fong (1994) asserts that in examining the social environments of some Asian cultures, such as the People's Republic of China, it is important to adopt a framework starting at the macro level of culture and communities to explain the impact of the mezzo level of family upon the functioning of the micro level individual system. In other words, to understand the abandonment of a female infant in China, professionals must understand the role of the family as it implements macro level policies reflecting historical societal attitudes toward women and female children.

The ecological framework is able to examine Chinese society in the era of the single-child policy, which has drastically changed the attitudes of the society, the functioning of the family, and the fate of female infants. The person-in-environment theoretical framework will be discussed from a macro level perspective—societal attitudes and practices toward female infants in the context of a Chinese paternalistic society based on Confucianism. The

Chinese societal attitude toward mental health is also important to consider at the macro level. The belief that poor mental health is due to dysfunctional family relationships implicates any parent-daughter relationship since Confucian ideals were based on the emperor-subject and father-son relationships. Finally, at the macro level, societal policies that are implemented to address a social problem, such as overpopulation, often create other social problems, such as female infanticide. This results from implementation of an inherently biased social policy in the historical and political context of a sexist society. The social policy is passed and implemented, like the single-child policy, but it dictates practices that have contributed to the unfair treatment of female infants.

At a mezzo level perspective, it is important to understand the Chinese family system and the changes made between traditional, feudalistic times and the era of the single-child policy when the Chinese family unit was conceptually and in practice drastically altered. Family size and the roles and functions of family members varied not only over time but by geographical location. For example, historically the nature of the mother-infant relationship was dependent upon the sex of the child. The children who were cared for best, and thus those most likely to experience positive mental health, were highly favored sons. Despite strong propaganda efforts to ensure that daughters were just as valued as sons, the single-child policy caused families of Mao's revolution to rethink the ideology that girls were equal to boys and "women held up half the sky" (Women of

China, 1985). Thus rural families allotted only one child were desperate to have sons to farm their land and take care of the parents and grandparents in their old age. Some rural areas were without a social security system, so the preference for sons increased and the disregard for female infants increased, making female infants highly vulnerable to abuse or neglect.

At the micro level, the only-child phenomenon has reduced the existence of female infants and girls to the level seen in feudal times, when females were expendable. The sexism that currently prevails threatens the existence of female infants, as evidenced by the recent reports of neglect and maltreatment. The person-in-environment theoretical framework explains risk conditions and protective factors in terms of the social environment of these infants, starting with the macro level of societal attitudes and practices, which at no point in time ever entirely removed the risk factor for any female since China culturally, historically, and even contemporaneously is a paternalistic, male-dominated society favoring sons and not daughters. An in-depth discussion of these macro level societal attitudes and practices follows, preceding the discussion on risk and protective factors.

The Sociocultural Context

Macro Level: Societal Attitudes and Practices

Chinese society is an evolving society. Historical times and events have made a difference in attitudes and practices toward infant mental health issues. In traditional society, which held sway from feudal times to 1949, Confucianism prevailed and practices reflected male dominance. Mental health concerns were focused on preference for sons. Female infanticide and female adult suicide were commonplace; females were devalued because they could not carry on the family name, nor did tradition permit them to perform important rituals honoring male ancestors.

From 1949 to 1979, an era when Communism and socialist ideology prevailed, the emphasis was not on the individual or the family but on the country, putting principles and practices of valuing the socialist state first. Infant mental health was revamped with an ideology that deemed females to be "holding up half the sky," and females were as important as males. During the Communist regime of Mao Tsetung and Teng Hsiao-p'ing, China's severe overpopulation brought about a policy decision that reversed attitudes toward female infants. In 1979 China implemented the single-child policy, limiting families to having one child. The preference for sons prevailed despite Communist efforts to eradicate what was labeled feudalistic, sexist thinking. Infant mental health immediately became a concern when reports surfaced of forced abortions or female infants being drowned or abandoned (Mu, 1986; Wei, 1992–1993; "Why Female Infanticide," 1983). The initial reports caused alarm, but China assured the world that the child maltreatment was monitored and negative infant mental health was under control.

Societal attitudes toward infant mental health throughout the history of China are grounded in cultural beliefs about mental illness.

CULTURAL MEANING OF
MENTAL ILLNESS

Chinese cultural values and behavior norms as they pertain to mental illness are useful in understanding infant mental health in China. Chinese folklore attributes madness or mental illness to several possible causes (Gaw, 1993; Lin & Lin, 1981). These include lack of hormones or vitamins, diminished brain functioning, and imbalanced *yin* and *yang*. Mental illness could also be a sign of the ancestral gods' wrath, or due to some misconduct requiring corrective behaviors or thinking (Lin & Lin, 1981).

Mental illness caused Chinese families to feel shame and guilt, often resulting in disharmony among family members. There was the belief that the imbalance of the *yin* and *yang* and the wrath of the ancestral gods were connected and often pointed toward dysfunctional relationships. Because the Confucian ideal favored the father-son relationship, poor mental health or mental illness in a family was believed to implicate any female relationship, whether parent-child, husband-wife, or mother-son. Mental illness thus jeopardized women's worth and their places as family members.

SEXIST FEUDALIST VALUES
AND PRACTICES

The history of the treatment of female infants in China can be divided into three distinct historical periods: traditional China (pre-China to 1949), Maoist era (1949–1979), and the single-child policy period (1979–present). During the traditional China era, girls were perceived as worthless. It was considered appropriate to kill them as infants, to sell them as young women, or to bind their feet from early childhood to older adulthood.

The mental health of females (at all stages of life development) was at its best during the Maoist era. In changing the traditional Chinese feudalistic beliefs that female babies were worthless, the Chinese government attempted to eliminate the sex bias, at least temporarily. However, population control became a major issue in the 1980s and economic reforms militated against the practice of limiting child labor when rural families needed the manpower to survive. Thus males were preferred to females, causing rural families to violate the attempts to control an overcrowded society. In the single-child policy era, the Chinese government wanted Chinese parents to believe that an only daughter was as good as, if not better than, an only son. However, sexist, feudalistic ideology prevailed as the single-child policy slowly lost its effectiveness when population control was becoming futile.

POLICIES PROMOTING SEXISM

In 1979, the Chinese government inaugurated the single-child policy as a means to curb population growth. Vice Premier Teng Hsiao-p'ing, soon to be China's most powerful leader, in 1977 advocated a two-child policy to cut rapid population growth because of limited food, water, and natural resources. Other concerns were reduced employment, declining capital accumulation, lowered living standards, lagging educational achievements, and hindering the Four Modernizations (an economic development program for modernizing China's agricultural, industrial, military, and scientific and technological sectors; Bongaarts & Greenhalgh, 1985).

In mid-1978 the single-child policy was discussed by top policymakers as the means to curb population growth, and in 1979 it became official national policy. In an effort to enforce population control and to keep the population under 1.2 billion through the end of the twentieth century, the government of the People's Republic of China mandated that Chinese married couples could have only one child. In 1980, Party Chairman Hua Guofeng announced the goal of stabilizing the population at 1.2 billion by the end of the century. In response, the State Council "deemed it necessary to launch a crash program during the next 20–30 years calling on each couple of the dominant Han nationality [93 percent of the Chinese population] to have only one child" (Bongaarts & Greenhalgh, 1985, p. 587).

Since there was not a uniform national policy, the 1979 policy emphasized diversity: It established different regulations for cadres (government and party officials), urban residents, rural dwellers, and national minorities. The policy differed for urban and rural areas, for different provinces, and for different situations within the same province (Croll, Davin, & Kane 1985; Davin, 1990; Jowett, 1989). Urban families received a number of economic incentives to have only a single child. Each couple received a certificate, which they had to sign, entitling them to only one child. If the couple conformed to the policy, they received a bonus averaging 8 percent added to their monthly income until the child was 14 years of age. An increment was added to the pensions of parents of single children. Maternity leave was longer for the first child than for subsequent children (6 months with pay as opposed to 56 days). In Guangdong province, women who gave birth late (at age 24 or older) were given an extra 15 days of maternity leave (Hardee-Cleveland & Banister, 1988). A single child received free health care and free education through senior middle school. The child was promised preference in job placement when she or he was old enough to work (Wolf, 1985).

In rural areas the incentives were different. The family of a single child would receive a monthly nutritional or welfare allowance in cash or work points, starting either from the birth of the child or from the time a parent signed a statement of commitment to the one-child policy. In "model townships," such bonuses usually continued for an average of 5 years after the child was born. In some places, the family of a single child would be offered a single payment. Sometimes they received paid maternity leave or extra paid maternity leave. Sometimes they were allocated a private plot of land or housing as a reward for complying with the population policy. Although economic incentives were officially available to any family in compliance with the single-child policy, either in urban or rural areas, researcher Elizabeth Croll

questions the feasibility of such economic incentives, that is, "the degree to which it is practically operative, particularly the source and extent of its funding" (Croll, 1985, p. 29). It seems fairly clear that the funding of incentives has varied widely, depending on the financial resources of localities and work units that had to pay the bill.

If economic incentives might accrue to those who abided by the policy, those who failed to heed its directives risked penalties, again differing by geographic location. For example, in urban areas, if a second child was born, the single-child certificate was withdrawn, and so was the subsidy. In the rural areas, the economic disincentives, known as "excess child levies," took the form of payments due the state and the collective for the extra burdens caused by the birth of additional children (Croll, 1985, p. 30). The disincentives included a deduction of 20 percent of a couple's pay from the date when a second pregnancy was discovered. Also deducted was a set percentage of the couple's wage until the second child reached a certain age. Country parents of more than single children also suffered reductions in their grain allocation, private plots, responsibility plots, and housing land. Penalties varied from province to province, but "the shared characteristic is to treat the second or third child as if it did not exist" (Wolf, 1985, p. 244).

In 1982, the national government announced a campaign to enforce family planning, especially by carrying out "technical measures" for birth control (Hardee-Cleveland & Banister, 1988, p. 14). These efforts included an increased number of sterilizations—from 5 million in 1982 to 21 million in 1983—mandatory IUD insertions, and required abortions for unauthorized pregnancies (Hardee-Cleaveland & Banister, 1988).

Factors hindering implementation of the single-child policy included the "feudal ideas" of the people—the age-old preference for sons over daughters. Even state policies could create problems: The new Marriage Law of 1980 lowered the age of marriage to 22 years for men and 20 years for women, thereby increasing the childbearing years of the average married couple. Finally, the transfer of agricultural production responsibility from collective farm to household put a positive value on having more children. For most peasants, a larger number of children would mean more hands to work the land, which in turn would mean monetary gains for a family (Bongaarts & Greenhalgh, 1985).

Due to the lack of policy uniformity and lax policy implementation procedures, Chinese leaders in the mid-1980s renewed their emphasis on planning. In 1987, in all of China only 16.2 percent of married women of childbearing age held a one-child certificate (Jowett, 1989). This may have been due to problems with early marriage and early childbearing as well as unregistered cohabitations, all of which disrupted China's family planning and population control program. Thus in 1991 the Central Committee of the Communist Party issued a document, "Decision on Strengthening Birth Planning Work and Strictly Controlling Population Growth," which called for a guaranteed stability of birth planning and an enhancement of ef-

forts to implement the family planning policy, especially in the rural areas (Greenhalgh, Chuzhu, & Nan 1993; Hardee-Cleaveland & Banister, 1988; Lei & Xiaobing, 1992). The results were forthcoming when in 1993 Peng Peiyun, minister-in-charge of China's State Birth Planning Commission (SBPC), announced birthrates dropping to replacement levels in 1992 (Greenhalgh, Chuzhu, & Nan, 1993).

However, China still faces a serious population problem with a population of 1.3 billion expected to reside in China by the middle of the next century (Wei, 1993). Peng Peiyun, Chairman of the State Planning Commission, predicts a population of 1.5 billion by 2025 and acknowledges the importance of continuing with the family planning program. The current policy encourages late marriage, giving birth at a later age, having only one child, and large differences in time between the two children of rural couples. Chairman Peng criticizes the one-child policy as an "oversimplification" because the family planning program is generally more lenient in rural and minority areas than in urban and Han-inhabited areas (Wei, 1992–1993).

Efforts to deal with the population problem continued. In June 1997 a new child quality law was passed. It allows authorities to impose sterilization and abortion on couples who will be having a child with mental, genetic, or infectious disease (Gemini News Service, 1997). The law reflects an intolerance on disabilities in newborns. It was originally called China's Draft Eugenics Law and is now known as the Law on Maternal and Infant Health Care. This law is another form of the state enforcing implementation of unrealistic policies that ultimately penalize the female infant.

Mezzo Level: The Single-Child Family

The single-child family results from the 1979 mandate to have only one child. This family system occurs in the People's Republic of China. The traditional Chinese family system of having lots of children, especially sons, and a big extended family exists for Chinese in Taiwan, Hong Kong, the United States, and other countries. It also existed in the People's Republic of China prior to 1979.

The single-child family is the usual nuclear unit with grandparents, uncles, and aunts but with only one child. There are urban and rural differences in compliance with the single-child family policy. Urban couples have responded more favorably, motivated by extra income incentives from workplace units. Rural families were influenced by feudalistic ideology, with grandparents perpetuating the need for sons. Economic demands for extra labor allowed rural families to pay extra tax levies for second and third children. Thus family size or family composition varied in urban and rural areas. Since the implementation of the single-child policy the demographics of female and male infants have been under scrutiny; the ratio of males to females is reported to be unbalanced at 110:100. Concerns for the shortage of female marriage partners have alarmed Chinese parents whose only sons are becoming of marriage age.

The income of single-child families has doubled in urban areas, so that couples have more money to spend on their only child. Rural couples are also spending money on the excess child levies and are able to have more than one child. Chinese couples are also able to make enough money to afford sonograms to determine the sex of the child. This frequently results in the abortion of females, despite strong warnings from the government and efforts to ban such practices. Chinese law does require couples to take medical tests that show the couple to be free of genetic, mental, or infectious diseases before they marry. This law is a result of government officials' seeing the need "to improve population quality," a policy that complements the single-child policy (Gemini News Service, 1997).

Micro Level: Infant Mental Health Problems

Several problems affect infant mental health in the People's Republic of China: sexism and female infanticide, abandonment and neglect, and special needs. These issues revolve around child maltreatment concerns, which will be discussed in this section.

SEXISM AND FEMALE INFANTICIDE

In traditional China, sexism and female infanticide were widespread. The Communist regime may curb such practices, but sexist discrimination has resurfaced with the single-child policy. The Chinese government was and remains concerned that it is still very important to Chinese parents, especially in rural areas, that their only child be male:

The more babies the better and baby boys are better than baby girls. That was the age-old idea of the Chinese parents. Since the early 1970s, however, the Chinese government has put emphasis on spreading family planning awareness. Although the influence of traditional ideas is still widespread, farmers' attitudes toward the family are changing, especially in the developed district. (Mu, 1986, p. 19)

The traditional preference for boys over girls created concern during the first few years of the policy, when increased incidents of female infanticide and wife abuse cases were reported (Jowett, 1989). In April 1983 *The Economist* ran two articles on the subject: "Massacre of the Innocents" and "China's She-Baby Cull." In one, American demographer Ansley Coale calculated 250,000 deaths of Chinese baby girls since the introduction of the 1979 single child policy (*The Economist,* 1983). Also that year, a Chinese government publication, *Women of China,* printed an article titled "Why Female Infanticide Still Exists in Socialist China," which stated that female infanticide was "related to the conventional idea of male superiority" ("Why Female Infanticide," 1983).

According to this article, the abuse of wives and female babies is not restricted to the countryside: It occurs in all places, for persons of all classes. "These incidents are not confined to outlying villages in mountains, but found in cities too. They have taken place not only in worker's or peasant's family, but also Party members, cadres or even fairly high-ranking officials too" ("Why Female Infanticide," 1983). In May 1983 *People's Daily* published a letter written by 15 rural women of Anhui Province who were mothers of only daughters and received abuse from husbands and in-laws and scorn from their acquaintances ("Why Female Infanticide," 1983). Many Chinese female babies or fetuses go missing or are aborted. Nancy Riley (1995) writes about China's "missing girls" who "ought to have been born but seem not to have been" according to census counts. She alleges they are aborted female fetuses.

Thus the single-child policy has not made it easier for the Chinese daughters or mothers to feel wanted, worthwhile, or even physically safe, because the age-old preference for sons continues to exist in the minds of many Chinese people. Chinese sources report estimates of an annual loss of 230,000 to 350,000 baby girls (Leng, 1989; Tsai, 1989). However, it is noteworthy that in 1995 the Chinese government did make amniocentesis illegal in an attempt to stop the aborting of female babies.

ABANDONMENT AND NEGLECT

The recent reports of female babies being abandoned in orphanages (Johnson, 1993, 1996; Spaeth, 1996) has caused national alarm. According to a recent report by the Human Rights Watch, *Death by Default* (1996), the mortality rate in welfare institutions that cared for abandoned children was between 50 and 80 percent in 1989 and 1990. However, China expert Kay Johnson (1993) asserts that this statistic is questionable, indicating that the national policy reported by the Human Rights Watch of "routine murder of children through deliberate starvation" is based on inconclusive evidence. Johnson details explanations for the high mortality rates other than starvation and medical neglect, lack of stimulation, high infant-adult ratios, and failure to thrive syndrome. She raises the point that a high percentage of infants arrive at the Chinese orphanages extremely ill or already suffering from malnutrition or exposure. Thus the orphanage itself serves as a hospice for parents who can no longer afford high hospital bills and medical costs. Severe restrictions on domestic adoptions (childless and over 35) exacerbate the problem; eligible childless couples are hard to find. Thus in the early 1990s international adoptions opened up.

Johnson (1993, 1996) asserts that the worldwide attention that Chinese adoptions and orphanages are getting can be focused on several levels in terms of problem solving. First, more money should be put into improving and providing the medical care that infants with disabilities need; second, there should be an easing up of the strict internal domestic adoptions restrictions; third, there should be more support for the staff who work in orphanages and who are affected by the emotional toll of dealing with dying infants; and fourth, reports put out by groups like the Human Rights Watch do not support China's efforts to deal with its domestic problems. Thus closer scrutiny needs to be given to the details of accusations made about China's atrocities.

ADOPTION AND SPECIAL NEEDS INFANTS
The Adoption Law of the People's Republic of China was adopted on December 29, 1991, and became effective April 1, 1992. The law states that the following categories

of children are eligible for adoption: orphans without parents; abandoned children whose natural parents can't be found; and children whose natural parents can't provide for the child because of an unusual hardship. Under this law, Chinese citizens who are more than 35 years old and childless are eligible to adopt a healthy child.

Adoptions in China have increased significantly since 1992. In 1996 more children were adopted from China than from any other country: 56 percent of the immigrant visas in the world were given to Chinese children adopted by U.S. citizens (see Table 7.1). As of March 1997, China had 40,000 welfare institutions, including orphanages, in rural areas; 100 orphanages in urban areas; and four SOS villages that provided care for orphans. The children who are available for adoption are Chinese only children from the children's welfare institutes with the Shanghai Children's Welfare Institute as the main orphanage in China's second largest city.

The Adoption Law of the People's Republic of China states that orphans under the age of 14 may be adopted. An orphan is defined as a child whose parents are deceased, have abandoned the child, or are incapable of providing for the child because of unusual hardship. However, researcher Steven Mosher hypothesizes that Chinese infants are abandoned because of "political imperatives not because of economic necessity." Mosher reported that over 90 percent of the Chinese orphanage population consisted of abandoned infant girls. Johnson (1993) reiterates that from 1988 to 1992, over 90 percent of the orphanages were filled with girls. Mosher

TABLE 7.1
U.S. Immigrant Visas to Chinese Orphans

Year	China	Total	%
1989	201	8102	2.48
1990	29	7093	.004
1991	61	9050	.006
1992	206	6472	.031
1993	330	7377	.045
1994	787	8333	.094
1995	2130	9629	22.01
1996	3333	5951	56.01

Note. More than half the total number of immigrant visas are assigned to Chinese orphans coming to the United States. Data tabulated from *International Adoption and Child Abduction.*

draws the following conclusions regarding the impact of the single-child policy: Female fetuses are selectively aborted; newborn baby girls fall victim to infanticide; abandoned infant girls who are not killed in utero or after birth are fortunate; older daughters get cast aside after a son is born; and an earlier born handicapped child will be abandoned for a healthier one. He maintains that the abandonment of girls defeats the single-child policy's purpose. The politics of the single-child policy also defeats the original purposes of the child welfare institutes (Fong, 1997). To deny the existence of the abandonment of female babies is to maintain a facade of the zero population growth.

Mosher mentioned the Shanghai Children's Welfare Institute situation between 1988 and 1993 when Dr. Zhang Shuyun, a former staff member, reported many cases of infants dying from neglect at the orphanage. Spaeth (1996) asserts that the orphanage staff at times decided to deprive an infant or a group of infants of care. The process is called "summary resolution,"

whereby the staff agree among themselves how to keep the ward population constant—that is, when a new ward enters the orphanage, staff members eliminate an infant, who may be handicapped or selected at random. The infant is denied food, medical care, or water. The infant may be sedated or removed to the "waiting for death room" (Spaeth, 1996).

It is also reported that orphanages demand a $3,000 donation for an adopted infant (Johnson, 1993). The orphanages in China are able to increase their financial resources with the fees collected from the international social service/adoption agencies (Gemini News Service 1997). Orphanages use this money to try to improve conditions in the orphanages (Johnson, 1993), but they also use it as a factor to determine which infants will be designated to be nurtured for adoption and which infants, who are deemed unadoptable, will be neglected because of poor health or ill appearance.

Some of the infants who are designated for adoption still suffer repercussions from the neglect or less than nurturing care environment of the orphanage (Johnson, 1993). These are usually special needs infants, who are placed in overseas Chinese and non-Chinese families. As of March 1997, China is struggling to define a special needs child and the medical conditions that qualify special needs. If a couple have children from the other marriages, they probably will be eligible to adopt another child if there are no children within the current marriage. Chinese American families or families that have already adopted from China will not receive special treatment in the adoption process, which usually takes longer than 6 months. Most adopting couples need to go through an agency rather than through private efforts.

Clinical Implications

Infant maltreatment in China has become a major concern since neglect is becoming a big problem for female infants. Neglect has usually been associated with parents who were not capable of caring for the child. In China, a new neglect situation is occurring because the parents can't afford the care that a physically handicapped child requires, or the single-child policy has led parents to revert to feudalist ways of preferring sons and devaluing daughters. New discussions need to occur to examine the traditional causes of child maltreatment and the traditional risk and protective factors in infant mental health. The situation in the People's Republic of China

may be creating a need for new definitions and interventions.

Child Maltreatment

Historically, child maltreatment is usually associated with uncaring parents, parents in absentia, or a society where the status of the child is unattended and tenuous (Mrazek, 1993). The typical types of child maltreatment are: physical abuse, sexual abuse, neglect, failure to thrive, fetal abuse, drowning or near-drowning, and Munchausen syndrome by Proxy (Mrazek, 1993). Failure to thrive and neglect are the most common in China. The infants who have been abandoned to the orphanages have been neglected by their parents; once they are in the orphanages, many of the infants not designated for adoption are also neglected by the staff members, with some infants starving and failing to thrive. The effects of maltreatment are significant, but the risk factors need to be reexamined in the case of China because some are caused by culture-bound traditional ideology and practices. This would call for new interventions that are not only culturally sensitive but also designed to ameliorate any further damage to the existence of the female sex.

Risk Factors

Risk conditions for these Chinese female infants exist. Identification of these conditions as well as risk factors will be critical for the development of culturally competent interventions. In their summary of studies of high risk infants and children,

Srinath, Girimaji, and Seshadri (1992) identified seven types of variables for identifying high risk groups: psychophysiological; neurological parameters; attentional processes; cognitive-intellectual functioning; social-interpersonal functioning; clinical-affective functioning; and obstetric complications. Mrazek (1993) analyzed studies done on risk factors affiliated with child maltreatment and found the following three variables to have high correlations with risk factors: (1) negative maternal attitude toward pregnancy; (2) high levels of perceived social stress; and (3) low socioeconomic status. The same article cited a number of other reasons for child maltreatment for which there was supporting evidence: lack of financial resources; low intelligence; parents' criminal record; loss of previous child; history of child maltreatment; negative maternal traits; and absence of social support and social isolation. (Mrazek, 1993, pp. 161–162)

The risk factors correlated with infant mental health in the People's Republic of China include two listed by Mrazek: a negative maternal attitude toward pregnancy and high levels of perceived social stress. If the Chinese mother is aware that the infant will be female, she may try to abort the child in hope of another pregnancy and a son. The social stress the mother is likely to experience is the pressure to produce a son, especially if the family is rural and needs the labor or is expecting the son to carry on the family name and maintain the traditional ancestor worship.

Although studies on risk factors of child maltreatment in China are difficult to conduct, they are much needed. If they were done, the findings would likely include the following risk conditions:

1. Sex of child. The female infant is likely to be at higher risk than the male infant because of the preference for sons.
2. Physical deformities. The developmentally disabled or physically scarred infant is at higher risk; an only child is to be perfect, especially a daughter who is to be married. In some rural areas the bride is still expected to bring in a hefty marriage dowry. A physically deformed female child will not bring in the needed income of the dowry that the boy's family is expecting.
3. Geographic location. Rural areas pose higher risks of maltreatment than urban areas because the urban parents are able to make more money and have less need of extra child labor to bring in income to the family. Rural areas may not have social security systems to support families, so there is a greater need to have sons to care for aging parents.
4. Age of the child. Infant maltreatment is more likely to happen during the first trimester, especially if the child is suspected to be female. Infants are especially vulnerable to being abandoned by parents and then neglected by caretakers in the orphanage.
5. Feudalistic ideology. Infants whose parents are influenced by grandparents or others with the feudalistic preference for sons over daughters are at a higher risk for maltreatment than those in families accepting the single-child policy. In Chinese families tied to the patrilineal location of the son as the primary care-

taker of the parents, infant daughters are at higher risk of maltreatment.

6. Financial resources. Infants born to rural couples who can afford to travel to urban areas to leave the infant at an orphanage are at higher risk of being abandoned.

7. Poverty. Poor families are more likely to want to be rid of a physically deformed child or may not have the money to care for a handicapped child.

In addition to the above maltreatment risk factors, there are biological, mental health, and parenting factors to consider. The major biological risks to Chinese infants are developmental delays experienced by the infants due to neglect and malnutrition. Children can experience both biological/maturational and psychological/developmental delays. The problems are compounded in the case of orphans; often nothing is known about orphans' perinatal care because the infants were abandoned and parental knowledge of pregnancy is not made available to the orphanage caregivers in China nor to the adoptive parents in the United States. Early detection of such delays thus is impossible and intervention may not be timely. This compounds the risk factor for these children: Studies on children with developmental delays warn that those with specific developmental delays are at higher risk for developing behavior problems (Srinath, Girimaji, & Seshadri, 1992). There may also be nonorganic failure to thrive issues (Vietze et al., 1980).

Gusukuma (1997) reports adoptive American parents citing developmental delays of as much as 6 to 8 months in Chinese infants. Deprivation symptoms were obvious, such as dehydration and malnourishment. Infants have been diagnosed as having pervasive developmental delay (PDD). The American parents report that the infants seem to thrive once they are in the care of their American adoptive families. However, the long-term effects and the extent of the damage of the developmental delays are not known.

Mental health risk factors for orphans are related more to the adult-child relationship. The affective relationship with the early primary caregiver is unknown since most female infants are left at the orphanages at a very early age. The attachment and bonding to a primary caretaker is at risk since the history is unknown and not available. Gusukuma (1997) cites American adoptive parents reporting Attention-Deficit/Hyperactivity Disorder with Oppositional Defiant Disorder as problematic.

Parental risk factors lie mostly with the Chinese biological parents and not with the American adoptive parents. The lack of maternal stimulation is a risk factor. The infants may have been ignored by the Chinese mothers and in the orphanages may have experienced another nonstimulating environment, prolonging the malnutrition and starvation (Johnson, 1993). Other parenting risk factors are societal. Unless China as a country decides to combat the feudal ideas that sons are necessary for family survival, females—infants or adults—are always at risk of being devalued or being replaced (Fong, 1990; Johnson, 1993; Riley, 1997).

Protective Factors

The protective factors can best be described as applying to individuals rather than groups, with sex often the decisive factor. For orphans, the major protective factor is adoption at a very young age. The adoptive American families are reporting Chinese infants thriving under good medical care and consistent family attention (Fong & Gusukuma, 1997). Another protective factor is early abandonment to the orphanage (so there is as little time as possible for parental maltreatment) and some sort of attention to the infant by the caretaker at the orphanage.

It has been posited that in examining risk factors, protective factors can act as "buffers against the risks" (Osofsky, Hann, & Peebles, 1993, p. 112). The buffering protective factors for Chinese infants are: (1) being born male; (2) living in urban China; (3) having parents who are educated and socialized to accept the single-child policy and who are content with a female child; (4) being born healthy without physical deformities; and (5) being eligible for adoption and being adopted fairly quickly during the first year of life.

Conclusion

The future of Chinese female infants is in the hands of the Chinese government, the adoption agencies, and the adoptive parents. China has a history of maltreatment of female infants and adult women. The Confucian preference for sons has greatly inhibited the valuing of females and strongly swayed the populace toward preferring sons, despite population control efforts.

China faces an imbalance of males to females. The immediate concern is ensuring the survival of female infants through measures to monitor or prevent child maltreatment in the forms of neglect, starvation, and failure to thrive. However, male children may be suffering from more subtle problems, such as being spoiled or obese, or being overstimulated with the expectation that the only child will someday have great achievements and will care for all elderly family members.

China is in transition and needs assistance with the problems of neglected female children and overly prized male children. Allowing foreign adoptions as an intervention is only a short-term solution, and not an altogether satisfactory one. For example, American adoptive parents are concerned about the adopted infants' failure to thrive while in the orphanages and about the infant's developmental delays (Fong & Gusukuma, 1997). China needs to review the risk conditions for infants and find ways to eliminate or ameliorate them. The protective factors need to be strengthened, but this does not seem possible in the short term. At present the most promising course is not to change the Chinese negative attitudes toward female children but to get the infants to interventions, such as positive adoptive placements, as soon as possible. It is inevitable that the rates of the adoptions from China to the United States will increase.

All signs point to an increase in the number of Chinese orphans adopted by U.S.

parents. Thus it is imperative that American mental health professionals be prepared to help adoptees suffering the consequences of China's discriminative maltreatment practices. Such repercussions of China's culture-bound traditions will likely continue to be felt until interventions that take the complexities of the situation into account have been developed and implemented, and to create interventions culturally designed to cope with the complex context of China's current situation.

References

Benoit, D. (1993). Failure to thrive and feeding disorder. In C. Zeanah, Jr. (Ed.), *Handbook of infant mental health* (pp. 317–332). New York: Guilford.

Bongaarts, J., & GreenHalgh, S. (1985). An alternative to the one-child policy in China. *Population and Development Review, 11,* 585–617.

Bronfenbrenner, U. (1979). *The ecology of human nature: Experiments by nature and design.* Cambridge, MA: Harvard University Press.

China's she-baby cull. (1983, April 18). *The Economist,* p. 36.

Coll, C., & Meyer, E. (1993). The sociocultural context of infant development. In C. Zeanah, Jr. (Ed.), *Handbook of infant mental health* (pp. 56–57). New York: Guilford.

Croll, E. (1985). Introduction: Fertility norms and family size in China. In E. Croll, D. Davin, & P. Kane (Eds.), *China's one child family policy* (pp. 1–36). New York: St. Martin's.

Croll, E., Davin, D., & Kane, P. (Eds.). (1985). *China's one child family policy.* New York: St. Martin's.

Davin, D. (1985). The single child policy in the countryside. In E. Croll, D. Davin, & P. Kane. (Eds.), *China's one child family policy* (pp. 37–82). New York: St. Martin's.

Field, T. (Ed.). (1980). *High risk infants and children.* New York: Academic.

Fong, R. (1990). *China's only child: The family and the school.* Unpublished doctoral dissertation, Harvard University, Cambridge, MA.

Fong, R. (1994). Family preservation: Making it work for Asians. *Child Welfare, 53*(4), 331–341.

Fong, R. (1997). Child welfare practices with Chinese families: Assessment issues for immigrants from the People's Republic of China. *Journal of Family Social Work, 2*(1), 33–48.

Fong, R., & Gusukuma, I. (1998, March). *From policy to practice: The adoption of Chinese children by U.S. families.* Paper presented at the Council on Social Work Education Annual Program Meeting, Orlando, FL.

Gaw, A. (1993). *Culture, ethnicity, and mental illness.* Washington, DC: American Psychiatric Press.

Gemini News Service. (1997). *International Adoption-China.*

Greenhalgh, S., Chuzhu, Z., & Nan, L. (1993). *Restraining population growth in three Chinese villages: 1988–1993.* (Working paper No. 55.) New York: United Nations Population Council, Research Division.

Gusukuma, I. (1998, March). *Intercountry adoptions: Past hopes present dreams, and future promise.* Paper presented at the Council on Social Work Education Annual Program Meeting, Orlando, FL.

Hardee-Cleveland, K., & Banister, J. (1988). *Family planning in China*. Washington: United States Bureau of the Census, Center for International Research.

Human Rights Watch. (1996). *Death by default: A policy of fatal neglect in China's state orphanages*. New York: Author.

Johnson, K. (1993). Chinese orphanages: Saving China's abandoned girls. *The Australian Journal of Chinese Affairs*, No. 30, 61–87.

Johnson, K. (1996). The politics of revival of infant abandonment in China, with special reference to Hunan. *Population and Development Review, 22*(1), 77–98.

Jowett, A. (1989). Mainland China: A national one-child program does not exist. Part One. *Issues and Studies, 25*(9), 48–67.

Karhausen, M. (1997). *Children in China*. Maryknoll, NY: Orbis Books.

Lei, Z., & Xiaobing, Y. (1992, April 13–19). China's Population Policy. *Beijing Review* (pp. 17–20).

Leng, S. (1989). *Changes in China: Party, state, and society*. New York: University Press of America.

LeVine, R. (1977). Childrearing as cultural adaptation. In P. Leiderman, S. Tulkin, & A. Rosenfeld (Eds.), *Culture and infancy: Variations in the human experience* (pp. 15–27). New York: Academic.

Lin, T., & Lin, M. (1993). Love, denial, and rejection: Responses of Chinese families to mental illness. In A. Kleinman & T. Lin (Eds.), *Normal and abnormal behavior in Chinese culture* (pp. 387–401). Netherlands: D. Reidel.

Malhotra, S., Malhotra, A., & Varma, V. (1992). *Child mental health in India*. Daryagani, New Dehli, India: MacMillan India Limited.

Mrazek, P. (1993). Maltreatment and infant development. In C. Zeanah, Jr. (Ed.), *Handbook of infant mental health* (pp. 159–170). New York: Guilford.

Mu, A. (1986). A family's smallness is its strength. *Beijing Review, 29*(48), 19–20.

Riley, N. (1995). China's missing girls. *The Honolulu Advertiser*. Honolulu, HI.

Riley, N. (1997). American adoptions of Chinese girls: The socio-political matrices of individual decisions. *Women's Studies International Forum, 20*(1), 87–102.

Sameroff, A. (1993). Models of development and developmental risk. In C. Zeanah, Jr. (Ed.), *Handbook of infant mental health* (pp. 3–13). New York: Guilford.

Spaeth, A. (1996, January 22). Life and death in Shanghai. *Time International*.

Srinath, S., Girimaji, S., & Seshadri, S. (1992). High risk children: Issues related to identification and intervention. In S. Malhotra, A. Malhotra, & V. Varma (Eds.), *Child mental health in India* (pp. 121–134). Daryagani, New Dehli: MacMillan India Limited.

Tsai, W. (1989). New trends in marriage and family in mainland China: Impacts from the four modernization campaign. In S. Leng (Ed.), *Changes in China: Party, state, and society* (pp. 225–246). New York: University Press.

Vietze, P., Falsey, S., O'Connor, S., Sandler, H., Sherrod, S., & Altemeier, W. (1980). Newborn behavioral and interactional characteristics of nonorganic failure-to-thrive infants. In T. Field (Ed.), *High risk infants and children* (pp. 5–24). New York: Academic.

Why female infanticide still exists in socialist China. (1983, May 1–2). *Women of China*.

Wei, J. (1992–1993, December 28, 1992–January 3, 1993). China still facing population problem. *Beijing Review* (pp. 16–18).

Whiting, J. (1977). A model for psychocultural research. In P. Leiderman, S. Tulkin, & A. Rosenfeld (Eds.), *Culture and infancy: Variations in the human experience.* New York: Academic.

Wolf, M. (1985). *Revolution postponed: Women in contemporary China.* Stanford, CA: Stanford University Press.

Women of China. (1987). *New trends in Chinese marriage and the family.* Beijing, China: China International Book Trading Corporation.

Zastrow, C., & Kirst-Ashman, K. (1997). *Understanding human behavior and the social environment* (4th ed.). Chicago, IL: Nelson-Hall Publishers.

Zeanah, C., Jr. (Ed.). (1993). *Handbook of infant mental health.* New York: Guilford.

8

Infant Mental Health in Brazil

Salvador Celia

8

Introduction

Brazil has almost 160 million inhabitants and a large population of children and youth (50 percent), many of whom are 3 years of age and under. It is a developing country with huge contrasts: It is among the 10 largest economies in the world, yet, the greatest concentration of income is in the hands of a small percentage of the population; that is, 10 percent hold the vast majority of wealth, leading to severe social problems. Among the most significant social problems is the lack of such basics as health care, education, and housing. Inevitably it is the child population that suffers most.

Although government efforts have reduced the levels of such important indicators as child mortality, malnutrition, and illiteracy, these are still significant factors, and we are concerned about the present conditions of survival under which our children live, and the level of development they attain. For instance, we now know that U.S. and European research studies on the development of infant brains have shown the importance of actions performed during the first moments and first years of life. We have also heard about the nationwide concern of the U.S. government manifested through its famous conferences of 1997, organized by Mrs. Hillary Rodham Clinton, where it was shown that urgent interventions were necessary in integrated health, education, and social welfare plans for the purpose of prevention, in order to achieve psychoprophylaxis for good infant development.

In Brazil we are still far from having this vision of national security for the effective development of the country, since investment in childhood has proved to be the culminating point of any child-oriented primary care plan. Although we are nowhere near achieving the desired level, we will describe our vision for this subject and ongoing intervention programs that give us hopes of better times for our child population.

Having participated in various political plans (Project Vida, Project Care for Pregnant Women and Infants) and education plans (training mental health agents, pediatricians, and, lately, medical students) during the last two decades, I describe a few thoughts, research studies, and results achieved in the course of our work with a few mental health colleagues.

I begin with a basic finding, as we look at the results of the Project Vida experience and the experience at the Leo Kanner Institute when, in 1991, we began providing health care to malnourished infants in the northern area of the city of Porto Alegre, the capital of the state of Rio Grande do Sul. This is a city with a good cultural and economic level, and we found a rate of 23 percent malnourished infants in a *favela* (slum); this led us to begin an integrated care project for infants and depressed mothers. The study was presented at the WAIMH congresses in Chicago (1992) and Tampere (1996). Today we can confirm the value of the intervention program. We find that in this *favela* the rate is now around 10 percent, as compared with other neighboring populations where it is around 23 percent.

The project was developed in partnership with the local community, and with the participation of technical people such as psychiatrists, psychologists, pediatricians, social workers, nurses, nursing aides, nutritionists, and health agents. Initially all the families (300) were studied, and we found children in migrant families from rural areas who had come to the capital to seek work and better living conditions. This caught our attention because many of these families, living in exactly the same social and cultural conditions, did not have malnourished infants. In the women we found relevant psychosocial factors such as loss of roots, lack of support by the pregnant woman's partner, the presence of mistreatment in the women's life, abuse, neglect, lack of food and affection, unwished-for pregnancies, attempted abortions, early weaning, and a difference in length of exclusive breast-feeding time between the control groups and the groups of mothers with malnourished babies.

The results of the applied Beck Inventory were very important and confirmed the significant rates of maternal depression as compared with the control group. After the initial overall study of the target population, intervention strategies were established, such as building a small, modest nutrition center, a program of nutrition education for the mothers, intensive pediatric care, checking the infant's weight and height, and careful psychological help to mothers and their interactions with their babies. The attention that was given consisted of approaches such as empathetic psychotherapy and interactive guidance, which greatly contributed to the improvement of mother-infant interactions, both for individuals and groups.

The program is still ongoing under the coordination of pediatrician Dr. Carmen Nudelmann, with the support of Project Vida and the Leo Kanner Institute. In this project, when we think about the work being done and the results achieved, we can see the value of the integration capacity of different specialists in health and education with the participation of the community itself, through its leaders and institutions (neighborhood association, religious organizations, etc.).

The idea that health care involves viewing the patient as an individual, as well as an object of psychological and somatic treatment, appears fundamentally important to us, and we find that all technical persons in their specialties are essential for a well-functioning project. This political position of the professional or technical specialist in these areas does not depend solely on financial resources but also on a mentality required to avoid the great likelihood of iatrogenizing our interventions. We could exaggerate our positions at any time, for instance saying "this pertains to the psychiatrist," or to the pediatrician, or to the social worker, forgetting that, even respecting the specific areas, all are part of an ecosocial system in which forces are interactive and do not exclude each other. At other times we iatrogenize our actions even when we "fight" to see who is going to coordinate the tasks or teams, forgetting to take a good look at the position of those who are best prepared to deal with the specific topics and the teamwork.

Personal Capacitation—Projects

I now describe some of the activities performed in what I am calling my reflections on personal capacitation (personal training).

I begin with the experience of training medical students. Since 1996 I have been a professor at the medical school of the Lutheran University of Brazil, whose main campus is in Canoas, adjacent to the city of

Porto Alegre. This medical school has included in its curriculum the discipline "life cycles," which, in the first year of the course, includes studies in the infant and its world. Practically upon entering medical school, each student is made responsible for a pregnant woman or infant aged less than 1 year, to observe, assess, and study the family and its social interactions. He or she takes care of them throughout the 6 years of medical school.

Currently the new medical school and course are in their 3rd year, and the results we find are most interesting. The students mostly dedicate their attention to interaction with social problems. Consequently, they have an improved view of family interactions, and they have a greater possibility of observing and being able to act as health agents who can recognize, from early on, the risk and protective factors in these families and communities. They are visibly concerned with humanistic aspects and take an integrative view of the areas of health, education, social aspects, and citizenship. They have a better understanding of their role in preventive work, psychoprophylaxis (prevention of mental disease), and social policies, as members of a developing society.

We also include a research program in the medical program, based on a suggestion from Prof. Brazelton at the White House Conference of 1997, to make use of the vaccination day in order to check on the infants' development. In October 1997, in the small town of Canela, population 27,000, with the support of the local town administration, we began our work with a look at 200 babies up to the age of 1 on na-

tional vaccination day. At that time our students performed 10- to 15-min interviews, checking on and evaluating the infant's interaction with its caregiver during and after vaccination (checklist). We divided the sampling into three levels: Group A, 69 percent, consisting of 129 infants with good interaction; Group B, 22.7 percent, 42 infants possessing less than three items from our reference table; and Group C, 7.5 percent, 14 infants possessing severe problems at interaction. The last group became the object of special attention, and 3 months later the infants were visited at home for reassessment. We found that our initial observations were 90 percent accurate. It was most interesting that, besides confirming the first study, we found other problems in the nine families visited: malnutrition, mistreatment, alcoholism, depression in family members, and even worrisome living conditions. In addition, there was an imminent risk of accidents because the houses were located in topographically dangerous areas. The results were sent to the technical staff of the local town administration, and they began to work with us by helping to care for this needy population.

I also began to coordinate another program to train professionals in mental health, in 1980, in the Department of Health of the State of Rio Grande do Sul. At that time we invited several specialists to participate in a state project for the care of pregnant women and infants up to the age of 3, to be seen at the Medical Dispensaries of the city of Porto Alegre and in the state of Rio Grande do Sul. The program consisted of theoretical and practical seminars with supervision, in order to allow us to take care of this needy population using individual or group techniques.

The first technicians were trained and, in 1983, when they began to work in their specific fields they multiplied the interactions and skills of new technicians at a time when one did not believe in infant care and psychoprophylactic techniques. The repercussions went well beyond the borders of the state of Rio Grande do Sul, since we began to participate in the National Program for Incentive to Breast-Feeding, with the visions of bonds and interactions which formerly had not been as well developed. I believe that the program even encouraged colleagues from Uruguay, Argentina, and Chile to organize psychoprophylactic studies.

Since 1984, at the Leo Kanner institute, we have tried to stress the importance of collaborating with pediatricians at a time when it was not usual to have them participate in child psychology. Since we view pediatricians as the main preventive agents in mental health, we have been working with Dr. Bertrand Cramer to evaluate the effects of our program. The constant interchange with colleagues in Uruguay and Argentina has been very helpful in learning more about and development techniques for prevention, intervention and treatment.

Conclusion

The need to provide attention in early infancy has become increasingly obvious, especially after advances in neurobiology.

Among those advances, the evidence provided by the White House Conference (1997) that "windows of opportunity" (the period in which the main central connections are formed) close around the age of 6, and that until the age of 3 the brain is even more malleable (Shore, 1997). The need for training health care and child education professionals in early prevention is increasingly apparent for the growth of the field of developmental psychology. It is necessary to support and educate families, parents, and caregivers to act with appropriate stimulation at decisive moments (touch points) for each infant during its development. The dissemination of knowledge in families must be broadened and reinforced. In this sense, the work performed in the Canela community yielded significant results when several mothers revealed that because they received a leaflet with information regarding interactions with their baby, on how to speak, touch, sing, and dance, they felt less depressed and their babies became healthier.

Because our research indicates high rates of maternal depression and child malnourishment, we must advocate the care of pregnant women. Because more and more families take advantage of day care centers due to the growing numbers of mothers returning to work, nurseries have become highly significant for children's social and cognitive development. We must, therefore, insist on the training of infant caregivers, be it in neighborhood homes or at day care centers.

Unfortunately, educational policies in Brazil stress child development from age 6 onward, with a few regions stressing ages

3 to 6. Therefore, insufficient attention is given to day care centers. Not only are there too few day care centers, but the quality of care is also lacking within the existing centers. There is a great need to provide constant supervision of day care attendants. Often, day care attendants are not qualified or acknowledged for their work. Some attendants may be performing duties they were not employed or trained to perform. Day care workers are sometimes also depressed and therefore, like the mothers who participated in our research studies, unable to interact appropriately with the babies.

I believe that primary care programs need to be developed for medical students as well as for professionals in the related humanistic fields of psychology, social work, speech therapy, nursing, pedagogy, and law. Training in these areas will benefit not only the students but also society as a whole. The multidisciplinary view, accompanied by learning about the ecological view, may have much to contribute to the improved understanding of protective factors, risk factors, and resilience.

Because intervention programs must begin early, the possibility of using vaccination day as a point of departure for action appeared very useful to us. Children's primary schools should become involved in children's development and family lives. Secondary schools should focus more on caring for adolescents, especially girls, and teaching human sexuality courses to prevent the increasing numbers of teenage pregnancies and sexually transmitted diseases.

As shown in our community programs in the *favela*, there is a great need for the integrated care of pregnant women, individually or in groups, which should be performed more frequently to prevent problems such as postpartum depression and malnutrition.

Hospital delivery methods should be improved and humanized. The number of unnecessary cesarean sections should be decreased. The participation of family members such as the father or grandmother should be allowed and encouraged, or even as Kennel showed us (Kennel & Klaus, 1993), the presence of the *doula*. The moments of initial interactions with the babies must be privileged, and it should be stressed that in countries where the grandmother is present for supporting the new mother, there is a lower rate of postpartum depression. Breast-feeding campaigns must be intensified to facilitate bonding while being sensitive to the guilt felt by mothers who do not manage to breast-feed. Maternity leave (4 months in Brazil) and paternity leave (5 days) need to be maintained and lengthened. It should be fundamental to provide places where infants can receive appropriate care. Mothers and infants in the dispensaries and in the *favelas* should be visited, supported, and guided by health care professionals.

The ecological systemic and humanistic view of health will now allow us to take better care of low income, needy communities. Independent of the social situation, everything we know today points to the fact that we have to begin intervention techniques in early infancy in order to have a more humane society with a better quality of life.

References

Celia, S., Alves, M., Bebs, B., et al. (1992). Malnutrition and Infant Development. Paper presented at the Fifth International Congress of the WAIPAD, Chicago.

Celia, S., Santos, A. M., Krowcauk, E., et al (1983). Assistencia Materno Infantil: Analise de uma experiencia: Perspectivas. In *A criança e o adolescents brasileiro da decada de SO* (pp. 13–28). Porto Alegre, Brazil: Ed. Artes Médicas.

Kennel, J., & Klaus, M. Pais. (1993). *Bebê: A formaçâo do apego.* Porto Alegre, Brazil: Ed. Artes Médicas.

Shore, R. (1997). *Rethinking the brain: New insights into early development.* New York: Families and Work Institute.

The White House Conference on Early Childhood Development and Learning: What new research on the brain tells us about our youngest children. (1997). Washington, DC: Author.

9

Infant Mental Health in Scandinavia

Pia Risholm Mothander

9

Introduction

Child-rearing patterns differ between societies, as well as within them. Today we believe that the study of variations in infant care can improve our understanding of the relationship between cultural patterns and early personality development. The contributions to this volume constitute examples of how caregiving descriptions from different countries can add to our knowledge of early development in different contexts. Kevin Nugent (1994) at the Brazelton Scale Training Center cited three important reasons for cross-cultural research on caregiving patterns. First, it contributes to our appreciation of different child-rearing patterns across the world by challenging our assumptions about the nature of child development and opening our minds beyond the ethnocentrism so easy to adopt when belonging to or working in a homogeneous culture. Second, it reminds us that experimental controlled studies are not the only means of gathering information about child development. Third, cross-cultural studies of child development increase our awareness of the cultural bias in our assessment tools and intervention programs and underline the importance of questioning each method or tool in the light of the cultural background of the children and families they are to serve.

Cross-cultural studies of the belief systems dealing with child-rearing practices are of interest to infant specialists but should be of value also to those more generally interested in the development of society. The most important "natural resource" of a society is its infants, since the children make up the next generation of adults and will guarantee the continued existence of the society. In this sense, child rearing reflects the inner core of a society's handling of its own resources. The way children are cared for is a measure of a society's developed level of responsibility for the future and the investment put into its children to create this future.

The importance of considering internal family dynamics in the light of a wide sociocultural environmental context has been further stressed by Jordan (1997). Representations of child care are not only dependent on family patterns but also on expectations outside the family, in the cultural and the environmental setting. This implies that infant mental health cannot be understood without taking into account the geographical, demographic, historical, and cultural framework in which the individual subject is produced. This has previously not been the most common approach in discussing infant mental health issues, and infant specialists have seldom focused on historical and demographic conditions when describing the inner life of babies. However, we believe that these data have a contextual relevance and are important in understanding the background of infant mental health. Our thoughts are based on the view that infant mental health is best captured through an understanding of the mental well-being of infants and parents within the early relation framework. Like a stone thrown into water, child care is surrounded by numerous ripples that also have to be described. The context in which child care takes place is constantly changing, as is the water into which a stone has been thrown.

In this chapter, infant mental health in Scandinavia will be presented in a very broad perspective. Scandinavia is originally the generic name for the central Nordic countries, Sweden, Norway, and Denmark. However, in the past few years it has been more common to include Finland as well as Iceland in what is called Scandinavia. Today there are differences among the Scandinavian countries regarding infant mental health issues, mainly due to different economic conditions, but we assume that compared to other regions in the world, the shared history still makes the similarities greater than the differences. The starting point and the main focus of the presentation will be Sweden, the cultural base of the author. When not specifically otherwise stated, our text deals with Swedish conditions. Scandinavia will be introduced as a geographical region with historically related states offering settings for families to raise their children. Typical features in child care patterns are highlighted and their development through history dis-

cussed. The chapter concludes with a discussion of how external changes in the present-day situation might affect the quality of parenting. Infant care will be looked upon as taking place within the first dyad, within the primary relationships, embedded in the family context, and surrounded by the cultural setting, as well as within the social and physical environment.

Theories about Parenting

Even if child care takes place in the home, it is not only a parental issue, but something shaped by a continuous intergenerational exchange of influences from both the public and the private sphere. When two people from two different families form a new family, two family traditions of child care are blended and have to adapt to variations in family expectations as well as to different environmental factors: family economy, job opportunities, etc. John Byng-Hall, family therapist at the Tavistock Clinic in London, discusses how family scripts, patterns of representations of family roles, develop from one generation to another (Byng-Hall, 1995). In his definition, family scripts are the family's shared expectations of how family roles are to be performed within various contexts. Byng-Hall claims that every new generation is obliged to rewrite its family scripts. Family life is a rehearsal for the next generation, he says, and the representations that a parent develops concerning how to take care of his or her child reflect the integration and recasting of expectations from the parent's own childhood environment. In this perspective, the representations of infant care can be seen as inner thoughts about who the parents themselves are and how they would like their lives to be.

Since parents' capacity for child care is rooted in the parenting behavior of the older generation, the process of change in this capacity is by definition slower than in many other behavioral structures. The conservative character of the family scripts helps to create stability even as it makes the scripts vulnerable to external changes. We can use the definition made by Byng-Hall and extend our thinking to the expectations that surround the family. Influences from the outside are represented by what we call society scripts. In every society parents are embraced by support systems that execute informal and formal control, expressing society's generalized representations or norms about do's and don'ts in child care. The society scripts are not as rigid as the earlier described family scripts; they are more adaptable to external influences and they change faster. However, when the society scripts change so fast that the family scripts do not have time to adapt, the consequence is a discrepancy between the inner and the outer world. In this case, the result might be a conflict between the child care beliefs of the individual and the demands from the environment. This conflict will have to be dealt with both on the individual and on the society level, otherwise the caregiving to children will be affected.

In this theoretical perspective, the development of parental identity can be seen as the result of a transactional negotiation process between individual and family needs, on different script levels. Two Swedish sociologists, Bäck-Wiklund and Bergsten (1997), describe the shaping of the new role identity as a collaboration project between the individual and the society. In a recent study about modern Swedish parenting, they discuss changes in people's attitudes to two dimensions: personal freedom and dependence. Based on interviews with parents, they conclude that the present dominating focus on the individual life project, reflecting the value put on individual freedom, complicates the development of the family project, which rests on feelings of dependence and lack of freedom. The authors suggest that the modern Swedish parenting role is bound to show ambivalence since the incongruity between individual development and family development is so prevalent.

When the individual life project shifts toward realizing the family project, the relationship to the individual's internalized reproductive capacity is activated. The development of an intrapsychic parental identity is a lifelong process, starting as early as when a child first thinks about a possible future baby of his or her own. The parental identity seems to focus on certain themes, themes that might be universal but are shaped by cultural influence. Daniel Stern has discussed these themes in describing the intrapsychic parental structure that he calls the motherhood constellation (Stern, 1995). The first theme deals with survival of the infant, and focuses on the maternal attention directed at keeping the child alive. In a society where the birth of every infant is based on a well-planned decision, as in a modern industrialized society, a mother has to prove that she has made the right decision in having a baby. Her project is to show that she can successfully give birth to an infant that is healthy and thrives. Her need to prove that she is a "real" woman who can produce a "real" offspring is based on her relationship with the earliest psychological levels of her own reproductive capacity. Lebovici writes about this early relationship, in psychoanalytical terminology, as a pre-Oedipal narcissistic relationship, where the mother is both mother and baby herself (Lebovici, 1983). The baby in this relationship is a *bébé fantasmatic,* and the verification of this baby constitutes an important psychological foundation for parenthood (see also Risholm Mothander, 1994). However, the relationship with the reproductive capacity cannot stay on the fantasy level, but must develop toward reality. When using the motherhood constellation concept and its definition as a lifelong phase, we have to anticipate an intrapsychic development over time. The woman must develop her narcissistic needs into caregiving needs and create space for the theme of identity reorganization, where she can form her caregiving maternal identity. During pregnancy the mother tries to ascertain her relationship to the ideal mother and the ideal baby, as well as the opposites, the worst ever mother and the worst ever baby, in intersubjective meetings with the role models of her own mother and other women. In these meetings she further investigates the possibilities of creating a supportive matrix and in doing so she activates both her private family and her shared society scripts.

Later the interaction with the real baby develops her capacity to develop the primary relatedness theme, as described by Stern. The development of a parenting capacity, as described by both Stern and Lebovici, illustrates how the parental identity is rooted in the parent's early experiences.

Given the conservative character of the development of the intrapsychic representations and family scripts of child care, and the many influences that have to be integrated in order to create secure parenting patterns, it is important that clinicians identify child care patterns that lack coherence as well as patterns that show marked conflicts between inner representations and observable behavior. A certain degree of discrepancy is natural and necessary to stimulate the development and rewriting of the family scripts, but if the conflict between parental representations of how they would like to take care of a baby (i.e., their representations of child care) and the actual child care they render dominates, the development of the child may be affected negatively. If the conflict between the parenting capacity and the society scripts for child care is too much in focus, the well-being of the children may be endangered.

The results of the parenting capacity invested in the children might not be revealed until the children are older, perhaps not until they are parents themselves. In attachment research this has been labeled as the tendency of history to repeat itself or that the individual adult caregiving capacity is dependent on the quality of the individual's own childhood attachment experiences (Fraiberg, 1980; Fonagy, Steele,

Moran, Steele, & Higgitt, 1991). It has been empirically established that maternal sensitivity to infant signals and communications, as expressed in early interaction with the infant, is an important foundation for the child's later socioemotional development (Bohlin, in press; Suess, Grossman, & Sroufe, 1992). Since the research findings are stronger for the negative side, that is, insecurely attached infants run a higher risk of negative socioemotional development than securely attached infants, child specialists have to be sensitive to identify early patterns of qualitatively deviant interaction.

Scandinavia

Geography and History

The Scandinavian countries are characterized by long coastlines, large forests, and numerous lakes. Scandinavia enjoys a climate more favorable than most countries of the same latitude. The climate is determined by the location in the border zone between cold arctic and warmer air masses. The western areas are affected by their proximity to the Atlantic with its warm Gulf Stream. In the north there are longer winters with more snow than in the south, and there is also a difference between the western more humid regions and the eastern dry inland climate. The extreme contrasts between the intense light of the long summer days and the equally long dark winter nights, with only a few hours of twilight, are typical. During summer, sunlight lasts around the clock in the areas north of the Arctic Circle, but even as far south as Stockholm, June nights have only a few hours of semidarkness.

During several periods of history Scandinavia was covered by inland ice. The most recent Ice Age ended only 10,000 years ago. The ice was heavy and during the thawing period, the jagged rocks in the mountains were polished and partly crumbled into a clay that rivers washed onto the plains, turning them into fertile agriculture areas. Plenty of water, trees for fuel and building shelters, and good conditions for farming during the summer made the land suitable for settlement. People migrated into Scandinavia from the south and from the east as the ice retreated. Gradually the inhabitants developed a fishing and hunting society, which later turned into a society based on agriculture. During the Viking Age, about A.D. 800 to 1100, a marked expansion took place: Expeditions departed in many directions and reached far-off destinations, both for trade and for pillaging. During this period the Scandinavians were an influence on distant cultures, but they also brought home new ideas from abroad. In spite of its geographic position on the outer edge of Europe, Scandinavia has never been an isolated corner of the world.

In the fourteenth century Denmark, Norway, which then included present-day Iceland, and Sweden, which then included present-day Finland, formed a union ruled by a queen of Danish origin which lasted for more than a hundred years. The following centuries were marked by conflicts between the central governments in the different countries represented by the royal families, the high nobility, the church, the burghers, and the peasants. During these years the political dominance shifted between powerful groups, and the borders between the countries were often changed. Cultural patterns became interrelated. At one period the present-day Baltic republics, as well as large areas of northern Germany, were included in the Scandinavian sphere of power. However, in the nineteenth century the period of Scandinavian dominance came to an end. Finland came under Russian rule and the Baltic states were incorporated into Germany. The borders of present-day Denmark were settled, and later a union was established between Norway and Sweden that lasted for about 100 years. Finland gained independence during the Russian Revolution. Both Denmark and Norway were under German occupation during World War II. Iceland became an independent state in 1944, after having been ruled by Norwegians and Danes for many hundreds of years. Scandinavia had found its present-day borders.

Population

Throughout history, the population of Scandinavia has with few exceptions been very homogeneous, but that does not mean that Scandinavia has been fenced off from neighboring areas. There have always been interregional population movements within the Scandinavian countries, and traders and merchants from all parts of Europe have over the centuries visited Scandinavia. One example was the technology of processing iron, which was taught by influential craftsmen from Europe who settled in Sweden during the seventeenth century. The Sami, inhabiting the northern portions of Scandinavia and the Kola Peninsula since ancient times, constitute a minority group in Scandinavian society, linguistically, culturally, and demographically. Formerly they were a nomadic people, but today many Sami have abandoned their traditional reindeer herding and have merged with the majority population. The Sami language is related to Finnish, which indicates that the Sami and the Finns originally migrated into the area from the east. However, the majority of the Scandinavians came from the south Swedish, Norwegian, Danish, and Icelandic, as well as the Faroese language, are part of the Germanic language group, all related and to some extent shared. The modern common Nordic labor market has facilitated present-day mobility, but until recently few people have immigrated from distant areas in larger groups.

In the nineteenth century the demographic changes in Scandinavia were dramatic. The death rate began to decline, partly due to medical advances and better agricultural output. Literacy increased and the growth of information made people more aware of economic inequalities and lack of religious freedom, factors that probably contributed to the great emigration wave toward the end of the century. More than one million people emigrated from Sweden between 1853 and 1873, when harvests were poor and famine gripped certain areas. Altogether nearly 1.5 million people, out of a population of between 4 and 5 million, emigrated from Sweden between 1851 and 1930, mostly to North

America. Additional emigrants came from Norway, and a few from Denmark. It took both courage and money to leave your home country. The emigrants knew they would most probably never return, and it has been said that the average traveler was a capable and strong individualist of fairly young age, determined to build a new future in what was considered to be the promised land.

Later, during the worldwide economic depression of the 1930s, emigration stopped and the population growth was again low. However, after World War II, the number of births increased in Scandinavia. As of the beginning of the 1990s the Swedish fertility level was slightly over two children per woman, a rate regarded as ideal in Sweden and in many other European countries. Infant mortality is very low: 4 deaths per 1,000 live births. The average life expectancy is 81 years for women and 76 years for men. Sweden today has a population of 8.8 million, Denmark 5.1 million, Finland 5 million, and Norway 4.3 million. Iceland has the smallest population of the Scandinavian countries, with 260,000 inhabitants.

Immigration has proved to be stimulating both for society and the economy. During and after World War II, refugees were on the move in northern Europe, and a period of labor immigration started in Sweden due to the rapid postwar industrial expansion. At the beginning of the 1970s immigration more or less stopped when economic conditions changed, but during the late 1980s and the early 1990s the numbers of refugees and their immediate families applying for asylum again added to the immigration figures. There have been differences among the Scandinavian countries regarding the willingness to accept refugees, but in general all the governments have today become much stricter regarding accepting foreigners than only a few years ago. However, international contacts and awareness have increased on all levels and in present-day Sweden every 20th inhabitant is a foreign citizen and every 10th was born outside the country. The multicultural society has come to stay.

Family Patterns in the Past

As in most countries, the caretaking of young children in Scandinavia has traditionally been a family matter. The history of infant care patterns has been described by historians as an integrated part of family life, typically the women's life. As such it was included with other gender activities and under the influence of the major economic and structural development of society. The historical focus was never on the child's perspective, in terms of what it means to a child to grow up in specific circumstances. Children were first studied as a specific group when physical health aspects were addressed in the combat against infant mortality. Later the focus was put on the exploration of the child's mind, more specifically on how to control it. Not until quite recently, perhaps as a consequence of international experimentally oriented multidisciplinary infant research, has the development and the inner life of the preverbal infant been emphasized. Psychologists and psychiatrists have gradually become more and more involved in infant mental health issues.

Over a long period of history, Swedish farmers lived together in small villages with common grazing lands and allotments on common arable land. The family pattern was that of an extended family, where members of different ages lived on the farm together with farmhands of both sexes. Infants were hardly ever mentioned as individuals in early historical documents; they constituted a natural part of a family and were specifically mentioned only in legislation concerning how family names and property were to be handed down. Infants in medieval society were probably not looked upon as individual beings, since the concept of childhood was not yet known (Ariès, 1980). They were seen as future people, not yet realized, but accepted as part of the everyday environment. Their physical needs were taken care of by the mother during the breast-feeding period of the first 2 to 3 years, but during that period no expectations were placed on the individual infant. However, the weaning period constituted a shift. When the infant could do without the constant solicitude of the mother, it automatically became part of the adult world. Now caregiving turned into a period of harsh fostering, executed by all family members, with control and punishment as major tools. DeMause describes the child-rearing attitude of Western societies during medieval time as "the ambivalent mode," meaning that children were seen as evil creatures who had to be beaten into shape by their parents and others (De Mause, 1976). However, this reading of history has been questioned as being too simplistic (Brembeck, 1986). A more pragmatic ex-planation of the policy of strict control would be that since a surviving child was an investment for future labor, it had to be protected from a dangerous environment not adapted to a child's mental and physical capacity. When parents were working, the children were looked after by older people, who did not have the capacity to attend to them all the time. Threats of both religious and pagan punishments were effective in controlling the physical activities of the children, who consequently grew up in fear of God, as well as of trolls, gnomes, and other creatures believed to inhabit the neighborhood. "The old man in the well" prevented the children from going near the water, "the trolls in the woods" made them stay close to home, etc.

During the nineteenth centuries, the Swedish government implemented reforms in order to accelerate the technical development of agriculture. The reforms had great social consequences since families were now supposed to move to new consolidated properties. Villages were split, settlements became more scattered, and families consequently became more isolated than before, which affected the situation of young children. Infant mortality was still high, and as late as 1810, 20 percent of Swedish children died before age 1. Child care attitudes were related to class. On average, children of educated parents were treated more humanely and child development as an issue slowly started to appear in European literature, for example in the writings of Rousseau (Ambjörnsson, 1977). However, among the uneducated classes in rural areas, the understanding of child care was minimal and many infants died because of pure negligence. In a study on traditional breast-feeding in Sweden, it was reported that in the poor coastal areas in northern Sweden, where women had to do the agricultural work while the men were out fishing, a mother without a caretaker for her child could hang the swaddled infant on the wall, or tie the toddler at the bedpost with a rope, within the warmth of the fire but out of reach of animals and other dangers. The baby could then be left without care for many hours. Older children who could feed themselves could be left for days while the mother went to the more distant fields (Gaunt, 1983).

When the industrialization period started all over Europe in the nineteenth century, infant care was also affected. Women became engaged in production, and breast-feeding was difficult to combine with long working hours. In the transition to a new society the children were the hardest hit by the changes. In some parts of Sweden famous for linen production, infant mortality was remarkably high among the weavers' children, a fact which has been explained as a result of local caregiving patterns (Lithell, 1985). Weavers' infants were not breast-fed, but were cared for by older siblings who fed them with cow milk from a cow's horn. Infants born during the summer months ran a higher risk of catching lethal infections than infants born during winter, since mothers frequently left their infants to other caretakers during the linen harvest, and bacteria in the cow horns thrived in the summer heat. Infants were exposed to what we today consider double dangers, for they were deprived of close maternal contact as well as antibody protection from breast milk.

Solomon and George (1996) have described the adult caregiving system as a goal-corrected behavioral system guided by parental representations of caregiving. The parent's evolutionary fitness depends on the survival of all her offspring. During good times, with plenty of food, the conflict within the caregiving system is not activated. A mother can bond to and lovingly enjoy every child she gives birth to. However, in bad times, having many young children and little food means that none can get enough to eat. This might endanger the life of all her children. In its most extreme form, optimal maternal caregiving could then be to let one infant die in favor of another child—perhaps a child not yet born. The theoretical thinking of Solomon and George can be applied to Scandinavian circumstances. Since the majority of parents in Sweden during the eighteenth and nineteenth centuries had experience of infant loss, the consequence was that mothers did not really invest emotionally in a newborn baby until it had proven its ability to survive. The first and major task for the newborn was to show the mother that he or she was worthwhile investing in, to stimulate the development of maternal feelings and invite the mother into caregiving behavior. Thus, the high infant mortality and the bonding process were transactionally negatively related, in that vulnerable infants who would have been in need of extra care did not get it since they did not signal to their mothers that they would survive. The postponed bonding could be seen as a parental defense, an emotional protection against parental bereavement in case of loss of the baby, but it also increased the risk for every baby. A baby had to be born with a strong positive affect signal system in order to be seen and taken care of. Mothers behaved according to their representations and family scripts for infant care, and they could not see that they themselves were in a position to have any influence on something that was considered to be God's will.

Having many children was a punishment, but having none would also lead to problems. Few families could feed 9 to 12 children, a normal number of births for a healthy woman during her fertile years. Gaunt (1983) refers to a Norwegian protocol from 1593 about a lawful divorce, the reason being that the parents had too many children. However, for most families the number of children was reduced due to infant mortality. The family constituted the basic economic unit and it was important to have children who could support the elderly. Having no children was consequently also a reason for divorce, as every farmer and landowner lived under the pressure to produce an heir. A new marriage had to be considered if there were no offspring.

When the child was weaned it was transferred to the status of future labor force. Child rearing during the nineteenth century has been evaluated differently in history, probably depending on the author's perspective. Historical documents reveal that upper-class people at the time were shocked, not by the way they themselves took care of infants, but by the lack of manners they noticed among the peasant children. Child care or child rearing was described as nonexistent and children were seen running loose and untamed as wild animals. However, many reports from the not-so-wealthy homes contain worries as well as parental joy and pride. Both accounts are probably true, reflecting the growing socioeconomic differences and lack of contact between the rich and the poor. In both groups there must have been warm feelings. From an evolutionary perspective, it would be a waste of human resources if parents did not like their children.

The church gradually became the major controlling norm system in the rural areas. In the nineteenth century, the Lutheran state Church of Sweden, to which the majority of the Swedish people still belong, decreed that children would grow lazy and sinful if not taught the value of hard work by their parents. The goal was to teach obedience in order to facilitate following instruction at work. The clergymen in the churches had the population in a firm grip; they taught and held examinations in every household to guarantee knowledge of the Ten Commandments and the content of the catechism. In 1842, the first law was passed obliging every community to organize primary school education. The schoolteacher soon became as important as the clergyman in controlling the population. Gradually the ability to read and write spread to all levels of the population, which, as mentioned earlier, not only made people read the religious message but also increased their awareness of the outside world.

The Swedish Welfare Model

The Birth of the Welfare State

At the turn of the century, industrialization and urbanization had changed living conditions to such an extent that the threats to poor children's welfare became obvious to government authorities. However, funding was lacking for intervention. In the cities, poverty and poor housing hit the children hard, especially during the long, cold, and dark winter months. Children's hospitals were built, financed by private donations, and they were quickly filled with poor and needy young children. Rickets, tuberculosis, and epidemics kept infant mortality figures higher in Stockholm than in other European capitals, and medical professionals expressed a deep concern over the need for preventive measures. Breast-feeding was encouraged, and in 1901 a private organization called the *goutte du lait* or milk drop was founded to help mothers who did not breast feed to get surplus milk from other women. From the milk drop a mother could borrow infants' clothes and get her baby examined by a doctor at no cost. A poor woman who could not breast-feed could get up to eight small bottles of breast milk per day free, usually carried home by an older sibling after school. Women who had plenty of milk could sell the surplus to the nearest milk drop and earn some extra money. The importance of the milk drops increased, so that by the end of the 1920s almost 25 percent of the infants in Stockholm were registered. Not until the 1930s, however, did the government begin to subsidize this activity. Gradually the milk drops turned into the present-day network of child health centers in the residential areas, where families can obtain parenting support and preventive health care for their infants.

Important initiatives to spread knowledge about poor people's living conditions and the needs of children came from socially radical intellectuals, in particular the co-operative movement, the feminist movement, and the temperance movement (Ohrlander, 1992). In a famous and influential appeal, the Swedish author Ellen Key in the year 1900 proposed the twentieth century as the Century of the Child. Interest in philanthropy became a fashion among wealthy people. The Swedish Poor Relief and Child Care Society was founded in 1906 with the vision to create

> a nice and comfortable society in the future, built on liberal economy, also but not only balanced by different public and municipal collective societies and responsible initiatives. Through co-operative initiative, unions and solidarity institutions, peaceful co-existence between the social classes was to be created. In idyllic family life in beautiful homes and gardens of their own, the children's growing up should be good and a life should be led, stamped by bourgeois ideals of education, self discipline, self governing and self fostering. . . . The social child care should be responsible for all children in need, protect them against the consequences of poverty and turn them into good members of society. (Ohrlander, 1992, pp. 305–306)

Every municipality created a child care board to which officials and district representatives had a duty to report on the welfare of children. Professional authorities sat together with laymen on the child care boards. This design gave scope for "good and respectable neighbors," as well as experts, to influence the implementation of the new norms. However, the attitude toward families as expressed in the child care board protocols from the 1920s was very patriarchal, especially with regard to unmarried mothers. Poor families, it was believed, should be made to improve their child care by force, directives, and punishment mixed with counseling and practical help. Society had set its goal: to protect children, extirpate poverty, and socialize the children. The aims were stated by society; the child care board was society's advocate; and if the aims did not coincide with those of the parents, the child had to be protected from the parents. If the home was not a good enough home it was the parents' fault. Many children were put in foster care far away from the cities. Growing up in the countryside was considered more healthy, and foster families were easy to find on the farms in the rural areas. Under the control of the child care boards children who were placed in foster care could be forced to work hard as farmhands, separated from their families of origin. Children were not seen in relation to their parents but rather in relation to the legislation about every child's right to proper care. Ohrlander (1992) describes this as a major value conflict between the old family and household principles and the new social territory.

Medical experts became gradually more involved in child welfare work, and there was a shift from regarding poor child care as a symptom of poverty to seeing it as a matter of deficiencies in parenting. Social problems were redefined, since poverty was now officially considered more or less

abolished and the standard of living for the working class was stated to be better than ever. However, population growth decreased during the 1930s, probably because of families' ambivalence about the future. The conflict between the individual's and society's responsibility was not solved but still active. The government was worried and introduced specific housing projects for families in order to encourage parents to have more children. The social state guaranteed children's right to care, proper upbringing, and education, but at the same time the government had difficulty bearing the cost. Influential conservative groups claimed that social policies were too expensive for the government to bear, but the members of the child care boards defended the notion that society has a responsibility to guarantee the welfare of children.

In this situation, pediatricians formulated an offensive program for improving child health care based on the involvement of medical professionals and rational scientific interest. Every child was to be diagnosed, for with proper treatment and care a child would stand a better chance of growing up to be a useful member of society. The check was to be conducted by pediatricians and pediatric nurses who would collaborate with the social welfare authorities. Parents were now given directives on how to care for their children: It was as if all bad behavior found in adults was congenital and ready to develop if not forcefully fought in childhood. Parents were told not to be too intimate with their infants, who had to learn from the first day how to reject desires and endure discomfort. Mothers were instructed to differentiate between the wants and the needs of their infants (Ribbens, 1994). Infants should not be spoiled with more physical contact than necessary. Infants should be fed at regular intervals and left in peace between meals. Crying was a normal way to strengthen lung capacity. The first infant specialists appeared in the field, claiming that children should be looked after at institutional day care centers by professional day care staff, rather than by unskilled parents in the homes. A few collective houses were designed in Stockholm by fashionable architects for the new class of modern and intellectual parents. In these collective houses, child rearing, housecleaning, laundry, and cooking were taken care of by employed professionals in order to leave the parents free to concentrate on their work. Children's cognitive and moral behavior was focused on and documented, but knowledge about early relationship development was lacking while experts focused on the scientific understanding of child development.

Since World War II, international contacts have increased on all levels and Scandinavian child care patterns have been influenced by research, literature, and information from many sources within and outside the region. Different trends in feeding, caring for, and early education of children have appeared and disappeared. However, the Swedish welfare system is still unique in the world with its aim of guaranteeing support to all families living in Sweden, regardless of cultural and educational background. The welfare system is integrated in and generally accepted as a Swedish society script for family life. People are taking support from the state for granted. The issue under discussion in this paper is the development of society scripts in a changing world. We know that with modern information technology many different sources have more influence than ever before. The surrounding world is changing faster than ever. Can the aims of the welfare system be kept unchanged? How do young people of today resolve the conflict between the need for individual freedom and the desire for a family? In which contexts are young people's parenting representations developing? How are the boundaries of having family scripts rewritten in the 1990s? It is assumed that somewhere in this transactional process of change we should look for the core of infant mental health.

Swedish Family Policy

Government policies reflect society scripts. One of the cornerstones of Swedish family policy of today is child care, together with parental insurance and a child allowance, which is paid monthly to families with children up to the age of 18. Society has further taken on a wide responsibility for other family-oriented domains, such as reproductive health and the health of preschool and school-age children.

In the 1930s the ban on birth control information and sale of contraceptives was lifted, and family planning was offered by the public health services. The aim was to increase the population and to educate people in what was normatively seen as healthy family life. Sex education was introduced and became a compulsory subject in the school curriculum in 1954. In the beginning it focused mostly on biological facts, protection against unwanted pregnancies, and venereal diseases. Sexual relations were condoned only within marriage. However, with the economic growth of the 1960s, social attitudes toward reproduction and sexuality changed. It became increasingly common for young people to live together without being married, and these informal unions were fairly soon accepted. Cohabitation became legally equal to marriage. Today, when a couple splits up, possessions acquired during the cohabitation period are to be divided according to the same principles as in a legal divorce. Nowadays, contraception services are free of charge and the price of contraceptives is subsidized, with greater subsidies for those under 25. Changes in abortion legislation have gradually taken place and under the 1974 Abortion Act, a woman has the right to an abortion up to the 18th week of pregnancy. In an effort to minimize the numbers of abortions, a prevention program has been developed that includes health education on sexuality, fertility, and gender differences. Many channels, such as health care and social services, the leisure sector, the church, and various nongovernmental organizations have been engaged in this program. The idea behind these efforts has been to put abortion in a broader context of sexuality and human relations, and to prevent unwanted pregnancies with the underlying message that every child has the right to be wanted.

Young men and women nowadays often live together for several years without intending to start a family. Modern contraception is widely used both for limiting the number of children and for timing childbearing, mainly to postpone the first child. The mean age for a woman having her first child is currently 27 years. The number of mothers aged 15 to 19 is low in an international perspective, less than 10 per 1,000. For fathers aged 15 to 19 it is even lower, 2 per 1,000.

Maternity health care throughout pregnancy is offered free of charge at the maternal health centers in residential areas, and subsequent health care for children from birth to school age is offered at child health centers, where infants' families are registered as soon as they come home from the maternity hospital. Home deliveries are rare. To visit the CHC is part of being a parent. More than 99 percent of infants' families attend a CHC on a regular basis for well-baby clinics with weight checkups, inoculation programs, and general advice about feeding, infant care, etc. Until only a few years ago CHCs were staffed by pediatric nurses and pediatricians, but today they have mostly been replaced by district nurses and general practitioners not specializing in pediatrics. However, pediatricians, child psychologists, and other experts are available as consultants. Medical services are free for all children. The controlling function of the CHC has been reduced. Today the main task of the nurse is to establish a trusting relationship with every family in her district. She offers an initial home visit to invite every family to the CHC when a baby is born, and she is active in giving information about daily telephone and visiting hours as well as the possibility of receiving home visits when needed. The family is offered parental education in support groups, together with other families in the neighborhood. In Stockholm, 60 percent of first-time mothers attended parental groups in 1997. The aim of the group activity is to create networks of parents and to prevent isolation during the stay-at-home parenting period. (For a more detailed presentation of the maternal and child health care in Sweden, see Risholm Mothander, 1998a.)

For many years now, Swedish family policy has concentrated on enabling both men and women to combine parenthood with gainful employment. This endeavor is prompted both by concern for the growing generation and by the pursuit of equality between the sexes. When a child is born, the law entitles the parents to a leave of absence from work. A parent can stay home with a child for 360 days, while receiving parental benefits. Leave can be taken at any time until the child is 8 years old. Each parent is entitled to 30 days with benefits equal to 85 percent of regular earnings. These benefits are personal and are not transferable between parents sharing custody. For another 210 days, the benefit rate is 75 percent of regular earnings, and for the remaining 90 days it is SKr 60 a day (about U.S. $7). The earmarking of a certain number of parental insurance benefit days was introduced in 1995, and the arrangement has been dubbed "father's month." It was intended to encourage all fathers to take parental leave, but so far it has had no such effect. During 1994, 78 percent of all fathers took at least part of their parental leave, and 11.4 percent of all

parental leave was used by fathers. The use of paternal leave is related to ethnic origin and level of education. Swedish fathers living in cities and with a high level of education exercise their right to parental leave more often than other fathers and they prefer to use it during summer. In addition, parents are entitled to a leave of absence from work for up to 120 days annually, at 75 percent of income, when their children are ill. This applies to children up to the age of 12, and in the case of disabled children up to the age of 21.

Most parents return to work at the end of their parental leave. The majority of Swedish households with children regard child care amenities as a natural adjunct to the family. Without these amenities it would not be possible for 70 percent of mothers with children under 7 to go out to work. However, a large proportion of mothers work part-time, that is, less than 40 hours a week.

Governmentally controlled and subsidized child care is offered to children from 12 months, at day care centers or in family day care. Expansion of child care facilities was regarded as the most important family policy issue of the 1970s, and the expansion enjoyed high priority. Day care centers are the form of child care that has expanded most, and today 39 percent of all children up to the age of 6 are looked after in this way. Most day care centers have one to four groups of children, the children being grouped either by age or in so-called sibling groups with mixed ages. Previously there were 12 to 15 children per group, but the economic situation has deteriorated and today one can find groups with as many as 24 children. Staffing ratios have thus diminished. Although child numbers have increased, there are still generally about three adults per group, but in some cases only two. More than half of the personnel are qualified preschool teachers, and about 40 percent are child care attendants. Children attend day care centers either full-time or part-time. Most day care centers are open for 8 to 12 hours per day, Monday to Friday.

Child care services in Sweden are distinguished by high standards and by the fundamental principle that they exist for all children. Both educational activities and practical care are provided. For example, two or three meals are served every day. Child care services further have a special responsibility toward children who require special support for their development for physical, mental, or other reasons. Children who are in need of special support are entitled to a place in regular child care services and, if necessary, are allotted special backup resources. At some day care centers there are special groups in which perhaps half the children have some kind of disability. These groups are smaller, and staff members have special training or experience in supporting children with special needs. Hospitalized children are also entitled to developmental preschool activities.

For families who do not want to have their children at day care centers, family day care should be available. A child-minder looks after children aged up to 12, usually in the minder's own home, while the parents are at work or studying. Child-minders can have groups ranging from a few children to about ten of various ages,

their own children included, often at different times of day. The proportion of children in family day care has gradually declined with the expansion of municipal day care centers. Stay-at-home parents or child-minders can further use a drop-in form of facility, the open preschool, where social and educational stimulus is offered. The open preschool is usually staffed by one preschool teacher and one child care attendant. The main purpose of the open preschool is to provide parents and child-minders with a meeting point and to give them the opportunity, together with the preschool teachers, to develop educational activities for the children. Often the open preschool is a hub of social contact for young families in the residential areas.

Traditionally, children start school at the age of 7 in Sweden, which is late by international standards. In a historically sparsely populated country with long dark winter months, children under 7 have earlier not been seen as psychologically and physically mature enough for schooling with its demands on social skills, such as taking part in group instruction, walking to and from school, and handling social challenges, such as having lunch in the school lunchroom. However, since 1997 children have been allowed to start school at 6 if their parents so desire. Naturally, the late school start has affected the preschool curriculum, which in many ways shows similarities to the curricula of lower grades in other countries' school systems. The transition from the preschool to school for the 6-year olds is facilitated by having the preschool and the school groups in the same premises.

The Crisis of the Welfare System

Like many other Western industrialized societies, Sweden experienced a growth of wealth during the 1970s and 1980s, based on a prosperous export industry. The improved economic situation affected both public and private life. It was a generally accepted political strategy in Sweden to further develop the welfare state and to give priority to the development of social insurance, health care, child care, education, and financial support to families. The values dating from the beginning of the century, when Sweden was a society with a small homogeneous population in transition from agricultural to industrial economy, had become integrated in both family and society scripts. Welfare was considered a necessary cost, and a tax-based system of transferring money was developed. Swedes have been described as the most heavily taxed people in the world. Families gradually became dependent on two salaries, but employment for both men and women was available and easy to find.

However, government welfare expenditure increased, and at the end of the 1980s the Swedish economy could no longer fully support the welfare system. The situation was known to a few, but the political situation was not stable enough to present a program based on cutbacks. The necessary reductions in the welfare system were postponed, which made the economic situation worse, so that when they eventually came, Swedish society was unprepared and shocked. Families who were hit by increased unemployment could no longer count on the financial support they had earlier received from the state. There were reductions in the levels of allowances to support families, including child allowance, sick allowance, and housing allowance. Fees for day care increased, and the number of staff in child groups, both in day care and schools, was reduced, which affected the quality of the education. Stricter rules for day care attendance were introduced in order to optimize the size of the groups. Many infant specialists, such as day care psychologists and mental health staff in schools, were withdrawn. The number of open preschools was reduced. Radical cutbacks in hospital care were made. The 4 to 6 days of postpartum care in the delivery clinics was reduced to 24 to 48 hours for cases without complications. Specialists in pediatrics in the CHCs were replaced by district nurses with broader responsibilities. When the pediatric specialists were withdrawn from the CHCs, the demand for the services of child psychologists increased dramatically (Risholm Mothander, 1998a). Children's mental health reflected the mental well-being of families. The referrals to psychiatric child and adolescent clinics doubled over a period of only a few years. Swedes are currently facing a transitional crisis, moving from a state of shock to gradually accepting that it is never going to be the same again. The level of unemployment is more than 10 percent, and the inequality between those who have a job and those who do not has increased the level of family stress.

Theoretically we can see how the present situation illustrates the slow process of change in the family scripts and in parents' representational world. The third parental generation after the birth of the welfare state has fully integrated the values of the responsibility of the state in their representational world, to the extent that they feel abandoned as parents when support is withdrawn. The conflict between the individual's and society's responsibility, current at the beginning of the century and described by Ohrlander (1992), has surfaced again, but in reverse. When parents need support from the state, help is no longer available and there is nowhere else to turn. Voluntary aid organizations are not as well developed in Sweden as in many other countries. Parents of today have to rewrite their family scripts in order to get them to fit with the new society scripts. They have to shoulder more of the parental responsibilities themselves and bridge the sudden and wide gap between their own parental representations and the support available from the state. In this process the well-being of infants is endangered.

Infants at Risk

A coherent society that cares for children is probably the best safety net for families. But even the best knitted net has its holes; no welfare system can provide a complete cover. In times of economical constraints, the holes in the safety-net might grow bigger and increase the risk for children to fall through. New patterns of risk factors might appear, patterns that might have been seen early by infant experts but identified only much later by politicians.

During the economical crisis in Sweden the social welfare system has been preoc-

cupied with its own cut-backs and the reorganization to a more limited economy. Infants who are at risk for developmental delays and emotional problems have not been supported enough. There are different types of risk patterns and they share the same complexity all over the western world. They are related to infants born preterm, infants with somatic problems, infants in refugee families, infants in families with poor mental or physical health and infants experiencing early separations. A few will be discussed below.

Of the 90,000 infants born in Sweden every year, approximately 4.5 percent are born preterm. The group of very preterm infants mounts to 0.8 percent and the extremely preterm infants, born before 29th gestation week, are 0.3 percent of the infants born in a year (Stjernqvist, 1999). This is a small group in comparison with international figures, but still 1,000 infants are born preterm or very preterm every year. Today with the improvement of the medical care more than 80 percent of the infants survive, but most of them need extensive hospital care. Some will have long lasting needs that put special demands on the environment. The stress placed upon a mother and a father suddenly turning into premature parents is easy to understand. Preparing for parenthood is a psychological process that has been described as a complex interaction between representations of different interpersonal and intrapsychic levels. For a present day couple, where family is defined as a planned and controlled project, a sudden premature birth is a trauma (Risholm Mothander, 1999). When cutbacks are made in hospital budgets medical care often gets priority over the care for the more hard to identify psychological needs of families. Family stress reactions do not disappear; they often remain when the infant has left hospital care. Out-patient staff at the Child Health Centers have just recently started to think about the biopsychological needs of this group of families, learning more about their fragility and designing special parental support groups, etc. However, when the work-load is increased it is hard for staff to allocate time for a new task. Another problem is the vulnerability to infections and stress among many of the children born prematurely. Since the majority of Swedish parents are gainfully employed and child care is concentrated to day care centers, fragile infants may have to spend many hours in groups that are not appropriate to their needs. Some infants show early regulatory problems. Others might not develop symptoms before they reach school age. Since the group of very preterm or extremely preterm children is a "new" population, meaning that they are a group of children that earlier did not survive, we do not yet have a lot of experiences or outcome data to show when arguing for smaller groups, more staff per child, etc.

Further, Scandinavian child specialists are worried over the increasing amount of children in daycare, preschools, and schools with attention deficit and regulatory problems. More children than ever need extra support in order to cope with their environment. Medication is rare but very much discussed. Children with neuropsychiatric problems have for some years mainly been a concern for parents or teachers of older preschool and school children, but gradually the knowledge is spreading that the individual difficulties might have an early origin. It is hard to judge whether this is a child's problem or if it is a societal problem. Quite a few experts would rather place the diagnosis on society than on the child. Bigger groups in schools and reduced number of staff makes it harder for vulnerable children to create inner models for relationships. It is difficult to identify single causes but parental stress, lack of structure, and over-stimulation through television and media have been discussed as adding to the problems.

Another group of infants that have come to be discussed in the infant mental health field in Sweden lately is the increasing amount of young infants having more than one home from a very early age. The rate of divorce is as high in Sweden as in many other western countries (approximately 40 percent). During the first infant year, 7–10 percent of Swedish parents live apart. In the year when the first-born child is turning two, over 4 percent of parents having lived together are split up (Statistika Centralbyrån, 1999). Earlier, the vast majority of infants stayed with their mothers. However, government has supported shared parental responsibility; the earlier mentioned father's parental benefit month is one example of this support. Attitudes have changed, and the present generation of fathers are more involved in child care than earlier. Problems arise when a marriage or a love relationship breaks up. A divorce always leads to feelings of abandonment and loss. When children are involved, the parental conflicts affect them. In the clinical field an increasing amount of cases are seen where the conflict between man and woman are acted out in the child's arena. Both fathers and mothers feel that they are capable of caretaking and society is supporting single fathers just as much as single mothers. Government has taken sides in this issue by creating a new law in 1998 stating that in case of divorce, custody is automatically shared between parents. The law does not say anything about shared living but many parents interpret the law as applicable to it and literally cut the baby's living arrangements into two equal parts. Everyone agrees that it is valuable for the child to have emotional and physical access to both parents, but too many parents have not shared their responsibility negotiated and reached a solution for the baby's living that is cognitively and emotionally acceptable to a growing child's mind.

Parenting in a Changing Context

Since young people in Sweden often live together for a couple of years before they start a family, they postpone having the first child until both have finished their studies or are established on the job market. A common goal among young people is to create an individual secure financial base before having children, and to reach a salary that will make the 75 percent parental benefit reasonable to live on. Since equality between sexes is one of the political foundations of Swedish society, both men and women find it natural to develop their personal careers and individual projects before they focus as a couple on having children. Many young couples

raised in the 1970s were born into a lifestyle based on a consumption-oriented economy. Two salaries with no children makes a high standard of living possible. However, the present unstable situation of the labor market has changed the conditions for economic family planning. Having children today puts a heavier burden on family finances than it did in the past, and most families must accept a lower standard of living than the earlier generation did when they became parents. The step toward the family project is thus more radical and needs more planning.

In this transitional period, when parents are forced to rewrite their family scripts for parenting and family life, postponing childbirth is one way of winning time. In the beginning of the 1990s the birthrate in Sweden was 2.3 children per woman. In 1997 the rate was 1.5 children per woman, which is the lowest figure ever recorded (the first statistical reports date back to the eighteenth century). It can be assumed that young people feel lost and are unconsciously hoping for the return of an economic situation more in accord with their representations of the context in which parenting roles are to be performed, that is, the context in which they grew up. However, the present situation of having children late might have long-term consequences on a societal level. If women postpone childbearing too long, they will not have enough time to give birth to the number of children they would wish. The birth figures will then continue to remain low.

When a woman gives birth to very few children, her caregiving capacity, as defined earlier, becomes very concentrated on the children she has. The pressure to be successful becomes more obvious. We assume that for a woman in her 30s who has her first baby, often with limited earlier experience of child care and after a long period of life focusing on individual projects, it is a major task to reorganize her inner structure and to make room for a new lifelong identity as a mother to a child. When the maternal identity is developing, psychological space for the motherhood constellation themes must be allowed, but there must also be room for other themes on a level where they can be regulated and not cause intrapsychic conflict. The woman must allow herself to develop her motherhood mindset without giving up her earlier identity. The developmental task for the Swedish woman becoming a mother is to develop an inner structure where the core identity is well-integrated and where different personal roles are allowed to coexist in a state of balance. A parallel situation applies to fathers. The society script for fathers implies that he takes part in family life and develops a parental identity based on equality and shared responsibility for child care and housework that balances an earlier male role identity. The intrapsychic regulation between different role identities is a major issue for parents in many industrialized Western societies today but could be of specific interest in a country like Sweden with its welfare model so heavily focused on infants' rights, equality between the sexes, and the development of the family.

With roots in a homogeneous traditional agricultural society, where the family has historically been the basic economic unit,

the general attitude in Sweden is still that a parent should take care of the infant in the home during the first year. Given this, most infants are taken care of by their mothers during the daytime, although fathers are encouraged to take an active interest. Bäck-Wiklund and Bergsten (1997) discuss how social reproductive activities, including the care of young children, have developed in the welfare state. When the responsibility for social reproduction became a shared responsibility between the family and the state, the individual, emotional, and public spheres became linked. The division of responsibilities between family and state was discussed and decided on in the political arena, and the relationship between men and women, which was formerly a private issue, became one of political importance as well. In public discussion, equality between the sexes and shared responsibility for the home and child care was brought forward as one of the major aims of the welfare state. Access to child care, that is, child care outside the home, was brought forward as one of the foundations of the welfare state, and the cost was heavily subsidized by the government.

However, housework, such as cooking, cleaning, and doing laundry, did not receive the same priority from the welfare state. This was considered to be part of every family's private responsibility, was not subsidized, and has remained the responsibility of the couple, since the system of taxation prevents families from employing help. The state responsibility for collective day care was the only issue that survived from the collective house ideology of the 1930s. The discrepancy between the ideas parents expressed about parenting and their actual parenting behavior is evident. The political declarations about equality between the sexes and the possibility for both men and women to combine parenthood with gainful employment, that is, the society scripts, do not reflect family reality. Family scripts are conservative: Mothers are still the primary caregivers and do most of the housework. Swedish fathers are very much encouraged to take part in child care today and are becoming more and more engaged in family issues, but more in attitudes than in actual behavior. This can be seen as reflecting a transitional conflict, since the new expectations for Swedish fathers are difficult to combine with older family scripts. We assume that this conflict between what the mother expects and what she can get from the father also influences her attitudes toward mothering. Swedish men spend twice as much time on work outside the home as women, and women spend twice as much time on housework as men. This pattern has been confirmed in a recent government investigation about division of power in the Swedish society (SOU 1998b). To conclude, child care in Sweden became a collaborative project between mothers and the state while housework remained the responsibility of the women. With society now changing the conditions for child care, the daily lives of children and women are affected most.

In their interview material Bäck-Wiklund and Bergsten (1997) analyze the maternal strategies of coping with the discrepancy between inner beliefs and outer reality. They describe one group of mothers who had managed to keep a feeling of coherence in their maternal functioning; the authors describe them as having a secure maternal attitude. Women in this group had a well-functioning social network and had created a private interpretation of their maternal role, rather conservative, but with no guilt for parts they could not keep active during their children's infancy period. Their expectations for the future were positive. A second group is described as being resigned, reflecting that the mothers in this group could not find a coherent meaning in what they were doing, how they were living, and how they would have liked to live. Both these groups were relatively small in number. The largest group had what the authors call an ambivalent attitude toward mothering. Women in this group expressed insecurity and were worried over both their present and future situation, the availability of child care, their own return to the job market, the development of the relationship with the partner, etc. They were preoccupied with plans and felt they achieved nothing. Many of them had earlier experiences of broken relationships. They felt that their present life situation was complicated and lacked coherence. The group that Bäck-Wiklund and Bergsten interviewed was small, only about 30 families, and generalizations are difficult to make from such a limited material. However, it is interesting that from a sociological point of view they identify a qualitative maternal identity pattern that has its equivalent in the attachment paradigm.

Given the Swedish model for family life

and infant care, with opportunities to develop a deep contact between mothers and infants over a full year with little stress from outside, and where the mother's role as primary caregiver is supported by society through the parental insurance system, there should theoretically be plenty of room for the development of a secure attachment between mothers and infants. According to the attachment theory, the base for the infant's inner model for relationships is formed during the first year, the time when Swedish mothers and infants spend their days together. However, a longitudinal study aimed at evaluating the influence of early interactive experiences with the primary caregiver on socioemotional functioning of Swedish children has yielded complex results. In this research, carried out at the Uppsala University by Bohlin, Hagekull, and their research group, 125 normal middle-class children were studied from the age of 6 weeks to 9 years, within the theoretical framework of attachment theory. At 15 months the Strange Situation was administered as a way of assessing attachment quality. Surprisingly enough, the results showed that the group of infants classified as insecure/ambivalent (C) was large, 21 percent, compared to the average of 6 percent reported for other Western European samples. The group of secure children (B) amounted to 62 percent, and 17 percent were assessed as insecure/avoidant (A). Bohlin and Hagekull raise the question of whether the time for assessing the attachment quality unhappily coincides with the time for shifting from parental to nonparental care (Bohlin & Hagekull, in

press). In Sweden this shift often takes place right after the child's first birthday. In that case the Strange Situation would not tap the child's experiences of earlier maternal sensitivity, as integrated in the behavior of the child, but rather the transitional imbalance in the mother-infant relationship during a period of increased stress. Of the infants classified as insecure/ambivalent, 50 percent had gone into nonparental care during the previous 4 months, as compared to 26 percent of the other children. This may of course be true, but we cannot avoid asking whether the high degree of ambivalence in the attachment quality did not also reflect some of the role identity stress put on mothers in Swedish society of today. This stress has been suggested to be more evident for well-educated women, like the Swedish, who want to continue their job careers, than for mothers who are planning to remain stay-at-home mothers as in many other Western European countries. It is true that the Swedish children, when exposed to the Strange Situation, were already exposed to an increased level of stress through starting day care, but they should still theoretically have been reacting according to their inner working model for relationships, based on earlier experiences of the quality of their mothers' earlier caregiving. The present situation should not change their inner working model of the use of the mother as a secure base.

In general, when the Swedish infant has reached its first birthday, the attitude is that mothers ought to start to think of returning to work or studies and that infants should go into some sort of day care. The parental insurance money is usually used up, and in the residential areas there are hardly any children at home during the day time. Mothers might miss the adult life and contact with job friends. Employers can put pressure on mothers to return to work. Many mothers experience this period as the peak of conflict between their maternal role and the job role, something they have feared (Risholm Mothander, 1994). The transition to day care is not taking place at an optimal time, neither for mothers nor for children. The mother has been the primary caregiver for her infant for a full year, and has experienced close contact with the child. The infant is in a developmental phase where the capacity for intersubjectivity is about to find its form and where the need of a secure base is very explicit in the child's exploratory behavior. Children at this age are sensitive to changes in relationships and environments, since they are in the process of creating inner working models for relationships. Regardless of which theoretical language is used, the psychological importance of the onset of walking, with its capacity to entertain "a love affair with the world," and the intensity of verbal development make it hard for a parent to separate from the infant and leave him or her in a day care group of perhaps 15 other toddlers, to be looked after by three attendants only. Many parents face the dilemma of leaving the infant in day care with ambivalence: They put their infants in peer groups with few adults and at the same time are preoccupied with how to make the infants feel that there are always attachment objects available to be used as a secure base.

From a theoretical caregiving perspective we may ask if children's security-seeking behavior during the time not spent in day care is encouraged by parents as a compensation for the daily separations they are introducing to the children. In the 1940s experts advised parents to avoid body contact with their infants since it would spoil them. Children were fostered to become self-contained. Dependence was seen as dangerous, a sign of weakness, and insecure children learned to become avoidant. Later Winnicott argued that the need for physical contact is a lifelong need, but that the inner meaning of the concept changes over time. He wrote a paper about how maternal trust in the child's capacity to cope with frustration during the second half of the first year helps the infant develop the capacity to be alone, something different from being lonely (Winnicott, 1958). Today the issue of physical contact between parents and infants in Sweden is important and very much focused. Parents are preoccupied with how to get their children to trust that they will not be left alone. Co-sleeping is common; more than 60 percent of infants under 36 months sleep in their parents' bed during a part of or the whole of the night (Nikolova, 1996). Many parents are satisfied with the way sleeping is organized in the family and express that sleeping patterns cause them no problems. On the other hand, perturbances and disturbances in children's sleeping patterns are by far the most common symptom for which parents seek pediatric and psychological advice during infancy. Very often these symptoms are related to parental problems of the same type that characterize the mothers with ambivalent attitudes toward mothering: lack of coherent role identity, depression, worries about the future, relationship problems in the couple, etc.

Synthesis

Facing the end of the Century of the Child, we have to conclude that the Scandinavian infant is a physically healthy baby. We have less knowledge about infant mental health, since there are no epidemiological data available. An infant born in Sweden today is most probably planned, welcomed, and in good physical health. He or she is the first or the second born of a couple most probably in their late 20s or early 30s. All Swedish infants are born at delivery clinics where fathers usually attend and the women giving birth are assisted by trained midwives. Medical doctors are called to the delivery room when required, and if an infant is in need of intensive neonatal care, it is available. The medical care of vulnerable infants, such as premature or sick babies, is of a very high technical standard, but their psychological care is seen by many professionals as threatened as an effect of harder economic conditions. When a mother goes home with her newborn after 24 to 48 hours, she is offered free support in the home, first by midwives from the MHC and later by nurses from the CHC. Most infants are taken care of in the home by the primary caregiver, normally the mother, for the full first year of life. The long period of maternity leave offers plenty of time for

bonding and attachment processes to develop. Breast-feeding in Sweden has been sensitive to trends over the decades but never declined as much as in many other Western countries. Most Swedish delivery clinics have earned the U.N. designation "baby-friendly hospital" for their encouragement of breast-feeding. As many as 70 percent of infants are today breast-fed at the age of 6 months.

When the child has reached the age of 1, the mother is expected to leave him or her at day care and go back to studies or work. If the child is sick, the parents have the right to stay home from work to look after the child. The majority of mothers will work part-time until the child has reached school age, to shorten the time at day care for the child and to be able to do housework at home. Women do twice as much housework as men. In spite of an animated discussion about the increasing rate of divorce among young families, more than 85 percent of children 0 to 6 years do live with both their parents.

In Sweden both parents are involved in social reproductive activities including child care, but fathers' involvement is reflected more in attitudes than behavior. It has been suggested that Swedish mothers experience a conflict that has turned into an ambivalent attitude toward mothering. This attitude is characterized by role conflicts, difficulties in putting pieces together, and a sense of lacking coherence. We can speculate as to whether this ambivalent attitude influences the quality of caregiving. The division between securely and insecurely attached children seems to be as in other European countries, but in a sample of Swedish infants, a larger number than expected were qualitatively assessed as insecure/ambivalent. There is not yet enough data to secure the hypothesis that Swedish infants have experienced their mothers' ambivalence and internalized it in their inner working model of relationships. It has been hypothesized that Scandinavian mothers, being more well-informed and educated, are more caught by the conflict between parenting and gainful employment than other European mothers.

We know more about infant physical health than about infant mental health. There are data on physical reactions to inoculations, the prevalence of children's diseases, and infants' dental status, but data on mental health during infancy is lacking. Diagnostic systems for assessing mental health and developmental status during infancy have not been available, and there has been great resistance to lifting the infant out of the relationship context to study it individually. The attitude Winnicott expresses as "there is no such thing as an infant" has characterized the attitude toward infant psychiatry in Sweden. Diagnosis has not been considered important during infancy, since it has been considered the responsibility of the state to support every infant family. A psychiatric diagnosis has been considered labeling and as more stigmatizing than useful.

Attitudes are gradually shifting as economic conditions change, and today every supportive intervention has to be evaluated in order to obtain funding. In the outpatient child and adolescent psychiatric units, diagnoses are not necessary for treatment, and have until recently seldom been used, especially not in the case of younger preschool children. However, voices have been raised in support of using diagnosis not only as a way of obtaining extra resources, such as day care, but also as a way to structure observations, use a common language, and plan interventions. This is a complicated issue, but so far the discussion has been mostly concentrated on how to avoid labeling and how to include the relationship with the parent in helping the infant to a better development. Still most clinicians believe that the best way to support an infant is to support the infant-parent relationship.

Epidemiological studies of Swedish school children indicate that as many as 10 to 15 percent are bearers of psychiatric symptoms (SOU; 1997a). It can be assumed that many of the problems have their roots in earlier years, even in infancy. Given a basically well-developed welfare system reaching every family, the data is upsetting. The high figures should constitute a challenge to the state to concentrate on measures to bridge the gap between parents' caretaking capacity and the available support from the state, that is, the gap between family and society scripts. We believe that the state cannot abdicate from its responsibilities. The recent changes in the welfare system have been too sudden and have not given families time to adapt to a different life situation. Therefore the state should not only be obliged to offer interventions to children who are suffering from psychiatric symptoms today but should also plan preventive measures for future generations. In order to reduce the risk for future poor mental health, well-integrated institutions reaching the whole population should have priority; they must be maintained and afforded the possibility of offering early support to families. The maternal and child health centers constitute a secure base for the majority of young families, and visiting them is integrated in the parental role behavior. In many places they function as a social matrix and act as a replacement for the support previously rendered by older women in the family group. Through the modern maternal and child health centers early interventions can be channeled to different groups at risk, based on a working alliance between families and infant specialists and without depriving the parents of the right to develop their own parental responsibility. At the close of the Century of the Child we have to conclude that babies born in Sweden stand a good chance of enjoying good mental health, but that infant specialists must continuously support parenting in a changing society and fight for the protection of a welfare system that acts as a secure base.

References

Ambjörnsson, R. (1977). Introduction to J. J. Rousseau (1762). *Emile eller om uppfostran.* Göteborg: Stegeland. 3–30. (In Swedish)

Ariès, Ph. (1980). *Centuries of childhood. A social history of family life.* New York: Vintage Books.

Bäck-Wiklund, M., & Bergsten, B. (1997). *Det moderna föräldraskapet. En studie av familj och kön i förändring.* Stockholm: Natur och Kultur. (In Swedish)

Bohlin, G., Hagekull, B., & Rydell, A-M. (Social Development, in press). Attachment and social functioning: A Longitudinal Study from Infancy to Middle Childhood.

Bohlin, G., & Hagekull, B. (1999). Behavior problems in Swedish 4-year-olds: The importance of maternal sensitivity and social context. In P. M. Crittenden (Ed.), *The organization of attachment relationships: Maturation, culture, and context.* Cambridge: Cambridge University Press.

Byng-Hall, J. (1995). *Rewriting family scripts. Improvisation and systems change.* London: Guilford.

Brembeck H. (1986). *Tyst, lydig och arbetsam. Om barnuppfostran på den västsvenska landsbygden under senare delen av 1800-talet.* Skrifter från Etnologiska Föreningen i Västsverige no 5. Göteborg. (In Swedish)

deMause, L. (1976). The history of childhood. London: Souvenir Press.

Fonagy, P., Steele, M., Moran, G., Steele, H., & Higgitt, A. (1991). Measuring the ghost in the nursery: A summary of the main findings of the Anna Freud Centre—University College London Parent-Child Study. *Bulletin of Anna Freud Centre* 14, 115–131.

Fraiberg, S. (1980). Clinical studies in infant mental health. The first year of life. New York: Basic Books.

Gaunt, D. (1983). *Familjeliv i Norden.* Malmö: Gidlunds. (In Swedish)

Havnesköld, L., & Risholm Mothander, P. (1995). *Utvecklingspsykologi: Psykodynamisk teori i nya perspektiv.* Stockholm: Liber Utbildning. (In Swedish)

Jordan, B. (1997). Gender politics and infant mental health. *The Signal*, 5(3), pp. 1–5.

Lebovici, S. (1983). *Le nourrison, la mère et*

le psychoanalyste. Paris: Le Centurion. (In French)

Lithell, U-B. (1981). *Breast-feeding and reproduction.* (Studia Historica Upsaliensia 120). Stockholm: Almquist & Wiksell.

Nikolova K. (1996). *Sover Barnet på Nätterna.* (Omsorgsnämndens rapportserie 96:2) Stockholm: Stockholms Läns Landsting. (In Swedish)

Nugent, J. K. (1994). Cross-cultural studies of child development: Implications for clinicians. *Zero to Three, 15*(2), 1–8.

Öberg, L., & Högberg, L. (1991). *Där de vita sängarna stå. Om barnsjukhuset Samariten.* (Exhibition catalogue). Stockholm: Stockholms Stadsmuseum. (In Swedish)

Ohrlander, K. (1992). *I barnens och nationens intresse* (Studies in education and psychology no. 30). Stockholm: Almquist & Wiksell. (In Swedish with English summary)

Ribbens, J. (1994). *Mothers and their children: A feminist sociology of child rearing.* London: Sage.

Risholm Mothander, P. (1994). *Mellan mor och barn.* Stockholm: Liber Utbildning. (In Swedish)

Risholm Mothander, P. (1998a). Psychotherapeutic work at the maternity and child health centres in Stockholm. *Infant Mental Health Journal, 19*(2), 220–228.

Risholm Mothander, P. (1998b). Samspel och utveckling. In B. Wrangsjö (Ed.), *Barn som märks.* Stockholm: Natur och Kultur. 74–102. (In Swedish)

Risholm Mothander, P. (1999). Premature mothers to premature infants—a relationship trauma. *The international Journal of Prenatal and Perinatal Psychology and Medicine, 11*(1), 33–40.

SOU, 1997:8. *Röster om Barns och Ungdomars Psykiska Hälsa.* Statens offentliga utredningar. (Delbetänkande av Barnpsykiatrikommittén). Socialdepartementet. Stockholm: Norsteds. (In Swedish)

SOU, 1998:6. *Ty makten är din.* Statens offentliga utredningar. (Betänkande från kvinnomakturedningen). Socialdepartementet. Stockholm: Norsteds. (In Swedish)

SOU, 1998:31. *Det gäller livet.* Statens offentliga utredningar. (Slutbetänkande av Barnpsykiatrikommittén). Socialdepartementet. Stockholm: Norsteds. (In Swedish)

Solomon, J. & George, C. (1996). Defining the caregiving system: Toward a theory of caregiving. *Infant Mental Health Journal, 17*(3), 183–197.

Statistiska Centralbyrån, SCB, (1999). Barnfamiljer 1997. Demografisk rapport. 1999:1. Stockholm: SCB.

Stern D. N. (1995). The motherhood constellation. A unified view of parent-infant psychotherapy. New York: Basic Books.

Stjernqvist, K. (1999). *Född för tidigt.* Stockholm: Natur och Kultur. (In Swedish)

Suess, G. J., Grossman, K. E., & Sroufe, L. A. (1992) Effects of infant attachment to mother and father on quality of adaptation in preschool: From dyadic to individual organisation of self. *International Journal of Behavioral Development, 15,* 43–65.

Winnicott D. W. (1958) The capacity to be alone. In J. Sutherland (Ed.), (1987), *The Maturational Processes and The Facilitating Environment,* No. 64, 29–36. London: Hogarth.

10

New Attitudes: Infant Care Facilities in Saint Petersburg, Russia

Rifkat J. Muhamedrahimov

10

Introduction

By the time the social work project Infant Habilitation received official approval in Saint Petersburg and the first early intervention program in Russia was organized, the national demographics, socioeconomic status, and health conditions of children had reached critically low val-

ues. According to the data of the governmental report "О положении детей в Российской Федерации (1993 год)" [*On childhood conditions in the Russian Federation*] (Russian Federation, 1994), there was a decrease in birthrate from 17.2 to 9.4 per 1,000 inhabitants in Russia from 1987 to 1993. In Saint Petersburg there was a corresponding decrease from 14.8 to 6.5 per 1,000. Whereas 73,200 babies were born in the city in 1987, in 1993 there were only about 32,400. The decrease in birthrates was accompanied by an increase in illness among neonates (173.7 babies per 1,000 live births in 1991 compared to 82.4 in 1980) and by increased infant mortality rates (the number of infants dying under the age of 1 year per 1,000 live births went up to 19.9 in 1993). In Russia, more than 60 percent of the infant mortality cases in the first year occur within the first month of life. Forty-five percent of those are neonates dying in hospitals within the first 6 days of life because of complications in the course of pregnancy and delivery. In Saint Petersburg, 80 percent of developmental delays are caused by an unfavorable uterine period of development, 12 percent are caused by posttraumatic phenomena or chronic illnesses, and 2 percent are attributable to genetically caused illnesses.

In 1991 in Russia, 75.1 percent of pregnant women suffered from ill health. Normal birth was registered in 40 to 45 percent of deliveries and for some Russian territories in only 25 percent of deliveries. The percentage of children born to women not officially married has gone up from 13 percent of total live births in 1988 to 18.2 percent in 1993. According to expert assessment, if the present tendency persists, by the year 2015 the percentage of healthy neonates in Russia may shrink to 15 to 20 percent, while the percentage of neonates suffering from inborn and acquired chronic diseases will increase to 20 to 25 percent.

Until recently, Russian infant facilities in general and those for at-risk babies in particular were characterized by priority of medical assistance and an absence of educational, psychological or social work. Because high risk children when left in the family had no access to medical assistance, families with severe risk babies were given virtually no choice between a segregated institution and keeping the child at home. Therefore, high risk babies were being taken away from the family and placed in special medically oriented institutions. In addition, infant facilities lacked screening techniques, ways of assessing babies' developmental level of functioning, and a system of spotting high risk babies early on. In addition, there were too few up-to-date publications on infant development available for either parents or professionals.

Until the present time, the universities and pedagogical institutes have been training specialists to work with children mostly over the age of 3. There are no places for training teachers (including special education) or psychologists for children ages 3 and under, and social work or any system of training social workers is virtually nonexistent. There is no professional training in such specialties as motility development or organizing the setting for children from birth to 3 years (physical and occupational therapy), which are prominent in developed countries.

A study of statistical data and of the existing facilities for children reveals the urgency of the need to develop and implement special programs focusing on the needs of children under the age of 3. The results also make evident the necessity of organizing a comprehensive system of coordinated social, pedagogical, psychological, medical, and other facilities for at-risk babies and their families. Trained specialists and new legislation are needed to make both the public and professionals aware of the importance of early prevention.

In 1992, extensive efforts in that direction led the city of Saint Petersburg to accept a citywide social work project, Infant Habilitation (Chistovich et al., 1996; Kozhevnikova, Muhamedrahimov, & Chistovich, 1995), for further development and implementation. In its original draft, the program consisted of organizing the screening of infants, assessing infants' functional development levels, and creating new services in several city districts to facilitate the development of children with developmental delay, or risk of potential delay, from birth to 3 years. The authors advocated that screening and spotting at-risk babies be carried out in local child polyclinics and organized a center for assessing the level of children's functional development, which has become the Institute of Early Intervention. Therapy with developmentally delayed or potentially delayed babies began in 1992 in Russia's first Russian-Swedish lekotek (a toy library for at-risk children in the early period; Stensland Junker, 1971), which was opened in one of the kindergartens of Saint Petersburg. This chapter sums up 5 years of experience in organizing an interdisciplinary family-centered caregiver-infant interaction–oriented early intervention program by the staff of this preschool establishment, and describes the resulting model of supplying assistance for special needs children and their families within the system of education.

Early Intervention Program in a Preschool Educational Establishment

Models Used in Creating the Early Intervention Program

During the period of experimental work in organizing assistance for high risk infants and young children, the interdisciplinary group of employees went through the following early intervention models.

1. Play interaction with at-risk babies, using educational handbooks for young children, and modeling play interaction for the mother and other members of the family. The possible models to follow here are the working system of a lekotek and any program of early education for special needs children (e.g., the Portage Guide to Early Education described in Shearer, 1987).

2. Organizing a sociopedagogical early intervention program on the principles of family-centered work of an interdisciplinary team of professionals. As a model, one can take early intervention programs for infants and young children in the United States (Education of the Handicapped Act Amendments, part H, 1986, 1991), and recent lekoteks (Bjorck-Akesson & Brodin, 1991). Both of these use a multidisciplinary, family-centered approach with staff members working together as a single team. Implementing that approach was one of the main tasks in organizing work with at-risk babies and families in the Russian-Swedish lekotek of Saint Petersburg.

3. Early intervention not only as a sociopedagogical program for high risk children from birth to 3 years (Education of the Handicapped Act Amendments, part H, 1986), but also as an early psychotherapeutic intervention arising from the traditions of child psychotherapy (Fraiberg, Adelson, & Shapiro, 1975). The object of psychotherapy in this case is the interaction between the child and parents (Lebovici, 1983), with the relationships of the baby, mother, other family members and the therapist being treated as a single system (Stern, 1995; Stern-Bruschweiler & Stern, 1989). It is shown that the functioning of this system may be changed through influencing any of its various elements, that the therapeutic effect may be achieved regardless of the psychotherapist's theoretical orientation or the point of applying intervention—be it the baby, the mother, or the interaction itself (Stern, 1991, 1995; Stern-Bruschweiler & Stern, 1989).

From our point of view, the use of theoretical concepts and accumulated rich psychotherapy experience with young children who are socioemotionally at risk may be promising in early intervention work with babies who are at risk for medical and biological developmental delay as well as with their parents. This becomes all the more clear when considering the data on interactional disturbances between mothers and premature babies and between mothers and babies with medical and biological risk factors (Beckwith, 1990; Field, 1987, 1990). It is noteworthy that psycho-

therapeutic early intervention itself has grown out of projects of working with partially sighted children and their parents (Fraiberg, 1971).

In this way the creation of new services for at-risk children brought an awareness of the importance of infants' mental health. The team's work became concentrated on combining the sociopedagogical and the psychotherapeutic approaches to early intervention. The team began focusing on extending the theory and practice of early psychotherapeutic intervention, originally developed mainly for babies with social and emotional risk (Fraiberg, Adelson, & Shapiro, 1975; Lebovici, 1983; Stern, 1991, 1995; Stern-Bruschweiler & Stern, 1989), to include both infants with medical and biological risk and their families.

The Early Intervention Program

At present there is an ongoing program of early intervention, existing within a preschool, in which different kinds of specialists constitute an interdisciplinary team using a family-centered, parent-infant interaction–oriented approach to facilitate the development of children from birth to 3 years with developmental delay or risk of delay.

INTERDISCIPLINARY TEAM WORK

One of the basic concepts for the early intervention program for special needs children and their families is that staff members should act as a team at all stages of the work. Three models of teamwork organization have been written on: multidisciplinary, interdisciplinary, and transdisciplinary teamwork (Hanson & Lynch, 1989; Rossetti, 1990). The multidisciplinary model, in which staff members represent different disciplines and work independently of each other, carrying out their part and their work virtually without cooperating or crossing professional boundaries, is the most widespread in the facilities for at-risk children in Russia. To organize a transdisciplinary model would demand considerable experience in early intervention program work, as well as time and financial outlay for training personnel. Such a model is especially effective when center-based facilities are combined with home visits. In the present conditions, it will be several years before the transdisciplinary model becomes feasible. The model we adopted was that of an interdisciplinary team, in which the members carry out their duties in the framework of established cooperation channels and which is characterized by a higher degree of coordination and integration of the service. To organize this model of teamwork, we found it necessary not only to bring together specialists representing different disciplines to cover the different aspects of work, and to make ourselves conversant with up-to-date information on infant development and early intervention, but also to do some intensive group work, in the course of which the staff members acquired the theoretical knowledge and personal experience of interaction in a group that was not included in their initial training. At present, the team of staff members involved in the early intervention program includes two preschool teachers, a psychologist, a physical therapist, and a pediatrician-neona-

tologist. Each of them has received additional training and has qualified in the area of infant development corresponding to the field of their initial training by taking part in seminars and meetings with professionals from Sweden, Norway, the United States, France, and the United Kingdom, organized within the framework of the city social work project Infant Habilitation. They have also completed the foundation course in psychological development and disorders of childhood conducted by the specialists of the Anna Freud Center. In order to make a study of group dynamics, the team members have completed the introductory course in group analysis held in Saint Petersburg by the Institute of Group Analysis (London).

One of the most essential concepts of the ideology of the family-centered approach to working with developmentally delayed at-risk babies is the way in which parents and other family members are made part of the early intervention team. In Russian medical, pedagogical, and social establishments, the prevailing practice is for parents to delegate full responsibility for their child's fate to specialists. Therefore, involving parents in the work of the team is yet another specific task, a practice entirely new in organizing facilities for special needs children in Russia.

Family-Centered, Caregiver-Infant Interaction–Oriented Early Intervention

THE IDEOLOGY

Until recently, the point of view most widespread among Russian specialists was the traditional model of socialization and seeing development as a result of a one-way influence of an adult upon the child. The most important factors in determining the establishment of infant psychology in Russia were the concepts that the source of a child's mental development is located in its relationship with an adult (Vygotsky, 1932) and that the main prerequisite of an infant's mental development is its communication with an adult, usually the parent (Lisina, 1961). It was believed that in communication a zone of proximal development is created, where cooperating with an older partner helps the child to realize his or her own potential. By the late 1970s, a child's social interaction at an early age was supposed to be regarded as a special, paramount type of activity, when the social interaction activity of the child had "another person, a partner in communication, as subject" (Lisina, 1986, p. 13). In spite of the existence of original national ideas and theories of infant development, the Russian special education teachers (defectologists) are still working mainly with children aged over 3 years, focusing on the child separately, and have very limited contact with parents and other family members. Unfortunately, up to now in Russia, those working with special needs children tend to ignore the fact that any organic damage "affects first and foremost the relations with other human beings" (Vygotsky, 1924, p. 5), so that a strictly medical view of a problem is too narrow, while the ignored social aspect "that tends to be regarded as secondary and derived, becomes in actual fact the primary and ruling one" (Vygotsky 1924, p. 7). There is also a lack of appreciation that even with the application of special educational techniques so frequently used in work with special needs children, "we must not forget we have to bring up not a blind person, but, before anything else, a child" (Vygotsky, 1924, p. 14).

To organize a new type of facilities for younger children, it was necessary to take into consideration the theoretical conclusions existing on the subject of early social interaction between infant and mother, which are not widely known in Russia, and the influence of that experience upon the child's further development (Mahler, Pine, & Bergman, 1975; Winnicott, 1960). It was also necessary to consider the data from detailed experimental studies of the process of interaction (Fogel, 1977; Kaye, 1977; Stern, 1977; Stern, Beebe, Jaffe, & Bennett, 1977), making it possible to define stages of an infant's developing sense of self during the first months of life (Stern, 1985). This caused infant development to be viewed within a broader frame of reference, regarded as part of the complex system of mother and infant (Osofsky & Connors, 1979) or family members and infant. In organizing the service, it was also necessary to consider the data from the studies of at-risk groups, which stressed, on the one hand, the special importance of the socioemotional sphere in the overall development of a child (Guralnick, 1992a; Guralnick & Groom, 1987; Odom, McConnell, & McEvoy, 1992), while on the other hand pointing out the difficulties of the family adapting to the situation (Krauss & Jacobs, 1990; Shonkoff, Hauser-Cram, Krauss, & Upshur, 1992), the severe disturbances in the mother-infant interaction and in the child's skill in establishing social contacts (Beckwith, 1990; Field, 1987, 1990). The staff members realized that their task was not only the selection of age-appropriate toys and organization of play activity, or choosing guideline books for the educational curriculum of a special needs baby (e.g., the Portage Guide to Early Education described in Shearer, 1987), but also that of providing a child with the chance to get the experience, so necessary for further socioemotional development, of sensitive interaction with the mother (Ainsworth et al., 1978) and family members.

EXPERIMENTAL DATA

Mother-Infant Interaction among Residents of Saint Petersburg

In order to organize a family-centered, mother-infant interaction–oriented early intervention program, an obvious prerequisite was to conduct a preliminary study of interaction between mothers and babies living in Saint Petersburg. It was necessary to define the main characteristics, the strengths and weaknesses, and the potential conflictual areas within the dyads' interactions.

In observing interaction in a structured learning situation (53 virtually healthy dyads, mothers aged 26.4 ± 4.3 years, level of education 14.2 ± 2.1 years, the age of children being 8.0 ± 2.2 months), it was found that only half the mothers in the sample allowed the child to study the task materials before giving instructions. Half of the mothers encouraged the child to perform the task. Only ⅓ of the mothers praised the child in general terms or for success in performing the task. About ⅔ of

the mothers did not stroke or pat the child and used an imperative style of teaching.

Assessment of the quality of interaction between mothers and 12-month-old babies according to the Parent-Child Early Relationship Assessment (PCERA) technique (Clark, 1985) in laboratory conditions (25 virtually healthy dyads, mothers aged 28.4 ± 6.5 years) has shown that the mothers' affective and behavioral involvement both in the structured task and in the free play segments was characterized by a moderate or less than moderate amount of positive physical contact with infants (average group assessment figures for the two segments being, respectively, 2.4 ± 0.9 and 3.0 ± 1.0; a 5-point scale was used), and by a moderate amount of negative physical contact, mainly consisting of physical restraint and interference with the child's actions (3.3 ± 1.0 and 3.4 ± 1.2). In structured play, the mothers tended to concentrate on the task and were less likely to initiate social interaction unconnected with performing the task (2.4 ± 1.1). Often, they expressed criticism toward the baby (3.6 ± 0.8). In the free play segment, mothers demonstrated difficulties in the structuring and mediating of the environment (3.5 ± 0.9). In both segments, the parental style was controlling and punctuated with instances of intrusiveness (3.1 ± 0.9 and 3.1 ± 0.8). The interactive style of the infants contained attempts to avoid parents' initiations (ratings in the avoiding, averting/resistance variable in structured and free play tasks are 3.5 ± 0.6 and 3.4 ± 0.7 respectively) and several instances of noncompliant behavior (3.5 ± 0.7 and 3.3 ± 0.7). Mutuality and positive emotional tone did not seem to be characteristic for the dyadic interaction as a whole (the average values of the dyadic variable of mutuality being 3.6 ± 0.8 and 3.3 ± 0.8, the affective quality 3.9 ± 0.8 and 3.8 ± 0.8). After the research project is completed, there will be more information available about the results of assessing interaction between mother and infant residents of Saint Petersburg. But even the preliminary figures serve to prove the point that the healthy children of healthy mothers are undergoing a conflictual interaction experience, which is inappropriate to their socioemotional developmental needs.

From the history of how the norms of family life were formed in the Russian society, there emerges evidence of a deeply rooted existing tradition that determines parental attitudes toward children starting at the earliest age. According to the *Domostroy*, an ancient Russian collection of instructions on maintaining order in the family and household,

> bring thy children up in forbiddance—and thou shalt find peace and blessing in them. Smile not at him, playing with him but rarely: easing him in a small matter, thou shalt suffer grief in a great one, and in future it will be like thorns that thou hast driven into thy soul. So give him not easement in his youth, but belay him on the ribs as he is growing up. ("Домострой" [*Domostrov*], 1994, p. 159; author's translation)

As witnessed by a publicist of the late nineteenth century, "We had the Domostroy reigning supreme everywhere, in all notions, in all strata of society . . . , everywhere, from a man's first steps he felt, how in all things was he oppressed and stifled, how his personal feeling was given no freedom or outlet, being squeezed like a kind of butter into the old, repellent forms" (Shelgunov, 1885, pp. 497–498). Even today there still exists an opinion that a child should be compliant, that he or she should not be overly cosseted and praised. Not only grandmothers or grandfathers, but the parents of today as well echo the traditional "Punish thy children in their youth, that they may be peace unto thee in thy old age" (Dahl, 1984, p. 298).

The more recent history of Soviet totalitarian rule shows abundant examples of ignoring the emotional needs of childhood. The notions of developing and shaping healthy children—the builders of a new society—in a collective, and the tenet that a female citizen should become free of family duties, have led to the creation of a wide network of establishments for the public upbringing of infants. By the late 1970s more than 3 million children aged from 2 months to 3 years were being brought up in crèches with 9 to 12 hr a day or a full 24-hr per day attendance. The focus of crèches, which were part of the health system, as well as in crèche-type preschools, was on cognitive rather than emotional development. Such an early separation from the mother coupled with the social deprivation experienced in crèches was bound to have an adverse influence on the forming of early relationships and the socioemotional development of several generations of children who are now parents.

The focus existing in the Russian maternity homes, of making sanitary norms the priority in assisting childbirth while ignoring the emotions and expectations of parents, may only worsen attempts to promote healthy emotional relationships between mother and infant (Chalmers, 1994). In the majority of maternity homes, the child is parted from the mother almost immediately after birth, and is then kept in another room; early breast-feeding is nonexistent; the child is swaddled; there is a rigid regime of feeding, out of any accord with the baby's feeling of hunger; the personnel supplement bottled formula between feeding times; and the contact of both mother and infant with other family members is limited or nonexistent (Bystrova, Widstrom, Lundth, Vorontsov, & Muhamedrahimov, 1997). A joint Russian-Swedish project on childhood development during the first year of life, initiated in 1994, has been conducted in Saint Petersburg. The project researches the effect of different maternity home regimes on the characteristics of mother-infant interaction after delivery. The goal of the study is to change the traditional ways of providing care for neonates in the Russian maternity homes.

Individual Traits of a Mother's Interaction Behavior

Analysis of interaction in a structured task situation shows that there exists considerable variation in mothers' social behavior toward their infants. It has been found that the mothers who were more sensitive to their children's signals were those with a higher level of empathy ($p < .05$) and a non-authoritarian way of relating to people ($p < .01$) according to the Interpersonal Diagnosis of Personality (Leary, 1954). Positive emotions, verbal and nonverbal expressions of positive attitudes toward the child, absence of negative comments, and praise and encouragement occurred more frequently in mothers with a predominantly nonpunitive reaction to frustration ($p < .01$) in the Picture-Frustration Study (Rosenzweig, 1944); they allowed themselves to be dominated and dependent ($p < .025$) according to the Interpersonal Diagnosis of Personality (Leary, 1954). Seeing another person as valuable, as well as having no marked changes in her emotional state on the Self-Rating Depression Scale (Zung, 1965) and Anxiety Scale (Spielberger, 1972), is of assistance to the mother in giving a more adequate response to her baby's anxiety ($p < .025$).

The results of our preliminary survey on individual personality characteristics of the mother, acquired through psychological testing (Leary, 1954; Rosenzweig, 1944; Spielberger, 1972; Zung, 1965), have also yielded information on the mother's social behavior and the baby's experience of primary relationships. This information, along with the information on the weak points in the interactions of mother and infant residents of Saint Petersburg, was used to help create a valid strategy for early intervention.

The Needs of Families with Young Children

A preliminary survey of mothers with young children residing in Saint Petersburg (20 mothers of children with medical and genetic risk having a developmental delay of more than 6 months, and 20 mothers of children without a developmental delay) using the Family Needs Survey (Bailey & Simeonsson, 1990) has shown that both suffer primarily from scarcity of information (81.4 percent and 68 percent affirmative answers, respectively) and from lack of community facilities (63.4 percent and 58.3 percent). Both parental groups have equally great need of information on how to teach the child (95 percent and 90 percent), on the facilities available at present (75 percent and 75 percent) or in the future (85 percent and 80 percent), and on how children grow and develop (60 percent and 65 percent). Mothers of children with developmental delays are especially interested in how to play or talk with the child (95 percent, as compared to 55 percent) and in information about any condition or disability the child might have (95 percent and 55 percent). They have a great need to communicate with other parents (60 percent, compared to 40 percent), for publications on families having a similar child (65 percent and 20 percent), and for meeting with a consultant (65 percent and 30 percent). Mothers of at-risk children are more reluctant to express a need to discuss matters of social support for the family. Thus, they were less willing to discuss the subject of helping the family members to support one another through difficult times (20 percent affirmative answers, compared to 55 percent for mothers of healthy children), having friends to talk to (45 percent and 60 percent), and finding more time to spend on themselves (40 percent and 55 percent). As for financial matters, those are problems that about ⅔ of the mothers of both groups are reluctant to discuss.

The results of administering the Family Support Scale (Dunst, Trivette, & Deal, 1988) have shown that half or more of the mothers of children with or without developmental delay regard as unavailable their own parents (50 percent and 60 percent), the husband's relations (55 percent and 65 percent), colleagues (55 percent and 55 percent), priests (65 percent and 80 percent; that is, mothers of at-risk children are more drawn toward the church), parental (75 percent and 85 percent) and social (75 percent and 90 percent) groups, and professional agencies (70 percent and 70 percent). This last response regarding the availability of professional agencies is probably caused primarily by the deficiencies and scarcity of such groups and agencies. Mothers of at-risk children, compared to mothers of healthy children, more frequently regard their own parents as unavailable (50 percent and 20 percent) as well as parents of other children (50 percent and 30 percent). Their friends are also less available or not always useful (40 percent and 5 percent). More mothers of both types see their husband as very helpful (65 percent and 60 percent), rather than unavailable (20 percent and 10 percent).

When assessing the family need and the level of social support with the help of questionnaires and scales, it is important to remember that the answers may depend not only on the actual situation, but also on the mother's condition and the notions she holds. Thus, for a group of mothers with special needs children, the results of assessment using the Zung depression scale (Zung, 1965) and data from the Family Support Scale were found to be positively correlated ($p < .05$). However, the data from the Family Support Scale and the results of the assessments using the measurement of meaning method (Osgood, Suci, & Tannenbaum, 1957) were negatively correlated. Those mothers of at-risk children who assessed the meaning of the concepts *family* and *husband* as low, regarded the sources of support for the family as more useful ($p < .01$ and $p < .05$, respectively). That is, if many of the sources of social support are reported as available and useful, it does not always mean they really exist and are useful. Those may be answers that reflect the condition and the beliefs of the mothers with special needs children, which are not found or are less pronounced for mothers of healthy children.

THE STAGES OF INFANT AND FAMILY SERVICE

The early intervention program created in a Saint Petersburg preschool educational establishment is targeted at facilitating the development of children between 0 and 3 years. For some of them, the appropriate diagnostic techniques have revealed a critical delay in development in one of the following areas: cognitive development, motility, language and speech development, self-support, or social and emotional development (Kent Infant Development Scale and Child Development Inventory; see Reuter & Bickett, 1985, as well as Chistovich et al., 1996). The program is also targeted at those living in physical and mental conditions aggravating the risk of developmental delay, including infants at risk for developmental delay due to a lack of early intervention.

As a result of several years of researching the most appropriate ways of organizing the program, the interdisciplinary team suggests that an infant and family service should consist of the following stages (Figure 10.1).

1. The family of the special needs baby may be given information and a referral to the program from the city association of parents of special needs children, from an organization (e.g., from a child's polyclinic, a maternity home, the Institute of Early Intervention), from an individual specialist, or lastly, the parents may contact the program directly.

2. The employees of the program accept the referral, enroll the child and parents on the waiting list, and initiate contact with the family.

3. In the next stage, one of the program staff members, a neonatologist, sees the parents (usually the mother) and, on the basis of their conversation, as well as the information gathered from medical reports brought from previous examinations, determines the cause of referral to the program. In addition, the staff member gets a family history including the primary data on pregnancy and delivery and the child's development up to the time of referral; finds out about the living conditions of the child and the family and the relations in the family, and discovers what the immediate social environment of the child and family is like. Based on the results of the interview, an individual card on the child and the family is filled out. There is sound reasoning behind the fact that the first

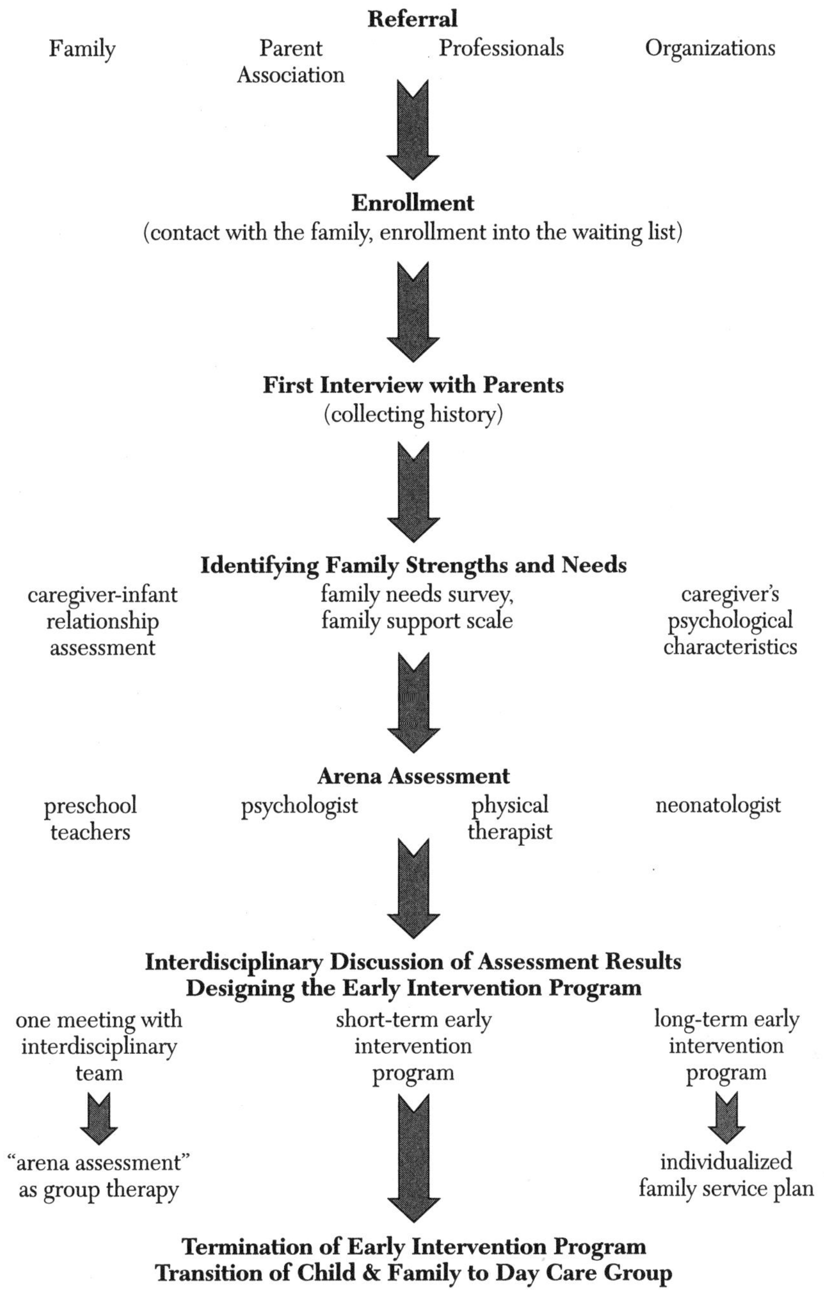

Referral

Family   Parent   Professionals   Organizations
Association

Enrollment
(contact with the family, enrollment into the waiting list)

First Interview with Parents
(collecting history)

Identifying Family Strengths and Needs

caregiver-infant   family needs survey,   caregiver's
relationship   family support scale   psychological
assessment   characteristics

Arena Assessment

preschool   psychologist   physical   neonatologist
teachers   therapist

Interdisciplinary Discussion of Assessment Results
Designing the Early Intervention Program

one meeting with   short-term early   long-term early
interdisciplinary   intervention   intervention
team   program   program

"arena assessment"   individualized
as group therapy   family service plan

Termination of Early Intervention Program
Transition of Child & Family to Day Care Group

FIGURE 10.1
Stages of the infant and family service

interview is conducted by a pediatrician, a neonatologist, as mothers traditionally expect questions on the course of pregnancy, the birth, and the child's condition to be asked by medics, based on their earlier experiences at medical establishments. Second, the neonatologist, with a view to the further interdisciplinary study of the problem, is trying to determine not only the medical, but also the social factors of risk in the child's development from the very first interview. The initial interview is concluded with setting the date for conducting the assessment of the quality of mother-infant interaction according to formalized techniques, and with handing out the blank forms and questionnaires used to determine the family's needs and the mother's individual mental characteristics.

4. Assessment of the quality of the relationship and of the mother-infant interaction characteristics is done with the help of the Parent-Child Early Relational Assessment (PCERA; Clark, 1985). This is also the stage at which the mother's individual characteristics are measured (using psychological methods), and the Family Needs Survey (Bailey & Simeonsson, 1990) and the Family Support Scale (Dunst, Trivette, & Deal, 1988) are administered. The reasoning behind organizing this stage of the program and its different elements in this particular way has been given earlier in the discussion of the family-centered, caregiver- and infant-oriented principles of early intervention.

5. The data resulting from all the preceding interviews with the child and family are reported to all the program staff members. Then an interdisciplinary team assessment is carried out, defining the main needs, as well as the strong and the weak points of the child and family (arena assessment; Rossetti, 1990). In the course of doing this kind of work, team assessment has fallen into stages that correspond to the stages at which a child's development would be assessed by separate specialists, as they are set out in the literature (Parker & Zuckerman, 1990). This assessment includes forming a therapeutic alliance with parents and child, collecting data on child and family, informal observation, conducting formal tests, formulating the strong and weak points of the child and family, and concluding with feedback and discussion.

6. The interdisciplinary team members discuss the results of their observations and assessment of the child and family; determine the possible forms and strategies of early intervention, the frequency of meetings, the duration of the program; and appoint a primary team member to work with the child and family. In discussing the matter of duration, there is a choice of three variants: one single session; a brief early intervention program; or a long-term early intervention program. In the first case, after the interview with the neonatologist and participation in the formalized procedure of assessment of the mother-infant interaction, it is sufficient for the parents and child to have one session with

the team, the arena assessment thus being regarded as yet another type of group therapeutic interaction. In a short-term program (and on the different stages of a long-term program), depending on the professional orientation and training of the team members, different models of short-term therapeutic intervention may be used (Clark, 1985; Cramer et al., 1990; McDonough, 1991). In some cases, these approaches may be suggested along with enrollment in special education programs, or speech, physical, or occupational therapy. A long-term early intervention program is necessary for babies with a considerable developmental delay. In long-term cases, it is necessary to create an individual plan of work with the child and the family (Education of the Handicapped Act Amendments, part H, 1986; McGonigel, Kaufmann, & Jonson, 1991).

A primary staff member is appointed to carry on the further early intervention, chosen usually with regard to the agreement between his or her professional orientation and the main need of the child and family and the main line of intervention. Thus, a preschool teacher may conduct a behavioral and educational program (separately for the child and for the caregiver, or for each of them in the other's presence, for just the two of them, or in a group of several mothers and children) and use it for, say, the model of play therapy and different strategies of communication-based intervention (Rossetti, 1996). According to their basic training, a physi-

cal therapist or a special education teacher may organize the individual setting or the special education of the child, providing for a new experience in the process of sensitive interaction, with the mother and other family members receiving training at the same time. A psychologist (psychotherapist) may organize the interaction of mother and infant, applying an appropriate model when therapy is carried out after the assessment of mother-infant interaction (Clark, 1985), such as interaction guidance, (McDonough, 1991), or psychotherapeutic interaction with the child and parents (Cramer et al., 1990; Lebovici, 1983; Lieberman & Pawl, 1993). When using the interdisciplinary approach, not only at the stage of assessment of the family and the special needs infant, but also at the stage of choosing the optimum form of intervention and carrying it out, representatives of different professions (or sometimes schools of approach) may conduct different variants of therapy. When needed, the other members of the team have consultations with the appointed staff member, and on some occasions join the work. In our view, such a model of concerted effort done by a cooperating team of workers whose different professional orientations are necessary to satisfy the multiple needs of babies of the developmental delay risk groups and of their families, best accords with the theoretical tenet of effecting functional changes within a system by applying intervention at different points, such as the observable behavior of the mother and infant, the interaction between them, and the representations of the mother and infant (Stern, 1991, 1995; Stern-Bruschweiler & Stern, 1989).

7. The last stage is the completion of the program and, in some cases, the transition of the child and family to another program.

Thus we are now changing over to a three-stage system of assessment of the baby's level of functioning and of the strong and weak points of the child and the family. If an additional session and observation of the child's functioning is needed after the arena assessment, the assessment system may consist of up to five steps. The task is to collect clear information on the extent to which the actual level of the child's development and the quality of functioning are determined, respectively, by the child's constitutional characteristics, his or her early developmental history, caregiver-child interaction patterns, family relationships, living conditions, etc. Before the proposed program reaches the stage of discussion by the interdisciplinary team of the form and length of early intervention and adopting an intervention plan, a differentiated diagnosis is made according to the new multiaxis system of diagnostic classification (Zero to Three, 1994). The experience of using this classification in our program so far has certainly proved that, precisely as its authors had expected, application of a common new classification system promotes mutual understanding among professionals, establishes a common language, and gets the work of the in-

terdisciplinary team organized in stages, from the collecting of data to creating and carrying out a plan of intervention.

On the basis of the 5-year experience of the functioning of the early intervention program, a regulations document has been drafted on the development of facilities for infants and early age children with special needs as a subdivision of a preschool educational establishment. The document outlines the aims, tasks, and content of the work to be done in the subdivision, defines the criteria for opening such a facility, and describes ways of financing and the requisite staff and hierarchy of administration. The regulations include a section on the handbooks to be used, a list of specialists and their duty regulations, and a list of documents necessary for having the service organized. Assistance is provided to families free of charge, apart from a number of specially stipulated cases. The legislative basis of the proposed model is article 18 of the Law on Education of the Russian Federation, the program of development for the educational system of the city of Saint Petersburg in the years 1996 to 2000, the City for the Little Ones project. In our view, creating subdivisions for the family-centered assistance for infants with special needs in educational preschool establishments is a sensible arrangement, as:

1. The personnel of kindergartens are oriented toward creating conditions not so much for treatment as for a child's development; however, every kindergarten has a unit to provide medical service for the children;

2. Usually parents bring a child to the

kindergarten daily, except on weekends, so that for the parents of special needs children it is natural to come with their child to such an establishment several times a week;

3. It presents a possibility of integrating the children with special needs into ordinary kindergarten groups; and

4. The network of educational preschool establishments is well developed and widespread. At the start of 1994 there were 6.8 million children enrolled in the 78,000 children's institutions of Russia. Kindergartens exist in every part of the city and are usually quite near to the family's home.

Throughout the organization of the program and thereafter, the staff have undergone a number of changes in mental state that have affected both the process of absorbing the relevant theoretical information and the therapy work with infants and families. During the preliminary period and the 1st year of the program everyone was full of enthusiasm, driven by a commitment to provide assistance to the babies with special needs and to organize the work on entirely new lines. Later, already during the 1st, and to a considerable degree the 2nd year, we came face to face with babies of severe genetic and medical risk, with their slow, fits and starts development, their regressions, and the depressed state of parents and family, all of which caused the staff members' defense mechanisms to be activated, bringing about shielding and resistance in the course of performing their duties (Osofsky, 1996). Creating the early intervention program and working with at-

risk babies and members of their family, the staff members were experiencing the emotions that are experienced by parents and members of a family at the birth of a special needs baby (Ditchfield, 1992). Given the virtual absence of supervision or any system of support for the professionals working with at-risk babies, there was a marked desire to return to the old, commonly accepted norms of providing assistance. The situation was made worse by the fact that outside the program the system of facilities for at-risk babies was left virtually unchanged, remaining undeveloped and rigid. After a lengthy period of group discussion within the team, the 4th year was the year of emerging awareness of the situation and of positive adaptation, when a process of restructuring the consciousness of the staff members began, so that the program came to be seen in a new way, and new plans for its further development were made.

The Existing Problems and the Further Directions of the Program

In the years when the early intervention program in a preschool was being organized, the team came against the natural difficulties caused by virtual absence of any social work whatever or any support for families of special needs children. One cannot avoid the question of what will happen to the family and child after the child reaches the end of the program at the age of 3 or 4 years. As a result of living within an undeveloped and rigid system of social facilities, it is possible that even after several years of keeping the severely retarded child in the family, the parents would be forced to place him in a segregated institution.

For several years, an alternative service has been functioning in the system of preschool education of Saint Petersburg, where children with special needs attend the special child groups organized for them in preschool establishments. Another possibility is creating integration groups for healthy children and children with special needs on the basis of the wide network of preschool establishments existing in society and in the kindergartens that are already in every district (Guralnick & Groom, 1987; McEvoy, Odom, & McConnell, 1992). This may be especially fruitful where there is also an ongoing early intervention program within the preschool. In such a case, it would be possible to organize a gradual transition of the child into a group in the same kindergarten, which would assure both children and parents a safe passage out of one program and into another, soften the process of adaptation to the new conditions, and achieve continuity of relations and social experience.

In 1995, in order to carry on the work with the children who had gone through an early intervention program, a project was initiated to organize joint attendance for special needs children and their peers in ordinary groups of the same preschool establishment. The shape this project took initially was determined, on the one hand, by the great numbers of children that had in the course of several years passed through the facilities of the early intervention program and still needed further assis-

tance after reaching the barrier age of 3 to 4 years, and, on the other hand, by the fact that only 5 families out of 100 attending the kindergarten agreed to allow their healthy children to consort with "invalids." Finally a group was formed, attended by 5 children with medical and genetic risk aged from 2.5 to 5 years (developmental level from 3 months to 2 years) and by 7 healthy children aged from 3 to 6 years.

Analysis of the video recordings of free play activities and those organized by the staff has shown that the children's being in an integrated group yielded positive results. In the 6-month period of attending the group, improvement was observed in the qualitative characteristics of interaction of the children with special needs in maintaining and developing play activity and in joining the play of their peers (Guralnick, 1992b). It turned out that the number of positive interactions between the healthy children and those with special needs was considerably higher than the number of negative ones. The healthy children showed a step-by-step change in the number of positive interactions, from equal numbers within their own subgroup and with children with special needs, to interaction among themselves only, to, by the 3rd month, equal numbers of positive interactions in both subgroups.

A 6-month observation of the integration group personnel has shown interesting dynamics in the number of interactions with the children. Initially there was a drop in the number of interactions between personnel and children compared to the starting level. Then there was a considerable increase in the number of contacts, especially marked in the interaction with at-risk children (the questionnaire of the U.S. National Academy of Early Childhood Programs, "Early Childhood Classroom Observation," was used, adapted and complemented with additional scales to assess interaction with at-risk children). The decrease in interactions with children coincided with lower spirits and increased anxiety levels in staff members. In other words, the personnel demonstrated several phases of changing mental state and of adaptation to working in the group. It has been found that the more an assistant teacher is oriented toward emotional interaction with the healthy children, the more often she establishes contact with the special needs children. According to the results of observations, ordinary kindergarten group teachers are oriented toward educating a child; consequently, they pay less attention to emotional interaction and view the child merely as an object for the educational process. This demonstrates the need for creating a new educational system to train staff that work with children of at-risk groups, as well as for providing the staff with some emotional and professional support.

The initial variant of integration gave the parents of healthy children a chance to look differently at the life of the families with special needs children and served as a good example for changing attitudes toward the problem of integration. Furthermore, it strengthened the commitment of all staff members toward changing their mode of work and including a special needs child in every preschool group. By now, the second variant of integration has been realized, in which every group of 12 healthy children includes one or two children with special needs, attended, in some cases, by a special assistant.

Thus, as a result of 5 years of interdisciplinary team members working in a preschool establishment, a new model of development for high risk children's groups has been created within the educational system. The model envisages stage-by-stage and continuity-preserving facilities for infants and children of early and preschool age in a preschool educational establishment. These facilities will consist of two departments: a department of interdisciplinary, family-centered assistance for infants and young children; and a department for the inclusion of children who have completed a program of early intervention in peer groups of preschool age.

In 1992, one of the tasks faced by the initiative group of professionals was to create an early intervention program alternative to segregating children in orphanages, and to provide the families of special needs infants with a chance for interdisciplinary assistance if the child remained in the family. At the termination of these 5 years, after creating a model of the early intervention program within a preschool educational establishment, the team members of this program are willing and able to address the conditions of infants and early age children in the orphanages. This decision is dictated in part by the fact that the overwhelming majority of parents of babies with medical and genetic risk of developmental delay, reject their children and have them placed into the network of orphanages under the Ministry of Health. Thus, in 1994 in Saint

Petersburg there were 44 Down syndrome children born; of them these 44, only 2 remained living in the family and were enrolled in the early intervention program organized by that time in the preschool establishment. The other 42 were relinquished by parents into orphanages.

The Condition of Babies in Orphanages and Guidelines for Early Intervention

The History of Orphanages in Russia

The first Russian home for the care and upkeep of "illegitimate and all kinds of foundling babies" was created by Mitropolite (Archbishop) Job in 1706 at a Novgorod convent. In 1715, Peter the Great issued an edict that fostering asylums were to be established in all the provinces. Those fostering asylums received their means of support mainly from charitable organizations and various collections and bequeathals. In the reign of Catherine II, the fostering asylums were included in the list of official state institutions, but continued subsisting on "charitable donations." In 1764, the empress personally inaugurated "a fostering asylum with a special hospital for the accouchement of destitute women" in Moscow, and in 1770, another in Saint Petersburg (Yuzhakov & Milyukov, 1904). The inmates were to be taught a craft and, by the grace of a privilege granted by the crown to this type of establishment, were reckoned free upon graduation, thus becoming people of the third estate, neither the landed gentry nor the peasant serfs.

Because of the great numbers of children being abandoned, and because of the inadequate care provided for the infants in the fostering asylums, in 1767, a practice was started of sending children to villages to be brought up in peasant families for a fee. That is, a system of family fostering of abandoned or orphaned children was begun. For the duration of the peasants' summer toil in the fields, they began to organize daytime crèches in order to take care of the children under 2 years of age (Shengelidze, 1900). The villages in which asylum children were placed formed districts, called *okrug*, in each of which an office of district inspector was created to watch over the children's health and to keep track of their upbringing. On account of the high rate of illness and mortality existing in the provincial fostering asylums, in 1828 the further establishing of fostering asylums was forbidden throughout the empire. Yet some of the asylums already established, including the ones in Moscow and in Saint Petersburg, survived, and the children were all concentrated in those large-city fostering asylums. Thus, in 1898 within the Saint Petersburg asylum alone, there were living about 30,000 children (Yuzhakov & Milyukov, 1904). The fosterlings of the imperial asylums could be restored to their mothers or, on the mothers' consent, to other persons, adopted, or in the case of the mother being dead, returned to relatives.

By the late nineteenth century the mortality rate among the children was still very high. Thus, according to the reports of 1898, out of the inmates of fostering asylums only 15.6 percent survived to reach the age of 22, the regulation age for leaving the asylum. Factors regarded as major causes of early childhood mortality included an insufficient number of wet nurses, the prevalence of epidemic illnesses, and the need to decentralize those fostering asylums that were too large. What was thought of as an important factor in securing the child's life was the mother's feeding of and constant care for the child, or "the mother's attachment to the child" (Rodulovich, 1892, p. 292). By the second half of the nineteenth century the practice of the child being fed by the mother herself in the fostering asylum was increasingly encouraged, as was that of sending the fosterlings out to be brought up in a rural setting. It was very soon found out that families took in such children almost exclusively for the money; only in a very few cases was it the absence of a child of their own and a wish to have one (Rashkovich, 1900). Beginning in 1837, instead of fostering asylums, children's asylums began to be organized in Russian cities, mostly attached to female almshouses, as well as district or regional hospitals, for the rearing of foundlings and waifs aged under 10 to 14 years. However, the lack of wet nurses or food for the babies, and a hurriedly ill-judged distribution of children from asylums to families, with no selection of the applying families, made this form of organizing care just as unsatisfactory as the other (Rashkovich, 1900).

The Soviet period of organizing facilities for foundling infants and orphaned children started after the 1917 revolution. All children's and fostering asylums, which had been for the most part supported by foundations and charitable organizations, were abolished. A network of state-supported establishments was then created within the system of health service. In 1918, in the first letter of the Department of the Defense of Motherhood and Infancy, newly created within the Commissariat of Social Support, the guiding principles for further activities were declared. Under these guidelines and in accordance with the ideology of the Soviet state, special attention was demanded of services for the laborer of the new social system, the mother "in the carrying out of her social function of procreation," and for the child "in his most difficult years of infancy" in a network of the freshly created mother and child homes (Konius, 1954, pp. 104–105). The letter also proclaimed the decision that henceforth all fostering asylums for infants without parental support were to be considered establishments of a defunct type and to be reduced to the minimum.

In spite of the first directive resolutions of the new state, very soon establishments of two types began to be created for the rearing of orphaned and foundling children up to the age of 3 years: asylums for children up to the age of 1 year, and asylums for children aged from 1 year to 3 years. Soon orphanages (baby homes) became widespread: mixed-type establishments where children from birth to 3 years were brought up. According to the resolution adopted in 1946, a baby home is an institution for the public rearing of orphaned children, children of single mothers, and children who have lost contact with parents or whose parents have been deprived of parental rights by the courts. Later there was included a provision that the orphanages would also accept children with defects in physical or mental development up to the age of 4 years for rearing and medical care, and there has been virtually no change in that up to the recent years (Ministry of Health of the USSR, 1986).

The transformations taking place within the society of Russia in the course of the last decade have made it evident that change is necessary in the system of facilities for children left without parental support. It has been agreed upon that family-type children's homes must be created (Council of Ministers of the RSFSR, 1988), some of them on the basis of peasant (farmer) households (Government of the Russian Federation, 1994), with children being reared in them wholly at the expense of the state. In 1993, 361 family-type children's homes were created in Russia, in which 932 natural and 2,282 adopted children were being brought up. The new Family Code of the Russian Federation (1996) makes provision for placing a child left without parental support into an adopting family for a contract period, with monetary payments being made to the family for the child's upkeep. Thus, in the new system of facilities for homeless children that is being organized in the post-Soviet period, one can see the ways and means that existed in prerevolutionary Russia of the second half of the nineteenth and the early twentieth century. However, the changes in the life of all strata of society, and the unstable and complicated economic situation in Russia are not conducive to the spread of new forms of organization for the life of children left without parental care. In Russia, orphanages are still the main establishments where infants and early age children are placed.

Condition of Infants in the Orphanages

The number of children in an orphanage is not less than 30 and not more than 100. Groups, depending on age, are supposed to contain from 10 to 15 children. The measures taken in recent years for changing the work in the orphanages envisage, while retaining the original number of staff a reduction of the number of children in a group to 6 (Council of Ministers of the RSFSR, 1994). Yet this is rather in the nature of a recommendation, and no additional financing is provided to support it. Every age group has its own regime. Communication between children of different groups with each other is limited. A child that has fallen ill is moved to a special unit, isolation ward, or hospital. Each group has its own personnel, consisting mostly of medical and nursery nurses. The personnel work in 24-hr shifts, 1 day in every 4. Transferring personnel from one group into another together with the children as they grow older is not allowed. Doctors carry out the management of the functioning of the establishment and the monitoring of the children's health. Since the orphanages constitute part of the health service system, the number of assistant teachers and educators is limited. There is no provision for including social workers or psychologists on the staff. Children from orphanages may be returned into the family of their biological parents or put up for adoption (including, since 1991, adoption by foreign citizens). Upon reaching the age of 3 to 4 years, the children are either transferred for further rearing into children's homes within the system of education, or, in the case of considerable developmental delay due to illness or genetic risk, passed on for medical care in the social security establishments.

In 1993, the total number of baby homes in Russia reached 253, with about 17,700 children as inmates. There were 3,150 aged to 0 to 12 months, 9,100 aged 1 to 3 years, and 5,450 children over 3 years of age. Out of these, 15,000 children evidenced delay in mental development, the majority being classified as the uneducable group of severely mentally retarded children. Delay in physical development was detected in 10,300 children. Out of the total number of children there are over 9,000 inmates of orphanages; that is, over ⅓ are orphans and children deprived of parental care. According to the governmental report "О положении детей в Российской Федерации (1993 год)" [*On childhood conditions in the Russian Federation*] (Russian Federation, 1994), about 1 percent of neonates become orphans in the first hours of life as a result of the mothers rejecting them in the maternity homes. The main causes of rejection of children are the social destitution of parents, their living conditions being inappropriate for keeping and rearing children, grave illness of parents, the mother serving a prison sentence, and serious disease in the child. In 1993, about 950 children residing in the orphanages of Russia died (half of them under 1 year of age). In that same year, 3,800 were taken from the orphanage back into the family, about 3,050 were adopted, 1,600 were transferred for medical care

into the social security organizations, and 1,950 were transferred into educational establishments. In 1996, in the 13 orphanages of Saint Petersburg, there resided about 1,500 children aged 4 years old and under.

The development of a program directed at changing the situation of children in the orphanages for the better should be based, apart from the analysis of history and statistical data, upon the results of observations of different aspects of life of the babies in the group and upon an analysis of the conditions of children and personnel in an orphanage. In the preliminary stage of our program, observations were carried out on the distribution of hours of work performed by the orphanage staff members. An analysis of the duration and quality of interaction of the personnel with the babies was completed. A study of the emotional state of the women employed in the orphanage and the ways in which that state affected their interaction with the babies was performed, as well as an analysis of the interaction behavior of babies with each other in a playpen. Finally, a data questionnaire was administered to the staff members on the needs of the children and the staff themselves and on their own views as to the ways of improving the life of children in the orphanage.

DISTRIBUTION OF WORK TIME OF THE ORPHANAGE PERSONNEL

Observation of the interaction of the personnel of the orphanage with children under 3 months (Group 1) and from 3 to 10 months (Group 2) was carried out in the course of 2 months. The interactions were observed once a week from 9:30 A.M. to 12:30 P.M. during the morning feeding and the children's waking hours. During the observations, the average amount of time spent by a medical or nursery nurse with the group in the following three categories was calculated.

1. Time spent interacting with the infants while performing the duties considered obligatory in the orphanage (e.g., feeding, changing, hygienic procedures, sponging)
2. The number of interactions initiated (e.g., talking to the child, picking up the child, displaying toys to the child)
3. Interaction in response to a child's behavior (e.g., crying, burping, vocalizing)

The results of the observation are shown in Table 10.1. It has been determined that the women looking after the babies, on the average, initiated free interaction for only 19 min if working with children aged from 3 to 10 months, and 16.8 min if working with children aged under 3 months. In a great majority of cases the women used separate initiations to start an interaction (13.1 min in Group 1 and 12.6 min in Group 2). Combining different types of stimulation while interacting with a baby was observed very seldom and took up a very small part of the working time (5.9 min in Group 1 and 4.2 min in Group 2).

It was found that women working in the orphanage virtually never responded to a baby's motions, change of facial expression, or attempts to initiate eye contact. They very rarely responded to the babies' vocalization, burping after breakfast, or crying.

The crying of a baby under 3 months continued unanswered on the average for 12 min, from 3 to 10 months for 10.2 min. On average, in the period of observation, the time of response to the babies' behavior took up only 2.3 min for women working in Group 1, and 1.1 min in Group 2. Part of the responses to the infants' behavior took place in silence (see Table 12.1).

It was found that in the three most favorable morning hours for interaction between the children and adults, staff members of the orphanage spent most of their time carrying out procedures necessary from the point of view of a medical establishment regime. On average, 90.7 min (50 percent of the time) was spent carrying out procedures when working in Group 1 with babies under 3 months, and 65.6 min (36 percent) was spent in Group 2 with children from 3 to 10 months. For only ⅓ of the time while carrying out the regulation operations and being in immediate contact with the children in Group 1, and a little over half of the time of contact with the children in Group 2, the women spoke to the children. The rest of the time the operations were performed in silence. During the morning 3-hr period of observation, out of the total time spent by staff members in carrying out the required actions, each baby under 3 months received, on average, only 12.6 min and each aged from 3 to 10 months received 12.1 min. The greater part of that interaction time was during feeding. During the 3 hr of observation, each child in Group 1 was given 5.8 min, on average, and each in Group 2, 5.1 min (see Table 12.1). Within the observed 3-hr period, the total time the nurse spent

TABLE 10.1

Length of Interaction between an Orphanage Staff Member and the Child
(Average per Shift from 9:30 A.M. to 12:30 P.M.)

	Group 1 M ± SD (minutes)	Group 2 M ± SD (minutes)
I. Interaction during regulation activities		
A. Feeding		
Time spent feeding the children	48.1 ± 16.4	30.1 ± 9.8
Talks while feeding	7.0 ± 7.9	15.0 ± 9.7
Does not talk while feeding	41.1 ± 19.0	15.1 ± 10.6
Time spent feeding one child	5.8 ± 1.3	5.1 ± 1.8
B. Changing		
Time spent changing the children	32.0 ± 15.0	27.0 ± 13.4
Talks while changing	19.2 ± 18.8	18.6 ± 12.4
Does not talk while changing	12.8 ± 17.0	8.4 ± 8.3
Time spent changing one child	4.2 ± 1.7	4.1 ± 1.4
C. Hygienic operations		
Time spent in hygienic operations	8.4 ± 4.9	6.2 ± 4.9
Talks while performing hygienic operations	1.7 ± 3.8	0.6 ± 1.3
Does not talk while performing hygienic operations	6.7 ± 6.2	5.6 ± 4.1
Time of hygienic operations per child	1.2 + 0.1	1.4 + 0.2
D. Sponging		
Time spent sponging	2.2 ± 2.0	2.3 ± 1.7
Talks while sponging the child	1.1 ± 1.6	0
Does not talk while sponging the child	1.1 ± 1.6	2.3 ± 1.7
Time spent sponging one child	1.4 ± 0.5	1.5 ± 0.6
Total:		
Time spent in regulation activities	90.7 ± 31.2	65.6 ± 23.1
Out of that, talking	29.0 ± 26.1	34.2 ± 19.4
Without talking (in silence)	61.7 ± 41.4	31.4 ± 18.0
Average time per child	12.6 ± 2.2	12.1 ± 2.4
II. Initiates interaction with child		
Talks to the child	5.3 ± 7.1	4.9 ± 3.5
Picks up	3.0 ± 3.0	2.4 ± 3.1
Displays toy	2.6 ± 2.3	3.3 ± 1.5
Tactile stimulation	2.4 ± 2.7	1.6 ± 2.2
Changes positioning	2.1 ± 2.7	0.7 ± 1.2
Winds up a mechanical sounding toy	1.5 ± 1.4	0.3 ± 0.4
Talks while busy with something else	1.1 ± 1.9	1.0 ± 1.1
Initiates by vocalizing	0.2 ± 0.3	1.0 ± 1.5
Plays with child with a toy	0.3 ± 0.4	0.3 ± 0.4
Uses other forms of initiation (total time for changes of facial expression, eye contact, vocalizing at a distance)	0.5 ± 0.8	1.3 ± 1.5
Total:	19.0 ± 14.9	16.8 ± 8.5
Different initiations used separately	13.1 ± 11.8	12.6 ± 7.1
Different initiations combined	5.9 ± 7.8	4.2 ± 3.7

(*continued*)

TABLE 10.1 (Continued)

	Group 1 M ± SD (minutes)	Group 2 M ± SD (minutes)
III. Behavioral response to child's signals		
A. The child's crying		
Responds by talking	1.4 ± 1.3	0.6 ± 0.8
Picks up in silence	0.3 ± 0.4	0
Period of crying without response	12.0 ± 14.7	10.2 ± 15.3
B. The child's burp		
Responds by talking	0.4 ± 0.5	0.2 ± 0.4
Wipes off in silence	0.2 ± 0.4	0
C. The child's vocalization		
Responds by talking	0	0.3 ± 0.4
Period of vocalizing without response	0.1 ± 0.2	0.1 ± 0.2
D. The child initiates contact by looking, moving,		
Change of facial expression	0	0
Total:		
Time of responses to the child's behavior	2.3 ± 1.1	1.1 ± 0.9
Out of them, talking	1.8 ± 1.3	1.1 ± 0.9
Not talking (in silence)	0.5 ± 0.9	0
Total:		
Length of interaction between an orphanage staff member and the children (average per shift in the hours from 9:30 A.M. to 12:30 P.M.	112 ± 39.3	83.5 ± 27.2

interacting with the children equaled 112 min when working in Group 1, and 83.5 min in Group 2. During the remaining observation time, the personnel cleaned the room, filled in the registration journals regarding the infants' medical state, brought food from the kitchen, washed dishes, and did other chores.

Thus, according to the results of the observations, the deprivation suffered by babies in an orphanage consists of an exceedingly small amount of time spent interacting with their caretakers. The orphanage personnel infrequently responded to the infants' signals and initiations for interaction and rarely interacted with the children during their silent carrying out of regulation procedures. The next step in the analysis of the children's conditions in an orphanage was the analysis of the interactions between child and adult that occur during feeding time. This is the most prolonged interaction, besides being repeated several times throughout the day.

INTERACTION BETWEEN ORPHANAGE STAFF AND INFANTS DURING FEEDING

Babies of the first group, under 3 to 4 months, are bottle-fed. Often, the infants are left in the cot and a pillow is used to support the bottle. In this situation, communication is reduced to a minimum and, in

TABLE 10.2

Characteristics of Interaction of Orphanage Personnel with Children in Group 2
(3 to 10 Months) during Feeding

Characteristics of interaction	M ± SD
1. Duration of feeding (minutes)	
duration of feeding	5.1 ± 1.8
time before and after feeding	2.0 ± 0.9
total period of interaction	7.1 ± 2.4
2. Feeding rate (times a minute)	
spoonfuls into the child's mouth	12 ± 3.4
spoon touching the child's face	30 ± 9.7
3. The child's initiations (times a minute)	
number of looks into the adult's face	1.0 ± 0.6
number of vocalizations	1.5 ± 1.4
total number of initiations	2.5 ± 1.6
4. Responses to the child's signals (times a minute)	
number of responses to a look	0.6 ± 0.5
number of responses to a vocalization	0.7 ± 0.6
total responses	1.3 ± 0.9
5. Initiating interaction with a child (times a minute)	
number of looks into the child's face	0.6 ± 0.6
number of verbal messages	3.6 ± 3.0
total number of initiations	4.2 ± 3.3
6. The number of communications with other staff members (times a minute)	1.0 ± 0.9

spite of the existing rules, as seen in Table 12.1, the feeding mainly takes place without talking. Starting at the age of 3 to 4 months, children are spoon-fed. The caregiver holds the child in her lap with the child's back toward her. In one hand she has the plate of food, in the other the spoon. The child's head and arms are pressed against the woman's body with her elbows, and often kept immobilized throughout the period of feeding. The results of analyzing video recordings of feeding the children from 3 to 10 months, by the 17 medical and nursery nurses working in this group, are presented in Table 10.2. The average time of interaction, from the moment the woman puts the child on her lap to the time she rises from the table, constitutes 7 min 10 s. Out of this, the time before the start of feeding (tying on of the bib, checking whether the food is too hot), and after the feeding (giving drink from a cup, wiping the face with a napkin) adds up to an average of 2 min. The feeding time proper for the child equals 5 min 10 s. Every 5 s of that period, the staff member pokes a spoonful of food into the baby's mouth (12 times a minute). The child does not have time to swallow the food and pushes it out with the tongue. The woman at once picks up the dropping food from the chin and pushes it back into the child's mouth. On average, in the group observed, a woman working in the orphanage does about two "pickups" after every spoonful of food into the mouth. Within the space of 1 min, she touches the child's face with the spoon 30 times. In such a coercive feeding situation, the baby attempts to draw the woman's attention and, on the average every 24 s (2.5 times a minute), initiates interaction either by looking into the adult's face (one look a minute), or by vocalizing (1.5 times a minute).

The women respond to only 51 percent of the children's signals (1.3 responses a minute, of them 0.6 to a look and 0.7 to the child's vocalization), ignoring and leaving unanswered the remaining part. It has been found that the women show more initiative than attention toward the signals of the child they are feeding. On average, in the group, they demonstrate initiative in communication 4.2 times a minute (once every 14 s). The frequency of initiations by look equals 0.6 a minute, and by verbal communication addressed to a child (for instance, saying in the imperative: "Eat, eat.") were observed 3.6 times a minute.

In summary, it may be said that even in the situation of the longest and the most intense interaction with adults, in the situation of feeding, the children and infants in the orphanages find themselves in a situation of deprivation. There is not only a lack of harmony in the mutual behavior between the women and babies, an insufficient number of initiatives and mutual responses, a broken pattern of attuning to each other's signals, but even violence in the situation of feeding. The orphanage staff members treat the infant as an object to be fed, into which they should shove the food off the plate as fast as possible. Depri-

vation and abuse are further exacerbated by the fact that during feeding the women are often distracted from the children, associate with the colleagues feeding the other children, and answer the signals of the babies awaiting their own turn to be fed.

INFLUENCE OF THE ORPHANAGE STAFF MEMBERS' PSYCHOLOGICAL CHARACTERISTICS ON THE INTERACTION WITH BABIES AT FEEDING TIME

An examination of the emotional state of the orphanage staff has shown that, in comparison to mothers of children under 10 months, they manifest a higher level of situational anxiety ($p < .025$; Anxiety Scale, Spielberger, 1972) and of depression ($p < .025$; Self-Rating Depression Scale, Zung, 1965).[1] It is probable that the daily work with and responsibility for infants abandoned by their parents, some of whom have medical or genetic risk of developmental delay, may result in a change of emotional state in the orphanage's staff. Also, many of the staff have children of their own to bring up, and often feel anxious about them while on duty. Some have to combine work in an orphanage with another job in order to improve their financial situation. A number of studies indicate that a mother's depressive state significantly disrupts the interaction behavior of mother and infant (Beckwith, 1990; Field, 1990). Undoubtedly, the depressive state and the heightened anxiety level of the women looking after the babies in the orphanage constitute yet another deprivation factor, which adversely affects the infants' development.

A correlation analysis of the parameters of interaction between the orphanage staff members and the infants during feeding has shown that the number of initiative looks directed by the baby toward the adult is greater in those cases when the feeding women, on the one hand, respond to those looks more often ($p < .01$), and, on the other hand, more often initiate interaction by addressing verbal communications to the child ($p < .03$). Analysis of the psychological factors affecting the interaction between the orphanage staff members and the babies has shown that the higher the index of depression and anxiety of the woman seeing to the child, the less frequently she responds to a child's eye contact, and the fewer looks initiating communication the child addresses to her ($p < .01$ and $p < .05$ respectively).

It has been established that a direct connection exists between such mental characteristics of the women as empathy (ability to share in another's experience, to feel compassion; Interpersonal Diagnosis of Personality, Leary, 1957) and expectation of positive result when establishing interpersonal contact (ability to attune, to display warmth, friendliness, support), and the number of vocalizations of the child initiating interaction ($p < .05$ and $p < .025$ respectively). The higher the caretaker's ability to empathize and the better her attunement with the baby, the more frequently she responds to the baby's vocal initiations, and in turn, the more the infant vocalizes during the feeding time ($p < .01$). The number of verbal communication initiations to the infant during feeding is greater in those women who tend to regard another person as valuable ($p < .025$) and who are trustful and characteristically feminine ("L" and "I" factors of the 16 PF Questionnaire, Cattell, Eber, & Tatsuoka, 1970; $p < .01$ and $p < .05$ respectively).

All these data indicate that the infants in the orphanage are sensitive and attuned to the mental state and characteristics of the women caregivers. Disturbances in the emotional sphere and the individual character traits of the orphanage staff members cause changes in the interaction behavior toward the infants and, consequently, disturbances in the interaction characteristics on the part of the infants.

Women working in the orphanage display a wide variety of individual traits, according to the list of characteristics of interaction at the time of feeding given in Table 10.2. Thus, the duration of feeding varies from 4.5 min to 11.5 min, the number of touches of the spoon against the child's face from 12 to 45 a minute, the number of interaction initiations from 0.9 to 12.5 a minute. Some women would respond to only 13 percent of the child's signals, while some others would react to every signal. It has been established that the women who would initiate interaction with the infant by a word or eye contact more than five times during the time of feeding, and reacted to more than ⅔ of the child's signals (23 percent of those surveyed), differ from the other staff members in regarding another person as valuable ($p < .001$), in femininity ($p < .01$), in a less dominating personality and greater emotional stability (factors "E" and "C" of the 16 PF Questionnaire, Cattell, Eber, & Tatsuoka, 1970; $p < .05$ and $p < .005$ respectively). It has been found that, compared with the other staff members, this group of women assesses the child in the orphanage as a better, more active, and stronger one ($p < .01$; the Measurement of Meaning method, Osgood, Suci, & Tannenbaum, 1957). It has been established that those women take longer to feed the child and less frequently touch the child's face with the spoon. However, they do not differ from the other staff members in the speed of feeding—that is, the number of spoonfuls a minute into the child's mouth—and the number of communications addressed to the side past the baby. It is probably the conditions of work in the orphanage, the necessity to feed a great number of infants in the time stipulated by the medical regulations, that determine the rhythm of feeding (one spoonful into the mouth every 5 to 7 s), which is adopted by all the staff members gathering at the same table to feed the children, regardless of their individual psychological characteristics. As for the increase of the overall time of interaction during the feeding, it happens mainly through the increased time of communicating with the child before and after the spoon-feeding proper ($p < .01$).

Among the surveyed orphanage staff members, there exists a group of women (41 percent of those surveyed) who display just as much initiative in communicating with the infants during feeding (like the previous group, initiating contact with the infant by word or eye contact more frequently than five times a minute), but remain insensitive to the children's signals. Another group (35 percent of those surveyed) demonstrates neither initiative, nor

sensibility toward the children's signals. In the case of a special intervention program being organized, it is probable that women of the middle group would move into the group of those with sensitivity and initiative.

INFANTS' ATTACHMENT BEHAVIOR IN AN ORPHANAGE

During the last several years preschool special education teachers and speech therapists have been involved in caregiving activity for children as young as 1 year old. They provide educational sessions with children five times a week individually or in a group. It is important to understand what attachment behavior infants showed toward teachers after several months of short but consistent meetings.

Attachment behavior was studied in 8 children who had been placed in one of the orphanages in Saint Petersburg for social reasons. The average age of the children at the time of investigation was 16.5 ± 3.7 months. They were placed in the orphanage at age 2.5 ± 2.5 months. According to the baby home pediatricians, five children were delayed in psychomotor development (not more than 3 months' delay) and three of the children had diagnosis of "encephalopathy." There were no genetic or marked medical problems observed.

In the attachment behavior investigation procedure, the speech therapist was identified as the caregiver for 5 of the children, with whom she had individual 15-min sessions five times each week. A special teacher was identified as the caregiver for the remaining 3 children who had not experienced individual sessions with the speech therapist. The special teacher worked with the children in 3- to 4-hr sessions five times a week. The average age at which the children began spending time with the caregivers was 11.8 ± 1.7 months.

The classical Strange Situation procedure developed by Mary Ainsworth (Ainsworth, Blehar, Waters, & Wall, 1978) was used to study attachment behavior. Infants' proximity- and contact-seeking, contact-maintaining, resistant, distant interaction, and avoidant behaviors were scored using a 7-point scale in Episodes 5 (reunion after the first separation) and 8 (reunion after the second separation).

Results indicated that average data for the sample of infants' proximity- and contact-seeking behavior was 3.2 ± 2.3 in the first reunion episode, and 3.7 ± 2.1 in the second. Contact-maintaining behavior was 1.8 ± 1.5 and 2.6 ± 1.6 respectively. Resistant behavior was 2.1 ± 1.3 in the fifth episode, and 2.1 ± 1.7 in the eighth. Average data for the sample of infants' distant interaction behavior was 2.1 ± 1.3 in the first reunion episode and 1.6 ± 1.1 in the second. Avoidant behavior was 3.9 ± 1.9 and 3.6 ± 2.0 respectively.

Three of the 8 observed infants showed a combination of evident avoidant behavior with the minimal proximity- and contact-seeking, contact-maintaining, resistant, and distant interaction behaviors. Three cases were a combination of the evident avoidant behavior with the active proximity- and contact-seeking behavior in at least one of the reunion episodes.

In the seventh case, the child showed the active proximity- and contact-seeking behavior in the fifth episode, and evident

wish of proximity and contact with the caregiver in the eighth. He didn't exhibit avoidance, but showed instances of resistance in the first reunion episode, and a high level of resistance in the second. This 14-month-old boy had been placed in the baby home at the age of 1 month. At the time of the Strange Situation procedure, the child had been meeting with the caregiver for 2 months in individual 15-min speech therapy sessions five times a week. According to the speech therapist, in spite of the short length of the sessions, she paid more attention to this particular child, and in fact preferred him over other children in the baby home.

Among the group of children was a 12-month-old girl who had lived in the baby home since her second month of life. At the time of the Strange Situation procedure, the special teacher had been visiting the girl's group of living for 3 months in 3- to 4-hour sessions five times a week, and paid more attention to this girl than to the other children in the group. In both reunion episodes the child showed very active proximity- and contact-seeking behavior, and active contact-maintaining behavior. There were no avoidant or resistant behaviors observed in the reunion episodes after the first and second separations from the caregiver. In this case, consistent group sessions coupled with the positive attitude of the caregiver toward the infant may favor the behavior of secure attachment.

INTERACTION OF INFANTS
IN AN ORPHANAGE

For a baby who is living in an orphanage under conditions of deprivation, who has low quality of interaction, who experiences a great number and frequent change of caretaking staff, and who lacks a primary caregiver, a peer becomes one of the main sources of social and emotional stimulation. Babies who stay daily, for long periods of time, within the same space with the same peers, are presented with a chance to use their skills to establish social interaction.

To explore the interaction of the babies in the orphanage (determining the interaction behavior parameters, changes in interaction as the children get older, discovering specific individual traits), six series of observations were conducted and videotaped of three children of the same age: 2 boys and 1 girl. The children were first observed at 3.5 months and last observed at 9.5 months (Muhamedrahimov, Palmov, & Nikforova, 1996). All three children had been placed in the orphanage by their mothers for social reasons. Birth history shows that the children were born at 40 weeks. Their Apgar scores, length, and weight were, respectively, 6/8, 49 cm, 2850 g (the boy K.), 8/9, 52 cm, 3600 g (the boy S.), and 8/9, 52 cm, 3400 g (the girl V.). The children were placed in the orphanage at the ages, respectively, of 32 days (K. had been in hospital for 27 days before entering the orphanage), 7 days, and 9 days. The children were first put out into a playpen with peers when they were about 3 months old. During observation time the babies were in the same playpen where they were usually put after they had their sleep and where they spent most of their waking hours. As the children got older, their interaction in the playpen without toys, which was standard in the orphanage for the ba-

bies in the first months of life, changed to interaction in the playpen with toys.

This section analyzes interaction among peers in the playpen without toys at the time when K. was aged 3 months and 27 days, S. 3 months and 16 days, and V. 3 months and 18 days. The children were laid down side by side, so that the baby in the middle could interact with the neighbor on the right or the left. The babies lying to either side of him or her could either interact with the infant in the middle or look into the mirror that was on the other side. Every 6 min the position of the children was changed in such a way that, during the six series of observations, each baby should on two occasions have different neighbors in the center, on the right, and on the left.

In analyzing the resulting videotapes for each child, depending on the series of observation, the time was calculated during which the child looked around or to the front, looked into the mirror on the right or on the left, and looked toward the peer on the right or left. This also included the length of face-to-face interaction, the number of manifested behaviors, and the percentage of observation time within the series when the child showed a definite type of behavior. Change in direction of looking within a definite section of space was regarded as connected with interaction behavior in this spatial direction. For instance, moving one's eyes from the neighbor's clothing to his or her hand was consigned to the period of time when the child was looking at his or her peer; moving one's eyes from the neighbor's hand to one's own hands. The interval during which the child changed from looking at his or her peer to looking forward or around was considered looking to the front. The variations of placing the children in the playpen in the different series of observation and the interaction behavior parameters of the babies in the defined spatial directions are given in Table 10.3.

On the strength of the information thus acquired, it has been found that, when placed between two peers, the babies would look at one of their neighbors for longer periods of time than they looked around or in front of themselves ($p < .01$). When placed on the side, the babies looked at the peer lying next to them or looked into the mirror longer and for a greater part of the time, than around or in front of themselves (in Series 1 and 2 for the babies V. and K.; in Series 3 and 4 for V.; in Series 5 for K., in Series 6 for S. and K.; $p < .01$; see Table 12.3). In 8 out of 12 cases of being placed between the peer and the mirror, the babies looked into the mirror rather than at the neighbor for a longer period and for the greater part of time (V. and K. in Series 1, 2, 3, and 5; S. in Series 3 and 6, but still $p < .06$; see Table 3).

It has been found that in three cases out of four when placed to the side (in Series 3, 4, and 5), the baby S. looked in front of him and around for a longer time than at his neighbor or into the mirror. Out of six series of observations, S. looked in front of him for longer and for a larger percentage of time than K. in five (in Series 2–6, $p < .05$; Table 3) and in four of them longer than V. (Series 2–5). In her turn, V. looked around and in front of her longer (Series 2–6, $p < .025$) and for a greater part of time (Series 3–6, $p < .05$), than K.

As a result of the observations conducted, it has been established that, out of the six series, a baby may look at the child lying beside him (in his or her direction) on average, from ⅙, when placed between a peer and the mirror, to ½ the observation time when placed between peers (see Table 12.3). This behavior has been observed to occur simultaneously in children lying side by side, with face-to-face interaction and eye-to-eye contact. In spite of the comparatively low frequency of face-to-face interaction, every baby has shown ability to form several different sets of successive changes in the type of mutual eye contact. There were registered a short and a long simultaneous look at each other, short and long spells of averting the gaze and turning it back to each other's face and eyes. The babies were found at times to be able, on the one hand, to keep their eyes fixed on a peer's face or maintain eye contact for scores of seconds without break. On the other hand, in the period of the peer maintaining a long look, periodically, with an interval of several seconds, they were found to avert the eyes and then turn them back again to look the partner in the eye (see Figure 10.2).

To draw a peer into interaction, the babies used a wide spectrum of behavior. In the series described, there were observed initiations of interaction from a distance (looks at the peer, attempts to establish eye contact, vocalizes, smiles, changes facial expression, moves lips, sticks out tongue, turns head, moves hands and/or fingers, moves feet, changes posture, arches body, etc.), as well as initiations by actually touching the peer (touches face, head, hands,

TABLE 10.3

Parameters of Interaction Behavior of Babies in a Playpen

(the boys K.—3 mo. 27 days and S.—3 mo. 16 days, the girl V.—3 mo. 18 days).

Types of Behavior/Parameters	Looks in the Mirror on the Right	Looks Around and Forward	Looks at the Baby on the Left	Out of That, Face to Face	Looks at the Baby on the Right	Looks Around and Forward	Looks at the Baby on the Left	Out of That, Face to Face	Looks at the Baby on the Right	Looks Around and Forward	Looks in the Mirror on the Left
SERIES 1		baby K.[1]				baby S.[2]				baby V.[3]	
M ± SD	36.6± 66.2	19.4± 57.2	27.0± 43.7	6.7± 3.9	16.7± 20.1	6.0± 9.3	40.3 ± 49.7	5.8± 4.6	20.1± 17.8	9.2± 12.3	45.7 ± 46.7
N[5]	9	12	5	6	15	21	8	11	11	17	7
%[6]	47.2	33.4	19.4	5.7	39.9	17.9	46.2	9.2	31.7	22.4	45.9
SERIES 2		baby V.				baby S.				baby K.	
M ± SD	77.1± 156.5	8.1± 10.3	6.7± 7.9	1.0± 0.0	18.9± 28.0	9.3± 8.1	58.1±132.4	1.0± 0.0	5.3± 6.6	5.4± 5.2	37.3 ± 67.6
N	8	12	6	1	9	19	7	1	4	19	17
%	81.5	13.0	5.5	0.1	22.5	23.5	54.0	0.1	2.8	13.5	83.7
SERIES 3		baby V.				baby K.				baby S.	
M ± SD	28.8± 50.0	7.0± 5.9	1.0± 0.0	0.0	57.0± 8.5	5.8± 6.5	21.0 ± 20.9	0.0	0.0	34.6± 70.7	32.2 ± 64.2
N	9	11	1	0	2	9	8	0	0	5	5
%	77.5	23.2	0.3	0.0	34.1	15.6	50.3	0.0	0.0	51.8	48.2
SERIES 4		baby S.				baby K.				baby V.	
M ± SD	3.5± 2.1	31.6± 38.2	5.7± 6.3	0.0	0.0	2.7± 2.7	49.7±51.7	3.6± 3.4	32.4± 35.9	9.5± 14.9	0.0
N	4	10	6	0	0	6	7	24	9	8	0
%	3.8	86.8	9.4	0.0	0.0	4.4	95.6	23.9	79.3	20.7	0.0

SERIES 5

	baby S.[2]			baby V.[3]			baby K.[1]		
M ± SD	15.3± 18.9	0.0	6.0± 6.3	11.9± 19.3	13.4± 8.4	12.5±14.8	3.0± 0.0	118± 79.9	0.0
N	11	0	10	7	10	2	1	2	0
%	73.7	0.0	26.3	34.3	55.4	10.3	1.2	98.8	0.0

SERIES 6

	baby K.[1]			baby V.[3]			baby S.[2]		
M ± SD	3.0± 0.0	131± 127	0.0	4.0± 1.0	27.6± 52.3	20.0 ± 7.9	3.5± 0.7	129± 178	0.0
N	1	2	0	3	7	3	2	2	0
%	1.1	98.9	0.0	4.5	72.8	22.7	2.6	97.4	0.0

AVERAGE FIGURES FOR SERIES 1–6

Children's position	baby on the right				baby in the center				baby on the left		
M ± SD	24.3± 30.2	1.3± 2.7	14.1± 10.4	29.6± 50.5	18.1± 20.4	10.8± 9.0	33.6 ± 18.4	17.7± 2.4	9.6± 13.6	10.9± 11.9	60.4± 51.5
N	5.0± 4.3	1.2± 2.4	9.5± 4.2	5.0± 3.2	6.0± 5.5	12.0± 6.4	5.8± 2.6	6.0± 9.8	4.0± 4.9	8.7± 7.7	5.5± 6.2
%	35.0± 38.8	1.0± 2.3	38.5± 34.2	26.6± 36.6	22.6± 16.8	31.6± 26.5	46.5± 29.5	5.5± 9.7	19.0± 32.1	18.7± 18.5	62.3± 38.4

[1]K., a boy aged 3 months, 27 days
[2]S., a boy, aged 3 months, 16 days
[3]V., a girl, aged 3 months, 18 days
[4]M ± SD: values in seconds for average duration of behavior within the series and the standard deviation
[5]N: number of occurrences of the behavior in question
[6]%: time percentage within a series of observation taken up by the behavior in question

Interaction between K. and S. (Example out of Series 1)

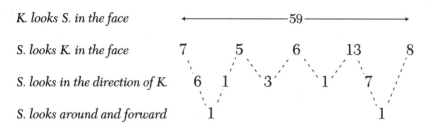

Interaction between S. and V. (Example out of Series 1)

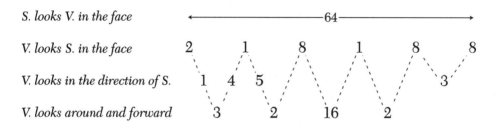

Note: K. is a boy aged 3 months, 27 days; S., a boy aged 3 months, 16 days; V., a girl aged 3 months, 18 days. Figures represent interaction behavior length in seconds. The left arrow indicates the start of a face-to-face interaction.

FIGURE 10.2
Interaction of babies in a playpen.

body; leans against, pushes, kicks, etc.). In some cases, indirect ways of drawing into an interaction were observed, for instance, when one of the peers would finger or suck the clothes the neighbor was wearing, or rhythmically hit the surface of the playpen with his feet. The same wide scope of social behavior was manifested in the babies' responses to a neighbor's initiations, evidenced by swerving toward the peer to draw him or her into interaction. A general change of activity level, such as focusing and change of look, change of facial expression, the beginning of vocalization, smile, change of movement, and attempts to touch one's own reflection were also observed when a child turned toward the mirror.

In the case of successful initiations and involvement of the infants in an interaction, not only the successive changes of look described above were observed, but also simultaneous vocalizations; short successive vocalization exchanges; short successive changes of facial expression; and smiles exchanged simultaneously, but alternating in the level of intensity turn by turn. Finger, hand, foot, and body movements were observed, either simultaneously executed by both partners or mutually and successively changed in the intensity of movement. In the time of interaction, infants could change the intensity and rhythm of behavior in accordance with the other's behavior. Peers demonstrated ability to focus attention both on each other and on the same point in space.

Thus, as a result of the observations, it has been established that the babies prefer to interact with a peer or to look into the mirror, "communicating" with their own reflection in it, than to look into space in front of and around them, devoid of social stimuli. The observed infants have actually shown a tendency to turn for longer periods and for a larger share of time toward their own reflection in the mirror than toward the neighbor, but not to a statistically significant degree. An individual specific characteristic of social behavior has been detected in the babies, manifesting itself in a greater (in S.) or smaller (in K.) inclination to turn to the space in front of him instead of interacting with peers. It has been found that, when interacting with each other, the babies not only make use of a successive change of social behavior usually observed in an interaction of a baby with an adult (Stern, 1977; Stern et al., 1977), but can even form, all by themselves, chain patterns of behavior, consisting of face-to-face interactions differing in length and type. They demonstrate an ability to keep their eyes fixed long on the peer, giving the partner a chance to vary behavior by averting the eyes and turning them back (see Figure 10.2). In other words, the infants demonstrate an ability to form asymmetrical social interaction with peers, comparable in its features to the known parameters of interaction between adults and infants (Brazelton, Koslowski, & Main, 1974; Fogel, 1977).

DATA FROM ANSWERS TO A
QUESTIONNAIRE FOR THE
ORPHANAGE PERSONNEL

A change from the system of segregation and strictly medically oriented facilities to socially oriented programs of development for children residing in the orphanages, demands a preliminary analysis of the living conditions and needs of the infants, as well as a study of views and needs of the personnel taking care of the children. Analysis of the data resulting from a survey conducted among staff members of one of the orphanages in Saint Petersburg (a group of 63 persons, consisting of medical nurses, assistant teachers, defectologists—i.e., special education teachers—nursery nurses, and doctors) with the help of a questionnaire specially designed for the purpose (see Table 10.4) has shown that, from their point of view, to improve the conditions of children there is not so much a need for an increase in medical assistance (that item was marked by only 5 percent of the staff members) or more special education classes (8 percent), but rather more communication and attention on the part of the personnel (57 percent), having an intimate person always available to the child (54 percent), and a change in living conditions (30 percent). Among the reasons for their insufficient communication with the children, the women have noted lack of time caused by their being too busy with their principal duties (57 percent; according to the regulations of the orphanages, these consist first

TABLE 10.4
Data from Answers to a Questionnaire for the Orphanage Personnel

Every item of the questionnaire you are holding contains six variant statements.
Please choose and mark two statements that are most relevant to you.

1. I work in an orphanage because
- 11   a) I do not want to be without a job.
- 9   b) I find the pay adequate and the working hours convenient.
- 59   c) The work corresponds to my professional interests.
- 19   d) I like the atmosphere.
- 78   e) I like working with small children.
- 9   f) Other (indicate what) _____

2. It seems to me that children in the orphanage
- 5   a) Need more medical attention.
- 8   b) Must have additional special education classes.
- 30   c) Need change of living conditions.
- 57   d) Need more communication, attention from personnel.
- 54   e) Need an intimate person available at all times.
- 3   f) Other (indicate what) _____

3. The children I work with would be better off living
- 13   a) In a common orphanage.
- 30   b) In a family-type orphanage.
- 14   c) In a common orphanage, changed according to family type.
- 27   d) In the family with biological parents.
- 71   e) In an adopting family.
- 2   f) Other (indicate what) _____

4. I seem to communicate with children very little because
- —   a) They do not need it.
- 2   b) It is outside my sphere of duties.
- 57   c) I have no time; too busy with my principal duties.
- 2   d) I do not know how.
- 37   e) I do not want attachment between the child and me.
- 24   f) Other (indicate what) _____

5. Sometimes I have difficulty interacting with the children
- 6   a) While feeding or changing.
- 3   b) During hygienic operations.
- 6   c) In the moments of free communication.
- 38   d) When a child frets or cries.
- 37   e) When I must leave the group.
- 25   f) Other (indicate what) _____

6. I could provide better work if
- 76   a) There were fewer children in the group.
- 30   b) Children were not passed on from group to group.
- 11   c) I had more information on the child's development.
- 30   d) I were trusted more and controlled less.
- 6   e) If it were not for the distress over the children in the orphanage.
- 6   f) Other (indicate what) _____

TABLE 10.4 (Continued)

7. **I would like to talk about my difficulties, discuss the emotions arising in the course of my work, with**
   - **13** a) Administration of the orphanage.
   - **44** b) Colleagues in my shift and staff members of the orphanage.
   - **27** c) Other early age specialists.
   - **37** d) Consulting psychologists.
   - **24** e) I feel no need to talk about my difficulties.
   - **—** f) Other (indicate what) _____

8. **If I could take a break during working hours, I would prefer to**
   - **41** a) Have a cup of tea in the group with colleagues in my shift.
   - **13** b) Have a cigarette in a specially allocated smoking room.
   - **62** c) Spend the time in a room organized for that purpose.
   - **5** d) Chat with friends I work with.
   - **38** e) Stay alone away from the group.
   - **5** f) Other (indicate what) _____

9. **In order that the break in the routine and the rest period have no adverse influence on the children and cause no disturbance for the staff, it is necessary to**
   - **27** a) Let the staff member decide for him/herself when to take a rest, depending on the current situation in the group.
   - **8** b) Include the rest period into the timetable of the shift for everyone at the same time.
   - **59** c) Provide a period of rest for every staff member on the principle of others standing in at the time.
   - **48** d) Provide a possible rest together with the children, for instance, take several children and go into a room where one can spend time as one would in the family.
   - **13** e) Think of changing the mode of working, since within the regime as it is at present any rest or distraction on the part of the staff cannot but affect the children adversely.
   - **3** f) Other (indicate what) _____

10. **Please state your position in the orphanage.**
    - **2** a) Doctor.
    - **53** b) Medical nurse.
    - **13** c) Nursery nurse.
    - **9** d) Defectologist—special education teacher.
    - **21** e) Assistant teacher.
    - **2** f) Another position (indicate what) _____

Thank you!

Note. the figures given on the left are the number of times a statement received a positive response.

and foremost of medical and educational work), and not wishing any attachment to be formed between them and the child (37 percent). Staff members are sure they could provide better work if there were fewer children in the group (76 percent), if the children were not passed on from group to group on their having reached the regulation age, into a strange setting and among people strange to them (30 percent), and if they themselves were given more independence and were trusted more and controlled less (30 percent). Only 11 percent of staff members have declared that improvement of work provided in the orphanages depends on having more information on childhood development. The personnel point out the necessity of reorganizing the system of orphanages and consider that the children they are working with would be better off living in adopting families (71 percent), in a family-type orphanage (30 percent), or with their biological parents (27 percent). Part of the staff members speak of the possibility of orphanages being reserved for children with severe medical and genetic risk of developmental delay (13 percent).

In an earlier research project, comparing women taking care of the infants under 10 months and mothers of children of the same age, it has been found that the emotional state of staff members of the orphanages tends toward a higher level of anxiety and depression. There is no doubt that the difference in state may be caused not only by working with at-risk children left without parental support, but also by working in an institution in which the organizational principles are not in accordance with the wishes and expectations of the staff members. As a result of the survey, it has been established that only 24 percent of the staff members feel no need to talk about difficulties and discuss the emotions arising in the course of work (see Table 12.4). The rest of the women would like to talk about their difficulties and discuss the emotions arising in the course of their work—most not with the administration of the orphanage an inclination customary for and characteristic of employees of an authoritarian medical institution (only 13 percent indicated a desire to do so), but rather with the colleagues in their shift and staff members of the orphanage (44 percent), with the consulting psychologists (37 percent), or with the other early age specialists (27 percent). The results of the conducted survey have to be taken into consideration in working out and implementing a program of early intervention for infants and early age children in the orphanages.

Suggested Guidelines for Early Intervention in Orphanages

Since 1994 the Swedish Adoption Center has been organizing seminars in a number of Russian territories (Pskov, Saint Petersburg, the Moscow region, and Karelia) for the administration and staff members of orphanages on the subject of development of infants and early age children and forms of early intervention. The experience of taking part in the organization of such seminars and the subsequent discussion and follow-up of the results have shown that supplying information may be very effective in changing the attitude of the staff, as a means of influencing the situation in the orphanages. However, this is only a small first step toward changing conditions for infants with special needs. Often, when the women get back to their orphanages, the routine and the accustomed type of relations leave no room for innovation, so that the old system persistently dictates its own rules of segregation and disregard for the infants' mental health. It is necessary not only to carry on the association with the staff of the orphanages, but also to organize joint work on creating programs of early intervention for the orphanage children. On the basis of the results of research described earlier, as well as having observed and associated with the children, and having discussed the results with the staff of the orphanages, the following directions may be suggested for the program.

Measures Unconnected with Changing the Organization Structure of Orphanages

Possible measures aimed at changing the attitude of personnel toward the children in an orphanage include:

1. Psychological and professional support for the personnel in the different periods of working with children in the form of individual or group support (for instance, encounter or discussion groups), supervision; support of the process of turning away from treating children as mere objects of medical or educational manipulations; verbaliza-tion and discussion of cases where staff members had close emotional relations established with the children, responding to the child's emotional need to have a primary caregiver;

2. Supplying up-to-date information on the development of infants and early age children, stressing the effect the socioemotional environment has upon the children's mental health, including the children living in an orphanage; supplying information on different approaches to organizing facilities for infants with special needs and on programs of early intervention;

3. Turning away from the priority of medical and neurological diagnosis in classifying children within the orphanages; change of approach in the child's assessment from the traditional way, focused on motility development, anthropometry, and some aspects of cognitive development, toward an interdisciplinary assessment of the level of functional development in the main spheres; understanding the problems of the infants' mental health;

4. Preparing the personnel and the children for parting in connection with the child's transfer to another group, adoption or return to the biological parents, the child's transition to other institutions;

5. Psychological and professional support for the personnel in different stages of changes in the baby home.

Measures aimed at changing the work of personnel with children in an orphanage include:

1. Training personnel in interaction with children, taking into consideration the data on the social behavior of infants, the social behavior of adults when interacting with infants, and the data on interaction models of adult persons with healthy babies and babies of different risk groups;

2. Creating various programs of changing the social environment of the children, including:

   • Creating opportunity for daily association with each child's most intimate caretaking staff member of the baby home, including interaction and social stimulation according to a definite program;

   • Turning from silent manipulations with children by the personnel in the regulation operations to comprehensive communication and complex stimulation at the times of feeding, changing, etc.;

   • Creating opportunities for peer interaction, organizing and supporting the interaction among peers;

   • Organizing a schedule of daily group classes of personnel with the children;

   • Organizing the setting in a manner appropriate for the child's functional level of development;

   • Organizing the child's personal space, making it possible for each child to have personal possessions and toys and providing a place for the children to keep those toys;

   • Collecting a child's personal album with snapshots and descriptions of that child, significant people, significant events, meetings, holidays, and birthdays;

   • Having the child conducted by a caregiver to any treatment procedures and functions beyond the living quarters or outside the orphanage.

In each of the programs listed above, when dealing with the infants with deficient motility, or medical or genetic risk of developmental delay, it is necessary to keep in mind the recommendations of special education and speech therapy (making use of symbols, pictograms, sign language), physical, and occupational therapy.

Measures Connected with Changing the Structure of Orphanages

To effect change from working on the principle of "all staff members, not every day, for all children" to working according to "constant caregiver, every day, for a small group of the same children" so that the children can experience an unbroken association with their own most intimate caregiver, it would be necessary:

• To put an end to the practice of transferring the children from one group into another, from one set of personnel to another;

• To organize groups of children with constant caregivers, providing for them to have the same living quarters throughout, to create living conditions close to family life;

• To change the working hours for personnel from the existing 24-hr shift timetable (one day in every four) to a morning, day, and night shift, to afford the infants and the women caregivers most intimate with them a chance to see and associate with each other every day;

- To provide for having fewer children in the group;
- To create conditions for integrating the children with medical or genetic risk of developmental delay with medically sound children, and for mixing children of different ages;
- To organize meetings of the children and the personnel of different groups;
- To encourage and to make provisions for parents' desire to visit and be with their children.

It is best to start carrying out the program in an orphanage mainly with a group of children in the first months of life, then gradually, as their development progresses, involve children and personnel of other groups. The experience of changing the life of babies and early age children in the orphanages may prove to be greatly valuable and necessary for changing the life of children in other segregated establishments as well. Any program directed at changing the present situation in the orphanages has to be regarded as only the first step toward totally abolishing the system of segregating children with special needs as well as providing them with conditions that would enable them to remain in the family environment.

The changes going on in recent years in the social, political, and economic system of Russia could not leave untouched the system of special institutions of segrega-tion, including the ones for infants and early age children. However, the process is extremely slow, and in many aspects the orphanages still remain the very image of Soviet socialism, evidencing the relations and the routine characteristic of the epoch of flourishing totalitarianism in our society. In order to make changes for the better and, in the end, to effect a transition from segregated institutions for at-risk children to a flexible family-centered system of facilities that allow the children to stay in the family, it is necessary to continue to study the experience of reorganizing the system of facilities for special needs children in other countries, as well as to make use of the experience, accumulating in Russia in recent years, of creating programs of early intervention. Besides reflecting the most general trends and directions of change in the facilities for infants and early age children, the new programs must take into consideration the peculiarities of different regions. In the territory of the 89 nations comprising the Russian Federation, people coexist who, on the one hand, are united by a common history and the use of the Russian language but, on the other hand, are separated by a different history of origins and formation, different religious beliefs, and different languages, cultures, and modes of life, all of which they have kept intact despite decades of totalitarianism. If the customary ways are followed, the development of new forms of infant facilities in Russia will be extremely circumscribed, in the manner of the Soviet society's practice of creating a program that may be new, but must be uniform for all. The early intervention program in a preschool educational establishment and our efforts to change the lives of babies in Saint Petersburg orphanages is only one example of the many possible programs that could be organized to attempt to change facilities for special needs children in a post-Soviet society. It is only the beginning of a long journey toward creating conditions conducive to mental health for infants and early age children.

Note

1. Psychological methods mentioned in this section have been adapted and are now widely used in the Saint Petersburg school of psychology.

References

Ainsworth, M. D. S., Blehar, M. C., Waters, E., & Wall, S. (1978). *Patterns of attachment: A psychological study of the Strange Situation*. Hillsdale, NJ: Erlbaum.

Bailey, D. B., & Simeonsson, R. J. (1990). Family Needs Survey. In M. J. McGonigel, P. K. Kaufmann, & B. H. Jonson (Eds.), *Guidelines and recommended practices for the individualized family service plan* (2nd ed.; Appendix D., pp. 3–6). Bethesda, MD: Association for the Care of Children's Health.

Beckwith, L. (1990). Adaptive and maladaptive parenting: Implications for intervention. In S. J. Meisels and & J. P. Shonkoff (Eds.), *Handbook of early childhood intervention* (pp. 53–77). Cambridge: Cambridge University Press.

Bjorck-Akesson, E., & Brodin, J. (1991). International diversity of toy libraries. *Topics in Early Childhood Special Education, 12*(4), 528–543.

Brazelton, T. B., Koslowski, B., & Main, M. (1974). The origins of reciprocity: The early mother-infant interaction. In M. Lewis & L. Rosenblum (Eds.), *The effect of the infant on its caregiver*. New York: Wiley.

Bystrova, K. S., Widstrom, A. M., Lundth, W., Vorontsov, I. M., & Muhamedrahimov, R. J. (1997). К обоснованию значения режимов общения матери и новорожденного ребенка для последующего развития и здоровья детей [The significance of mother and neonate infant communication regime for the children's further development and health]. In А. И. Захаров (Ed.), "Перинатальная психология в родовспоможении" (pp. 102–113). Saint Petersburg, Russia: Gloria.

Cattell, R. B., Eber, H. W., & Tatsuoka, M. M. (1970). *Handbook for the Sixteen Personality Factor Questionnaire*. Champaign, Ill.

Chalmers, B. (1994). *Childbearing practices in different cultures (from a psychosocial perspective)*. Paper presented at the Riga WAIMH. Conference on the Mental Health of Infants, Children and Parents, Riga, Latvia.

Chistovich, L., Chistovich, I., Guralnick, M., Kozhevnikova, E., Muhamedrahimov, R., Reuter, J., Risberg, A., & Suleymenova, R. (1996). Early intervention in the new independent states (NIS) of the ex-Soviet Union. In A. Guedeney, P. De Château, P. Kaukonen, & T. Tamminen (Eds.), *World Association for Infant Mental Health VI World Conference Abstracts, July 25–28, 1996* (p. 209). Tampere, Finland: Vammalan Kirjapaino Oy.

Clark, R. (1985). *The Parent-Child Early Re-*

lational Assessment. Madison: Department of Psychiatry, University of Wisconsin Medical School.

Council of Ministers of the RSFSR. (1988). "О создании детских домов семейного типа. Постановление Совета Министров РСФСР от 18 ноября 1988 г." [On creating children's homes of a family type. Resolution of the Council of Ministers of the RSFSR of 18 November 1988]. No. 475.

Council of Ministers of the RSFSR. (1994). "О мерах по улучшению работы специальныхучебно-воспитательных учреждений для детей и подростков, имеющих недостатки в физическом и умственном развитии. Постановление Совета Министров РСФСР от 24.05.91 г." [On measures toward improvement of work in special education and training establishments for children and adolescents having defects in physical and mental development. Resolution of the Council of Ministers of the RSFSR]. No. 278.

Cramer, B., Robert-Tissot, C., Stern, D. N., Serpa-Rusconi, S., DeMuralt, M., Besson, G., Berney, C., & D'Arcis, U. (1990). Outcome evaluation in Brief mother-infant psychotherapy: A preliminary report. *Infant Mental Health Journal, 11*(3), 278–300.

Dahl, V. I. (1984). "Пословицы русского народа" [Russian Folk Proverbs]. Moscow: Художественная литература.

Ditchfield, H. (1992). The birth of a child with a mental handicap: Coping with loss? In A. Waitman & S. Conboy-Hill (Eds.), *Psychotherapy and mental handicap* (pp. 9–45). London: Sage Publications.

"Домострой" [Domostroy]. (1994). Издание подготовили В.В. Колесов, В.В. Рождественская. Saint Petersburg, Russia: Наука.

Dunst, C. J., Trivette, C. M., & Deal, A. G. (1988). *Enabling and empowering families: Principles and guidelines for practice.* Cambridge, MA: Brookline Books.

Education of the Handicapped Act Amendments of 1986, Pub. L. No. 99-457.

Field, T. (1987). Affective and interactive disturbances in infants. In J. D. Osofsky (Ed.), *Handbook of infant development* (2nd ed., pp. 972–1005). New York: Wiley-Interscience.

Field, T. (1990). *Infancy.* Cambridge: Harvard University Press.

Fogel, A. (1977). Temporal organization in mother-infant face-to-face interaction. In H. R. Schaffer (Ed.), *Studies in mother-infant interaction* (pp. 89–117). London: Academic.

Fraiberg, S. (1971). Intervention in infancy: A program for blind infants. *Journal of the American Academy of Child Psychiatry, 10,* 381–405.

Fraiberg, S., Adelson, E., & Shapiro, V. (1975). Ghosts in the nursery: A psychoanalytic approach to the problems of impaired infant-mother relationships. *Journal of the American Academy of Child Psychiatry, 14,* 387–421.

Government of the Russian Federation. (1994). "О мерах государственной поддержки детских домов семейного типа, созданных на основе крестьянских (фермерских) хозяйств. Постановление правительства Российской Федерации от 5 июля 1994 г." [On measures of state support of family type children's homes created on the basis of peasant (farmer) households. Resolution of the Government of the Russian Federation of 5 July 1994]. No. 786.

Guralnick, M. J. (1992a). A hierarchical model for understanding children's peer-related social competence. In S. L. Odom, S. R. McConnell, & M. A. McEvoy (Eds.), *Social competence of young children with disabilities* (pp. 37–64). Baltimore: Brookes.

Guralnick, M. J. (1992b). *Assessment of peer relations.* Seattle, WA: University of Washington, Child Development and Mental Retardation Center.

Guralnick, M. J., & Groom, J. M. (1987). The peer relations of mildly delayed and non-handicapped preschool children in mainstreamed playgroups. *Child Development, 58,* 1556–1572.

Hanson, M. J., & Lynch, E. W. (1989). *Early intervention.* Austin, TX: Pro-Ed.

Kaye, K. (1977). Toward the origin of dialogue. In H. R. Schaffer (Ed.), *Studies in mother-infant interaction* (pp. 89–117). London: Academic.

Kozhevnikova, E., Muhamedrahimov, R. J., & Chistovich, L. A. (1995). Санкт-Петербургская программа "Абилитация Младенцев"—первая в России программа раннего вмешательства [Saint-Petersburg "Infant Habilitation" program—the first Russian program of early intervention]. "Педиатрия," *4,* 112–113.

Konius, E. M. (1954). "Пути развития советской охраны материнства и младенчества" [The ways of development of Soviet defense of motherhood and infancy] (1917–1940). Moscow: Центральный Институт усовершенствования врачей.

Krauss, M. W., & Jacobs, F. (1990). Family assessment: Purposes and techniques. In S. J. Meisels & J. P. Shonkoff (Eds.), *Handbook of early childhood intervention* (pp. 303–325). Cambridge: Cambridge University Press.

Leary, T. (1954). *Interpersonal diagnosis of personality.* New York.

Lebovici, S. (1983). *Le nourrisson, la mere et le psychoanalyste: Les interactions precoses.* Paris: Editions du Centurion.

Lieberman, A. F., & Pawl, J. H. (1993). Infant-parent psychotherapy. In C. H. Zeanah (Ed.), *Handbook of Infant Mental Health* (pp. 427–442). New York: Guilford.

Lisina, M. I. (1961). Влияние отношений с близкими родственниками на развитие ребенка раннего возраста [The influence of relations with family members on the development of early age children]. "Вопросы психологии," *3,* 117–124.

Lisina, M. I. (1986). "Проблемы онтогенеза общения" [Problems of communication ontogeny]. Moscow: Педагогика.

Mahler, M. S., Pine, F., & Bergman, A. (1975). *The psychological birth of the human infant.* New York: Basic Books.

McDonough, S. C. (1993). Interaction guidance: Understanding and treating early infant-caregiver relationship disturbances. In C. H. Zeanah (Ed.), *Handbook of Infant Mental Health* (pp. 414–426). New York: Guilford.

McEvoy, M. A., Odom, S. L., & McConnell, S. R. (1992). Peer Social Competence Intervention for Young Children with Disabilities. In S. L. Odom, S. R. McConnell, & M. A. McEvoy (Eds.), *Social competence of young children with disabilities* (pp. 113–133). Baltimore: Brookes.

McGonigel, M. J., Kaufmann, R. K., & Jonson, B. H. (Eds.). (1991). *Guidelines and recommended practices for the individualized family service plan* (2nd ed.). Bethesda, MD: Association for the Care of Children's Health.

Ministry of Health of the USSR. (1986). "Положение о доме ребенка" [Regulations on baby homes]. No. 1525.

Muhamedrahimov, R. J., Palmov, O. I., & Nikiforova, N. V. (1996). Infant-infant interaction in orphanage. In A. Guedeney, P. De Château, P. Kaukonen, & T. Tamminen (Eds.), *World Association for Infant Mental Health VI World Conference Abstracts, July 25–28, 1996* (p. 152). Tampere, Finland: Vammalan Kirjapaino Oy.

Odom, S. L., McConnell, S. R., & McEvoy, M. A. (1992). Peer-related social competence and its significance for young children with disabilities. In S. L. Odom, S. R. McConnell, & M. A. McEvoy (Eds.), *Social competence of young children with disabilities* (pp. 3–35). Baltimore: Brookes.

Osgood, C. E., Suci, G. J., & Tannenbaum, P. H. (1057). *The Measurement of Meaning*. Urbana, IL.

Osofsky, J. D. (1996). When the helper is hurting: Burnout and countertransference issues in treatment of children exposed to violence. *Zero to Three, 16*(5), 35–38.

Osofsky, J. D., & Connors, K. (1979). Mother-infant interaction: An integrative view of a complex system. In J. D. Osofsky (Ed.), *Handbook of Infant Development* (pp. 519–548). New York: Wiley-Interscience.

Parker, S. J., & Zuckerman, B. S. (1990). Therapeutic aspects of the assessment process. In S. J. Meisels & J. P. Shonkoff (Eds.), *Handbook of early childhood intervention* (pp. 350–369). Cambridge: Cambridge University Press.

Rashkovich, M. P. (1892). К вопросу о призрении подкинутых детей общественными учреждениями [Toward the question of providing for foundling children by the public foundations]. In "Труды четвертого съезда русских врачей в память Н. И. Пирогова" (pp. 296–316). Moscow: Печатня С. П. Яковлева.

Reuter, J., & Bickett, L. (1985). *The Kent Infant Development Scale manual.* (2nd ed.). Kent, OH: Kent Developmental Metrics.

Rodulovich, V. I. (1892). О призрении брошенных детей вообще и в Орловском земском приюте в частности [On the care of abandoned children in general and for those in the Orel municipal orphanage in particular]. In "Труды четвертого съезда русских врачей в память Н. И. Пирогова" (pp. 290–295). Moscow: Печатня С. П. Яковлева.

Rosenzweig, S. (1954). La mesure experimentale des types de reaction a la frustration. In H. A. Murray et coll. (Eds.), *Exploration de la personnalité* (Vol. 2, pp. 575–588). Paris: P.U.F.

Rossetti, L. M. (1990). *Infant-toddler assessment: An interdisciplinary approach.* Austin, TX: Pro-Ed.

Rossetti, L. M. (1996). *Communication intervention: Birth to three.* San Diego, CA: Singular.

Russian Federation. (1994). "О положении детей в Российской Федерации (1993 год)" [*On childhood conditions in the Russian Federation (1993)*: Governmental report]. Moscow: Russian Federation.

Russian Federation. (1996). "Семейный кодекс Российской Федерации с изменениями и дополнениями на 1 мая 1996 г" [Family code of the Russian Federation supplemented and augmented of 1 May 1996]. Moscow: Teis, 1996.

Shearer, D. E. (1987). The Portage Project:

A home approach to early education of young children with special needs. In J. Roopnarine & J. Johnson (Eds.), *Approaches to early childhood education* (pp. 269–282). Columbus, OH: Merrill.

Shelgunov, N. V. (1885). "Очерки русской жизни" [Sketches of Russian life]. СПб.

Shengelidze, V. V. (1900). Организация трудовой помоши в Казанской губернии [Organization of labor assistance in the Kazan region]. "Журнал русского общества охранения народного здравия, 9," 1–12.

Shonkoff, J. P., Hauser-Cram, P., Krauss, M. W., & Upshur, C. C. (1992). Development of Infants with Disabilities and Their Families. *Monographs of the Society for Research in Child Development,* 57(6, Serial No. 230).

Spielberger, C. D. (Ed.). (1972). *Anxiety: Current trends in theory and research* (Vol. 2). New York.

Stensland Junker, K. (1971). *Lekotek: A program for training through systematic play activity.* Unpublished manuscript.

Stern, D. N. (1977). *The first relationship: Infant and mother.* Cambridge: Harvard University Press.

Stern, D. N. (1985). *The interpersonal world of the infant: A view from psychoanalysis and developmental psychology.* USA: Basic Books.

Stern, D. N. (1991). Maternal representations: A clinical and subjective phenomenological view. *Infant Mental Health Journal,* 12(3), 174–186.

Stern, D. N. (1995). *The motherhood constellation.* New York: Basic Books.

Stern, D. N., Beebe, B., Jaffe, J., & Bennett, S. L. (1977). The infant's stimulus world during social interaction: A study of caregiver behaviors with particular reference to repetition and timing. In H. R. Schaffer (Ed.), *Studies in mother-infant interaction* (pp. 177–202). London: Academic.

Stern-Bruschweiler, N., & Stern, D. N. (1989). A model for conceptualizing the role of the mother's representational world in various mother-infant therapies. *Infant Mental Health Journal,* 10(3), 142–156.

Vygotsky, L. S. (1924). К психологии и педагогике детской дефективности [Toward the psychology and teaching of childhood defectivity]. "Вопросы воспитания слепых, глухонемых и умственно отсталых детей" (pp. 5–30). Moscow: СПОН НКП.

Vygotsky, L. S. (1932). Младенческий возраст [Infancy]. In *L. S. Vygotsky's family archive.* Manuscript.

Winnicott, D. W. (1960). The theory of the parent-infant relationship. *International Journal Psycho-Anal.,* 41, 585–595.

Yuzhakov, S. N., & Milyukov, P. N. (Eds.). (1904). Воспитательные дома [Fostering asylums]. In "Большая Энциклопедия" (4th ed., Vol. 5, pp. 523–526). Saint Petersburg, Russia: Prosvesheniye.

Zero to Three. (1994). *Diagnostic classification: 0–3: Diagnostic classification of mental health and developmental disorders of infancy and early childhood.* Washington, DC: Author.

Zung, V. (1965). Self-Rating Depression Scale. *Arch. Gen. Psychiatry,* 12, 63–70.

11

Cross-Cultural Perspectives on Infant Mental Health: Germany, Austria, and Switzerland

Peter Jaron Zwi Scheer and Marguerite Dunitz-Scheer

Introduction

Cross-cultural thinking shares a basic problem with history: Our view of the past is influenced by the way we look at things today. Johann Wolfgang von Goethe pointed this out when he wrote (*Faust,* part 1): "Was ihr den Geist der Zeiten heibt, das ist im Grund der Herrn eigner Geist, in dem die Zeiten sich bespiegeln!" ("What you call the spirit of a time is nothing but the spirit of yourself, in which time is reflected!"; authors' translation.) Culture may be treated as a mixture of historical processes, traditions and events, creations of research, literature, art, and drama, and the development of techniques, from handicraft up to most modern inventions (Gehlen, 1820; Popper, 1964). Current Austrian and German culture is still strongly influenced by the centuries of monarchism and the revolutions following World War I. Democracy still seems unfamiliar, not only in politics, but also in daily

life. Switzerland, in contrast, has a long history of democracy, after liberation from the Austrian-Habsburgian regency in 1292. As a result of these different traditions daily family life, including infancy, is quite different in these three countries. Different history, different landscapes, and the different development of social welfare systems have led to considerable variation in the infant mental health scene today.

The differences among the three German-speaking countries are greater than might be expected. Leydendecker (1997) discusses the "zoom factor" of comparative psychology: that is, how an observer's distance from an object affects the object's appearance. Seen from the United States, the German-speaking countries may seem very similar, but in fact they have very different traditions, upbringings, situations, styles, and local cultures. For example, the Swiss writer Gottfried Keller (1819–1890) wanted to stop the trend of young Swiss men going abroad to earn their living. He pointed out that

We would like to express our thanks to Susanne Macari, PhD, University of Virginia and Graz, and Professor Jack David Dunitz, University of Zurich, for their help in linguistic matters as speakers of standard American English living in German-speaking countries. In addition, we also thank Markus Wilken, PhD, University of Osnabrück and Graz, for his constructive help.

Switzerland could become rich if people became proud of their country and introduced tourism and trade. He showed his people the beauty of Switzerland, made them self-confident and proud, and inspired a new national feeling. "Alii belli gerant, tu felix austria, nube!" ("May others fight in wars; you, happy Austria, marry!") was one of the main political mottos of the old Austrian monarchy. Such an outlook is far from democratic ideas of engagement, motivation, self-fulfillment, and personal and political awareness. Germany is today one of the eight major economic countries (referred to as the G8 states) of the world. In spite of the economic recovery, the former German core identity has been lost.

The German-speaking countries have undergone significant changes in this century: The two world wars started here. The first changed Germany from one of the world's leading nations to a shadow of its former self. The destruction of the multinational former Austrian empire brought economic chaos and poverty. The second war brought poverty, destruction, and the expulsion of the intellectual elite from Austria and Germany. The language in which Goethe wrote became subject to bias, hate, and mockery. These changes engraved themselves in the history of the developing science of psychoanalysis and its offspring, infant mental health. Sigmund Freud himself was a child of the Austrian monarchy: In his time—the fin de siècle—one might well have imagined that monarchy would be everlasting. Freud's interest in psychodynamics and his first theory of human drives (Freud, 1900) can be understood

only in light of the governmental system of his time. He thought everything could be cured by recall memories: Genealogy was a widespread interest at that time, especially among wealthy Jewish families (Roberts, 1984).

Psychoanalysis started in Vienna at the turn of the century: *Traumdeutung* arrived on the market exactly in 1900. Although it was published in 1899, Freud thought the book should be dated 1900, to indicate that it was intended for the coming century. As time went on, psychoanalysis increasingly reflected the contemporary scientific literature. Individuals such as August Aichhorn (1924), Siegfried Bernfeld (1921), Alfred Adler (1922; see also Pfabigan & Scheer, 1983), and Jakob Moreno (1946/1969) challenged the tenets of psychoanalysis and provided examples of the ways in which psychodynamic evaluation, assessment, and intervention must be viewed within its cultural and historical context. René A. Spitz studied an orphanage in the ninth district of Vienna and found further evidence for the importance of early caregiver-infant relationships (Spitz, 1965).

This rough outline of the historic roots of psychodynamics suggests that psychodynamic evaluation, assessment, and intervention can only be discussed and understood in terms of the historical background of a given culture and the development and current state of the field. In this chapter we highlight some transcultural aspects of childrearing and infant development from our perspective as psychoanalytically and behaviorally trained pediatricians.

Evolutionary Approaches in Cross-Cultural Perspectives

The acknowledgment of a biological perspective in cross-cultural comparisons is common in many handbooks on infancy, by both English- and German-speaking authors and research groups. In a handbook on cross-cultural psychology, W. R. Thompson (1980) contributed a chapter on cross-cultural uses of biological data and perspectives. His terminology refers to the basic biological nature of human beings, in the sense that behavior and experience in interaction with the social and physical environment are rooted in an organismic ground. Of course, this also applies to infancy: There is a neuroendocrinological system; a physiological system with anatomical features; and there are inborn behavioral characteristics, such as reflexes and basic drives including hunger, thirst, sleep, sleep-wake rhythm, and sexuality, all functioning according to homeostatic principles. Behind all of this is the developing brain with its multiple functions for behavioral regulation. As Keller (1997) points out, the application of a meta-perspective, namely an evolutionary view, is not so common in mainstream psychology. Psychological analysis by its nature is proximate, but evolutionary considerations introduce an additional dimension, providing a perspective on human behavior (Bischof, 1985) and activity as strategies to maximize reproductive success (Belsky, Steinberg, & Draper, 1991a,b). The key concept of reproductive success is the optimal representation of an organism's own genes in future generations.

In *The Selfish Gene*, Dawkins postulates (1976, 1994) that evolution takes place at the level of the gene. But he acknowledges that for humans, since the evolution of language, memes are more important than genes. Modern times change faster than human evolutionary processes can occur. Factors other than genetically determined fitness are important and decisive for reproduction. In human society, the process of adaptation has shifted to a cultural level. Our culture rewards those who are able to transmit and expand ideas, creations, and value systems into successful projects. Success gives access to increased resources, promoting further expansion and more success.

Infants in the German-speaking countries are adapted to the society, culture, and ecology of middle and northern Europe. For example, in Europe it is taken for granted that infants need milk for growth. Without milk, it is thought, infants will not grow up to be healthy and happy adults. In Japan, in contrast, traditionally nobody drinks milk, but infants nevertheless thrive and grow up. Attachment and the process of development of relationships is very different in Europe, South America, India, China, or Japan (IJzendoorn & Kroonenberg, 1988, 1990). Even within Europe, comparative studies of attachment in Germany and Italy show differences (IJzendoorn & Kroonenberg, 1988). Cooperative studies of infancy where Western countries participate must be conceptualized by taking national differences into account (Bronfenbrenner, 1981; Harwood, 1996; Keller, 1994).

However, such consideration for naturally, ecologically, and culturally closed communities becomes less critical as the transglobal influence of modern communication media grows each year. The concept of the global village gains in reality, as no spot on the globe is now inaccessible to modern information transfer. The future prospect of obtaining valid data on large cross-cultural differences is thus diminishing rapidly. In all countries and cultures in the world today the media, being more or less independent of cultural censorship, have the potential to influence the goals and visions of parents more than the teachings of their own parents (Goodnow & Collins, 1990; Keller, Chasiotis, & Runde, 1992).

Classical thinking on these matters is static. The evolutionary approach, in contrast, implies a shift to a functional, goal-directed assessment that treats psychological processes as a whole (Bischof, 1985). This approach offers a conceptual integration in which the evolutionary theory of natural selection generates hypotheses about the design features of the human mind (Belsky et al., 1991b). Such an approach is considered crucial for the discovery of new knowledge (Berry, 1992). It stimulates the formulation of questions in one discipline and their application to the knowledge base of another discipline, as well as the use of knowledge developed in one discipline to solve problems of other disciplines. This sort of integration goes beyond multidisciplinary in its contribution to the field of infant mental health as it has developed in the past 20 years (Barkow, Cosmides, & Tooby, 1992).

Two contrasting orientations are signifi-cant for evolutionary approaches, especially when applied to cross-cultural psychology: emphasizing the centrality of the comparative method and applying naturalistic observations—that is, using whole individuals as units of analysis (Thompson, 1980). A metaperspective on cross-cultural knowledge and findings seems to be desirable from the standpoint that cross-cultural psychology does not refer to tight theories, but merely to an abundance of theoretical frameworks, often leading to theoretical eclecticism. The multiplicity of underlying cultural and biological influences on human behavior has been described as a function of the additive influence of genes, environment, and the interaction of the two. Although widely accepted, the term *general interaction* is ambiguous: It is nothing more than a preliminary descriptive statement and does not give direction to empirical research.

The more refined conceptualization proposed by Reese and Overton (1970) does not transcend this dichotomy. The authors describe two major philosophical models that provide the basis for assumptions about human development: organismic and mechanistic. Organismic refers to the concept of an active organism that develops through processes of qualitative change. The approaches of Piaget (1977) and Freud, although different, can both be subsumed under this theoretical heading. Mechanistic, in contrast, stresses quantitative change and the active role of processes happening outside the primary control of the individual. This view refers to the external stimulus environment as the primary source of developmental change. Behavioral or learning theorists, including Bijou and Baer (1976), make use of this approach.

The more recent model of development as an interactive process includes both the organismic and mechanistic models of development. The model presents a continuous, dynamic process involving both active and reactive events between the infant and caregivers. This model is postulated by many infancy researchers, including Emde, Zeanah, Crittenden, Stern, and Bretherton. From a conception of a biological or evolutionary perspective, the genotype can no longer be understood as expressing fixed, deterministic relationships between genes and behavior (Plomen, Owen, & McGuffin, 1994). Instead, "genetic preparedness" conveys the idea that behavioral acquisition (learning) is framed according to time windows for the acquisition of specific skills and information.

Plasticity, the capacity to be molded in different ways by different environments, is a main feature of human development. In order to clarify the discussion of genetic influences in evolutionary theory, the behavioral genetic approach must be understood. Human ethology marked the beginning of the tremendous impact of biological thinking in psychology. It has become especially important for cross-cultural research, since its major endeavor consists of identifying various behavior universals across cultures. Two kinds of universals are discussed: behavioral universals and universal contexts of development. Eye contact between caregiver and infant during early socialization is an example of a behavior universal. Universal contexts of development are discussed in terms of attachment theory and research, which has led to the introduction of a differential perspective, as is illustrated, for example, by patterns of gaze aversion.

The ethological approach can be questioned from the perspective of evolutionary or socio-biological theory. To fully understand the sociobiological approach, it is necessary to understand both the role of adaptation and the concept of culture. Since reproductive success is central to evolutionary theory, the parameters of reproductive decisions must be elaborated. The differences between evolutionary thinking and classical ethology become apparent when issues related to the quality of attachment are linked to different reproductive strategies (Keller, 1997).

Many children in the Western world learn more from television than from their parents, and what they learn spans a full range of knowledge, from quality information to rubbish. Nevertheless, certain internal representations and abstract visions of fantasy in various countries still remain distinctly different. For example, American history and culture are influenced strongly by the idea of liberty. For the child, this idea emphasizes the ability to choose what one wants to be. American parents can offer their child the conviction that exercising willpower can affect the child's future. A European parent may, of course, also try to implant this idea into his or her child, while also trying to promote secure bonding to give the child a good start in life. The effect, however, will be different because of the more complicated and multi-influential European view of the world.

This view seems more sensitive to many factors, of which human willpower may be one. American society as a whole reflects much more mixed cultural roots than European communities. American cities often contain great racial and ethnic mixtures of recent immigrants. In contrast, European urban structures may differ socioculturally from one city to the next, but the cultural conformity of any given place is usually relatively stable. This trend of local stability can persist over many generations, resulting in a rigidity that may lead to substantive differences between neighboring towns or districts.

For example, in a typical American upper-middle-class family living in New York, the wife may be from Texas and the husband from Washington state. Their three adult children could have been raised in Chicago but now, due to their several occupations, reside in Seattle, Maine, and Houston. The life of a single individual can reflect great flexibility, variability, and adaptation to large geographical separations. A typical Bavarian, in contrast, might have met his wife in Bonn, and the couple now live with their three children in Munich. It would not be unusual at all for the children to grow up and then raise their families in Munich. Because there is so much less mobility, the culture is subject to fewer dramatic changes.

A cross-cultural perspective views the process of human evolution as occurring on a wide dynamic spectrum, ranging from a microbiological-biochemical level to an abstract philosophical one. In this respect there are some basic differences: The biological and evolutionary aspects can be assumed to be cross-culturally stable and independent of cultural deformation, whereas moral development and psychoanalytical and philosophical aspects may reflect cross-cultural differences.

Definition of Infant Mental Health in German-Speaking Countries

Human development is, in a sense, a culture of its own, yet it is influenced by any given culture. Following Immanuel Kant, German authors write about the *competent* infant (Dornes, 1993; Keller & Meyer, 1982), or about an innocent empty page of creation, similar to John Locke's concept of the tabula rasa. Either approach influences the cultural expectations parents, researchers, and clinicians have for infant behavior and for adult-infant relationships. A cultural norm is a complex of traditional views and new trends, information, and knowledge, which combine in what we regard as common sense. The influence of new information from research depends largely on the level of education. The main focus of attention in modern German handbooks of developmental psychology is on cognitive development (Oerter & Montada, 1995; Trautner, 1991).

Jean Piaget's (1947) cognitive developmental theory is still given great importance respecting the child's academic achievements. Many concepts based on Piaget's work still influence modern research projects and his descriptions of his own children's development are often quoted in modern developmental and educational works (Piaget, 1936). Many diagnostic and developmental tests are based on his theory (Hoppe-Graff, 1997; Uzgiris & Hunt, 1987). Although many researchers continue to emphasize the importance of cognitive developmental skills, Piaget's overall influence is diminishing as investigators turn their attention to emotional, affective, and interactive aspects of development.

Influenced by the paradigms and theories of the cognitive revolution, evolutionary developmental psychology, and the theory of constructivism, research themes in the German-speaking countries have turned toward social cognition (Silbereisen, 1995), empathy (Bischof-Kohler, 1989; Borke, 1971), the theory of mind (Sodian, 1995), and language (Grimm, 1997). Another new factor is the theory of attachment and bonding, as introduced by Bowlby (1969) and developed by Ainsworth, Blehar, Waters, & Wall (1978). In Germany, this research was promoted widely by Grossmann and his group (Grossmann et al., 1997; Spangler & Zimmermann, 1996). Grossmann's research has had a key influence on developmental psychology in Germany. Although the German perinatal-pediatric community has yet to be heavily influenced by his work, this is not the case for Austria and Switzerland, both of which tend to be more interdisciplinary in their focus. In the meantime, it is now regarded as common sense to assess an infant together with his or her caregivers, since the infant's compliance, abilities, and performance are influenced by the presence of the caregivers. Assessment of the infant depends on social, cog-

nitive, and motor performance, and it also depends on the interactive context in which the assessment is done (Grossmann et al., 1998). By context we mean a chosen setting conceptualized as an ecological system (Bronfenbrenner, 1981) with regard to the caregivers (Walter & Oerter, 1979). Other factors are the ecological, behavioral, and evolutionary concepts we have already described. Such concepts place human behavior in the context of Darwin's theory of evolution, which stresses positive and negative behaviors as adaptive functions.

Development in infancy can be seen from any one of a number of widely divergent viewpoints reflected in parents, neurologists, psychologists, or pediatricians. Because of the variety of different and divergent research groups in the German-speaking countries, a generally accepted developmental assessment battery for infancy does not exist. All published tests concentrate on signal items, such as bonding, attachment behavior, motor development, or neuromotor functioning. Diagnostic tools such as that produced by Brazelton for neonatal assessment or the Zero to Three Diagnostic Classification system (ZTT DC) are not widely used in routine work in Germany. Integration and combination of "American style" assessment batteries is mostly unheard of, except for selected research centers within a few university pediatric hospitals (e.g., Graz, Ulm, Basel), where developmental aspects are integrated in research projects and study designs (Dunitz, 1998; Keller, 1997; Wilken, 1998).

German-speaking parents watch their

developing infants and toddlers and wait for the commonly known simple motor milestones: sitting unassisted at the age of 6 months, rapprochement and crawling at 8 to 9 months, walking and the first spoken words at 12 months, and the beginning of oppositional behavior at age 2. The concept of individuation, of growing need for autonomy, of bargaining and detachment from parental control, are experienced but less readily accepted as necessary developmental milestones. Another important milestone is the achievement of sleeping through the night, be it for the self-esteem of the mother or for her baby. A baby who has learned to sleep through the night is considered mature and well-developing. This is expected to happen within the first 2 to 3 months.

A caregiver is considered successful if the baby sleeps through the night and can play by itself at an early age. Parents expect these things, wishing to help their child become a well-adapted member of society. To be quiet and well-adjusted is a common aim. In contrast to well-studied cultures of Israel, Italy, or Greece, the German-speaking countries must be viewed as being distinctly maladapted to the cues, needs, and daily habits of small children. The terms *kindgerecht* (appropriate to the needs of small children) and *nicht kindgerecht* are commonly used to describe public areas such as shops, public gardens, or restaurants. It is extremely awkward to visit such places in the company of a typical lively infant or toddler. Children are expected to be silent, to sit still, and to whisper their wishes. More natural behavior is mostly considered disturb-

ing and improper. Parental expectation of the public conduct of infants and toddlers, although not yet studied cross-culturally, differs in other Western cultures.

Infant mental health has been translated as *seelische Gesundheit in der frühen Kindheit,* a term that focuses more on emotional health than on mental aspects of development. The word *seele* is not easily translatable, even though it is one of the most widely used and common concepts of human spiritual life in the German language. It means "soul," although *seelisch* may be translated as "spiritual" or "mental." So *seelisch Gesundheit* means essentially spiritual health; but what is meant is an emphasis on emotional and developmental issues in infancy.

Infancy in Austria

Mozart, Schubert, Freud, the Vienna Philharmonic Orchestra and the Viennese Waltz, the Emperor Franz Josef and Empress Elisabeth—these are all associated with Austria up to 1918. What has remained? Music and psychoanalysis. What has happened since? What has changed? The greatest change was undoubtedly the transformation from a vast eastern European multinational and multicultural empire to a small Catholic social-democratic democracy. The implications of this change for individual and family life were substantial. Austria traditionally has had a very strong family-focused ideology. One factor is the predominance of the Catholic faith, which encourages young people to marry early, establish stable and long-lasting relationships, and raise children in small family systems. The possibilities for families to move from one city (or even part of a city) to another are very restricted. Tax laws make buying and selling of real estate very difficult: Tax rates are as high as 10 percent and mortgages are difficult to obtain. Thus, families tend to stay in the same village, city, and region (e.g., Tyrol) for hundreds of years. Security and stability are assured at the price of rigidity and inflexibility.

Another factor is the social-democratic policy of the past 25 years, which has introduced and organized a unique, effective, and countrywide social welfare and medical care system. This system has had from its inception a specific focus on the enhancement and protection of rights of mothers to raise their children at home, at least during the first 2 years of life. Since 1995 the same privileges and rights have been granted to fathers. Infants in Austria benefit from one of the world's most intensive social care and medical screening programs, including nationwide early intervention and screening for medical and developmental issues. Every mother is registered as soon as the pregnancy has been confirmed. After the 12th week of pregnancy a "mother-child passport" is issued as the first document of the fetus. During pregnancy, eight or more medical examinations are recorded thereon, including the infant's birth in a special section. The passport is then used to document data from the baby after birth. The pediatrician or general practitioner documents at least four examinations per year of the developing child over the first 4 years. Each mother was paid the equivalent of

US$200–500 per year as a bonus during the first 4 years of her child's life, an amount that was reduced to US$200 a couple of years ago. Mothers also receive their full wages from their employer or from social security (which is obligatory in Austria) and must stay at home for at least 2 months before the birth is expected and at least 2 months afterward. These 4 months are defined as "motherhood protection time," and it is forbidden to employ a mother for any job within this period. Every employer, public or private, must guarantee employees the legal period of parenthood to raise their babies for 18 to 24 months and employees' jobs must be reserved for their possible return for at least 3 years after a baby's birth. During this period, the state pays about US$1,000 per month to the parent remaining at home with the baby, be it father or mother. Mothers giving birth to two or more infants often interrupt their careers for 5 years or more before returning. The national opinion is that a baby should be raised by its parents and that good parents take care of their children themselves, especially during the first years of life.

One of the positive effects of the Austrian system is that pregnancy and childbirth do not cause prospective parents additional stress concerning the retention of a job and the security of returning after a job break. A prerequisite for this privilege is that one has to have been working for at least 6 months before pregnancy is declared.

One of the negative aspects of the system is the greater social isolation of mothers and the lack of professional and organized extrafamilial help, such as nannies or group day care for toddlers. Motherhood in Austria does not present a threatening social situation for a working woman. The possibility of work, even a career, and small children is probably one of the most secure in the world. Social security and family protection programs with subsidized living and other benefits are taken for granted and can be found in every political party program. Of course, the financial situation of young families with more than two children is more difficult, and families with four or more children often live on the edge of poverty.

The motherhood leave granted during the first 2 years after childbirth is intended to allow for the upbringing of most Austrian infants. Problems of appropriate day care start at the age of 2 and last until kindergarten, which traditionally begins at age 4 or 5. These problems are especially acute for families without intrafamilial resources like grandmothers to look after the toddlers adequately. This deficit is the focus of much political discussion. To date, programs that various political parties have proposed to alleviate the problem have not been put into practice.

Interdisciplinary attempts in the field of infant mental health are developing. Over the past 80 years, throughout the country, pediatricians have collaborated intensively with the child and adolescent section of the social welfare system. Every child born to an adolescent mother, or to unmarried or single parents, is protected by law and monitored individually by a social worker, who tracks developmental issues and offers help and structure as needed. In a country-wide study started under the lead of one of the authors (M. D. S.) in 1996, 700 families with babies between the ages of 8 and 12 weeks in six Austrian centers have been involved in an assessment program that includes ZTT DC (1993) diagnosis, a Zeanah interview (Zeanah & Anders, 1987), and the collection of socioeconomic data. The study is financed by the government campaign to decrease violence in families and is subsidized by the Austrian Family Ministry. Preliminary results confirm the impression that the assessment program itself serves as an early intervention act and opens the way to guidance and counseling for parents who would not otherwise have had access to help. In Austria, unlike the United States, there is traditionally strong resistance to admitting the need for psychological help of any kind. After an encounter, as experienced in the course of the described governmental study, early relationship disturbances and disorders can be detected at an early stage, so that a few sessions of intervention usually lead to complete recovery. Another result is the possibility of early detection of regulation disorders and other disturbances on an individual level. The immediate referral for further evaluation sets new standards countrywide for a better understanding of early intervention in infancy.

Infancy in Germany

After the Holocaust, a wave of insecurity washed over Germany. People asked themselves whether, as children of the Nazis, they could raise their infants and children with love, respect for their parents, and with a mutual sense of pride and enjoyment. We still encounter professionals in the United States today who basically doubt that much has changed in the past half century. During and after the war, a generation of future parents grew up fatherless, with the dyad as their basic relationship model and no triad to interact with. Returning fathers had to reintegrate themselves into a country marked by destruction and chaos. All real and moral value systems were destabilized. An entire generation broke with values and beliefs including bonding and attachment. How could one transmit security onto the next generation after what had happened? Much more than Austria, Germany was forced directly and indirectly to deal with and confront responsibility for the tragedy. Children in each family asked their parents what had happened, where they had been, how they had survived, who had helped and who had harmed or perished. After the destruction, the country endured a wave of rebuilding and renewal, and with it a chance for long-needed changes.

Germany was divided into two parts from 1945 to 1990. In the western Bundesrepublik a modern democracy was installed and integrated into the community of First World countries. The smaller eastern part, the German Democratic Republic (DDR), was integrated into the Soviet bloc. The two parts developed very differently and when their separation was ended, Germany was faced with enormous problems of reunification. The east was confronted with economic disaster, the west

with an economic recession. The birthrate fell drastically in the former DDR and slowly recovered until it reached its former level in 1996. The two nations, formerly one and now reunited, had to readapt to each other, a process that is still under way.

As to child psychiatry and developmental psychology and allied disciplines, postwar Germany started up again with a clear preference for values introduced by the new world and a return of the expelled "Jewish-centered" psychoanalysis. The reintroduction of attachment and bonding research to Germany in such renowned centers as Munich, Regensburg, and Osnabrück in the 1980s cannot be viewed without a historical and transcultural discussion.

In Germany, pregnant mothers are privileged and protected legally and economically by a social system similar to that in Austria. As soon as pregnancy is confirmed, a medical checkup is made monthly. The duration of a work-free period of motherhood protection with full wages and social security including all medical examinations is 6 weeks before and 6 weeks after birth. After this period, mothers or fathers are able to stay at home with their infant for 1 to 3 years, during which they receive an equivalent of US$500–700 per month and are guaranteed that they can return to the former job or be accepted for an equivalent one. Mothers choose this possibility of child care more than fathers. Sharing of the infant's day care between both parents is possible too. At a first impression, young parents in Germany seem more self-reliant and secure nowadays than parents in Austria, but we do not have studies to confirm this.

Infancy in Switzerland

Heidi, Edelweiss, William Tell, watches, money, banks, mountains, and beautiful lakes: We associate all of these with Switzerland. Stability, fortune, and independence also characterize this nation, as does Swiss self-confidence and stubbornness, a national characteristic that is perceived as a virtue. In contrast to Austria and Germany, there is hardly any awareness of difference between prewar and postwar history in Switzerland. The centuries since the unification of the three original cantons by the famous Rütli Schwur in 1292 have passed as a continuum. Many Swiss families can trace ancestors back for hundreds of years and possess pictures, coats of arms, and children's cradles passed down through many generations. Many grow up in the house where a parent grew up.

We should expect secure bonding to be predominant for Swiss infants. Their lifestyle is stable almost to the point of inflexibility and rigidity; tradition is transferred constantly and slowly. The traditional Swiss mother is securely attached to her infant, offering her offspring a highly secure home base in terms of economic, social, and family resources. In some Swiss families the intensity of tradition and stability seems to have become too great, so that young mothers seek distance and independence at the cost of greater

social instability. In spite of a high per capita income, there is a small but growing group of working mothers who have to return to work 2 months postpartum and receive few national and social concessions. The rate of birth is 1.3 per female, which is not appreciably different from Austria or Germany. In contrast to Austria and Germany, Switzerland offers no social security for an extended period of time after birth. Only 2 months before and after birth are jobs reserved. After this period a woman must decide to return to a full-time job or to ask for dismissal with little chance of returning later to the same job. It is the very good economic situation, represented in a countrywide high employment rate, that serves as indirect but quite effective protection for women in motherhood. The most common form of day care for women returning to work is the day care foster mother. Such women mostly care for their own children and a small number (one to three) of infants of working mothers. A day care system like the creches now common in France is unheard of in Switzerland, even though some firms organize internal kindergartens for their own employees.

Two categories of people live and grow up in Switzerland: Swiss citizens or *Inlaender* (Schwiizer), and foreigners or *Uslaender.* Children grow up aware of belonging to one or the other group. Within these two groups, mental, language, and motor skill development are alike, but the development of affect, bonding patterns, emotions, and a sense of self, security, and belonging are very different. In contrast to children of immigrants in the United States, all children of immigrants in the three German-speaking countries grow up bilingual, although their parents seldom acquire the local language. A sense of being nationally assimilated, even to those granted citizenship, is rarely acquired within the first generation.

There is a clear difference in the feeling of national identity in the three countries. Since Austria was a multinational state up to World War I, children of immigrants obtain a feeling of Austrian identity by the second generation, especially when they have attended the Austrian school system. In Germany, the process takes at least a generation longer; the various national unofficial ghettos remain much more closed. In Switzerland, the sense of Swiss identity starts to develop only after several generations. Some Swiss families engage in serious rivalry as to which family can trace its roots back furthest. In such contests, time spans of over 500 years are not uncommon!

Infant mental health research in Switzerland traditionally has had two centers: the French-Swiss groups in Vevey, Lausanne, and Geneva, and the German-speaking group in Basel. Zurich, which has perhaps the highest density of psychoanalysts and psychotherapists in the world, lacks a scientific interest in the early years. The pediatric scene is advanced in neonatal intensive care and other organically oriented subspecialties of infancy, but interactional themes are not yet considered to be a responsibility of pediatricians. Education and training for pediatrics and for child psychiatry are strictly separated, with little overlap as yet.

Techniques and Methods of Diagnostic Assessment and Evaluation

There is always a gap between the best possible situation of diagnostic and therapeutic intervention for a specific baby with a specific problem and the worst possible scenario for the same problem. For example, we will discuss the common situation of an overinvolved, anxious mother aged about 40 with her first child presenting with insecurity about feeding. She could choose a variety of solutions in search for help. For example, she could:

- Talk to her own mother or mother-in-law and receive good advice.
- Talk to a female friend who has experienced and solved similar problems.
- Talk to her husband, who might reassure her or take over the feeding himself.
- Talk to her husband, who cannot help or is unwilling to, resulting in exacerbation of the problem and alienation of the parents from each other.
- Talk to her pediatrician and receive advice on changes in technical details.
- Talk to her pediatrician, get on the pediatrician's nerves, and be sent to the hospital:
  - where the infant would be evaluated, found to be healthy, dismissed, and returned home with a mother who would continue to be insecure about feeding, or
  - where the mother would be referred to a team responsible for assessing and treating interactional dependency problems.

The problem in question might then be classified as feeding behavior disorder, overinvolved mother-infant relationship, postnatal adaptation problems after caesarean delivery, no severe psychosocial stress, and good functional emotional developmental level (ZTT DC : 0–3). The result would be an intervention consisting of several sessions of mother-infant guidance, optimizing chances of resolving the problem. This team approach best describes the experiences of patients in our clinical setting.

Another problem could involve a different baby: an 8-month-old infant from a family of low socioeconomic class, with four siblings, who had been diagnosed as developmentally delayed during a routine examination. The underinvolved mother herself presents no specific problem. For this infant-mother pair, the individual performing the routine examination might:

- Consider the symptoms to be within an acceptable normative range of variation
- Assign a social worker to introduce an early intervention program and schedule an appointment to check the baby sometime in the future.
- Tell the mother to stimulate her baby more.
- Refer the mother and baby to a specialized developmental disorder team for a specific assessment.

The last option could lead to diagnosis of an affective disorder due to interactional deprivation, at risk for multisystem developmental disorder, underinvolved mother-infant relationship, general developmental delay, severe psychosocial stress, and not age-appropriate functional emotional level (ZTT DC : 0–3). In view of the main findings and developmental deficits the baby would be referred to a multidisciplinary stimulation intervention and guidance program with weekly house visits and reevaluation of possible developmental progress in 2 to 3 months.

The methods we use and administer in a standard diagnostic assessment include a primary session on an outpatient basis with the whole family of the presenting infant. A psychoanalytically oriented or systemic attempt at primary contact is chosen, depending on the training of the interviewer. A first impression of the interactional style of communication and developmental stage of the infant within the familial context, including its dyadic and triadic abilities, is obtained. A thorough medical checkup, including neurological examination of the baby itself, will follow. Before or after the first encounter with the infant mental health professional, a videotape is made by an assistant in training or a research fellow, showing a generally less stressful situation such as dyadic play in the playroom, as well as a more stressful situation, such as a feeding scene or the interactional task of undressing the baby. The videotaped scenes are limited to three to five sequences of 3 to 5 min. each, showing a variety of situations.

In a second session, the parents are interviewed individually, in absence of the baby, using the "child working model interview" (Zeanah & Anders, 1987), which was translated into German for clinical application in 1994. Thus, the assessment phase lasts for two or more sessions with the infant and its family. Then we decide whether or not the presenting problem requires inpatient treatment, for which mother and infant are admitted together. In contrast to other countries, the financial coverage for combined admission for parent and child is uncomplicated and requires only an official standardized multiaxial diagnosis explaining the necessity of inpatient treatment. In cases of imminent abuse or predictable physical or psychological breakdown of a parent or the baby, admission to the hospital is immediate. Intake procedures should include an assessment of the treatment wishes and needs of the parents themselves as well. The techniques and methods of diagnosis and early intervention currently used and administered in the field of infancy in Austria, Germany, and Switzerland are similar to those in the tradition of the United States.

What will be done in a specific situation clearly depends on the nature of the presenting problem, the concern and decision of the assessing diagnostician, the parents' understanding of and ability for therapeutic cooperation, and the resources and demands of the referral center. The younger the baby, the higher the probability of a pediatric consultation. Parents seeking help during the first 3 months of life usually prefer to first consult their pediatrician or general practitioner. The most frequent presentations and symptoms in this period are functional problems, such as feeding and sleeping disorders, regulatory problems, and problems of adaptation to the new family situation.

Throughout the three countries, so-called *Mütter-beratungsstellen* and *sozial-pädiatrische Zentren* have developed in the course of the past 100 years. These have both a strong social and medical orientation. For years, these counseling centers have been offering their services free. They are available to anyone without an appointment and are competent for any problem or question concerning babies: growth rates, weight, size, food, skin, clothing, sibling problems, etc. In the last two decades, these centers have been enlarged and the services offered updated: Special groups have been introduced for parents of twins, for fathers, for toddlers and pets, for breastfeeding, and the like. The centers are located throughout the regions, so that for any parent seeking help the distance to a center will rarely exceed 20 to 30 miles. Other than those specified in medical referrals, these centers are the primary referral centers, and they will recommend further specific referral if necessary.

Developmental issues, questions, and concerns about relationship and communication difficulties are generally presented first in such centers, and then sent on for differential diagnosis. Nearly every counseling center is staffed by a pediatrician, a nurse, a psychologist, and a social worker. If there is need for a specific examination, both parents and the baby will be seen as soon as possible. The standard assessment procedures for an infant up to the age of 3 includes: (1) a general impression about the problem of the referred clients in a family-therapeutic assessment style, and a definition of the main concern; (2) a general impression of the baby as seen by the rater, based on a physical, sensory, and neurological examination; (3) a medical history and collection of all prior reports; (4) an interactional diagnosis of mother with infant and father with infant in both stressful and less stressful situations (for example, play and feeding situation); (5) an assessment of psychosocial stressors in an interview; and (6) an assessment of representational issues, based on an interview with the parents in the absence of the baby. The representational interview focuses on conscious, preconscious, and imaginary internal representations.

The goal of the first part of the assessment is to define the presenting problem in a multifactorial standardized manner, such as that offered by the ZTT DC : 0–3. This has become a standard instrument for communication, teaching, training, and clinical work with some Austrian pediatric centers for infant mental health issues. In the center for interactionally dependent disorders of infancy at the university hospital in Graz it has been a part of the routine assessment battery since 1994 (the final translation into German has been completed and was slated for publication by Springer-Verlag in May 1998), and it is used for patient-centered communication with social workers, therapists, medical colleagues, and early interventionists outside the hospital. It is important to be able to meet both the baby and the parents in a variety of scenes and moods, and thus include a dynamic time factor of their adaptive resources in the assessment. The whole diagnostic assessment will last two or three sessions. The parents are asked to bring to the first consultation, if possible, a home video of 5 to 10 min. duration show-

ing their view of the troublesome symptom. These videos, made by the parents themselves, are a valuable source of information during the assessment phase. The first meeting must also provide the parents the opportunity to define the presenting problem independently from the rater. In the therapeutic intervention offered at the end of the first session, a feasible compromise that considers all parties' views and concerns must be found.

The five-axial diagnostic system provides recommendations and instructions on where and how to intervene. All described difficulties must be hierarchically ordered as to severity and relevance of the specific finding. In some cases, a single session of counseling will be enough to relieve the severity of interactional distress. Medical risk factors concerning the infants, such as premature birth, perinatal complications, postnatal surgery, and neonatal intensive care showing up with an Axis III diagnosis, present a clearly higher risk for interactional stress. Long lasting interactional stress is more likely to progress into interactional disturbance and disorder. There is a clear correlation between Axis III diagnosis in infancy and Axis II pathology. In a large group of infants (N = 214) with postnatal problems requiring surgical or intensive care involving more than 3 days of hospitalization, we found a high percentage (48 percent) of interactional distress with PIR = GAS scores of 40–60, and 35 percent scoring 40 or less (Wilken, 1998). Another study (Dunitz, 1997) investigated parental interactional distress and psychiatric disorders in parents of 82 infants in the course of treatment of their infants for severe nonorganic failure to thrive. The reversibility of the parental reactions could clearly be shown in the course of successful treatment of the infant's problem.

In most cases with lasting mental and physical handicaps, intermittent interactional distress was found to progress into lasting interactional disorders. The development of Axis I pathology, except for the regulatory disorders, seems also to be directly correlated to the occurrence and aggravation of Axis II and Axis III pathology. Infants with patterns of severe interactional problems and relationship disorders are more likely to develop eating and sleeping disorders, adjustment disorders, and affective disorders.

The importance of interdisciplinary training in interactional issues for nurses and all psychological and medical professionals cannot be overemphasized. We consider the introduction of a diagnostic classification system such as ZTT DC : 0–3 a vital requirement for this group to insure appropriate treatment regarding emotional, medical, developmental, and psychosocial issues in all treatment settings, including hospitals, private practice, and counseling centers.

Available Therapeutic Services for Early Intervention

A variety of trained professionals can administer early intervention for problems presented in infancy: pediatricians, midwives, early interventionists (*Früh-*

förderer), and physical or occupational therapists. Such intervention can occur in the context of infant-parent guidance therapy, family therapy, individual therapy for one or both parents, couple therapy, inpatient treatment for infant and mother, and counseling by specially trained social workers and family intervention programs with as much as 40 hours per week of home-based support and intervention for a limited period of time. The introduction of family-based intervention has promoted a revolution in the management of infant mental health. Until recently, the placement of an at-risk infant in an extrafamilial setting such as a foster family was almost the only intervention possible in emergency situations. However, for the past 10 years there has been a new nationwide trend toward increasing support of families within the family system. Financial and professional resources may be applied in high-risk situations for up to 40 hours per week of home-based psychosocial support and additional professional counseling on a trial basis, with the efficiency of such treatment reevaluated at short intervals. In 1990, the *Psychotherapie-gesetz* was introduced. This is a new law concerned with the regulation of psychotherapy as a profession in its own right, in addition to the work of medical professionals with psychotherapeutic training. The new law allows people trained in a variety of listed methods of psychotherapy to offer treatment covered by insurance. Depending on their specific social security and insurance, patients receive a refund of US$40–100 per psychotherapy session. Thus, psychotherapy has become more or less accessible for everyone.

The therapeutic aim in all cases of diagnosed interactional stress and relationship disorders is to (1) reduce the rate of severity of the disorder, (2) diminish the negative impact on the infant's developmental milestones, and (3) normalize the quality of the diagnosed relational pattern. The specific methods differ according to the underlying pattern of relationship disturbance and the parents' capacity for therapeutic accessibility. They must always respect the infant's individual, emotional, representational, and cognitive characteristics, developmental phase, regulatory pattern, and personality.

Interactional Disturbances and Disorders Seen from a Cross-Cultural Perspective

The variety of relationship patterns and relational disturbances between different cultures is most probably not greater than the spectrum within a given culture. The range of social and representational aspects and contents within a given culture is certainly much wider than the range of normal or pathological patterns between different cultures. An overinvolved parent in Boston will be more like an overinvolved parent in Zurich or Tokyo than like an underinvolved one in the same country.

The criteria for diagnostic classification for overinvolvement in parent-infant relating in the ZTT DC : 0–3 system show clear tendency to be more critical of the parent in his or her activities than the infant. In this kind of relationship, a parent's caregiving system is activated, be it by stress, danger, or anxiety, and strikes the observing examiner as being overinvolved. The overinvolvement can be expressed in different ways: high-pitched voice, intensity of bodily closeness; verbally, physically, or emotionally expressed intrusiveness, or impatience in cue response before initiating the next communication cycle with the baby. However, an activated attachment system on the part of the infant can also be the source of overinvolvement.

Discussions with hundreds of so-called overinvolved mothers seeking help make it clear that the symptom of overinvolvement is often a matter of insecurity. Sources of insecurity vary individually and are culturally dependent. Insecure mothers in the German-speaking countries show some similarities. The resource system that a large, multigenerational family offers mothers with babies no longer exists. The pressure of role confusion between career and motherhood is great. There are also high expectations of doing the job of motherhood well or even perfectly. If there is a tendency toward too much on various levels, many sources of stress can be found.

The overinvolved mother may also be preoccupied by the topic of women's liberation and role expectation in particular. Here again, we find cross-cultural differences: As reflected in equality of wages and career changes, women's liberation in German-speaking countries lags behind that in the United States by at least a generation. On the other hand, protective factors, such as job protection and the concept of paid parenthood, are more advanced in Europe. Overinvolved parents seek more and frequent medical help. However, the positive association of amelioration by high-tech medical equipment such as monitors, values of blood sample testing, and many other devices, endanger the relationship of overinvolved parents and their infants by making them more vulnerable to a certain kind of abusive behavior with the medical system. The need for more and more security is fulfilled by increasing the number of examinations up to the point where irritation stops the process. In the German-speaking countries, where medical help is provided by social security systems and does not depend on the parents' financial situation, this pattern of institutionalized overinvolvement is common.

Underinvolvement, in contrast, can be observed in depressed or detached parent-child relationships. Prolonged and undiagnosed postpartum depression and exhaustion are the most common factors, but poverty, social insecurity, social isolation, and any other severe psychosocial stressor can be involved. The parent seems distant, entangled in a world of worries, unable to react to the discrete and distinct cues stemming from the baby. In some cases of medically ill or retarded infants, underinvolvement is stronger on the part of the infant. Its medical condition does not allow the full range of reaction and cue emission, its attention span is shortened, and its capacity for mutual engagement is lowered. In many cases of hospitalized neonates and infants we find both processes: The baby's illness, combined with an undiagnosed parental emotional exhaustion and restricted outer uptake, results in underinvolvement on both sides. Hospital teams

tend to react slowly and resentfully to this pattern of parent-infant relationship, often condemning the parent without appreciating the underlying nature of his or her psychological state. Another factor is that overinvolved parents tend to receive much attention from professional teams in contrast to underinvolved parents, who can often be neglected and forgotten. This interaction aspect between professional teams and different kinds of parent-infant relationships has not been studied much and will hopefully be a subject of focus in the near future. From a cross-cultural perspective, there could be a tendency to rate a "normal" parent-child interaction of a German-speaking mother as being underinvolved in contrast to that of a mother from the United States because of the German-speaking mother's tendency to talk less with her baby.

Current State of Infant Mental Health in the German-Speaking Countries

In 1996 an affiliation of the WAIMH was founded to connect Austria, Germany, and Switzerland in the realm of infant mental health. Currently, there are approximately 300 members in the affiliate. There are various regional groups and currently six specific work groups have been formed to address important topics in infant mental health. The work groups focus on (1) infants from high-risk families, (2) feeding, sleeping disorders, and the screaming baby, (3) psychoanalysis and psychotherapy, (4) research, (5) infants of parents with psychiatric illness, and (6) training and teaching issues.

The center for teaching the techniques of the assessment of intuitive parenting qualities is in Munich, where the research group of Hanus and Mechthild Papoušek (1987) offers a postgraduate training program with multiple seminars and workshops. The second training and teaching center is Graz, where seminars and courses on diagnostic assessment with ZTT DC : 0–3 and interactive therapeutic intervention techniques are taught in weekly courses in a bedside teaching manner. The Austrian Society of Pediatrics has introduced and accepted these courses on interactional issues in pediatric counseling, headed by the authors, as part of updating annual training for residents and pediatricians in private practice. Two German universities have a long-standing research tradition in developmental psychology: Regensburg (Grossmann & Grossmann, 1997) and Osnabrück (Keller, 1997). Within large pediatric university hospitals, two groups have gained clinical acceptance in research topics, psychoanalytic thinking, and psychosomatic or psychotherapeutic assessment in routine clinical pediatric work: Ulm (Kächele and Brisch) and Graz (Dunitz & Scheer, 1997). In Switzerland, it is Basel (Bürgin) and Geneva (Stern and Bruschweiler-Stern), where researchers have been involved intensively in the field of infant mental health research for more than two decades. The nearly 300 members of the GAIMH know one another countrywide, and there is much communication with several regional and content-defined meetings held annually.

Conclusion

Comparative cross-cultural observation of infants and their caregivers, of different kinds of attachment behavior, of various ways and methods of parental protective behavior and cue answering, is one of the most interesting, stimulating, amusing, and fascinating subjects. We are aware of the danger of mis- or overinterpreting results obtained up to now, since most study designs focus on one or a few items and cannot incorporate the complexity of cultural factors. Whatever differences we find, as long as we are studying human beings and their infants in the early years of development, it will never be possible to discriminate completely among cultural, individual, genetic, and interactional variables. Nevertheless, the cross-cultural perspective definitely widens the rater's horizon and enhances reflection of intuitive patterns and pathways, be it as parent, observer, or study designer.

References

Adler, A. (1922). *Theorie und Technik der Individualpsychologie.* Hamburg: Fischer.

Aichhorn, A. (1924). *Verwahrloste Jugend.* Bern: Huber.

Ainsworth, M. D. S., Blehar, M. D., Waters, E., & Wall, S. (1978). *Patterns of attachment: A psychological study of the Strange Situation.* Hillsdale, NJ: Erlbaum.

Barkow, J. H., Cosmides, L., & Tooby, J.

(1992). *The adapted mind: Evolutionary psychology and the generation of culture.* New York: Oxford University Press.

Belsky, J., Steinberg, L., & Draper, P. (1991a). Childhood experience, interpersonal development, and reproductive strategy: An evolutionary theory of socialization. *Child Development, 62,* 627–670.

Belsky, J., Steinberg, L., & Draper, P. (1991b). Further reflections on an evolutionary theory of socialization. *Child Development, 62,* 682–685.

Bernfeld, S. (1921). *Der Mythos des Sysiphos.* Wien: Deuticke.

Bijou, S. W. & Baer, D. (1976). *Child development: A systematic and empirical theory* (Vol. 1). New York: Appleton Century Crofts.

Bischof, N. (1985). *Das Rätsel Ödipus.* München: Piper.

Bischof, N. (1996). *Das Kraftfeld der Mythen.* München: Piper.

Bischof-Köhler, D. (1989). *Spiegelbild und Empathie.* München: Huber.

Bowlby, J. (1969). *Attachment.* New York: Basic Books.

Bronfenbrenner, U. (1981). *Die Ökologie der menschlichen Entwicklung.* Stuttgart: Klett-Cotta.

Dawkins, R. (1976). *The selfish gene.* New York: Oxford University Press.

Dawkins, R. (1994). *Das egosistische Gen.* (Rev. ed.). Berlin: Spektrum Akademischer Verlag.

Dunitz, M. (1997). Psychiatric diagnosis in infancy: A comparison. *Infant Mental Health Journal,* 12–24.

Dunitz, M., & Scheer, P. (1997). Interaktionsdiagnostik. In H. Keller (Ed.), *Handbuch der Kleinkindforschung* (2nd ed., pp. 643–655). Bern: Huber.

Dornes, M. (1993). *Der kompetente Säugling.* Frankfurt: Fischer.

Freud, S. (1900). *Die Traumdeutung.* Wien: Deuticke.

Goodnow, J. J., & Collins, W. A. (1990). *Development according to parents: The nature, sources, and consequences of parents' ideas.* Hillsdale, NJ: Erlbaum.

Grossmann, K. E., Becker-Stoll, F., Grossmann, K., Kinder, H., Schieche, M., Spangler, G., Wensauer, M., & Zimmermann, P. (1997). Bindungstheorie. In H. Keller (Ed.), *Handbuch der Kleinkindforschung.* Bern: Huber.

Grimm, H. (1997). Sprachentwicklung. In H. Keller (Ed.), *Lehrbuch der Entwicklungspsychologie.* München: Springer.

IJzendoorn, M. H. van, & Kroonenberg, P. (1988). Cross-cultural patterns of attachment: A metaanalysis of Strange Situation. *Child Development, 59,* 147–156.

IJzendoorn, M. H. van, & Kroonenberg, P. (1990). Cross-cultural consistency of coding the Strange Situation. *Infant Behavior and Development, 13,* 469–485.

Keller, H., Chasiotis, A., & Runde, B. (1992). The existence of intuitive parenting programs in German, U.S.-American, and Greek parents of three-month-old infants. *Journal of Cross-Cultural Psychology, 23,* 510–520.

Keller, H. & Meyer, H.-J. (1982). *Psychologie der frühen Kindheit.* Stuttgart: Kohlhammer.

Keller, H. (Ed.). (1997). *Handbuch der Kleinkindforschung* (2nd ed.). Bern: Huber.

Leydendecker, B. (1997). Frühe Entwicklung im soziokulturellen Kontext. In H. Keller (Ed.), *Handbuch der Kleinkindforschung* (2nd ed., pp. 149–170). Bern: Huber.

Moreno, J. (1946/1969). *Psychodrama.* Beacon: Beacon House.

Oerter, R., & Montada, L. (1995). *Entwick-*

lungspsychologie (3rd ed.). Weinheim: PVU.

Papoušek, H., & Papoušek, M. (1987). Intuitive parenting: A dialectic counterpart to the infant's integrative competence. In J. D. Osofsky (Ed.), *Handbook of infant development* (2nd ed., pp. 669–720). New York: Wiley.

Pfabigan, A., & Scheer, P. (1983). Das Geheimnis des Traumes oder die Couch in der Berggasse. In K. Sottriffer (Ed.), *Das größere Österreich* (pp. 104–112). Wien: Tusch.

Piaget, J. (1977). *Understanding causality.* New York: Norton.

Piaget, J. (1936). *Das Erwachen der Intelligenz im Kinde.* Stuttgart: Klett.

Piaget, J. (1947). *Psychology der Intelligenz.* Zürich: Raschen.

Plomen, R., Owen, M. J., & McGuffin, P. (1994). The genetic basis of complex human behavior. *Science, 264,* 1733–1739.

Popper, K. (1964). *The open society and its enemies.* New York: Basic Books.

Reese, H. W., & Overton, W. F. (1970). Models of development and theories of development. In L. R. Goulet & P. B. Baltes (Eds.), *Life-span developmental psychology.* New York: Academic.

Roberts, M. (1984). *Sigmund Freud und seine Zeit.* München: Droemer.

Silbereisen, R. K. (1995). Soziale Kognition: Entwicklung von sozialem Wissen und Verstehen. In R. Oerter & L. Montada (Eds.), *Entwicklungspschologie.* Weinheim: PVU.

Sodian, B. (1995). Entwicklungs bereichs- spezifischen Wissens. In R. Oerter & L. Montada (Eds.), *Entwicklungspsychologie.* Weinheim: PVU.

Spitz, R. (1965). *The first year of life: A psychoanalytic study of the development of object relations.* New York: International Universities Press.

Thompson, W. R. (1980). Cross-cultural uses of biological data and perspectives. In H. C. Triandis & J. W. Berry (Eds.), *Handbook of cross-cultural psychology: Vol 1. Perspectives* (pp. 205–252). Boston: Allyn and Bacon.

Trautner, H. M. (1991). *Lehrbuch der Entwicklungspsychologie.* Göttingen: Hogrefe.

Uzgiris, I., & Hunt, J. McV. (1987). *Infant performance and experience: New findings with the ordinal scales.* Urbana: University of Illinois Press.

Wilken, M. (1998). *Was die klinische und die Entwicklungspsychologie von einander lernen können.* Unpublished manuscript. University of Osnabrück.

Zach, U. (1997). Familie und Kindheit. In H. Keller (Ed.), *Handbuch der Kleinkindforschung* (2nd ed., pp. 287–314). Göttingen: Huber.

Zeanah, C. H., & Anders, T. F. (1987). Subjectivity in parent-infant relationships: A discussion of internal working models. *Infant Mental Health Journal, 8,* 237–250.

Zero to Three National Center for Clinical Infant Programs. (1993). *Diagnostic classification study manual.* Arlington, VA: Author.

12

Work Projects toward Infant Mental Health in a Child and Adolescent Psychiatric Clinic

Miguel Cherro Aguerre

12

Introduction

The objective of this chapter is to present the method of work of a child and adolescent university clinic that has developed projects in the area of infant mental health during the last 9 years. Our intention is to open areas for discussion and interchange that, in the light of other experiences, allow us to express opinions about the positive or negative aspects of this methodology and work. In order to meet our objectives, we first describe the characteristics of our daily work, the conditions and specific premises of its framework, and then we explain the specific work of the groups that implement those projects.

Although the main theoretical reference of the clinic has traditionally been psychoanalysis, use of pluralism was initiated during recent years. So we can say that at present, there is a coexistence of groups with diverse orientations: psychoanalytic, cognitive-behavioristic, systemic, interactional, biological, and so forth. Our work includes teaching, treatment, and research, plus an administrative component that in the last few years we have seen as inseparable from the other three components, perhaps even influencing the success of each of them.

The teaching area involves graduate studies of psychiatry, other graduate studies (pediatrics and neuropediatrics), and undergraduate studies (medical and psychomotor treatment students). During their first year, graduate students study normal development, carry out observations of the child at different ages, and study a baby from the last trimester of gestation until the age of 4, through a systematic follow-up that includes observations and interviews. The treatment area is in a clinic set up in a children's hospital of the Ministry of Public Health through an agreement with the School of Medicine of the University of the Republic. We are the only public center with these characteristics, and we serve as a reference for all of Uruguay. Our country has a population of 3,200,000 and an area of 187,000 square kilometers with distances no larger than 600 km between the farthest points of the territory. There is also a centralism in the distribution of the population, meaning that approximately half of the inhabitants live in the capital city, Montevideo.

In our clinic we treat an ambulatory outpatient population. Additionally, we treat patients from all pediatric services of the hospital, in a system referred to as liaison psychiatry. We work directly with pediatric teams, providing them with advice based on our specific professional knowledge, and supporting them in their daily work with strategies. This model of work is known as the care of the caregiver, and we will describe it when we refer to involvement in the community.

In 1985, after the restoration of democracy in the government of the university, there was a change in the educational-care models in respect to health. The declaration of Alma Ata, 1978, introduced the dimension of the human individual as a biopsychosocial being. Thus, although past concerns centered exclusively in illness, medical care nowadays includes similar concerns about health, its promotion and preservation. Similarly, the classical model of inpatient medicine is now considered off center and the field has opened up to outpatient medicine. This initiated a new model of work that involves opening to the community, "working there where people live," and participating in first care strategies.

Culturally, this process entailed great confrontations and difficulties both with professionals and the population since it also meant entering into a field in which there was no experience. This involved creating or devising completely new solutions.

For us, the change meant trying to find a place in the community to develop our educational-care function first of all. However, the cultural models that operated traditionally formed our greatest barrier. There was no physical or conceptual place in the peripheric health centers for our mental health teams. Our students and professors lost the shelter of the hospital, not only from the point of view of comfort, but also in respect to working guidelines. In the hospital we all "knew the script," whereas in the community we had to write it. It was there that we realized the importance of a model of work that includes the care of the caregiver.

After a period of hardship with marches and countermarches, we were finally able to settle down with our project in the community day care centers, where we could learn a lot about infants and their caregivers, both institutional and natural. Institutional caregivers are those who belong to educators' and pediatric teams. Natural caregivers are parents, relatives, or whoever takes that role. To us, as a mental health team, this framework means working not only with the child, but also with those who take care of him or her. Caregivers, both institutional and natural, have specific needs that should be met. Those needs might include:

- Knowing the characteristics of each child regarding his or her stage of development.
- Being able to handle specific problematic situations brought about by the child's own development, by conflicting relationships with the environment, or by the child's institutionalization.
- Receiving orientation, guidelines, and instances of reflection when facing tensions resulting from the characteristics of the work itself, or by working in groups.

In all our projects, either inside the hospital in the framework of liaison psychiatry, or in the community, this care of the caregiver is rigorously included.

Concerning the research area, which is an essential component that contributes to the achievement of the preceding ones, in our country and field it has traditionally had little development. From our point of view, there were mainly two reasons for this fact: one, that neither medically nor socially has mental health been prioritized; and the other, that in our disciplines of mental health there has not been concern for methodological rigor in terms of statistical validation. The emphasis has traditionally been on the individual case study in depth. In this respect, we have to acknowledge the support of WAIPAD at first, and

WAIMH later in the research projects that we were able to carry out.

Since 1983 we have received valuable comments and orientation from Prof. Serge Lebovici. Since 1987 we have had the constant support and assistance of Profs. Robert Emde and Joy Osofsky, who have supervised and discussed all our lines of research with great dedication and generosity. At present, we have not achieved results of strong scientific consistency. However, we have advanced in accepting methodological demand, and we have been able to sensitize a large number of members of our team in respect to the need to carry out studies of this kind.

Finally, regarding the administrative component, the experience of these last 9 years drove us to assign it a relevant role. The challenge of forming multidisciplinary teams as well as the growing need for both intra- and interinstitutional coordination demand the acquisition of skills that permit handling the administrative steps in an accurate manner.

Institutionally and clinically, our work is not exclusively directed toward infants, since we also have to give care to children and adolescents. Nonetheless, there are various projects directed either totally or partially toward infants. The six articles incorporated in this chapter represent the projects that we consider the most relevant for their focus on infants or their caregivers. The first of these is "Experience of Community Involvement of the Child and Adolescent Psychiatric Clinic." Next, in the frame of what we understand as liaison psychiatry, we will focus on three topics: "The Somatic Patient: Clinical and Thera-peutic Aspects," "Liaison Psychiatry in Pediatric Intensive Care Units," and "The Psychosocial Aftermath of the Perinatal Death of a Twin." Finally, we will present the results of two research studies we have conducted, "Violence among Kindergarten, Elementary, and High School Students in a Private School" and "Early Bonding in Adolescent Mothers."

Experiences of Community Involvement of the Child and Adolescent Psychiatric Clinic

Dora Musetti, Gabriela Garrido, Yosana Guichon, Madelon Rodriguez, Sara Sadownik, Miguel Cherro Aguerre

Introduction

The community interventions of our clinic have been implemented with the following basic criteria:

- *Continuity*, which means sustained and permanent presence of our mental health teams, as opposed to impact policy, which we consider less effective in the consistency of incorporated skills. In some centers we have been working steadily for 5 to 8 years.

We acknowledge the collaboration in this work of: M. Pereyra, M. Tato, N. De Leon, C. Pivel, C. Garmendia, A. Ledda, A. Martinez, A. Medori, L. Russi, B. Golluchi, M. Pazos, A. Goodson, R. Berger, S. Tabo, E. Zimmer, I. Centurion, F. Serdio, and E. Ripa.

- *Case policy,* which is transmitting knowledge to the caregivers' team through group discussion of concrete and specific cases.
- *Second-level protagonism* in respect to the caregivers' team (educators or pediatricians), which means that in first care strategies caregivers have a leading role. Our role is to support and consult.
- *Coordination and integration,* which means striving for integrated, multidisciplinary, and coordinated models of work, previously discussed and agreed upon by the multidisciplinary team, and implemented by the caregivers' team.

These first care strategies of community mental health are developed through a municipal program of first infancy attention, and implemented through a net of initial educational community centers that care for children between 45 days and 5 years of age 4 to 8 hr a day. This program, called "Our Children," provides food, health, growth development control, and psychosocial stimulation, and promotes active participation of parents and neighbors.

This joint work of a university clinic and the government of the city of Montevideo was made possible thanks to an agreement that shows the interest of each of these institutions in offering services to the community "there where the people live." In 1994, the first agreement to provide attention in seven centers of initial education was signed. The framework aimed at four main levels: clinical, educational, research, and administrative. The actions of our mental health teams include the child and the caregivers, either natural (parents or

whoever takes that role) or institutional (educators and pediatricians), and as much as possible the neighborhood commissions that manage the centers. These first care strategies at the community level were implemented by psychiatric-psychological teams according to the model that the psychiatric clinic had been developing for 5 years in a pilot center. This experience continues to develop and has integrated 23 initial educational community centers from different neighborhoods from the periphery of Montevideo.

Levels of Action of the Mental Health Teams in the Initial Education Community Centers

First care strategies at the clinical level are directed toward the children themselves, the educators' teams, parents, and the neighborhood commissions. Strategies directed toward children include:

1. Control of the child population (primary and secondary prevention) through control of development, risk detection, and early diagnosis. Our tools include individual and group observations, application of scales of evaluation of development, and analysis of emerging cases in cooperation with educators.
2. Direct care of the child in the day care center. For individual children, this involves simple situations that do not constitute serious pathologies of the child or his or her family. Tools include observation of the child, analysis of the case together with the educator, and inter-

views with parents limited in number and frequency. Direct care for groups focuses on problems that involve a significant number of children. Tools include story workshops, gardening, or other activities planned together with the educators' team.

3. Indirect care of the child. Emerging cases are analyzed in cooperation with educators, an activity that also serves as professional development. The most complex cases are studied in multidisciplinary meetings with educators, pediatricians, social workers, nursing staff, and so forth. This is accomplished in the cases in which it is feasible to coordinate with the municipal health services of the Periphery that assign resources to the day care centers.

4. Support from our field to the integration of the child with severe difficulties: children with severe developmental disorders, mental retardation, and so forth (secondary and tertiary prevention). This is achieved through detection of cases and early diagnosis, follow-up through observations, specific information about the pathology, work with the educator, transfer to individual care at the secondary level, and coordination with other levels of the program, disciplines, and institutions.

5. Coordinated transfers to second and third levels of care. Since very few health centers of the periphery have child and adolescent psychiatry, children are sent to the Psychiatric Clinic of the Pereira Rossell Hospital.

6. Participation in the planning and implementation of children's activities inte-

grated with other disciplines. These activities include psychomotor activity workshops, music or pedagogical activities, instances of dialogue and listening to different topics that emerge, and integrated and coordinated workshops with different fields.

Strategies directed toward the educators' teams include:

1. Attention directed to the team itself, in the framework of the model of care of the caregiver. Areas of concern include integration of the group, functions and roles that emerge, conflicts, competencies, and anxieties provoked by the work of the group. This is achieved through periodic meetings coordinated by the mental health professionals.

2. Professional development through discussion of cases and participation in thematic workshops. Group discussion of specific emerging cases is intended to improve the comprehension of the specific case, to acquire guidelines for the detection of risk or the early detection of pathology, and to provide tools and knowledge to face other situations. It is performed through joint analysis of individual cases with educators and through the observations that the educator in charge proposes. The objectives of thematic workshops are: to favor the expression of knowledge, feelings, and experiences of the team in respect to the topic; to promote the collective creation of knowledge and contribute specific information about the topic; and to enable educators to carry

out activities with parents and/or the community in general concerning any topic related to infant mental health. Topics of such workshops or talks include limits, habits, development of sexuality, aggressiveness, and language.

3. Striving for a creation and systematization of knowledge from interdisciplinary collaboration. Mental health teams organize and implement workshops and athenaeums together with the educators' teams and participate in the joint production of written works presented at meetings or published.

4. Providing psychiatric-psychological support to those educators who need it. The primary resource is the adult psychiatry area of the Child and Adolescent Psychiatric Service of the Pereira Rossell Hospital. Educators may be sent there or to other university services for orientation and instruction.

5. Help in regaining their self-esteem, by emphasizing the relevance of the social role they perform.

Strategies directed toward parents include:

1. Paying attention to specific demands concerning their children. Tools include listening interviews, orientation, and facilitating other levels of care.

2. Participation in talks or workshops, organized with educators, about topics of interest to parents. The objectives may include interchange, information, recreation, expression, work, comradeship, and similar goals. We stress that

such activities be carried out integrated with other disciplines, with special attention to planning, facilitating, and watching their participation and ensuring the continuity of any actions that are implemented. The focus is on giving relevance to these integrated workshops where different triggers and group dynamics can be used, leading to diffusion talks about a specific topic of interest for the group. There is also emphasis on maintaining an open ear to other topics or concerns that arise, and directing participants as needed, for example, to new workshops.

3. Facilitating psychiatric-psychological care to the parent when it is pertinent. Resources include the adult psychiatry area of the Pereira Rossell Hospital and other services.

4. Using questionnaires about child-rearing styles. The objective is to investigate the cultural guidelines concerning child-rearing and action styles, in order to adapt our suggestions to local practices. We have developed forms about feeding and sleep that parents receive through educators and fill out individually and anonymously.

The initial education community centers, integral to the Our Children project, form part of the plan for administrative decentralization of the municipal government of Montevideo. For this reason, they are managed and regulated by neighborhood commissions supported by professionals of the city government, and funded by the city. Strategies involving these neighborhood commissions include:

1. Coordination with the commission by providing information on different aspects of the actions developed by mental health teams, professionals, and the commission itself. Not all commissions have been included and the level of coordination and support varies. This is achieved through regular meetings with some members of the commission, the presence of mental health professionals in commission meetings, and integration of commission members at the regular interdisciplinary meetings at the day care center.

2. Implementation of activities in accordance with the commission.

The educational level of action by mental health teams is implemented in only one center since it requires the presence of a large number of highly qualified professors that the clinic cannot ensure throughout all the program. First-level graduate students

- Gain practical experience of observation techniques with further analysis of them. The objective is the acquisition of knowledge of the normal development of the child between 45 days and 5 years of age.
- Participate in research tasks developed in the day care center.
- Reach a first approximation to semiology and pathology through the assistant-ships carried out by residents and fourth-level graduate students.
- Are in contact with group coordination tasks and interdisciplinary work developed by child and adolescent psychiatrists in day care centers.

Educational strategies include individual and group observations, application of evaluation scales, preparation of topics to facilitate staff development, and individual supervision of students' work. Residents and fourth-level graduate students have the opportunity to display techniques and strategies acquired in psychiatric care, if necessary modifying them so they can be used in an initial education center for children of a low socioeconomic environment. They are supervised by professors. Students learn to apply a repertoire of semiological and clinical resources acquired throughout the different levels of education and care, directed mainly to the promotion of health in the community.

At the research level, this center is used by the School of Medicine, through the Child and Adolescent Psychiatric Service, to develop actions at the community level; for this reason, research, inherent in university work, is essential. It has been difficult to put that statement into practice, and after several years of work, we are worried and question whether we will be able to develop research methods that study the transformations that action itself generates. We do not have a solid formation in this field, and the situation is even worse in the field of social sciences. However, we understand that research in the different areas of development is vital. Robert Emde has supervised and provided us with orientation at this level. We are working on defining indicators of progress and more rigorous methods of evaluating the results of actions that we implement. We presented two projects requesting economic support from the university in order to conduct research studies in both the control of development and moral development in the child.

Because the work of the day care center together with our team is part of an agreement between the city government and the School of Medicine, the administrative level is indispensable. It includes coordination, discussion, and agreement that facilitate action. To accomplish this, professors of our clinic meet periodically with the directors of the Our Children project, who represent city government.

In addition to action at the clinical, educational, research, and administrative levels, mental health teams strive for coordination with other disciplines. The objective of this coordination is to obtain interdisciplinary action and to avoid overlapping as well as the invasion of the educational center by the different discourses and methodologies of each discipline. This process is difficult because finding opportunities to meet at a common place and time is not always possible. We understand that there have been advances at the local level, coordinating some actions, and also at the general level, with the coordinators and professional teams of all day care centers. The objective of the coordination is to come to general thematic and methodological agreements. Actions are planned and developed according to the private plans of each center. Monthly multidisciplinary meetings at each day care center have proven to be the most effective coordination, even though this is not always possible. Professionals, then, meet personally or communicate by phone, and educators record their daily activity in notebooks.

Evaluating the Performance of the Mental Health Teams

We will finally develop some aspects connected to research in respect to the possibility of evaluating the actions and improving the intervention of mental health teams. In order to evaluate the development of this experience that today includes 23 centers in Montevideo, a group of more than 20 professionals during several years of work have considered several indicators. Most of them are process indicators, and they refer to the evolution of certain variables depending on the level to which the actions are directed.

WORK WITH CHILDREN

1. Evolution of the stability of the group of children. At two of the centers of the program, we recorded the index of rotation of the children's population. We observed that throughout the years, as the service became more organized and the program more permanent, the number of children who dropped out during the year decreased. This variable was affected by the high rate of nomadism of the marginal population; however, in one of the centers the rotation decreased from 44 percent to 26 percent in 4 years.

2. Direct care. Although our actions at the centers are oriented toward the promotion of health, our work has always included direct care of the child. There are several reasons for this: nonexistence of a national plan of mental health, little previous training of the educators in the project, the population's

lack of access to other levels of care, and so forth. Nonetheless, we have observed throughout this work, that as long as the educators received more training and development, and more meetings were held with parents, the demands for direct care decreased. In 1994, 23 percent of the children required direct care. That level fell to 14 percent in 1996, and we believe that it may continue to decrease.

3. Performance of the children after leaving the centers. This is the first indicator of results that we have intended to register; however, there have been controls for only one center and in one year. These data are not significant, but we mention them since the follow-up may be relevant. In 1996, the educators of one of the centers studied the children who had left the center through interviews with their first grade teachers. We obtained the following data:

- In a total number of 21 children there was 0% repetition, in a school in which the repetition rate for 1996 was 33 percent.
- The teachers mentioned that the children had good results in four areas: socialization, performance, companionship, and motor skills.

This indicator of results should be used in more centers with the same criteria for follow-ups. Some educators have reported that when children leave the center they have difficulty integrating into the school environment, since the attention in the center is integral and individualized. This does not happen in schools where the number of children per teacher does not permit it.

WORK WITH EDUCATORS

1. Evolution of permanence and stability of the teams. This indicator varies for teachers (graduate professionals) and educators (non-graduate community members without previous formal training). The stability of educators is high. We found 3 services in 12 with slight instabilities (change of one educator during the year). In the case of teachers, we detected a serious instability in seven centers (change of three teachers during the year).

2. Evolution of the interest in professional development. This indicator is mainly qualitative. We observed the interest and participation of educators and teachers in noncompulsory instances of development. These were not paid, and many take place outside of working hours. A number of educators participate in those instances, and they also demand formal training in the system.

3. Evolution of absenteeism. Our data, although not complete, suggest a decrease in absenteeism due to more development and compromise with the work and the program. Perception of the atmosphere as safe is also a factor.

4. Evolution of the reasons for consulting. Other aspects in which we have observed variations are the reasons for and frequency of caregivers' teams' consulting mental health professionals. We have registered a decrease in the consultations due to behavior problems, from 45 percent to 20 percent in 2 years,

including all services. This may indicate that the services are working better, with improved organization and resources as a result of a growing professionalism of the staff. This aspect has been fostered from the very beginning of the program. Having overcome previous problems, other disorders such as maturation retardation, learning problems, the acquisition of habits, and social adaptation become more evident. There are new reasons for consulting, such as serious family dysfunctions, requests for orientation, and situations of family violence. In 1996, "orientation to parents" ranked sixth among those reasons. We consider that this may be due to the advances of our integration with those centers, and the diffusion through workshops and parents' meetings of topics related to the child's mental health. Likewise, there is an increase of parents' trust in the team, which leads to more consultations. This increases the likelihood of detecting and dealing with serious situations, such as child abuse in general and sexual abuse specifically.

WORK WITH PARENTS

During the second semester of 1994, there were information meetings with parents in 50 percent of the services, in which 50 percent of the children's parents participated (approximately 150 parents.) In 1995, there was one meeting per semester in 100 percent of the centers, and approximately 350 parents participated each semester. That meant 700 parents a year. In 1996, there was an average of three meetings per center a year. As the number of centers increased to 16, there were about 50 workshops with parents. Since the average attendance at each workshop was 25 parents, the global participation of parents climbed to 1,250. In 1997, the number of workshops was similar, but two aspects showed significant improvement. There was more parent participation, with a better quality of interchange, and the activities were interdisciplinary, with the participation of the professionals of different disciplines that serve as consultants in each center. This way, the parents received integrated training, planned and evaluated by the team of educators and support teams. The parents' consultations were mainly about their own or their children's worries, such as the mother's depression, mourning, family dysfunction, orientation in case of separation, or illness of one of the parents. Between 10 and 20 percent of the parents consulted during the curricular year. However, this specific practice will be directly affected by the reduction of the resources that have been assigned to the program for next year.

Conclusion

From the balance of our intervention, we have to mention that we found positive points in implementing a model of community work directed to both children between 45 days and 5 years of age, and their caregivers, natural and institutional. Those positive points, which may be scientifically evaluated, are mainly reaching a larger population with the promotion of health, and providing a better education to professionals in the area of mental health.

The Somatic Patient: Clinical and Therapeutic Aspects

Silvana Abatte, Marisa Abeledo, Raquel Baraibar (Supervisor), Soledad Cabrera (Coordinator), Rosario Lores

Introduction

For centuries, man has tried to comprehend the health-illness process and the relationship of the factors involved in that process. Different trends have alternated in the quest for that understanding. While the Greek philosopher Anaxagoras (500–428 B.C.) introduced the distinction between psyche and some, Epidauro devoted himself to the restoration of health, keeping in mind the dynamics of the personality of the ill, who slept in the place and whose "incubation dreams" were interpreted (Haynal & Pasini, 1984).

Modern medicine dates from the end of the eighteenth century with the prominence of the clinic look: "The eye becomes the receiver and fountain of clarity" (Foucault, 1963; authors' translation). In caring for somatic patients today, the clinic look is still king, but it is accompanied by instruments and theories that, administered in a discrete way, enrich it. From these instruments and theories, we have chosen the clinical interview and the psychosomatic theory of the Pierre Marty Institute, articulated with the experience in a child and adolescent hospital of Montevideo.

In 1992, the Group of Approach of the Somatic Patient (GAPSO), formed by child and adolescent psychiatrists and psychologists, was created. The objective of GAPSO is to care for the child and adolescent (somatic patients) and their families. The approach is focused on the patient in the context of his or her particular family environment, and particularly in the child's mind. In the case of an infant (0 to 30 or 36 months), the focus lies on the mother's mind as well as the vulnerability of the environment to the infant's risk of becoming ill.

We are referring to a patient who has a real somatic illness, and whose mental functioning makes him or her more or less fragile. We direct our work to the mind. Our objectives are reanimating the patient and promoting his or her imaginative life, reflective capacity, and mental resources to elaborate and express the different events of his or her life in manners that do not represent a threat for his or her body. This practice is accompanied by a medical diagnosis that contributes to the strategies to be carried out, since the organic condition of the patient is always kept in mind. We might say that the team, more than resorting to one or another discipline depending on the patient's condition, has its foundation in a somatic view of the patient. For this reason, the medical look and the clinical look are present, and all the members are heard independently of their original profession.

The Strategy and Its Basis: The Interview

After a year of exhaustively reviewing the national and international trends in relation to psychosomatics, we decided to carry out therapeutic conversations in the Gessel chamber together with an experienced consultant. Our aim was to learn the mode of approach transmitted by the consultancy in practice and the theoretical basis that sustains it.

The group adapted to that style of work, and two professionals carried out the interview while the rest of the team remained behind the camera. Both the patient and the person who accompanied him or her had been informed of this practice. Then the therapeutic session to approach the somatic patient began. After determining the patient's capacity and limits through the analysis of dynamic, countertransferential, and institutional aspects, the group decided to exclude those somatic patients with infectious, contagious, or oncologic diseases.

In our practice the concept of "interview" is linked to an approximation method, to a technique of dialogue whose aim is, in broad terms, to know the child and his or her family in their individual characteristic aspects, their lifestyle, and how they value the problem for which they seek help. It consists of a formal meeting of approximately 1 hr 30 min that starts with an invitation to explain the reason for coming to the session. The discourse of the patient is followed with an alert listening, and our interventions have a colloquial tone so as to decontract and facilitate the opening of both the child and his or her companion (generally the mother). Our objective is to help them describe their daily life with rich tones.

We work on points of urgency, trying to promote a psychic elaboration from both of them, and to identify risk factors and resources for the reorganization of the psychosomatic balance. We evaluate relationships among the family and with the environment in order to detect bonds or circumstances that might also have a regulating character of support to the therapeutic process. We establish a series of periodic interviews, more frequent at the beginning and at longer intervals as therapy progresses. Our work is focused on re-establishing a more adequate mental processing of life experiences.

Theoretical Basis

Our practice is sustained mainly by the conceptions of Pierre Marty, Leon Kreisler, and Rosine Debray, for whom "a stable neurotic functioning, although pathologic, has a defense value in front of somatization. The economic role of the treatment of anguish, that is to tolerate it, negotiate it, and elaborate it, belongs to mentalization" (Kreisler, 1994; authors' translation).

The interventions, then, try to promote mental functioning while being careful with the mental symptoms the patient makes use of and evaluating their economic value for his or her psychosomatic balance. Keeping in mind that the theory highlights the existence of risk structures for somatic disturbances, which refers to the concept of structure as mode of functioning, it is necessary to identify the characteristics of the patient's mind, considering the malleability, the possibility of change, and the reversibility that characterize these stages.

As a reference, we maintain Leon Kreisler's classification, which assumes that the quality of father-mother-baby interactions has a strong influence in shaping the child's mind. The quality of the care (adequate, lack, or overload) would have an influence on the child's own resources, especially the first case; it would affect the quality of preconscience, heir of the function of paraexcitement inherent in the maternal role, which might guarantee or challenge the resources for good mental functioning (Kreisler, 1987).

This mental functioning, which becomes autonomous at a given moment, depends initially, as we pointed out, on the father-mother-baby interactions as well as the mother's mind. For this reason, the entire period of gestation, pregnancy, childbirth, the first stages of the child's life, and their influence on the mother is of paramount importance.

Rosine Debray has mentioned the risk of the "pressure situation" affecting the mother. This situation might be triggered by traumatic or destabilizing events during those periods and that consequently influence her disposition toward her pregnancy and the baby. We might mention here Andre Green's concept of "dead mother," that is, the mother who is present but not available because of some painful situation that involves her. For example, moving, losing a job, economic problems, the loss of significant figures, or mourning previous loss of a child, as well as normal contingencies of the mother-child encounter (e.g., handicapped child, separation of the parents, etc.) might hinder the father-mother-baby early interaction process, thus affecting the quality of care and risking a negative effect in the role of the mother to organize the baby in its functions and behaviors. The psychosomatic organization that the infant must achieve consolidates in a fragile way,

and from then on, the baby's mental life is at risk.

Kreisler, going deeply into the different styles of encounter and the diverse characteristics of mental functioning, elaborates his classification, constructing a psychosomatic nosography of child risks (Kreisler, 1987).

- Behavior neurosis, or behavioral functioning, refers to children with little imaginative richness. Their play and social relations are not filtered through a rich and personal inner life, and the functioning is concrete and immediate with a lack of affect. This mode of functioning is called empty behavior. It is as if their inner life cannot flow.

- In certain neurotic functionings, currently known as uncertainly mentalized neurosis, we perceive a weakening of the mental defenses when facing the different and varied traumatic situations that may lead to psychosomatic disorganization.

- States of disorganization indicate that the child is unable to decode and understand the affections and emotions he or she goes through, so that the body becomes the place to discharge those nonelaborated or wrongly mentalized excitements.

- Allergic structure is defined by the quality of the object relationship. This concept is taken from the description of the essential allergic personality (Marty, 1958), which describes a need and easiness of contact with people and the environment (fusional contact), avoidance of conflicting situations with a restraint of aggressiveness, and a quick, almost instant substitution of a valued object by another one. In the light of these works, the allergic functioning of the child is observed and elaborated (Marty, 1992). It is necessary, then, to identify traumatic situations that may have surpassed the child's resources for elaboration, either because of the nature of the trauma or the patient's fragility, and to harmonize the techniques (signaling, interpretation, confrontation, support, or others) that promote the recovery.

The concept of trauma (Freud, 1926) is a theoretical reference that is present in this approach. It is generally identified in the family history and has great impact on the key stages of the child's development. In order to identify it, and to understand the quality of family relationships, it is especially relevant to apprehend the history of the child in the family network. That is why the characteristics of the generation previous to that of the parents is included in the research.

As we mentioned previously, GAPSO members base their practices on the ideas proposed by Pierre Marty (psychoanalytic); nonetheless, we also include concepts used by cognitivism. We would like to highlight the relevance of psychological stress as a "result of a relationship between the subject and the environment, which is evaluated by the individual as threatening or surpassing his/her resources, thus endangering his or her well-being." Concepts such as cognitive evaluation (evaluation processes of the individual that mediate between confronting and responding to the stressor), cognitive reevaluation, capacity to confront, vulnerability, the chronology of stressing events in the longitudinal history and in relation to the vital

cycle, and the characteristics of the stressor (predictability, imminence, ambiguity, duration, uncertainty, biographical chronology) (Lazarus & Folkman, 1986) have been of great value at the clinic. We also take into account the hidden events and the summary of minor events. These conceptions do not contradict the psychoanalytic theory from which we depart; moreover, they have broadened our point of view as well as our capacity to understand the problems of our patients and the elaboration of a strategy of a therapeutic approach that suits each individual case. We will illustrate this approach with a clinical vignette.

Venancio, 4 years of age

Venancio and his mother came to the first session when the child was 4 years old. We were impressed by the chaotic situation: The boy was messy, did not make himself understood, and did not play. His mother explained what life had been for both of them, spending 3 months in the hospital with a son who had asthma attacks, convulsions, and hypoglycemic crises. "I *plug in* the bottle every 3 hours, he does not want to take his medicine. He becomes bad and aggressive," she said, talking about the first bonds with her son. He was not in school. According to his mother, this was accepted due to his health problems. She emphasized how dramatic their situation was by coming by ambulance, since they were from the interior of the country.

We tried to recognize the tiredness of the mother; we communicated that we understood how difficult the situation had been for her, especially because Venancio was born exactly 9 months after his older sister. Likewise, we valued the image of the son

339

and incorporated him into the dialogue. Voicing the difficulty of the situation and recognizing the trauma of the birth of her son, with somatic problems, only 9 months after the previous birth, was crucial.

This started the reanimation of the mother's mental resources, and her capacity to reflect about the 4 years in which taking care of Venancio's imbalances had driven her focus only on the disease and lose the perspective of seeing him as a child. The mother had focused her attention on the operant aspects of the treatment and her ability to identify hypoglycemia by changes of behavior. But she was unable to contact the expressive characteristics of the child's affections. As Debray points out, the reality of the illness blocked the free circulation of fantasies.

Preventive Aspects

In our work, we deal with four levels of care:

1. That of the natural caregivers. We work simultaneously with the child and the parents. With infants, we work through therapeutic father-mother-baby interviews. With older children, we work together with the family, but we also reserve private time for the child. In this way we try to protect the group from changes in the psychic economy of each member as the therapeutic process advances.

2. That of the team that carries out the somatic treatment of the patient. We try to identify the characteristics of the relationship of the team with the patient and his or her family. When communicating with our team we promote a reflective dialogue that enables them to develop their practice through a better organization of the patient involving less emotional cost for them. Thus, we facilitate the comprehension of that emotional cost, for example, by eliminating guilt, orienting them to set limits to the risk of an excessive affective involvement, and incorporating them into the therapeutic process.

3. That of the mental health team (GAPSO). The multidisciplinary nature of the team facilitates the comprehension of the patient and the visualization of difficulties. Each professional becomes enriched by the vision the others can give from their own perspectives. Periodical meetings that deal with theoretical, professional, transferential, and scientific aspects, as well as the role of affect in the interrelation, constitute a factor of protection for the mental health of each team member.

4. That of others (community members, extended family, teachers, etc.). Depending on the case, it may be necessary to refer to other people linked with the patient in relation to the reason for seeking help (grandparents, teachers, institutional caregivers, etc.). In order to coordinate efforts, exchange opinions, and make specific indications, we hold occasional synthesis meetings and create an annex team that is formed spontaneously. This team will offer extended care with more tools and less emotional cost.

Conclusion

Thanks to the convergence of the different schools of thought to which we subscribe, we make an effort to carry out an approach to the somatic patient that includes the three levels: intrapsychic, interactional, and the outside world. We aim at being able to capture the individual from different axes, establishing the most complete vision, and elaborating courses of action that produce a reanimation of the psychic life of the patient as soon as possible, with deep and broad results that are at the same time long lasting. That means enabling the individual to face future situations with more resources and a better understanding of his or her inner processses as well as those of the environment and the interaction between them.

The group is currently reviewing clinical histories and sending out questionnaires to track the evolution of all treated patients, whether they continue under treatment, finished the treatment, or stopped the treatment voluntarily. This evaluation will be personal, through mail or telephone, and the responses will provide quantitative data relevant to further studies. Clinically, in most of the patients we have noticed a remission of the somatic symptoms with an enrichment of the mental life of the patient.

Liaison Psychiatry in Pediatric Intensive Care Units

Aurora Fuentes, Rosario Lores, Monica Silva

Introduction

In our school of medicine, general practitioners and pediatricians get their degrees with little knowledge about mental health. For this reason, the patient is not always approached with a balanced attitude concerning biological, psychological, and social aspects. The result might be either a dissociation between a strictly organic medicine and an integrative one, or a somewhat dehumanized medical practice (Ferrari & Luchina, 1977).

In ancient Rome the medical doctor was aptly defined as *vir bonus medendi peritus,* that is, a good man expert in the art of healing. The expertise refers to the professional accuracy in medical practice, whereas the human goodness defines the moral and ethical accuracy in that practice (Gracia, 1995). Pediatric liaison psychiatry serves specifically the child and those who care for him or her through the model of care of the caregiver. As has been previously explained, care of the caregiver means giving care not only to the child but also to the family and the mental health team. In the case of pediatric intensive care, the model has some specific implications:

- For a child with a somatic pathology, it is necessary that we not be considered only as specialists in reactive pathological complications. That means not letting the pediatrician free him- or herself after consulting with us, but involving him or her so as to treat the child together.

- For a child with a psychiatric pathology, it is also important to treat him or her together with the pediatrician. Proceeding this way in these two types of cases will familiarize the pediatrician with the concept of integrative medicine.

- Because we work in multidisciplinary teams, we have to offer the best conditions for the team to coordinate actions, to have moments for reflection, decision making, and synthesis, and also to face and elaborate the tensions caused by the characteristics of the work and the fact of working in groups. That is why it is necessary for the mental health team to collaborate, shift passes, and report to the family (Granger & Stone, 1991; Hayez, 1991).

The advantages of this model of liaison psychiatry can be evaluated through indicators. The indicators that are mentioned internationally show that by working this way, the time and frequency of the periods of hospitalization are reduced, as are morbidity rates. In addition, there are indirect indicators:

- Standing and increasingly frequent requests for consultation from pediatricians.
- Consultations are carried out from the moment a patient is admitted and after the pediatrician's first evaluation, rather than after the patient is dismissed from the hospital.
- The residents' and graduate students' incorporation of concepts that facilitate the handling of some situations together with the mental health team: suspicion of abuse, sticking to treatment in the case of chronic diseases, sleep disturbance while in the hospital, frequent admissions to the hospital, intoxication, accidents, and so on.
- An increasing number of invitations to participate in seminars and conferences of pediatrics.
- Requests for a resident psychiatrist in some units with special psychosocial im-

pact, such as burns, hematology, and intensive care units (ICUs).
- Parents' permanent attendance to neonatal ICUs. This attendance is fostered by pediatricians and nurses, and continues after the baby is dismissed.

Clinical Aspects

Intensive care is an area of special impact for the child, the family, and the professional staff. The patient's risk of death causes a special situation of chronic stress conducive to burnout in everyone involved (Novali, Urman, & Sola, 1988). In addition, since the 1960s there has been an increased capacity to mechanically maintain vital functions, which has led to a medicalization of the initial and final stages of life, and even to a reformulation of the concept of death. This has brought about new ethical conflicts in the practice of medicine as well as new challenges for the patient and his or her family, who should not only obey the doctor's orders, but also assume that they are active participants in the healing process.

In order to organize this communication we are going to describe the clinical aspects of each of the receivers of liaison psychiatry: the child, the family, and the team.

THE CHILD

Admittance to an ICU, whether because of an acute or chronic disease, an accident, prematurity, or a congenital disease, always involves a dramatic rupture in the continuity of life that affects the child's body. Consequently, there is a psychic shock expressed through different signs depending on the characteristics of the child and the environment. Characteristics of the child include age and stage of development (level accomplished), previous admissions, and previous psychoaffective disorders. Characteristics of the environment that affect the child directly include previous deaths (siblings, abortions), reaction of the family to the child's disease (depression, negation, guilt, anger, etc.), and, where applicable, lack of a support group (collective accidents, disaster situation, abandonment, or an abused or institutionalized child). These factors, previous to admittance, determine the child's resistance to hospitalization, and they explain, at least partly, why some children do not need psychiatric support.

During the first years of life, the child reacts to hospitalization with anxiety originating in separation from his or her attachment figures and the loss of trust in the omnipotence of parental care. This situation frequently generates regressive reactions that constitute a healthy and restorative response. It is necessary to follow these cases closely in order to foster a gradual process of restoration of acquired independence and avoid situations of regressive overprotection. Oppositional manifestations express the struggle against the aggressions of an environment that the child cannot understand. The feared analytical depressions of the second year of life, which aggravate the somatic evolution, are not very frequent, because relatives have an almost permanent presence in our ICUs. As the child grows up, understands the situation, and acquires the concept of death as an irreversible fact, the most frequent symptomatic reaction is depression.

Dismissal from the ICU also deserves special attention, since it implies a loss of the security that is given by technology. The patient should recuperate his or her body as his or her own and assume its control. Often depression or intense anguish appear at this time, and should be treated carefully. It is also at this time that posttraumatic stress syndrome appears, which is why the somatic dismissal of the patient does not imply concluding care by the mental health team.

THE FAMILY

We should especially mention parents with children in the perinatal ICU. Here we have a situation with a double crisis: the crisis due to puerperium and the crisis due to hospitalization of a seriously ill child (crisis over crisis) (Lores, Correas, & Rodriguez, 1994). These parents have a lot of anxieties related to the unexpectedness of the situation, with feelings of guilt and disappointment in respect to the baby, that overlap with the necessary recognition of the puerperium as a special period. These parents are in an especially vulnerable situation.

Lebovici (1989) described the concepts of the real, imaginary, and fantasized baby. Clinical work proves the need for a balance among these three concepts so that early attachments develop normally (Cherro Aguerre, 1995). Sometimes the anticipated mourning ends with the abandonment of the baby or the family's withdrawal. At other times, the same situation arises due to the impotence that the parents feel in respect to technology, leaving the care of the baby to machines (Fuentes & Lores, 1994). Moreover, depending on how the parents develop the mourning for the fantasized and imaginary baby, the image of "harmed child" may crystallize. This image may develop into the vulnerable child syndrome, a relatively frequent situation in children who have been in an ICU. After dismissal, these children reenter the family dynamics with the label of unhealthy and are treated as such. This family will worry about any banality as if the child's life were at risk. Then family bonds vary, the setting of limits becomes difficult, and the development of the child changes.

THE TEAM

The common denominator of the reactions of the care team is burnout (Fuentes & Lores, 1994). This is described as a set of reactions that includes a loss of motivation to work, a lack of compromise and creative capacity, somatic expression disorders, and a deterioration of social activity. It appears in those persons who have tasks that are intensely related to others who require care (Maslach, 1982).

In the case of the ICU health team there are other elements among which we highlight the role of the medical doctor in society. In 1900 it was strange not to find a priest beside a moribund's bed, whereas the doctor was rarely present. Today the situation is the opposite: Death has become medical, and we expect from technology what we used to expect from religion or magic (Barran, 1992). The medical doctor has not only the power to heal, but also knowledge, so the anguish of not knowing how or not being able to avoid death appears.

Facing a possible death, we can find two reactions of the team in respect to the patient or his or her family. One of them is reducing the relevance of the disease, understating the seriousness of the situation, highlighting the healing possibilities, and minimizing the risk of a fatal outcome. It is common to rationalize this by saying that this is done in order not to cause the patient or the family excessive pain. The result is that the doctor takes care of the situation him or herself, and does not share the anguish with the parents. He or she keeps distant from them (Elman, 1994).

Another mechanism is increasing the seriousness of the pathology and indicating the situation to be worse than what the doctor perceives. The rationalization here is "in order not to create false hope," but it seems more an intent of self-protection against anguish if the patient dies. Furthermore, in the ICU the ethical challenges add other sources of stress: making the decision of not reviving, of discontinuing assisted respiration, and soon (Oberfield & Gabriel, 1991). Children in an ICU, with the constant presence of death, are hardly gratifying. Moreover, if they do not die but get better, they leave the unit fast, denying the ICU team the pleasure of seeing a completely recovered patient. All this has an extremely high cost, both physical and emotional, conducive to burnout.

Therapeutic Aspects

WITH THE CHILD

The objectives are generally limited to the immediate situation of crisis and have a brief duration. In respect to the methodology, the child is interviewed on an individual basis as well as together with the rest of the family. The crisis situation is contextualized from a dynamic comprehension without disregarding the subject and his or her history. The objective is for the patient to achieve a real view of the situation. It is known that what the child imagines surpasses reality, and that is why it is better to transmit truthful information, expressed with clear words according to his or her level of development.

It will also be necessary to create and foster the psychic defenses necessary to endure the treatments, which are generally cruel and invasive. Informing the patient about the manipulations that will be carried out, and respecting the time he or she needs to accept them, become relevant in the therapeutic process. This helps the patient not to lose the status of subject completely by keeping at least in part control over his or her own body. A crucial point of the treatment involves giving support to the patient in leaving the unit or accompanying him or her if he or she is going to die.

Play is both therapeutic and an indicator of health, since it allows the child to express a wide variety of feelings. Rarely are children found with whom it is not possible to play through a look, a smile, words, or toys. Integrating the family at play is important, since it fosters child-parent communication and helps parents to lose fear of harming their child's body, limited as their contact is by machines they do not know how to operate.

It is important to mention that the majority of children respond to being in an ICU adequately, and they teach real lessons to the adults that surround them.

WITH THE FAMILY

In respect to the family, we work in two different ways: with each family, or with groups of family members. In the first case, we work with those parents who request help or those who are in an unusual or difficult situation, such as those who are quarrelsome with the medical team or absent from reports. The objective is to help parents acquire the most realistic view, to clarify feelings, and to allow the team to detect each parent's projections, either to the health team (doctors, nurses), the child, the spouse, or him- or herself.

It is also necessary to act at the preventive level, taking into account that the crisis situation might produce rupture in the couple or generate a psychiatric pathology in parents or siblings (Baraibar 1991a, b). At the perinatal ICU it is necessary to make an accurate evaluation of the vicissitudes of the newly born–family encounter. The parents' expectation during pregnancy is an especially relevant point. The parents expect a child that they imagine in different ways. At childbirth, there is a reality that forces an adjustment from what was previously imagined: The real child appears. The adjustment to that reality implies a loss that should be elaborated. In the case of the unhealthy newborn that loss is even greater, demanding more intense psychic work in order to be elaborated (Lax, 1972). In this frame, the type of pathology that the baby presents is important in establishing the relationship.

The parents' personal histories are another important aspect. It is necessary to consider the histories of the families of both sides at the same time, especially in respect to illnesses, hospitalizations, deaths, and previous mourning (Baraibar, 1991). The attachment mode that develops is going to be influenced by these transgenerational elements, which might determine, for example, the role that the child will have in the family, becoming either overprotected or receiver of all evils. Furthermore, it is necessary to evaluate the parents' personalities, their capacity to handle the situation, and their defense mechanisms in respect to how healthy and flexible these are, and whether or not they permit a certain emotional balance.

The baby is also in a stressful situation, both from an environmental and an emotional point of view (Als, Tronick, Adamson, & Brazelton, 1976). There is a lack of skin-to-skin contact and body holding, which are the basis for self-image. This seems to develop through painful and bothering stimuli, rather than through the libidinization of the skin as happens in the healthy baby. The parents are not in the best situation to detect and meet the baby's needs, and they fail to act as a barrier to those stimuli (Bowlby, 1989).

Fostering interaction with and attachment to the baby in the ICU, as painful as it might be, contributes to creating a child-parents common history, inserting the baby in the family history. This interaction reduces the possibility that in case of death, this child will be searched for in the following children. We try to avoid the "replacement child" who annuls the new and different child and conforms to a specific psychopathology.

The parents should correct their idealized mental expectation so that it agrees with the thin, wrinkled, and weak prema-ture baby, or the baby with external malformations. The mother is afraid to see her child with an abnormality, and suffers when she thinks that she will be criticized for having gestated a weak, imperfect, unfinished child. Guilt and anger appear, and they might be self-assigned or projected on to other members of the family, in general the spouse. That projection might also be directed onto the health team, a fact that does not contribute to a good hospitalization or a good resolution of the bond with the child.

The parents might stop going to the unit due to the anguish generated by what they consider an imminent loss. This constitutes a risk of attachment and abandonment that should be detected early, in order to work specifically with the parents: exculpate, maintain hope. Other times we observe an overly optimistic view in the parents, which might determine a pathologic mourning. That is why it is necessary that they achieve a realistic view.

The place is not adequate for the mother-father-child encounter: It is too illuminated and noisy, it has too much steel and glass, and it is full of strange smells, noises, and men and women. The parents go from incubator to incubator and look at the babies with serious faces. To make things worse, the baby is full of wires and tubes, and is sometimes in restraints. Parents are afraid of harming their child even more, of carrying microbes into the unit, of touching the baby, and so on. Our reality shows a poor building structure to lodge these parents, who sometimes spend long periods in rudimentary waiting rooms, often without proper places for medical reports.

The apparent omnipotence of science and technology generates feelings in the parents of worthlessness and disapprobation of their child. It is common to find parents who feel that the machines and doctors will take better care of their child, or who feel very insecure when the baby is going to be moved to another area where they have to assume more participation and care. In this situation, there might be more or less hidden rivalries with the health team: envy toward the role of nurses, and at the same time fear of fantasized reprisals from the health team.

Parents do not always understand completely and accurately what they are told, either because that information contains many technical terms, or because their own psychic mechanisms do not allow them to. As a consequence, the team complains of having to give the same report several times. However, repetition is important since it allows parents to achieve a realistic view.

The groups of parents of perinatal ICU are open to all parents who wish to attend. These parents might either have their children in the ICU, in an intermediate area, or at pre-dismissal. Some parents even attend meetings after the baby is at home. Meetings are held weekly, and they last 2 hr. Professionals of both the mental health and pediatrics teams are present.

Meetings begin with a time open to parents' participation in which there is an avalanche of questions about the condition of each child, why different maneuvers and treatments are carried out, and so on. Later, feelings such as guilt, ambivalence, and insecurity appear. Parents often return to the group looking for reassurance in the face of their insecurity regarding their capacity to take care of a child who

was seriously ill many times after dismissal. It is frequent to see the group divided in two subgroups: parents whose children are in serious condition, and those whose children have favorable evolution. The latter are inhibited about expressing their joy, and part of the work of the mental health team is to help the verbalization of all feelings, not just the negative ones. This way the group offers support and permits hope.

The group serves several purposes:

- It provides mutual support.
- It offers a specific place to express feelings and become aware that all of them have similar feelings and go through the same stages.
- It allows the pediatrician and nurse attend the meetings to grasp the parents' feelings in a different situation. Since they do not protect themselves with technology to inform, they become closer.
- It permits the prevention and detection of specific risk situations: vulnerable child syndrome, anticipated mourning, and so on.
- It gives the opportunity to work out the situation with the rest of the family, especially siblings.

WITH THE HEALTH TEAM

Our interventions are at two levels: the medical team and the nursing team. This implies formal meetings to discuss specific topics with each team as well as informal meetings to facilitate communication and reciprocal exchange of information about patients. It is important to exchange the feelings that these patients inspire in those who work with them, since either detachment or excessive close contact is deleterious to the doctor-patient relationship.

Earlier in this work we mentioned burnout; now we describe some factors that permit workers to resist it:

- Social support, group work, the discussion of concrete cases in order to relieve the tensions that a particular patient produces.
- Improvements at the workplace: the environment should be as comfortable and functional as possible. Institutional changes in respect to place and working conditions reduce the rate of burnout.
- Incorporation of more resources.
- A more equitable division of work: rotation of roles and tasks, schedules, and so on.
- Suggesting individual treatment to those team members who need it.
- Fostering personal initiative and research so as to feel productive. This improves the quality of care, allows the confirmation that good results are obtained, and reduces pessimism.

What Happens with Our Team?

Psychiatrists, like the rest of the workers in the area of health, are vulnerable to burnout. That is why it is important to carry out intense personal work in order to help the professional identify the tasks that he or she cannot achieve, as well as to recognize his or her personal limitations. In this respect, the technical aspects should support the individual. So, for example, carrying out interviews in pairs allows flexible dynamics in the interaction with the patient since each professional can stay back and rely on the other when he or she needs it. Likewise, it might be necessary to replace a team member when the situation becomes intolerable for one of the therapists. Knowing when to step aside and let another participate is very important. The selection of team members should be slow and careful. They should be professionals with an orientation toward medical rather than biological work, who do not get overwhelmed by illness and death. In this respect, study and theoretical support constitute tools to know what happens and how to handle the situation better. The group behaves as referent and might be the place to detect when the work is too tainted by personal factors.

The Psychosocial Aftermath of the Perinatal Death of a Twin

Denise Defey

Abstract

Though the issues of birth of twins and perinatal loss of singleton fetuses or infants has been widely studied and management guidelines are available to clinicians and parents, this is not the case for the perinatal death of one of more twins. This situation,

This paper summarizes the work and conclusions of an interdisciplinary team integrated by child psychiatrists (Miguel Cherro Aguerre and, at a later stage, Aurora Fuentes) and psychologists (Pia Correas, Denise Defey, Rosario Lores, and Graziella Zito).

once considered rare, has become wide-spread due to the early ultrasound scanning of twins—⅔ of which will be lost in the first trimester—and the ever-spreading use of assisted reproduction techniques, which both increase the rate of twin pregnancies and introduce the practice of feticide in high-order multiple pregnancies. Since health care staff has gained such a relevant role in the subject, the research presented here seeks to ascertain what management attitudes may increase the psychosocial risk involved in losing one or more twins both for parents and the surviving child(ren). Habitual clinical management both in obstetric and pediatric care is analyzed and guidelines are provided in order to protect the mental and physical health of both the parents and the surviving infants.

Introduction

The fact of expecting, bearing, or rearing twins has always filled humans with excitement and a mixture of enjoyment, pride, fear, and an overwhelming sensation of having too much too near. However, the dark side of twinning is not very well known by laypeople, nor are the psychological implications habitually well handled by health care staff. This becomes especially dramatic in the perinatal death of one or more twins, the impact of which tends to be underestimated by relatives, friends, and staff. Since one child or more is alive, it is assumed that the loss will be overridden soon and the joy of parenthood will cast light on the family's life. In fact, the aftermath of the death of a twin during or soon

after gestation is always burdensome and casts shadow instead of light over parents' feelings and over their relationship with the surviving twin(s). Even when the loss takes place during the first trimester of pregnancy, this is bound to affect the way parents view their child and themselves for a very long period, sometimes lingering for a lifetime.

The Facts

Even though they account only for 1 to 2 percent of all births, twin pregnancies contribute 10 percent to global perinatal mortality rates (Ellings, Newman, Hulsey, Bivins, & Keenan, 1993). This is partly due to their pathological nature: The only normal human pregnancy is one that produces a single fetus. All twin pregnancies are medically considered high risk, a fact of which most lay people are not aware. Not only are risks increased for the embryos or fetuses but for the mother as well. Because early ultrasound scanning is routinely applied to pregnant patients, twinning is generally assessed in the first trimester. Two thirds of these pregnancies will reach term with only one fetus alive due to the vanishing twin phenomenon, in which one embryo or fetus is reabsorbed without any clinical evidence that parents could perceive on their own. Nature has spared them the corresponding grief: No sign is evident of this second fetus's existence or of its demise. However, technology has upset nature's protection and introduced the news of this child's existence into the parents' world. The news that they are expecting twins will be rapidly spread among family, friends, and coworkers, and thus the loss will become much more dramatic, affecting parents' attachment process and turning them into the object of other people's pity instead of joy. This will cast a shadow upon an otherwise perhaps undisturbed pregnancy course.

Fetal demise may happen later in pregnancy, producing the so-called fetus papyraceus, in which the dead fetus becomes fully dehydrated and mummified. If twinning has not been detected earlier, this appears as a most distressing finding at the moment of delivery. In the third trimester, stillbirth has a frequency estimated at 0.5 to 6.8 percent (Jauniaux, 1988) and the surviving twin's risk of dying in the first year has been estimated to be as high as 18 percent (Van den Veyver, Schatteman, Vanderheyden, & Meulyzer, 1990) and 28 percent (Szymonowicz, Preston, & Yu, 1986). The surviving twin is affected in his or her physical health in 46.2 percent of cases, 20 percent of which suffer neurological sequelae (D'Alton, Newton, & Cetrulo, 1984).

Another technology-induced source of perinatal loss in multiple pregnancies has arisen from the increasing use of assisted reproduction techniques. The technique of transferring several embryos in order to improve the chance of successful implantation has caused the rate of multiple pregnancies to increase. The higher the number of fetuses, the greater the risk of losing the whole of them by miscarriage, extremely low birth weight, or severe prematurity. In order to reduce these risks, several countries legally accept that such

pregnancies be reduced to a maximum of two or three fetuses. In some countries, such as the United States, this is strictly regulated, and only a few centers across the country are allowed to perform this kind of intervention, which the staff involved describe as "heartbreaking" for them as well as for most patients. (Manuel Alvarez, personal communication). In many centers of different countries the "reduction" of some of the fetuses (performed by puncturing the fetus' heart at three months' gestation) is performed upon the parents' request, which has led some of the staff to personal crisis and resignation from their posts. Scientific papers published in journals of obstetrics and gynecology are in the vast majority centered on the different reduction techniques and their rates of success, with complete dissociation from parents' feelings or reactions. Parents' anxiety, when acknowledged, has been assigned simply to the use of an "unfortunate misnomer," given to the procedure by calling it selective reduction (Berkowitz & Lynch, 1990).

Selective reduction, in fact, refers to the case when the fetus to be reduced is not randomly chosen but "selected" because of some defect (e.g., Down syndrome) that accounts for the decision not to continue bearing it. Since reduction in this case may happen after the first trimester, this fetus becomes mummified and pregnancy continues with both the living and the dead fetuses, which must be delivered. Psychosocial research in this field is practically nil, partly because parents tend to defend themselves from such bizarre and uncanny situations by extreme mechanisms such as complete secrecy and thorough denial, often refusing to be helped or even interviewed.

A situation that may not be readily perceived as the loss of a twin but in fact is so is the destruction of frozen embryos after a period of preservation when parents do not renew their contract to keep them, as happened to 3,000 embryos in Great Britain on August 1, 1996. Though these embryos seem to have fallen into complete oblivion so far as the parents are concerned (or, in psychoanalytic terms, to have been decathexised), they were the object of intense interest at some previous time, and the present lack of concern is precisely due to the fact that the parents did manage to bear and rear at least one other child.

Relevance of the Subject for Infant Mental Health

These facts make the subject most relevant for infant mental health professionals since this loss will affect parents, remaining offspring, and the rest of the family in various deleterious ways, reappearing at different moments of their lives. The psychosocial aftermath of the perinatal loss of a twin may have deleterious effects on infant mental health in a wide range of areas and situations:

- Parents' self-esteem and their perception of themselves as providing life or bringing about death will mold their representations of themselves, the dead child, and the surviving twin(s) and thus have consequences on actual interaction both with the latter and their other children.

- Since early interaction with the surviving twin(s) coexists with the grieving process, both parents will be undergoing depression while developing their bonding to their newborn infant, an occurrence that has been widely demonstrated to have deep and lasting consequences for the child.

- At the time in which the loss occurs (gestation or postpartum period), parents are undergoing an especially vulnerable period, with primary preoccupation (Winnicott, 1958) exposing them to a kind of hypersensitization that makes them vulnerable to events related to parenthood.

- The paradoxical quality of the loss (the end before or encompassing the beginning, life and death coexisting) and the demand on parents' feelings posed by the presence of the surviving child, make the mourning process likely to become disturbed, thus further affecting parenting and the mental health of the survivor(s).

- Partly due to its unfamiliarity and partly because of the lack of cultural traditions on how to deal with this problem in a way that is protective for both adults and children, the perinatal loss of a twin tends to be silenced and become a family secret, which makes it pathogenic for the protagonists and the generations to come.

The Current Status of the Perinatal Loss of a Twin

In recent decades, the subject of perinatal loss has been extensively studied; it no longer seems ethically acceptable to deprive groups of patients of empirically proven interventions shown to be effective in alleviating parents' suffering and protecting normal grieving processes (Zeanah, 1989). Partly due to educational interventions addressed to the health team staff and medical, midwifery, and nursing students (Defey, 1995), clinical management of the situation has changed so that perinatal death can no longer be termed a "non-event" (Lewis, 1976) or an "overlooked catastrophe" (Lewis & Page, 1978).

In the same way, the issue of bearing, delivering, and rearing twins has received scientific and lay attention for many years, and professional recommendations have become standard practice for many parents since they are now widespread and accepted as applicable scientific knowledge. Unfortunately, the same cannot be stated in the case of the loss of a twin. Relatives, friends, and staff underestimate parents' suffering since they do have what they had originally wanted: a living child. They fail to recognize that this situation imposes upon parents an almost impossible psychological task: to attach and detach at the same time, to feel sorrow and joy simultaneously, to receive congratulations and condolences from the same people at the same moment of their lives. The lingering memory of their lost child becomes a "sin" to their expected joy of parenthood, thus increasing their risk of pathological grief and intensified perinatal depression. Table 12.1 is based on a comparison of relatively new evidence to previously known facts concerning live twins and perinatal loss of a single baby that may help in understanding the similarities and differences among the three situations.

Risks to Surviving Twins, Parents, and Others

Some figures show how risky losing one or more twins in the perinatal period may be for parents' mental health. Much of the evidence available refers to mothers; fathers' reactions remain an issue in need of research, though clinical evidence points at extremely pathological reactions such as addictive or suicidal behavior.

An estimated 50 to 80 percent of women undergo benign postpartum depression (Romito, 1990); 10 percent will undergo severe depression in the first year of the child's life (Manzano, 1993). This has a 2.5-fold increase in the case of the mother having undergone high risk pregnancy—as all twin pregnancies are (Burger, Horowitz, Forsyth, Leventhal, & Leaf, 1993)—and has also been found to be more frequent among mothers of twins (Thorpe, 1991). Any relevant loss in the previous year and psychosocial stress are strongly associated with postpartum depression (Romito, 1990), which contributes to the fivefold increase in severe mental health disturbances in the puerperium as compared to other periods in a woman's life.

Low birthweight due to both prematurity and intrauterine growth retardation are the main sources of neonatal mortality. Stress in the mother has repeatedly been shown to increase the incidence of both. Furthermore, twins have been found by several researchers to be a high risk population with regard to mental health. The characteristic processes of confounding agglutination and complementing cleavage described by Cherro and his research

TABLE 12.1

Comparison of Reactions to Live Twins, Death of a Twin, and Death of a Singleton

Live Twins	Death of a Twin	Death of a Singleton
Pride in hyperfertility	Failure of parenting project	Narcissistic breakdown
Underlying representation of twinning as splitting of single child	Dead baby becomes a "ghost in the nursery"	The uncanny: mother produces death, not life
Cultural idealization/ destruction of twins	Horror/disavowal/ idealization of dead twin	Stillbirth or neonatal death as a nonevent
Difficulty in coping with double attachment	Simultaneous attach- ment/detachment	Hypercathexis of lost child
Upbringing as a demand- ing task	Grieving as a difficult, untimely, or impossible process	Grief process instead of upbringing
Confounding agglutination/ complementing cleavage: radicalization or fluent al- teration of both	Loss of twinship as a global unit	Indiscrimination: dead child inside
Ambivalent feelings	Self-blaming	Self-blaming

team (Cherro, 1993) pose a special danger as concerns bonding and later parent-infant interaction, which is at permanent risk of becoming too close or too distant in the case of each twin. The children undergo the additional risk of lack of discrimination between them and difficult identity assumption.

Neonatal and pediatric staff are seldom fully aware of the emotionally demanding nature of rearing twins, let alone of rearing a surviving twin. Their lack of perception of how twinning affects each single twin's existence is reflected in the fact that, once one of the twins has died, it is not uncom-mon to find that they often forget entirely that the dead twin ever existed. Long-term clinical management deficiencies in this sense include not mentioning the twin origin of a child in his or her clinical records. Furthermore, replacement and vulnerable child syndromes are not considered in the living child's assessments by medical staff.

The pregnancies in which feticide (which is fortunately not a practice in Uruguay) is performed or at least proposed to parents are more often than not the product of assisted reproduction techniques. This may consist of simple ovulation induc-tion or complex procedures such as in vitro fertilization and embryo transfer. In these cases, parents are faced with the (in a way, forced) transition from sterility to hyperfertility and finally end up in mourning over perinatal loss of one or several of their much wanted offspring (Schreiner-Engel, Walther, Mindes, Lynch, & Berkowitz, 1995). It is worrisome that there is practically no literature on the mental health status of the surviving children, which is underestimated to the point that asking parents over the telephone about the well-being of their children is considered scientific evidence reliable enough to be published by mental health professionals and quoted as stimulating data concerning the use of these techniques.

When situations like perinatal loss become part of the work routine for health care staff, the sheer number of cases plus the lack of adequate preparation for dealing with their own and the parents' distress can lead perinatal technical and nontechnical staff to emotional exhaustion. This, in turn, leads to depersonalization of their relationship with patients and parents, also increasing the risk of discord among the health team and several illnesses (especially cardiovascular). Work absenteeism becomes a way to protect themselves from the painful stimuli arising from everyday contact with death and distress. These reactions constitute a job-related pathology and have been termed burnout syndrome (Maslach, 1982).

Review of the Literature

As early as 1964 (Cain & Cain) and 1972 (Poznanski) the first papers appeared on

replacement child syndrome, parents' attempt to cope with the loss of a child by massively displacing onto another the feelings, expectations, and attitudes originally meant for their dead child. This concept was complementary to that of vulnerable child syndrome, in which the death of one child (especially if it was unexpected) leads parents to overprotect the other(s) since they are obsessed with the idea of illness and risk. This leads to an overmedicalization of the child which, as a sort of tragic paradox, finally does increase the child's health risks through unnecessary medical intervention or side effects of the treatments or medicines prescribed.

Bourne (1968) and Lewis and Page (1978; see also Bourne & Lewis, 1983) were the first to describe health care staff's reaction to perinatal loss, which Lewis and Page termed an "overlooked catastrophe." Extensive research followed these pioneering papers, and in many countries techniques of clinical management of this crisis situation were adapted to parents' needs after national and international institutions (such as WHO) became interested in the subject (Defey et al., 1985). The loss of a twin, however, has received less attention. Few papers on the subject can be found in the literature, none of them present prospective, longitudinal, or randomized control studies.

The observational studies published emphasize the intensity and special quality of parents' grief, which is in no way lessened by the presence of the living twin, who often suffers profoundly from the loss and may need lifelong support (Brian, 1995; Wilson, Lawrence, Stevens, & Soule,

1982). In fact, the effect of co-twin presence has been studied in the context of both twin-twin interaction and the effect of the presence or absence of one twin on the mother's attachment processes (Lewis, 1988; Lewis & Bryan, 1976, 1979; Gottfried, Seay, & Leake, 1994; Stiermas, 1987; Swanson-Kauffman, 1988).

When a twin dies before or after birth, parents feel this almost as a physical blow, and the presence of the living twin may be underestimated when contrasted with the death of its sibling. Parents have not only lost a child: They have lost the whole of a pair, their projects and fantasies concerning their fulfillment as parents of twins. The surviving twin(s) inevitably becomes the reminder of the missing sibling(s), and each developmental achievement becomes a sad evidence of what the other twin(s) missed. Feelings toward the living child are filled with ambivalence, since parents may feel that it has robbed its sibling of the chance to live. This is especially intense when the living one has been severely affected in its physical health status. The living child may even become the object of parents' rage and frustration through "unfair competition" by its dead sibling, who may become an idealized angel who does not busy its parents with misbehavior or further worries (Segal & Bouchard, 1993; Stiermas, 1987).

Concerning the special case of perinatal loss of one or more twins by multifetal pregnancy reduction, studies are few and methodologically feeble, ranging from alarmed reflections on clinical observations to studies centered on mothers' reactions but underestimating the study of risks

for the surviving children. The process has been described as highly stressful but "well tolerated." "Sadness and guilt may persist, especially for an identifiable subgroup" (younger women and those who were not convinced about the inevitability of the procedure); "Normal maternal bonding and achievement of parenthood goals facilitate grief resolution" (Schreiner-Engel et al., 1995, p. 541).

Using semistructured interviews, Nantermoz et al. (1991) describe mothers' reaction as distressful, with a lingering concern over their lost fetuses and uneasy feelings continuing throughout the pregnancy. After birth, attention seems to be more strongly focused on the sterility treatment and the reduction than on the living children who survived it. The attending medical team also becomes central in parents' discourse, with an emphasis on their warmth and understanding of parents' distress over the procedure. No severe depression, however, was detected in mothers.

Prevention-Focused Interventions

Considering prevention as the main aim of infant mental health interventions (Fonagy, 1996), our efforts are being addressed to generating changes in clinical management of perinatal loss of a twin among obstetric and neonatal staff. This is in connection with the disciplines involved in the research on this subject: child psychiatry and health psychology (or medical psychology, as it is also termed).

Considering the present situation concerning technological developments in medicine, the practical means by which these objectives seem likely to become fulfilled cover different areas of medical practice: ultrasound scanning, ovulation induction, embryo transfer, neonatal intensive care, and pediatric follow-up. Since mental health professionals are seldom aware of the biological risks and rate of fetal loss in twin pregnancy, specific training also seems necessary for a preventive approach geared to the potential or actual consulting population as a whole.

OVULATION INDUCTION

This is often the first therapeutic measure undertaken by general practitioners or gynecologists when faced with a woman's anxiety when she assumes she is sterile—sometimes without proper proof of it. Patients are more often than not unaware of the consequences of their undergoing ovulation induction, not only concerning the higher probability of multiple pregnancy but also for their general health status. They are even less conscious that multiple pregnancy is always of a pathological nature, or of the likelihood and consequences of the eventual loss of all or some of their offspring should a high-order multiple gestation occur.

Our work in this area is directed at changing the over-the-counter overuse of ovulation induction by using the following resources:

- Helping consumers become more conscious of the risks involved (direct preventive work with the population and patients through health education).

- Contributing to the legal enforcement of patients' formal informed consent prior to ovulation induction prescription; information should include not only the risks for their bodily health but also for their mental health.

- Educating medical students and staff in regard to the psychosocial risks involved in multiple pregnancy and eventual perinatal loss related to it.

ULTRASOUND SCANNING

Since the news of twinning in the first trimester elicits an enthusiastic—almost manic—response from the parents' affective milieu, it seems advisable that the assessment be expressed in a dubious manner, allowing for a confirmation in the next ultrasound session. Probably parents would be best advised to keep the news of eventual twinning to themselves until confirmation.

Appropriate ways in which to convey this message to the technical staff involved seem to be the following:

- Providing ultrasound clinics or specialists with informative sessions about this issue, including patient management guidelines such as the ones mentioned; this can be part of their global curricular training or a specific focused training session to be performed at their workplace, during scientific meetings, and so on.

- Including these guidelines in the training of under- and postgraduate students of medicine, midwifery, radiology, or any other profession likely to perform ultrasound scanning as part of their work.

- Providing ultrasound clinics or departments with written guidelines.

EMBRYO TRANSFER

Transferring embryos up to a limit of three per procedure seems a wise measure for prevention of such aggressive and disturbing procedures as multifetal pregnancy reduction. However, the rate of embryo loss is dramatically high, whether because they do not become implanted (around 70 percent) or because they are lost after implantation. The rate of success ("baby in your arms") is at best 17 to 18 percent, which leaves a vast majority of patients devoid of any kind of support for facing the loss of "babies" of whom they are able to keep only sad memories and an album of photographs taken during their eight-cell stage.

Interventions likely to produce impact in this field seem to be:

- Providing patients undergoing high-complexity assisted reproduction with equally highly specialized psychosocial support not only in the case of reproductive success but also in the case of reproductive failure.
- Training assisted-reproduction specialists to become better aware of the needs of patients whose treatments have failed, as well as of their own need for support in these situations, which also bring about painful frustration for them.

NEONATAL INTENSIVE CARE

Since up to 46 percent of surviving fetuses are affected by the intrauterine death of their sibling (many of them with severe necrologic sequelae) and some of the surviving infants die in their first year, many of these children need special medical care during their first stages of extrauterine life. Staff may be helped in several ways, both in their role of caregivers to infants and their parents and in their own needs arising from job-generated stress.

One of the ways in which the staff attempt to cope with their anxiety and anguish over anticipated mourning in parents is by emphasizing the negative aspects of their patients' condition and offering a somber prognosis. This diminishes the actual chances of survival since the infant must deal with parents' depression or abandonment while trying to overcome its condition—whatever it may be—and adapt to extrauterine life. Should the infant die, the parents' working through their grief is more likely to be complicated by guilty feelings over their early giving up hope and, consequently, their child's care.

Frequent shifts of medical staff hinder personal follow-up of cases and militate against awareness of the twin nature of the infants being cared for. The inadequate though frequent practice of stimulating anticipated mourning in parents becomes especially dangerous in these cases, which concern both attachment to the surviving twin and the possibility of overcoming the loss of its sibling. Since the parents are already depressed and overwhelmed, the announcement of their living child(ren)'s likely death may be more than they can stand and they often are flung into desperation and hopelessness. This, in turn, actually reduces the likelihood of survival of the living infant(s).

Interventions devised to protect both the parents and the staff may include:

- Emphasizing the relevance of this type of loss to the outcome of the surviving child's health status both formally and informally in staff meetings and in curricular training of the neonatal medical and nursing staff.
- Including nonmedical staff (secretaries, registry attendants, cleaners, etc.) in the provision of sensitization to the problem since they are likely to be in contact with parents during the most stressful periods and—especially in state-run hospitals—are likely to have the same sociocultural status as the parents and may, therefore, achieve better communication with them.
- Protecting the staff from the deleterious effects of burnout syndrome by routinely talking over the task of dealing with the emotional turmoil parents are undergoing; it is also useful to provide medical and nursing staff with means of handling the situation.

PEDIATRIC FOLLOW-UP

Since the surviving twin(s) are likely to be perceived by the parents as vulnerable, the pediatrician(s) in charge of their developmental control and eventual medical interventions should be aware of the potential distortion in parents' description of the child's condition. Medicalization of the surviving twin is often the way in which parents seek comfort for the ever-present uneasiness arising from what they feel is the perma-

nently impending danger of losing the child whose life has been spared. Given both the increased biomedical and attachment risks involved in his or her being a surviving twin, the adequate balance in assessment and in intervention is a most delicate item.

Interventions that may diminish the aforementioned risks include:

- Regular training of pediatricians concerning the relevance and risks of perinatal loss of twin pregnancy for the surviving child(ren) as well as practical training in clinical management of parents' anxiety. Such practical training can both enable pediatricians to show awareness of twinship and the loss and protect staff from parents' emotional breakdown that they may not be able to handle.
- Alerting pediatric staff concerning replacement and vulnerable child syndromes likely to appear in the surviving child as well as suggesting measures to prevent them, such as emphasizing the individual identity of the surviving twin in their comments to parents and being careful not to medicalize the child.
- Including in both lay population health education and in pediatric staff training fundamental preventive measures such as letting the surviving child know about his or her sibling's existence and loss.
- Granting psychosocial follow-up for the surviving child and his or her parents as a regular complement to pediatric consultation.
- Providing early therapeutic parent-infant intervention whenever necessary.
- Including in the surviving child's clinical records a written report emphasizing his

· or her twin origin and the specific risks involved in each case.

The Role of Mental Health Professionals

Evidence does not allow for recommendations concerning which way of handling the mourning process seems best for parents, surviving twin(s), and their siblings. Research on this is obviously needed, and it is a task to be carried out in countries with a higher incidence of twin loss than can be expected in Uruguay, which has only three million inhabitants and a small proportion of people in their fertile years. As the present situation stands, the most advisable goal seems to be helping fathers and mothers, both as individuals and as a couple, find their best personal way of coping with the loss and the parallel task of rearing their live child(ren). This may be burdensome in the cases with an affected surviving twin, in which the double task of undergoing mourning and adapting to their child's needs may be simply too hard an emotional effort to be carried out. We believe mental health staff should be careful to respect parents' timing, not "inoculating" them with the burden of grief when they are still not ready for it. In these parents, denial may be an essential survival strategy and, therefore, an effective coping mechanism.

Health education seems to be an area in need of intensive intervention from mental health professionals. The lay population needs to be alerted to the relevance and consequences of this kind of loss and thus become a more effective source of psychosocial support when this type of loss takes place among their families or friends. On the other hand, both students and staff in disciplines such as midwifery, nursing, obstetrics, neonatology, pediatrics, psychology, and social work need to be informed about the consequences and risks involved as well as approaches with the potential to fulfill parents' needs and prevent further damage to the attachment process and the surviving child's health.

However, dealing with the subject of the perinatal loss of a twin and its aftermath as concerns both mental and physical health of those involved is no easy task. The account of the stages that our work has undergone may be of help to others. In the first stage, this subject seemed a distant reality, affecting an unlucky few whose drama seemed very distant and somewhat obscure. Starting to realize that this loss might affect many people because of the number of twin pregnancies undergoing the vanishing twin phenomenon in the first trimester led to the awareness that this situation was not so distant from our everyday life. Some members of the group remembered patients or hospital cases who had undergone this situation, and some were even able to recall forgotten or silenced stories concerning their own families. The countertransferential feeling induced by this subject could be defined as awe: a mixture of horror and fascination at becoming witnesses to the drama of life and death coexisting within a woman's body, where somebody has lived and died in silence and all the human tragedies of filicide, fratricide, and parricide have been displayed, often unknowingly even by those directly involved.

Violence among Kindergarten, Elementary, and High School Students in a Private School

Miguel Cherro Aguerre (Coordinator), Dora Musetti, Beatriz Toledo, Luciana Muiño, Beatriz Estable, Ema Wolff, Myriam Tato

Introduction

In this communication we present some results of a research study on violence conducted jointly by our clinic and a private school. In the project we worked with three age levels: preschool, elementary, and high school. We are interested in presenting some of the results in a book about infant mental health because the infant is raised and grows up in a family, with parents and siblings of different ages, in institutions, and in a social environment that offer determined models among which the violent model worries us particularly.

The objective of presenting these results is to enable us to act directly and indirectly in the prevention of violence at early ages. Directly, because the work with preschoolers, for example, showed not only changes in the conceptualization of violence, but also some changes in behavior. Indirectly,

because the work with the parents of this age level also showed behavioral changes in the family. The results, discriminated by gender and age, permit us to detect risk groups and orient preventive actions at various levels: individual, group, family, institution, and community. At each age level, the professional team will always have to take gender differences into account.

Summarized Data of the Research

The study was conducted during 1995. The intention, shared by the school authorities and the clinic, was to verify whether a determined type of intervention might bring about changes in the case of violence. The objective of the research was the modification of the conceptualization of "being violent" in students between 5 and 18 years of age through reflection workshops, in an action integrated by students, educators, and the mental health team. Students' parents also participated in some instances. The population was formed by 27 preschoolers of 5 years of age, 115 primary schoolers between 6 and 11 years, and 279 secondary school students between 12 and 18. We used a longitudinal design of pre- and posttest to evaluate the intervention.

In the first application we obtained descriptive data of the different variables studied, and we analyzed the influence of gender on them. The evaluation instrument was a multiple choice questionnaire applied in groups and self-administered, which was adapted to the different age levels. Through this instrument we studied general data of the population, the most frequent type of violent behavior and its causes, places of par-

The results of this research, which was supervised by Prof. Joy Osofsky, were presented for the first time at the International Meeting of Canela, Brazil (May 1997). We acknowledge the active participation in this research of authorities, teachers, students, and students' parents of the Colegio Latinoamericano of Montevideo. We acknowledge the collaboration in this work of Dra. S. Curotti, Ps. N. De Leon, Dra. M. Pazos, Dra. C. Pivel, and A. Rattin.

ticipation in violent acts, violence in and out of the home, the feelings that it generated, its justification, the opinion about social violence, and the motivation to change. The results were presented in relative frequencies and the influence of the variable *gender* was measured by chi square test as an association measurement. The levels of significance were between .01 and .05. We have chosen some of the results of the pretest that we consider interesting, since they illustrate the points to take into account when planning prevention. All the results that we will present have statistical significance.

GENERAL DATA OF THE FAMILY, THE COMMUNITY, THE SCHOOL AND THE CHILD

Violence in high school students arises without a stimulus that provokes it (63 percent of the youngsters surveyed between 12 and 18 years of age admitted it). In preschool years, 60 percent of the boys used verbal violence and 65 percent physical violence to settle their interpersonal problems. In adolescence, 43 percent chose verbal violence and 26 percent physical. Eleven percent of the children and youngsters used violence "without motive," and 43 percent of the high school boys used violence for revenge, as did 11 percent of the grade schoolers. Sixty percent of the high school boys and 41 percent of the girls this age felt "pressured by the peer group" to be violent. Sixty percent of the 5-year-old children and 45 percent of the adolescents mentioned their home as a violent place. They attributed that violence mainly to their parents. The students who were abused by their par-

ents are the ones who respond with violence less (only 15 percent of the preschoolers and elementary school students, and 35 percent of the high school students respond with violence). Violence among siblings is admitted by ¾ of all the children and adolescents. Almost all the adolescent boys are violent on the street or in dancing places. Forty percent of the preschoolers are also violent outside their home, but only 15 percent of the elementary school students admit it. Thirty-four percent of the high school students admit to being violent with their friends, as do 60 percent of the preschoolers and 26 percent of the elementary school students. For high school students, the school ranks second as a place of participation in violent acts, following the dancing places. Seventeen percent of the elementary school students also perceive the school as a violent place. In 27 percent of the elementary and 26 percent of the high school students, the response to parents' violence is "submission with anger." Seventy-one percent of the adolescent boys do not feel remorseful when they respond to a provocation with violence, but 26 percent do not feel remorseful when they act with violence without provocation. Three fourths of the adolescents and preschoolers accept or respect the violent person. On the other hand, ¾ of the elementary school students reject violent students. Sixty-eight percent of the adolescents consider society today more violent than in the past, 62 percent think that violence is impossible to eradicate, and 22 percent of the boys even consider it necessary (great pessimism in adolescents).

DIFFERENCES ACCORDING TO GENDER

Girls use less physical and verbal violence than boys at all age levels (45 percent vs. 85 percent). When girls are violent, only 10 percent of them at all age levels admit choosing physical violence. A higher percentage of boys (40%), on the other hand, admit choosing it. High school girls are more violent than boys at home (59 percent vs. 31 percent), and less violent outside the home (92 percent vs. 57 percent). In addition, they feel less forced by the peer group to be violent (60 percent vs. 41 percent). Preschool girls fight less with friends than boys (29 percent vs. 60 percent). They are also less violent than boys when they face their parents' violence (25 percent vs. 0 percent). More girls than boys regret being violent, whether provoked or not (29 percent vs. 43 percent if they are provoked, and 74 percent vs. 93 percent if they are not provoked). Fewer girls justify violence in general, in all age groups (39 percent vs. 65 percent). Fewer high school girls than boys think that violence in the world is necessary (22 percent vs. 8 percent). More girls than boys at all age levels believe in the existence of nonviolent alternatives to violence (66 percent vs. 50 percent). Girls are more motivated to change than boys in all age groups (55 percent vs. 32 percent).

DIFFERENCES ACCORDING TO AGE

Preschool boys appear more violent than older boys (60 percent preschool, 30 percent elementary school, 34 percent secondary school boys). Preschool girls, on the other hand, appear less violent than older girls (15 percent preschool, 29 percent grade school, 24 percent high school girls). Primary school students use violence for revenge less than high school students (12 percent vs. 50 percent). High school students feel more forced by the group to be violent than younger students (51 percent vs. 4 percent). Preschoolers are more violent at home than older students (60 percent vs. 40 percent). More preschool and elementary school students than high school students feel that their parents are violent (75 percent vs. 58 percent). Preschool and elementary school students are less violent with their parents than high school students (15 percent vs. 26 percent). High school students are more violent outside their home than preschool and elementary school students (75 percent vs. 25 percent). Preschoolers are more violent with their friends than older students (44 percent vs. 30 percent).

Preschool boys fight more with girls than among themselves. In older ages, fighting among boys increases, while fighting with girls decreases. However, the percentage of boys who fight with girls increases again in high school. Preschool girls are not likely to fight among themselves, but their violent behavior increases gradually with age. Likewise, preschool girls are not as likely as older girls to start fights with boys.

Fewer preschoolers than high school students try to persuade their parents when they become violent (47 percent vs. 66 percent). On the contrary, they submit more than high school students (70 percent vs. 25 percent). More high school students than younger students respond with violence to their parents (40 percent vs. 15 percent).

Fewer preschoolers than high school students justify violence (22 percent vs. 80 percent). More younger students than high school students believe in the effectiveness of nonviolent alternatives to violence (88 percent vs. 28 percent). They are also more motivated to change (53 percent vs. 25 percent). For this reason, they are more receptive to intervention.

Characteristics of the Intervention

There are reasons to think that intervention conducted at the preschool level might achieve relevant conceptual changes in relation to violence. These changes are essential if we hope to obtain modifications in conduct later. The objectives of the intervention were to promote the alternative concepts of solidarity, justice, empathy, and ethics. At the same time, we tried to model adequate ways to solve conflicting interpersonal situations. These objectives were met through symbolic play and stories that propose moral dilemmas. If we accept that violent behavior may be learned through imitation of models, and that the home is the main source of models for children, the need to work with parents is evident. This work was carried out through workshops, in which there were opportunities for reflection, comprehension, self-evaluation, and compromise to change. Analyzing the differences of results between the evaluation before the intervention and the one after it,

	Before	After
Boys	92%	38%
Girls	71%	44%

FIGURE 12.1
Sibling rivalry: Rate of children that quarrel with their siblings.

we can find that there was a favorable change in the children. These changes led us to propose prevention policies toward violence. As we mentioned at the beginning of the chapter, these preventive policies should be framed in the care of the caregiver mode, which means that we will take care not only of the child, but also of natural or institutional caregivers. We will now mention the most relevant details.

Results of the Intervention in Preschoolers

The percentage of boys that fight with siblings decreased from 92 percent to 38 percent, and girls from 71 percent to 44 percent. This was verified as a behavioral change during the intervention (Figure 12.1). Physical aggression in boys fell from 65 percent to 38 percent. Verbal aggression in boys dropped from 60 percent to 29 percent and in girls from 31 percent to 11 percent (Figure 12.2). The percentage of boys

	Before		After	
	Boys	Girls	Boys	Girls
Physical Aggression	65%	0%	38%	22%
Verbal Aggression	60%	29%	31%	11%

FIGURE 12.2
Use of violence.

	Before		After	
	Boys	Girls	Boys	Girls
No Lending Children	35%	28%	0%	11%
Poorly Solidaristic Children	25%	0%	12%	0%

FIGURE 12.3
Identification with the aggressor.

who identify with the aggressor decreased. Facing the "child that does not lend," boys using violence dropped from 35 percent to 0 percent and girls from 28 percent to 11 percent. Confronting the "child who is not solidaristic," boys using violence dropped from 25 percent to 0 percent, and girls from 12 percent to 0 percent (Figure 12.3). The percentage of children who formed groups to fight descended from 35 percent to 0 percent in boys and from 29 percent to 11 percent in girls (Figure 12.4). Fewer boys agreed with violence in traffic (45 percent to 60 percent). Girls never agreed with it (Figure 12.5). Perception of the home as a violent place decreased in boys from 64 percent to 38 percent, and in girls from 57 percent to 42 percent. Violence among siblings also decreased, from 82 percent to 41 percent. The percentage of boys that fight with friends fell from 60 percent to 43 percent; of girls, from 29 percent to 0 percent.

Conclusion

In general, we can say that the main objective of the study, which was to measure the changes that a workshop activity might bring about in the students of a private school, was met. Analysis of those changes from the point of view of the developmental continuity of the three age levels, reveals a determined intrinsic logic. Those results permit the devising of preventive policies that take into account the development of the different ages, and offer them institutional models adapted to the specific needs in respect to the issue of violence, offering opportunities for discussion and reflection. In order to obtain an effective preventive policy in respect to violence, the institutional model should involve not only the school as an institution, but also the family and society as institutions. The changes observed in our population in general refer to the conceptualization or rep-

	Before	After
Boys	35%	0%
Girls	29%	11%

FIGURE 12.4
Children who formed groups to fight.

	Before	After
Boys	45%	6%
Girls	0%	0%

FIGURE 12.5
Agreement with violence in traffic.

resentation that the students have of violence. In only a few cases can we suppose that, besides the change in conceptualization, there was a change in attitude or behavior. Many parents confirmed this is in the area "fights with siblings," affirming that those fights decreased in frequency and intensity after the workshops. Many teachers also reported that there was a decrease in the area "students' fights" while the workshops were taking place. The same situation was not verified a year after the workshops finished. Those two results are highly positive, and they even have implications that may lead to program strategies with a scientific basis oriented toward decreasing violent styles of communication.

According to the results that we obtained, even though preschoolers appear more violent, we are conscious that in older ages violence continues and with more dangerous consequences. It is important to consider gender differences, since our data, which show that women are less violent than men, agree with other international research studies. The risk group toward which we should direct special attention is boys, who seem to be granted, culturally, more permission to use violence from birth. To make things worse, boys are more pessimistic in respect to alternative solutions and present less motivation to change. We consider that the strategies for working with this group will have to include the search for more efficient ways to modify those culturally incorporated schemata. However, we should not underestimate the work with girls, since they become more violent with age, even though they do not lose their hope and will to change.

Finally, and as a consequence of what we previously explained, we emphasize the importance of starting prevention as early as possible in all the areas and levels recommended internationally: the child, the family, the institution, and the society.

Early Bonding in Adolescent Mothers

Miguel Cherro Aguerre (Coordinator), Liliana Burgueffo, Laura Cuore, Nilda Rebuffo, Vivian Rimano.

Introduction

This article presents part of our research study on precocious pregnancy and early bonds in adolescent mothers. First, we will describe the relevance of adolescent pregnancy in our country; second, the methodology we applied; and finally, the results and conclusions. We would like to highlight the incidence of adolescent pregnancy in our country. In 1994, 24.5 percent of births at the Pereira Rossell Hospital were to adolescents between 12 and 19 years of age (Da Luz et al., 1996). If we consider the total number of births in urban areas of our country, we find that 6 percent of

This research was collected with the constant supervision and support of Profs. Joy D. Osofsky and Robert N. Emde. We acknowledge the collaboration in this work of Dra. Maria del Lujan Alvarez, Ps. Pia Correas, Dra. Currito Gonzalez, Dra. Alice Goyen, Dra. Amelia Miller, and Ps. Lucia Pierri.

them were to adolescents under 17 years of age. This figure increases in the poorest homes (Laurnaga, 1995). For this reason, poverty might be an element related to adolescent motherhood. Ninety-five percent of the adolescents take care of the rearing of their children (Group for the Advancement of Psychiatry, 1986).

Concerning the seriousness of the problem, adolescent pregnancy has been considered risky from the biopsychosocial point of view. From the biological point of view, studies in our society show that pregnancy in adolescents younger than 15 years of age is a risk factor (Pons, 1991). In respect to baby risk, children's mortality is higher in children whose mothers are under 20 years of age than in children of women of the following decade. Risks increase for both the mother and the baby due to the lack of obstetric control (Pons, 1991). This constitutes a source of preoccupation for neonatologists and pediatricians, and motivated a research study in our service in the framework of liaison psychiatry. From the psychological point of view, many authors consider adolescent mothers less capable than adult ones of providing their children with a positive psychoemotional environment since the specific conflicts of development might interfere with their parental capacities. It has been mentioned that their self-esteem is lower than that of adult mothers and that they are more prone to depression. They also have less autonomy than nonpregnant adolescents (Osofsky, Hann, & Peebles, 1993). The consequence in their children is a higher probability of developing disorders in conduct, depression, and distur-

bances in attachment (Osofsky, Hann, & Peebles, 1993). The mother-child relationship is characterized by poor verbal exchanges and a predominance of physical contact, which would provide the child with a poor cognitive and linguistic environment. This would be made evident during school years, possibly manifesting itself in learning problems (Elster, 1979; Levine & Garcia Coll, 1985; Osofsky, Hann, & Peebles, 1993).

From the social point of view, adolescent maternity might be a disadvantage as it becomes an obstacle to personal and professional development, thus reducing the opportunities of social insertion (Laurnaga, 1995). In middle and high socioeconomic levels, the family sends cultural messages that tend to avoid a precocious maternity that might endanger the fulfillment of a personal project. The incidence of births in adolescents at these levels is very low, due to the fact that most of the adolescents have a personal project that transcends maternity. The problem in these adolescents would be a higher incidence in abortion rate. When pregnancy in fact occurs, it is more determined by the life situation of the adolescent than by social guidelines, with which it is at variance.

WHY DO ADOLESCENTS GET PREGNANT?
One of the causes that contributes to the occurrence of adolescent pregnancy is precocity in sexual relations (Colombino, 1991; Gomensoro, 1991). It is hard for an early adolescent who is sexually active to understand the consequences of her sexual activity. Likewise it is difficult for her to use contraceptives effectively when she has not

reached the formal operational stage of her cognitive development (Group for the Advancement of Psychiatry, 1986). Moreover, adults, including the medical team, resist viewing sexual precocity as valid, so they do not put adequate contraceptive resources at the disposal of early adolescents (Pons, 1991). Many adolescents feel that they did not have resources to avoid pregnancy and blame their parents for not having taken good care of them. This reproach is directed toward the contradiction of an education characterized by an excess of sexual stimulation and liberty, and the adults' denial of the precocity of their daughters.

In marginal levels sexuality is highly linked to gestation, and fertility is a synonym of femininity. In these levels, young girls construct their identity through the model transmitted by their mothers. This model is that of the woman who reaches adulthood precociously through maternity, a socially respected value that turns the adolescent into an autonomous and socially respected being. Through pregnancy, and based on familiar and social tradition, these adolescents intend to solve their identity dilemma (Laurnaga, 1995). Nonetheless, their expectations of autonomy are not fulfilled, so they paradoxically end up being more dependent and poor than before (Osofsky, Hann, & Peebles, 1993). These adolescents, from a level that has socioeconomic and cultural deficits, perceive little benefit in both putting off gratification and planning for a future they view with a lack of perspective since work is low-paying and studies do not provide immediate economic benefits. The absence of specific projects for youth makes motherhood the only vehicle to fulfill a life

project (Group for the Advancement of Psychiatry, 1986). Sometimes pregnancy fills up a real emptiness, restoring the loss (by death or abandonment) of a significant figure, or fills up the emptiness of a deficient infancy. Adolescents who had a history of affective abandonment frequently need to act out the anguish they suffered, attributing a restorative function to the child. Through identification with the child, the adolescent mother hopes to be able to start a new life that corrects past frustrations. Paradoxically, this way conducts them to new frustrations.

Objectives of This Study

In this framework, we propose the following hypothesis: that adolescent mothers have more difficulties in interacting with their children than adult mothers. For this reason, they may constitute a risk dyad. The general objective of this study is thus to contribute as much as possible to the knowledge of the psychological and social factors related to adolescent pregnancy, maternity, and early mother-child bond in the most needy levels of our country. The specific objectives of the study are:

1. To study the causes of adolescent pregnancy.

2. To investigate the effect of the mother's age and prenatal control of pregnancy on the characteristics of the mother-child bond during the first year of life, evaluating the interactions of adolescent mothers and comparing them to those of adult mothers.

3. To try to evaluate other factors that have

an effect on the mother-baby bond, such as the socioeconomic level, social support, the mother's educational level, and the type of bond that the mother has with her partner and parents.

4. To elaborate, based on the interview, a predictive hypothesis about the potential capacity of the mother to raise her child and then compare it with the results obtained in the following stages, thus detecting an eventual risk.

To evaluate the mother-child interaction we used the concept of Emotional Availability (EA), which consists of the following elements:

- Sensitivity, that is, the mother's ability to perceive and interpret the child's signals and respond empathetically to the child's needs. This requires the ability to see from the child's perspective.
- Accessibility, which refers to the extent to which the mother is psychologically accessible to her baby and responds to the child's signals even though there may be other demands.

The mother's sensitivity and accessibility, conjointly, form the concept of Emotional Availability proposed by R. Emde. A good emotional availability implies that the mother is emotionally ready for her baby, responding to his or her demands over her own. This way it is possible to develop a safe and reliable attachment.

POPULATION

We studied 18 adolescent mothers between 14 and 16 years of age (mean age 15.28) who consulted the gynecological clinics of the Pereira Rossell Hospital between the months of May and December 1994. Half of them were controlled (over 5 obstetrics controls) and the other half were not. In order to polarize the sample, the age limit of the adolescent was fixed at 16 years 11 months, presupposing that the highest biopsychosocial risk is in this age group. As a control group, we studied 13 mothers over 20 years of age (average age 23.31), treated in the same clinics, in order to control the socioeconomic environment: 8 of them were controlled and 5 were not. All the mothers of the sample weds. All the babies were newborns (NB) at term, through normal births, with a weight over 2.500 g and without neonatal pathologies.

METHODOLOGY

We applied a structured interview during the last trimester of pregnancy to the controlled mothers, and immediately after childbirth to the noncontrolled. The protocol of the prenatal interview contains 11 thematic areas:

1. Personal information
2. Couple bond
3. Attitude toward pregnancy—expectations in respect to the child's future
4. Attitude toward child rearing
5. Attitude toward childbirth
6. Attitude toward breast-feeding
7. Social support and the father's role
8. Contraception
9. Wish to be pregnant—wish to have a baby
10. Project of life
11. Evaluation of the interview

From the interview, we elaborated predictive hypotheses about the possible EA of the mother in respect to the baby. Then we compared those results with the scores of EA obtained in the evaluation of the following stage. Through this, we tried to evaluate the effectiveness of the instrument (prenatal interview) to detect early, in the first contact with the pregnant adolescent, a possible risk for the future mother-child interaction. The purpose would be to implement therapeutic prophylactic measures toward the bond in those adolescents considered at risk.

EVALUATION OF THE
MOTHER-BABY DYAD

We studied the mother-baby bond through video recording and observation of the interaction, which included, if possible, the exploration of a feeding situation. This exploration was carried out between 24 and 48 hr after childbirth. The video was evaluated according to the Scale of Emotional Availability developed by Osofsky et al. (1987). This scale was designed for 6-month-old babies, but the group adapted it to NBs with Osofsky's approval. The Scale of Emotional Availability divides the dyad's interaction into five areas:

1. Motor area, which evaluates the mother's type of holding, the amount and quality of physical contact (caressing, touching, rocking), and the aptitude in functional care (feeding and other caring for the baby).
2. Verbal area, which evaluates the frequency and quality of verbalizations.

3. Look, which evaluates the type of look of the mother at the baby.
4. Encounter, which refers to the mother's perception of the baby's signals and her acting upon them. It includes who determines the feeding rhythm and how, the mother's response to the baby's signals, and the effectiveness of the mother's response to the baby's crying.
5. Expressions of affect of the mother to the baby, which include expressions of positive affect (smiling, caressing, etc.) and expressions of negative affect (anger, mistrust, frustration, impatience, or disgust).

Applying this scale, we assign the mother a score from 1 to 5. Scores 1 and 2 correspond to a low emotional availability, score 3 is satisfactory, and scores 4 and 5 imply a good and very good emotional availability. When possible, we carried out successive evaluations: the first one month after the baby was born; the second after 6 months; and the third 1 year after the baby's birth.

RESULTS OF STATISTICAL ANALYSIS

This analysis was made by Prof. Nelly Murillo. In order to compare the groups and determine the statistical significance of the differences, we used t test and chi square test. The significance level was 95 percent.

Education

In relation to schooling, there is a tendency in adolescents to complete their education less, even though the difference between adolescents and adults is not significant (Table 12.2).

TABLE 12.2

Completion of School by Adolescents and Adults

	Did Not Complete Primary		Completed Primary		Did Not Complete Secondary	
	N	%	N	%	N	%
Adolescents	5	29	8	47	4	23
Adults	3	23	5	38	5	38
	NS		NS		NS	

Interruption of Education Due to Pregnancy

X = 7.1

Of 17 adolescents of our study, only 18 percent (3) abandoned their education due to their pregnancy, whereas the other 83 percent (14) left school before getting pregnant. This difference is statistically significant. We would like to emphasize that the adolescents of this socioeconomic level discontinue their education before pregnancy and not due to it.

Employment

Eighty-three percent of the adolescents (10 out of 12) do not have a job, while only 33 percent of the adults are in that situation.

Socialization

The majority of the adolescents mention a lack of friendly relations.

Family

The adolescents show a strong tendency to continue living with their families, with or without their partners: 61 percent (11 out of 18), to 31 percent of the adults. Thirty-nine percent of the adolescents live only with

their families, without a partner, whereas only 15 percent of the adults are in this situation. Twenty-two percent (4 out of 18) of the adolescents live only with their partners, but the percentage of adults in that situation climbs to 54 percent (7 out of 13).

Couple Bond

Eighty-five percent of the adult mothers have a partner, and in all the cases the relationship has lasted more than a year. Sixty-one percent of the adolescents have a partner and only half of these have a relationship of over a year. Although this difference is not statistically significant, we observe in adolescents a stronger tendency to lack a partner and have less stable relations. Another verification is that the adolescents that have a partner control their pregnancy more than those who do not have one. The baby's father was over 19 years of age for 70 percent of the adolescent mothers.

Marital Status

Marriage is not frequent in this socioeconomic level. Only 11 percent of the adolescent and 15 percent of the adult mothers are married.

*Factors That Contribute to
Adolescent Pregnancy*

Exploring the conscious wish to get pregnant, 50 percent of the controlled adolescents wanted the pregnancy, to 12 percent of the non-controlled. The percentages are similar in adult mothers. In this case the differences (not statistically significant) are not related to age but to the presence of prenatal control. The absence of control of the pregnancy is related to an unwanted gestation. We studied the antecedents of abandonment due to separation or death of significant figures, on the hypothesis that early pregnancy might be linked to the unconscious desire to restitute a loss. We found a higher frequency of deaths in the history of pregnant adolescents (33 percent) compared to adults (12 percent). In respect to the accomplishment of an adult role in childhood, 53 percent of the adolescent mothers had performed adult roles at home, and in the rearing of younger siblings. In the adults, this antecedent was present in only 22 percent of the cases.

Attitude of Others Toward the Pregnancy

We observed that there was rejection of the pregnancy from the baby's father only in adolescents. The highest percentage was among those who did not control their pregnancy (33 percent). Initial rejection by grandparents occurred only for adolescents.

ANALYSIS OF EMOTIONAL AVAILABILITY

As we mentioned earlier, our research studied the mother-baby interaction using the Emotional Availability Scale. The average results of EA were 2.94 in adolescent mothers, and 3.34 in adult mothers. This difference is not statistically significant, so, globally, both adults and adolescents behaved similarly in EA. Discriminating the sample by age and prenatal control, the results were the following: The group of controlled adolescents had a satisfactory level of EA (3.12); however, it was below the score of the adults, either controlled (3.39) or not (3.27). The group of noncontrolled adolescents presented values below the satisfactory level (2.76). Although this difference is not statistically significant, it may indicate the noncontrolled adolescents as a group with a higher risk. From a qualitative point of view, fewer adolescent mothers than adult mothers achieved high scores. They were the only ones with scores 1 and 2, and very few of them scored 4. The low scores in adolescent mothers were due to the noncontrolled group, since most of the controlled adolescents behaved in a way similar to the adults; most of their scores were satisfactory. That did not happen with the noncontrolled adolescents, whose scores were lower, although not to a statistically significant degree. This characteristic was present in individual EA areas as well as overall EA.

STUDY OF THE AREAS OF
EMOTIONAL AVAILABILITY

It is important to mention that due to the small size of the sample the statistical results only show tendencies. The greatest score differences were found in the two adolescent groups (controlled and noncontrolled).

1. In the motor area, which explores motherly support, the values in the adolescent and adult dyads did not have statistically significant differences.

2. In nonfunctional manipulation, an area that evaluates behaviors such as touching, caressing, and rocking, both groups had scores below 3 (2.52 for adolescents and 2.84 for adults), which is considered satisfactory for a good psychoemotional development for the baby.

3. The study of the verbal area did not show statistically significant differences between the adolescent and adult dyads in respect to number of verbalizations. Surprisingly, not only adolescent mothers, but also adult mothers spoke very little. The interaction was highly silent in all dyads. Of the 18 adolescents, 78 percent (14) did not utter anything during the 15 min they were recorded. Adult mothers behaved similarly, and all scores for this item presented values much below what is considered satisfactory. The average scores were 1.47 for adolescents and 1.61 for adults.

4. The study of the look showed satisfactory values in both groups, without statistically significant differences between them.

5. Considering the mother's response to the baby's signals, we found statistically significant differences between the two groups of mothers. Adolescent mothers responded less to their baby's signals, with a score of 2.93, whereas the value for adult mothers was 3.61.

6. When we studied the expression of positive affect, such as smiling, caressing, and hugging, we did not find statistically significant differences between adolescent and adult mothers. The average in adolescents did not reach a satisfactory score, since it was 2.88. Adult mothers, on the other hand, reached an average score of 3. Discriminating the sample by age and control, in the group of adults we did not find differences in respect to whether they were controlled or not. However, in adolescents, those who were controlled had a score of 3.5, similar to that of adults, but those who were not had a very low average, 2.3. This difference, which is statistically significant, indicates that there is a group of adolescents with higher risk, which is related to the absence of prenatal control. We consider that this may be related to the higher frequency of unwanted pregnancies in this subgroup. This finding agrees with what was published by other authors, who found little positive affect in adolescent mothers in general.

7. The expression of negative affect was similar in both groups, with satisfactory scores.

In sum, studying the dyad of primiparous adolescent and adult mothers and their newly born children, we found a silent and calm interaction, with little interchange in general, and an almost null verbal interchange. The adolescent group presented more difficulty than the adult one in recognizing and responding adequately to the baby's signals. Among the adolescents, the noncontrolled group had very low scores in the expression of positive affect.

CORRELATION OF DATA

When we correlate the values of EA with the educational level, we find that the adolescents who did not complete primary school have the lowest EA score: 2.5. From a statistical point of view, this constitutes a tendency that needs to be confirmed with a larger sample.

The best result of EA is found in the adolescents who live with their partners and families; the worst, in adolescents who live only with their partners. Although the results are not statistically significant, the adults' behavior is opposite: The ones who achieve the best EA results are those who live only with their partners, and the ones who achieve the worst are the ones who live with their partners and families.

One might wonder whether our findings, based on mother-baby interactions during the first days of their babies' lives, reflect a constant; perhaps these interactions change with time. It may be possible that as the baby grows up interaction becomes more fluent and active, with more evident encounters and separations of the dyad. In order to study this, we implemented a follow-up one month later. From the 30 mothers only 12 were available: 7 adolescents and 5 adults. We observed a slight fall of the EA score in adolescents, while adults' average score was higher. The change in EA from that immediately after childbirth was not statistically significant in adolescents in general, even though it was significant in the noncontrolled adult group.

Examining the areas separately, we found an increase in verbalizations in both groups. The 7 adolescents, whose values were 1 at postchildbirth, had an average score of 2.4. The increase was even more evident in the adults, whose values changed from an average of 1.2 to 3. So, while the adults achieved a satisfactory level when the baby was 1 month old, the adolescents improved, but did not reach a satisfactory level. The follow-up a year later was only attended by 4 dyads, 3 adolescents and 1 adult. We carried out the Reaction toward the Stranger, but we cannot draw conclusions due to the size of the sample. We will only mention that the children of the 3 adolescents showed an insecure attachment, whereas the daughter of the adult mother showed a secure one.

Conclusion

SCHOOLING

The low educational level in both the adolescents and adults of our sample is common in the socioeconomic level where the study was conducted. This finding coincides with other research studies carried out in our society (Da Luz et al., 1996). Several authors (Levine & Garcia Coll, 1985) have mentioned the relation between low educational level and difficulty of motherhood in adolescents. In our study, we found lower average global scores of EA in adolescents with less instruction [did not complete primary school ([$M = 2.59$, SD 9.72])], compared to those who had more instruction [completed primary school and did not complete secondary school ([$M = 3.1$, $SD = 4.18$])]. However, this difference is not statistically significant.

INTERRUPTION OF SCHOOL DUE
TO PREGNANCY

In our study, we found that the majority (14 out of 17) of the adolescents had left their studies before pregnancy, not due to it. Authors of the First World, in contrast, have found that adolescent pregnancy causes leaving school. In addition, there is an absence of a project of life that includes the intention of continuing a formal education, with a consequent lack of qualification that makes it difficult for them to enter the job market. Eighty percent of the adolescent mothers of our research were not in school or worked. Moreover, there was a lack of friends in almost all the cases. In these conditions, their social contact suffers, and it is reduced almost exclusively to intrafamiliar bonds, leaving exposure to mass media as their only form of socialization. The consequence is an impoverishment in both the possibility of achieving personal development and acquiring resources to apply in the rearing of their children. Due to the predominant social guidelines the mother's family naturally assumes the rearing of the baby. This way, they help the adolescent solve the paradox of being biologically ready for procreation but emotionally immature to be mothers. According to Osofsky, the larger the number of persons available to support the mother, the higher is her self-esteem and the lower the possibility of depression, all of which would lead to a better emotional availability.

The low incidence of legal marriages found in the sample may reflect the frequent change of partners characteristic of this population, a fact that we verified in the families of origin. In addition, there has been a change in social values during recent years that has yielded a decrease in the stigma attached to being born to unmarried parents. However, the consequence for the adolescent and her child is worse than for the adult, since, according to our laws, it is impossible for her to register her child under her surname. According to Sarue and Fortuna (1994), 25 percent of the illegitimate births of our country correspond to adolescents below the age of 19. The rejection of the adolescents' parents is more frequent among those who are controlled. This might be due to the fact that these families are more involved with their daughters, and perceive that an early pregnancy may harm these girls by changing their projects of life.

Several authors have pointed out that maternity in adolescence might be a way to legitimate a maternity so far performed in the rearing of younger siblings. In this way, the young girl reevaluates a role she has already been performing although underestimated by the familiar and social environment, thus obtaining a personal gratification that raises her self-esteem. The lack of verbal communication between the adolescent mother and her child that we found, has already been mentioned by several authors (Osofsky, MacAnarney, Garcia Coll). The lack of verbal interchange between adolescent mothers and their children, combined with the qualitative aspects of the verbalizations, might contribute to a lower development in the language and intellect of the children of these mothers. Nonetheless, in our society, there have been studies that agree with ours, pointing out that the verbal communication deficit in situations of poverty does not only belong to adolescent mothers. Ceruti and Canetti also found in the majority of the mothers they studied, both adolescent and adult, an emphasis on visual and physical contact, and a disregard of oral communication. Another aspect to consider is the significant difference found in respect to a lower response of the adolescent mothers to the baby's signals. This item seems very valuable in evaluating EA, whose definition, as we previously mentioned, refers to the mother's capacity to perceive the emotional signals of her baby and to implement consistent and proper responses based on them.

A good EA implies that the mother is emotionally available to interpret and satisfy the baby's demands. When, due to her own needs, the mother distorts or does not respond to her child's messages, the development of the child may be disturbed. One hypothesis that we proposed to interpret these results, is that adolescents, whose own growth implies narcissist attitudes focused on themselves, do not have enough energy to dedicate to the baby. Neither do they possess the necessary flexibility to put themselves in the baby's place, since that would imply a regression to very early stages, a fact that is in opposition to their normal tendency toward growth.

On the other hand, adolescents need to keep being daughters and receive care and attention instead of giving them as mothers. During the first stages of life, the messages the baby sends, although very similar, are vital, since they are the only language through which the baby can express emotions and communicate them to the envi-

ronment. It is through her EA that the mother communicates that she recognizes her baby as a real presence and that she is capable of responding empathetically and properly. This mother-child encounter creates a needed frame for the baby's differentiation and representation of emotions and needs, so he or she can feel supported by the mother.

An aspect that we studied but have not been able to quantify yet is the lack of a good model of motherhood for the majority of adolescents studied. This lack makes it difficult for them to identify with an adequate mother because motherhood develops from the experience lived in that respect. In explaining adolescent mothers' difficulty in perceiving their babies' messages as a phenomenon of multifactorial causality, we have to mention that there is a cognitive as well as an emotional factor. We may suppose that our adolescents, either because of their age or the poor environment they come from, have not yet reached the last stage of cognitive development described by Piaget (formal operational thought). For this reason, it might be difficult for them to develop realistic expectations and attitudes of care toward their babies. They thus would not be able to understand that maternity requires an intense, prolonged, and sensitive interaction. Another perspective that was statistically significant indicates a relationship between higher risk adolescents and the absence of prenatal control, factors that we consider may be linked to a higher frequency of unwanted pregnancy. This finding agrees with what was published by other authors, who found few positive affects in adolescents in general.

To finish, we will say that even though the adolescents in our sample scored lower than adults, that does not mean they failed at rearing their children. Many of them did have good results in EA. Forty percent of our adolescents did not have partners, and the rest had unstable relationships that did not last very long; however, when the partner was present and participated in the support of the family, he acted as an emotional support for the dyad, thus favoring the mother's EA. Likewise, the lower autonomy of the adolescents from the original family seems to be a desirable characteristic that favors adolescent parenthood. The lack of verbalizations observed in the adolescent mothers' dyads might lead to poor cognitive and linguistic ability in their children, conditioned by the mother's age and educational level and the few stimuli received by these children during the early stages of development. This situation, transmitted transgenerationally, constitutes another factor of poverty.

Finally, we would like to mention that considering adolescent maternity as precocious implies not only a biological and psychological evaluation, but also cultural one. In the high and middle socioeconomic status groups, the productive and reproductive roles are separated, and the first one is emphasized. On the other hand, in the low socioeconomic status groups, those personal projects do not exist; furthermore, there are no opportunities to accomplish them. The project of personal fulfillment that the adolescent from that level has is

maternity, the only possession and richness she can aspire to. Besides, it is the only possible project of life that agrees with social guidelines.

References

Als, H., Tronik, E., Adamson, L., & Brazelton, T. B. (1976). The behavior of full term yet underweight infant. *Developmental Medicine and Clinical Neurology, 18,* 590.

Assanelli, M., & Defey, D. (1994). Psicopatologia del puerperio. In D. Defey (Ed.), *Mujer y maternidad: Aportes para su comprensión desde la psicologia medica* (Vol. II, pp. 107–150). Montevideo, Uruguay: Roca Viva.

Baraibar, R. (1991). Intervencion psicologica en crisis. Reflexiones desde el trabajo en Centro de Tratamiento Intensivo Pediatrico: Reunion Mensual de la Sociedad Uruguaya de Psicologia Medica y Medicina Psicosocial.

Baraibar, R. (1991). Acciones psicoterapeuticas en Centro de Tratamiento Intensivo Pediatrico. Descripción y fundamentos teoricos. *Archivo de Pediatria del Uruguay, 62*(1–4), 29–40.

Barran, J. P. (1992). Medicina y sociedad en el Uruguay del novecientos: H poder de curar. Montevideo, Uruguay: Ed. Banda Oriental.

Beal, S. (1989). Sudden infant death in twins. *Pediatrics, 84*(6), 1038–1044.

Berkowitz, R., & Lynch, L. (1990). Selective reduction: An unfortunate misnomer. *Obstetrics & Gynecology, 75,* 873.

Berkowitz, R., Lynch, L., Chitkara, U.,

Wilkins, I., Mehalek, K., & Alvarez, E. (1988). Selective reduction of multifetal pregnancies in the first trimester. *British Medical Journal, 38*(16), 1043–1047.

Bernardi, R., Schwartzman, L., & Canetti, A. (1992). Adolescent maternity: A risk factor in poverty situations? *Infant Mental Health Journal, 13,* 211–219.

Botting, B., MacDonald, I., & MacFarlane, I. (1987). Recent trends in the incidence of multiple births and associated mortality. *Archives of Diseases in the Child, 62,* 941–950.

Bourne, P. (1968). The psychological effects of stillbirths on women and their doctors. *Journal of the Royal College of General Practitioners, 16,* 103–1112.

Bourne, P. (1972). The psychological effect of stillbirths on the doctor. Psychosomatic Medicine in Obstetrics and Gynecology, 3rd International Congress, London 1971, pp. 333–334. Basel: Karger.

Bourne, P., & Lewis, E. (1983). Support after perinatal death: A study of support and counseling after perinatal bereavement [Letter to the editor], *British Journal of Medicine, 286,* 144–145.

Bowlby, J. (1980). *Loss.* New York: Basic Books.

Bowlby, J. (1989). *Una base segura, aplicaciones clinical a una teorie del apego.* Buenes Aires: Paidos.

Bryan, E. (1995). The death of a twin. *Palliative Medicine, 9*(3), 187–192.

Burger, J., Horowitz, S., Forsyth, B., Leventhal, J., & Leaf, P. (1993). Psychological sequelae of medical complications during pregnancy. *Pediatrics, 91*(3), 566–571.

Cain, A., & Cain, B. (1964). On replacing a child. *Journal of the American Academy of Child and Adolescent Psychiatry, 3,* 443–455.

Canetti, A., Navarrette, C., & Da Luz, S. (1993). Maternidad adolescente: Los obstaculos en el camino hacia la autonomía. Punta del Este, Uruguay: Encuentro Internacional de Psiquiatria del Lactante, el Niño y el Adolescente.

Cherro, M., Buka, D., Grobert, M., Herrera, M., Katzcovich, E., & Zito, G. (1988). Los gemelos o las vicisitudes de un punto de partida doble. *Revista de Psicoterapia Psicoanalitica, 2*(4A), 359–384.

Cherro, M., Defey, D., Correas, P., Zito, G., Lores, R., & Fuentes, A. (1996). Perinatal loss of a twin. *Proceedings of the IV WAIMH World Congress, Tampere, Finland.* WAIMH. pp. 2–3.

Cherro Aguerre, M. (1992). Quality of bonding and behavioral differences in twins. *Infant Mental Health Journal, 13*(3), 206–210.

Cherro Aguerre, M. (1993). *Acaso mellizos?* Montevideo, Uruguay: Roca Viva.

Cherro Aguerre, M., et al. (1995). Early relationship in adolescent mothers. *Symposium WAIMH in the International Congress of the International Society of Adolescent Psychiatry, Athens, Greece.*

Correas, P., Cherro, M., Defey, D., Lores, R., & Zito, G. (1994). Perdida perinatal de un gemelar. *Proceedings of une international symposium: "Mental Health of Infants, Children and Adolescents in the XXI Century" (1993), Punta del Este, Uruguay.* pp. 133–143.

D'Alton, M. E., Newton, E. R., & Cetrulo, C. I. (1989). Intrauterine fetal demise in multiple gestation. Acta Medica Semellal (Vol. 37, pp. 43–49).

Da Luz, S., Canetti, A., Navarrette, C., Lamstein, I., Mila, J., Neves, N., & Camporeale, N. (1996). Seguimiento interdisciplinario del binomio hijo-madre adolescents. *Archivo Pediatrico Uruguayo, 67*(I), 5–35.

Davis, J. (1988). Management of perinatal loss of a twin [letter to the editor]. *British Medical Journal, 297,* p. 87.

Defey, D. (Ed.). (1994, 1994, 1996, 1996). *Mujer y maternidad: Aportes pare su comprension desde la psicologia medica* (Vols. 1–4). Montevideo, Uruguay: Roca Viva.

Defey, D., Diaz, J. L., Friedler, R., Nuñez, M., & Terra, C. (1992). Duelo por un niño que muere antes de nacer. Montevideo, Uruguay: Roca Viva.

Defey, D. (1995). Helping health care staff deal with perinatal loss. *Infant Mental Health Journal, 16*(2), 102–111.

Defey, D., Diaz, J. L., Friedler, R., Nuñez, M., & Terra, C. (1985). La muerte de un niño antes de nacer [Videotape]. Montevideo, Uruguay: Latin American Center of Perinatology (CLAP—PAHO/WHO) and School of Medicine, University of Uruguay.

Defey, D., Diaz, J. L., Friedler, R., Nuñez, M., & Terra, C. (1986). Larga muerte de una vida breve: Muere un recién nacido [Videotape]. Montevideo, Uruguay: Latin American Center of Perinatology (CLAP—PAHO/WHO) and School of Medicine, University of Uruguay.

Dugas, M., Mouren-Simeoni, S., Huet, S., & Menet, M. (1987). Etude retrospective de jumeaux examines dans un service de psychiatrie de l'enfance et de l'adolescence. *Neuropsychiatrie de l'Enfance, 35*(4–5), 201–220.

Ellings, J., Newman, R., Hulsey, T., Bivins, H., & Keenan, A. (1993). Reduction in very low birthweight deliveries and perinatal mortality in a specialized, multidisciplinary twin clinic. *Obstetrics and Gynecology, 81*(3), 387–391.

Elman, M. (1994). El pediatra frente a la muerte. *Actas del Congreso de Pediatria Humanista* (pp. 293–298). Buenos Aires, Argentina.

Elster, A., McAnarney, E., & Lamb, E. (1983). Parental behavior of adolescent mothers. *Pediatrics, 71,* 494–503.

Engel, G. (1975). The death of a twin: Mourning and anniversary reactions: Fragments of 10 years of self-analysis. *International Journal of Psychoanalysis, 56,* 23–41.

Evans, M., Fletcher, J., Zador, I., Newton, B., Quigg, M., & Struik, C. (1998). Selective first-trimester termination in octuplet and quadruplet pregnancies: Clinical and ethical issues. *Obstetrics & Gynecology, 71* (3 Pt. 1).

Feichtinger, W., Breitnecker, G., & Frolich, H. (1989). Prolongation of pregnancy and survival of twin B after loss of twin A at 21 weeks' gestation. *American Journal of Obstetrics and Gynecology, 161,* 891–893.

Ferrari, H., Ferrari, I., & Luchina, I. (1977). *La interconsulta medico psicológica en el'marco hospitalario.* Buenos Aires: Nueva Vision.

Fonagy, P. (1996). Prevention: The adequate target of infant mental health. Plenary address at the IV WAIMH World Congress, Tampere, Finland.

Foucault, M. (1963). *Naissance de la clinique: Une archeologic du regard medicate.* Paris.

Fuentes, A., & Lores, R. (1994). Impacto de la muerte y burn-out en el pediatra neonatologo. X Curso de Actualizacion en Neonatologia. Montevideo, Uruguay.

Fuste~fberg, Brooks-Gunn, J. (1989). Find aged pregnancy and childbearing. *American Psychobiologist, 44,* 313–320.

Gall, S. (1988). Embarazo gemelar. *Clinicas de Perinatologia,* No. 1.

Gardner, S., & Merenstein, G. (1986). Perinatal grief and loss. *Neonatal network, 4,* 7–15.

Gifford, S., Murawski, B., Brazelton, B., & Young, G. (1966). Differences in individual development within a pair of identical twins. *International Journal of Psychoanalysis, 47,* 261–268.

Gonen, R., Heyman, E., Asztalos, E., & Milligan, J. (1990). The outcome of triplet gestations complicated by fetal death. *Obstetrics & Gynecology, 75*(2), 175–178.

Gonen, R., Heyman, E., Asztalos, E., Olhsson, A., Pytson, L., Shennan, T., & Milligan, J. (1990). The outcome of triplet, quadruplet, and quintuplet pregnancies managed in a perinatal unit: Obstetric, neonatal, and follow-up data. *American Journal of Obstetrics & Gynecology, 162,* 454–459.

Gottfried, N., Seay, B., & Leake, E. (1994). Attachment relationships in infant twins: The effect of co-twin presence during separation from mother. *Journal of Genetic Psychology, 155*(3), 273–281.

Gracia, D. (1995). Etica Medica: Farreras, P., & Rozman, C. Madrid, *Medicina Internal, 1,* 33–38.

Granger, H. R., & Stone, E. (1991). Collaboration between child psychiatrics and pediatricians in practice: Baffimore, Child and Adolescence Psychiatry; A comprehensive textbook. (944~8).

Groothuis, J. (1985). Twins and twin families: A practical guide to outpatient management. *Clinics in Perinatology, 12*(2).

Group for the Advancement of Psychiatry. (1986). *Crises of adolescence, teenage pregnancy: Impact on adolescent development.* New York: Brunner Mazel.

Hann, D., Osofsky, J., Stringer, Sac., & Carter, S. K. (1988). *Affective contributions of adolescent mothers and infant to the quality of attachment.* Poster session presented at the International Conference on Infant Studies on Washington, DC.

Hayez, J.-Y. (1991). La psychiatrie de liasson apliquee a l'enfance: Principes et exercise quotidian. In *La psychiatrie a l'hopital d'enfants* (pp. 121–134). Paris.

Haynal, A., & Pasini, W. (1984). *Medecine Psychosomatique.*

Hildebrad, W., & Schreiner, R. (1980). Helping parents cope with perinatal death. *American Family Physician, 22,* 121–125.

Jauniaux, E., Elkazen, N., Leroy, F., Wilkin, P., Rodesh, F., & Hustin, J. (1988). Clinical and morphological aspects of the vanishing twin phenomenon. *Obstetrics & Gynecology, 72,* 577–579.

Jauniaux, E., Elkazen, N., Vanrisseklberge, M., & Leroy, F. (1988). Aspects anatomocliniques du syndrome du fetus-papyrace. *Journal de Gynecologie Obstetrique et Biologie Reproductive, 17,* 653–659.

Keith, L. (1994). Mortality and morbidity among twins: Recent observations from the United States. *Acta Genetica Medica Gemellol, 43*(1–2), 25–31.

Kilpatrick, S., Jackson, R., & Croughan-Minihane, M. (1996). Perinatal mortality for twins and singletons matched for gestational age at delivery at 30 weeks or older. *American Journal of Obstetrics & Gynecology, 174,* 66–71.

Klaus, M., & Kennel, J. (1982). La relacion madre-hijo. Buenos Aires: Panamericana.

Kreisler, L. (1987). *Le nouvel enfant du desordre psychosomatique.* Paris.

Kreisler, L. (1994). L'enfant sur le chemin de la connaissance psychosomatique esquisse pour un hommage. *Revue Française Psychosomatique, 6,* 120–138.

Laurnaga, M. E. (1995). *Uruguay adoles-*

cente. Ed. Trilce, Instituto Nacional de la Familia y de la mujer.

Lax, R. (1972). Some aspects of the interaction between mother and impaired child: Mother's narcissistic trauma. *International Journal of Psychoanalysis, 53,* 339–344.

Lazarus, R., & Folkman, S. (1986). *Estres y procesos cognitivos.* Barcelona, Spain.

Lebovici, S. (1989). Les liens intergenerationnels (transmission, conflits). In S. Lebovici & F. Weil-Halpern (Eds.), Psychopathologie du bébé. *J. Les interactions fantasmatiques* (pp. 141–146). Paris: PUF.

Levine, L., & Garcia Coll, C. (1985). Determinants of mother-infant interaction in adolescent mothers. *Pediatrics, 75*(1).

Lewis, E. (1976). The management of stillbirth: Coping with an unreality. *Lancet, 2,* 619–620.

Lewis, E. (1979). Mourning by the family after stillbirth or a neonatal death. *Archive of Diseases in the Child, 54,* 303–306.

Lewis, E., & Bryan, E. (1988). Management of perinatal loss of a twin. *British Medical Journal, 297,* 1321–1323.

Lewis, E., & Page, A. (1978). Failure to mourn a stillbirth: An overlooked catastrophe. *British Journal of Medical Psychology, 51,* 237–241.

Lipitz, L., Frenkel, Y., Watts, C., Ben-Rafael, Z., Barkal, G., & Reichman, B. (1990). High-order multifetal gestation: Management and outcome. *Obstetrics and Gynecology, 76,* 215–218.

Lores, R., Correas, P., & Rodriguez, S. (1994). Recien nacido patologica. En D. Defey (Ed.), *Mujer y Maternidad, Vol II,* pp. 59–90.

Lumme, R., & Saarikoski, S. (1988). Perinatal deaths in twin pregnancy: A 22-year review. *Acta Genetica Medica Gemellol, 37,* 47–54.

Lynch, L., Berkowitz, R., Chitkara, U., & Alvarez, M. (1990). First-trimester transabdominal multifetal pregnancy reduction: A report of 85 cases. *Obstetrics & Gynecology, 75,* 735–738.

Macdonald, R., & Watters, J. (1994). Successful intra- and extrauterine IVF twin pregnancy. *British Journal of Obstetrics & Gynecology, 101,* 458–460.

Malavaud, B., & Moron, B. (1991). Divorce et embryons congeles. *Neuro-psychiatrie de l'Enfance, 39*(6), 233–237.

Manzano, J. (1993). Depresion puerperal. *Proceedings of the Encuentro Internacional Cambio y Desarrollo: El Lactante, el Niño y el Adolescente en el Siglo XXI, Punta del Este, Uruguay.* pp. 130–139.

Marty, P. (1992). *La psicosomatica del adulto.* Buenos Aires, Argentina.

Maslach, C. (1982). *Burnout: The cost of caring.* New York: Prentice-Hall.

Melgar, C., Rosenfeld, D., Rawlinson, K., & Greenberg, M. (1991). Perinatal outcome after multifetal reduction to twins compared with non-reduced multiple gestations. *Obstetrics & Gynecology, 78,* 763–767.

Minde, K., Corter, C., Goldberg, S., & Jeffers, D. (1990). Maternal preference between twins up to age four. *Journal of the American Academy of Child & Adolescent Psychiatry, 29*(3), 367–374.

Nantermoz, F., Molénat, F., Boulot, P., Hedon, B., Roy, J., & Visier, J. (1991). Implications psychologiques de la reduction embryonnaire sur grossesse multiple: Reflexions preliminaires. *Neuropsychiatrie de l'Enfance, 39*(11–12), 594–597.

Neifert, M., & Thorpe, J. (1990). Twins: Family adjustment, parenting and infant feeding in the fourth trimester. *Clinical Obstetrics & Gynecology, 33*(1), 102–112.

Novali, L., Urman, E., & Sola, E. (1988). Relacion de apego, muerte neonatal y sindrome de desgaste. Buenos Aires, Argentina: Ed. Cientifica Interamericana.

Oberfield, R., & Gabriel, P. (1991). Prematurity, birth defects, and early death: Impact on the family. In M. Lewis (Ed.), *Child and Adolescent Psychiatry* (pp. 954–963). Baltimore.

Osofsky, J., Culp, A., & Eberhart-Wright, A. (1988). *Final report to Kenworthy.* New Orleans, LA: Foundation Menninger Clinic, Topeka Medical Center of Louisiana, Louisiana State University.

Osofsky, J., Eberhart-Wright, A. (1988). Affective exchanges between high risk mothers and infants. *International Journal of Psychoanalysis, 69,* 221–231.

Osofsky, J., & Eberhart-Wright, A., Ware, L. M., & Hann, D. M. (1992). Children of adolescent mothers: A group at risk for psychopathology. *Infant Mental Health Journal, 13,* 119–131.

Osofsky, J., Hann, D., & Peebles, C. (1993). Adolescent parenthood: Risk and opportunities for mothers and infant. In *Handbook of Infant Mental Health* (pp. 106–119).

Osofsky, J., & Osofsky, H. (1970). Adolescent as mother: Result of a program for low-income pregnant teenagers with some emphasis upon infant development. *American Journal of Orthopsychiatry.*

Osofsky, J., Osofsky, H., & Diamont, M. (1988). The transition to parenthood: Special task and risk factors for adolescent mothers. In G. Michaels Goldberg (Ed.), *The Transition to Parenthood* (pp. 209–234).

Pons, J. E. (1991). Cuan riesgoso es el embarazo en la adolescencia. In J. Portillo, L. Martinez, & M. Banfi (Eds.), *La adolescencia* (pp. 236–239). Montevideo, Uruguay: Ed. Banda Oriental.

Porreco, R. (1990). Gestacion gemelar. *Clinicas obstetricas y ginecologicas, 1.*

Porreco, R., Burke, S., & Hendrix, M. (1991). Multifetal reduction of triplets and pregnancy outcome. *Obstetrics & Gynecology, 73,* 335.

Porreco, R., Harmon, R., Murrow, N., Schultz, L., & Hendrix, M. (1995). Parental choices in grand multiple gestation: Psychological considerations. *Journal of Maternal-Fetal Health, 4,* 111–114.

Poznanski, E. O. (1972). The "replacement child": a saga of unresolved perinatal grief. *Behavioral pediatrics, 81*(6), 1190–1193.

Prompeler, H., Madjar, H., Klosa, W., du-Bois, A., Zahradnik, H., Schillinger, H., & Breckwoldt, M. (1994). Twin pregnancies with single fetal deaths. *Scandinavian Acta of Obstetrics & Gynecology, 73*(3), 205–208.

Powers, W., & Kiely, J. (1994). The risks confronting twins: A national perspective. *American Journal of Obstetrics & Gynecology, 170*(2), 456–461.

Reis, J. (1988). Children-rearing expectations and developmental knowledge according to maternal age and parity. *Infant Mental Health Journal, 914.*

Robin, M., & Josse, D. (1987). Quelques aspects de la relation mere-enfant a la suite d'une naissance gemellaire. *Neuropsychiatrie de l'Enfance, 35*(8–9), 369–377.

Robinson, J., & Litile, C. (1994). Emotional availability in mother-twin dyads: Effect on the organization of relationships. *Psychiatry, 57*(1), 22–31.

Romito, A. (1990). Post-partum depression and the experience of motherhood. *Scandinavian Acta of Obstetrics & Gynecology, 69*, 154.

Santem, J., Swaak, A., & Wallenburg, H. (1995). Expectant management of twin pregnancy with single fetal death. *British Journal of Obstetrics & Gynecology, 102*, 26–30.

Sarue, E., & Fortuna, J. C. (1994). Caracteristicas demograficas de la adolescencia en el Uruguay, decada del 90. In *Adolescencia, salud integral y embarazo precoz.* (Documento especial No. 3). Montevideo, Uruguay: Republica Oriental del Uruguay, Ministerio de Salud Publica.

Schreiner-Engel, P., Walther, V., Mindes, J., Lynch, L., & Berkowitz, R. (1995). First-trimester multifetal pregnancy reduction: Acute and persistent psychological reactions. *American Journal of Obstetrics & Gynecology, 172*, 541–547.

Segal, N., & Bouchard, T. (1993). Grief intensity following the loss of a twin and other relatives: Test of kinship genetic hypotheses. *Human Biology, 65*(1), 87–105.

Stiermas, E. (1987). Emotional aspects of perinatal death. *Clinical Obstetrics & Gynecology, 30*(2).

Swanson-Kauffman, K. (1988). There should have been two: Nursing care of parents experiencing the perinatal death of a twin. *Journal of Perinatal & Neonatal Nursing, 2*(2), 78–85.

Szymonowicz, W., Preston, H., Yu, V. Y. (1986). The surviving monozygotic co-twin. *Archive of Diseases in the Child, 61*, 454–458.

Tabsh, K. (1993). A report of 131 cases of multifetal pregnancy reduction. *Obstetrics & Gynecology, 82*(1), 57–60.

Thorpe, K. (1991). Comparison of prevalence of depression in mothers of twins and mothers of singletons. *British Medical Journal, 302*, 875–878.

Timor-Trisch, I., Peisner, D., Monteagudo, A., Lemer, J., & Sharma, S. (1993). Multifetal pregnancy reduction by transvaginal puncture: Evaluation of the technique used in 134 cases. *American Journal of Obstetrics and Gynecology, 168*, 799–804.

Van den Veyver, I., Schatteman, E., Vanderheyden, J., & Meulyzer, P. (1990). Antenatal fetal death in twin pregnancies: A dangerous condition mainly for the surviving co-twin. A report of four cases. *European Journal of Obstetrics Gynecology and Reproductive Biology, 38*, 69–73.

Wilson, A., Lawrence, J., Stevens, D., & Soule, D. (1982). The death of a newborn twin: An analysis of parental bereavement. *Pediatrics, 70*, 587–591.

Winnicott, D. W. (1958). *Escritos de pediatria y psicoanalisis.* Barcelona, Spain: Laia.

Zaner, R., Boehm, F., & Hill, G. (1990). Selective termination in multiple pregnancies: Ethical considerations. *Fertility and Sterility, 54*(2), 203–205.

Zeanah, C. H. (1989). Adaptation following perinatal loss: A critical review. *Journal of the American Academy of Child & Adolescent Psychiatry, 28*(3), 467–480.

Zeanah, C. H., Dailey, J., Rosenblatt, M., & Saner, N. (1993). Do women grieve following termination of pregnancies for fetal anomalies? A controlled investigation. *Obstetrics & Gynecology, 82*, 270–275.

Author Index

Author Index

Subject Index

Subject Index

Subject Index

Royal Alexander Hospital for Children (RAHC)
infant studies, 106
Royal Children's Hospital, 113
Royal Commission into Mental Health, 101
Royal Commission on Human Relationships, 96, 104
Royal Commission on the Decline of the Birthrate, 100
Royal Hospital for Women, 108
Russia
infant care facilities, 245–290

Saint Vincent de Paul Hospital, 131
Scale of Emotional Availability, 369
Scandinavia
infant mental health, 213–242
school establishment
in Australia, 99–100, 101
School Medical Services
in Australia, 100–101
second child
penalties in China, 190
second-level protagonism
in infant mental health clinics, 329
sectorization, 127–130
securely attached infants, 238
selective reduction, 350–351
self-mutilation
and sexual abuse in Lakota, 167
Self-Rating Depression Scale (SDS), 45–46, 256, 274
self-sensorial manifestations, 134
semantic no, 15
sensorial representations, 138
sensory-perceptual abilities
experimental, 7–8
sensory-perceptual responsivity, 7
separation, 13
in Australia, 101, 103–104, 115–116
Aboriginal people, 115–116
from mother
in Japan, 50
neonatal, 84–85
neonatal period
in Australia, 104–105
and later outcome measures, 66
prolonged
in boarding schools for Lakota children, 165
sex of child
as protective factor in maltreatment, 199
as risk factor for maltreatment, 197
sexism
female infants in China, 187, 192–193
sexual abuse
American Indians, 167
in boarding schools for Lakota children, 165
in China, 196

Shanghai Children's Welfare Institute, 184, 194, 195
shoshi-ka, 41–42
single-child policy, 184
in China, 186–192
single mothers
in Australia, 96–97
single mother's pension, 98
single parenthood, 21
and alcoholism in American Indians, 168
in Australia, 99–100
skin-to-skin contact, 69
and child health, 71
smile, social
as organizer of psyche, 15
social-cultural contexts
multiple, 11
social-emotional systems
organization of, 11
social-interpersonal functioning, 197
social networks
differentiation of, 11
social support
adolescent motherhood, 368, 370, 373
social welfare
in Australia, 99–102
Social Welfare Board Register, 81, 82, 84
socialization
in infant mental health clinics, 334
Society for Research in Child Development, 20
sociobiological approach
infant mental health, 302
somatic expression disorders, 344
somatic patients, 336–341
and liaison psychiatry, 341–348
theoretical foundations of practice, 337–340
Spanish Society of Psychoanalysis, 131
speaking, 305
special needs children
in China, 185
in Russia, 263–266
support from infant mental health clinics, 330
in Sweden, 234–235
specialized hospital centers, 128
split type of mother, 47
spoiling
of only children
in China, 185
St. Marianna University
Western Yokohama Hospital Neonatal Center, 58–59
starvation
in boarding schools for Lakota children, 165
State Birth Planning Commission (SBPC), 191
still face situation, 144–145
stimulation
of child in Intensive Care Unit, 346

violence in private schools, 360–365
   age differences, 362–363
   gender differences, 362
   intervention, 363–364
   statistics and research, 360–364
vital functions, 342
vocalizations
   preverbal
     in autistic children, 79
vulnerability, 339
vulnerable child syndrome, 344, 353, 354

walking, 305
welfare
   in Australia, 97–99, 101–102
welfare model
   Sweden, 225–240
welfare system
   in Sweden
     crisis, 232
well-baby clinics, 229
widow's pension, 98

Winwanyang Wacipi, 162
Woope Sakowin, 162, 170–172
work methods
   in child and adolescent psychiatric clinic, 321–376
World Association for Infant Mental Health
   (WAIMH), 5, 58, 59, 111–115, 133, 136, 137–139,
   146, 148, 149, 328
   German-speaking affiliate, 316–317
   history of, 17–21
World Association for Infant Psychiatry and Allied Disciplines (WAIPAD), 17, 18–19, 20, 40, 43, 109–110,
   111–115, 149, 327
World Association for Infant Psychiatry (WAIP), 19,
   108, 136–137
World Health Organization (WHO), 127, 128, 129,
   130, 131, 355
World War II, 7, 13, 41, 49, 126, 128, 137, 146, 222, 228
   in Australia, 98
Wounded Knee Massacre, 163

yin and *yang*, 188
Yokohama National University, 58